The Shipwreck Sea

Love Poems and Essays in a Classical Mode

ᛊ

"The only sea I saw Was the seesaw sea With you riding on it. Lie down, lie easy. Let me shipwreck in your thighs."

– DYLAN THOMAS, *Under Milk Wood*

For Keith, A Voice for our Times and for all time!

The Shipwreck Sea

Love Poems and Essays in a Classical Mode

Ever,

Jeffrey

4/1/2019

Jeffrey M. Duban

CLAIRVIEW

Clairview Books Ltd.,
Russet, Sandy Lane, West Hoathly,
W. Sussex RH19 4QQ

www.clairviewbooks.com

Published in Great Britain in 2019 by Clairview Books

© Jeffrey M. Duban 2019

A CIP catalogue record for this book is available from the British Library

Print book ISBN 978-1-912992-00-3
Ebook ISBN 978-1-912992-01-0

Edited, designed, and typeset by Rachel Trusheim
Chariot illustration on p. 164 by Kati Gyulassy
Printed and bound in Malta by Gutenberg Press Ltd.

For Jayne E'er

Reader, she married me.

Contents

Acknowledgments

LOVING THANKS TO my dear wife, Jayne Connell, who read and corrected the work more than once in draft and who, with her English-teaching skills, saved me more than once from error, while guiding my explorations of the nineteenth-century American and British novels.

My love and sincere appreciation to my brother and professor of English, James Duban, for his literary-critical review of the entire manuscript in draft.

Sincerest thanks to abiding friend, Shlomo Shyovitz, for corrections and often probing comments on the Preface and PART I.

My gratitude, as ever, to lifelong mentor and support, Michael Putnam, and former colleague and enduring friend, Janice Benario, for their critical readings and approvals of PART V.

My sincere appreciation to friend and "Sappho soprano" Jennifer Klauder for the book's cover design and for her diligence in obtaining all artwork permissions and images. My thanks as well to Andrew Morgan for his splendid full dust-jacket realization.

I thank Hellenophile Alessandra Masu Swetzoff, of Boston and Rome, for permission to reproduce herein Artemisia Gentileschi's *Aurora*, "the favorite daughter of [her] collection of woman artists."

My love to my daughter, Jean Petrek-Duban, for remembering her mother's heart and the heart of her poem.

As previously in her handling of *The Lesbian Lyre*, I remain altogether indebted to my editor, Rachel Trusheim, whose care for my work and literary well-being is untiring; whose insight and judgment are uncanny; and, in that connection, one of whose roles (shared with Jayne) is that of occasionally saving me from myself.

Finally, admiringly, and enduringly, my appreciation and thanks to Sevak Gulbekian, Chief Editor, Clairview Books, for his continued confidence in my work, for his expertise and integrity, and for his ever discriminating and always affable ways.

Abbreviations

abl.	ablative (case)
adj.	adjective
acc.	accusative (case)
act.	active (verbal "voice")
decl.	declension
dat.	dative (case)
dep.	deponent (verb with passive form, active meaning)
fem.	feminine
fut.	future (verbal "tense")
gen.	genitive (case)
indic.	indicative (verbal "mood")
masc.	masculine
neut.	neuter
nom.	nominative (case)
part.	participle (verbal mood)
pass.	passive (verbal voice)
perf.	perfect (verbal tense)
pl.	plural
pres.	present (verbal tense)
pro.	pronoun
sing.	singular
voc.	vocative (case)
Eng.	English
Fr.	French
Ger.	German
Gr.	Greek
Heb.	Hebrew
Lat.	Latin
PIE	Proto-Indo-European
Aen.	*Aeneid*
Arg.	*Argonautica*
DRN	*De Rerum Natura*
Ec.	*Eclogue*
El.	Elegy

G.	*Georgics*
Gen.	Genesis
Il.	*Iliad*
Juv.	Juvenal
Met	*Metamorphoses*
Od.	*Odyssey*
PA	*Palatine Anthology*
PL	*Paradise Lost*
Sid.	Sidonius
Th.	*Theogony*
TLL	*The Lesbian Lyre*
WD	*Works and Days*
c.	abbreviation, Lat. *circa* 'around'
cf.	abbreviation, Lat. *confer* 'compare'
lit.	literally
n.s.	new series
*	without footnote, a lingustic symbol indicating a verbal root

Guide to Pronunciation

(For detailed treatment, see *The Lesbian Lyre*, xvii–xxii)

Name (transliteration)	Pronunciation (transcription)
Achilles	A-kil'-leez
Aegean	A-gee'-an
Aeneas	A-nee'-us
Aeneid	A-nee'-id
Aeolic	Ee-o'-lic
Anacreon	A-na'-cree-on
Archilochus	Ar-kil'-o-kus
Athenaeus	A-then-ee'-us
Briseis	Bri-see'-is
Carmina Burana	Car'-mi-na [*not* Car-mee'-na] Boo-ra'-na
Chryseis	Chry-see'-is
Cleïs/Kleïs	Clay'-is
Dionē	Di-ō'-nay [or Di-ō'-nee]
Heroides	He-rō'-i-deez
Hesiod	Hee'-see-id
Neoboulē	Ne-o'-boo-lay [or Ne-o'-boo-lee]
Riphē	Ree'-fay [or Ree'-fee]
Sappho	Sa'-phō

Artwork Credits

GRATEFUL ACKNOWLEDGMENT is made to the following for permission to reprint images. Below is the order in which they appear, cited and numbered as "plates" within the text.

Cover: Sir John Edward Poynter, *Cave of the Storm Nymphs* (painting, 1647–1652). Norfolk Hermitage Museum; HIP / Art Resource, NY.

1. Gian Lorenzo Bernini, *The Ecstasy of Saint Teresa* (sculpture, 1647–1652). Cornaro Chapel, S. Maria della Vittoria, Rome; Scala / Art Resource, NY.

2. Anne-Louis Girodet de Roussy-Trioson, *The Sleep of Endymion* (painting, 1791). Louvre, Paris; Erich Lessing / Art Resource, NY.

3. François Auguste Rodin, *The Hand of God* (sculpture, 1907). The Metropolitan Museum of Art, New York, NY.

4. Artemisia Gentileschi, *Judith Slaying Holofernes* (painting, 1614). Museo Nazionale di Capodimonte, Naples; Scala / Art Resource, NY.

5. Artemisia Gentileschi, *Susanna and the Elders* (painting, 1610). Schloss Weissenstein, Pommersfelden; Fine Art Images / Alinari Archives, Florence.

6. Alessandro Allori, *Susanna and the Elders* (painting, 1561). Musée Magnin, Dijon; © RMN-Grand Palais / Art Resource, NY.

7. Tintoretto, *Susanna and the Elders* (painting, 1555). Museo de Prado, Madrid / Wiki Commons.

8. Artemisia Gentileschi, *Aurora* (painting, c. 1627). Private Collection of Alessandra Masu Swetzoff (Boston and Rome).

Of all the poets of the world, of all the illustrious artists of all literatures, Sappho is the one whose every word has a peculiar and unmistakable perfume, a seal of absolute perfection and illimitable grace. In her art she was unerring. Even Archilochus seems commonplace when compared with her exquisite rarity of phrase.

– HENRY T. WHARTON, *Sappho*

Sappho's Muse . . . is passionately tender, and glowing; like oil set on fire, she is soft and warm, in excess.

– EDWARD YOUNG, *On Lyric Poetry*

Poetry is the place where language performs, and so poetry shows us most clearly what a language can do, and what it likes to do . . .

– WILLIAM FITZGERALD, *How to Read a Latin Poem, If You Can't Read Latin Yet*

Preface

THIS BOOK EXPLORES both the vicissitudes of love—its exhilarations, perversions, and often catastrophic results—and the "battle of the sexes" vis-à-vis artistic creation. It expands as such upon the concerns of *The Lesbian Lyre: Reclaiming Sappho for the 21st Century.* I begin with an essay titled: "Female Homer and the Fallacy of Gendered Sensibility" (PART I). Taking my lead from Samuel Butler's *The Authoress of the Odyssey* (1897), I disavow the notion of gendered creativity, that is, of any difference appreciable to eye or ear between works created by men or by women. My position is that the process and product of artistry is invariably gender-neutral. Artistic sensibility, with possible passing exceptions, is neither male nor female, but *human*, ideally reflecting humane values and serving humane ends. Civilization is itself "the idealized goal and outcome of art." This inquiry, within a necessarily bounded scope, traverses literature, painting, sculpture, and music.

The inquiry was spurred by the claim, inhering in feminist studies, that topics by, or pertaining to, women are of particular concern to women; and more, within their particular purview *because* they are women. The corollary is that male involvement in such areas, including the pervasive scholarship of the past, is and has been biased *because* male; that male views thus require correction or revision; that males were little suited and are now little welcome to the discussion. This is payback for traditional male dominance in the arts and in academe. Proprietary claims to the humanities by "women and minorities"—politically exclusionary in privileging the so-called "underrepresented"—are divisive and destabilizing, whence the "culture wars."

Classicist and Sappho scholar Thomas McEvilley (1939–2013) designated "a contemporary academic *thiasos*," i.e., 'band' or 'coterie', of Sappho scholars (by analogy to the coterie postulated for the "Sapphic circle" itself). The resultant field, says McEvilley, "has almost become what it studies, a new 'female initiatory discourse . . . conducted in the sheltered atmosphere of the *thiasos*'—the *thiasos* in this case being the sheltered and cultic atmosphere of classical studies in academia." The process, seeking to establish the primacy of women's scholarship vis-à-vis the premier woman poet of all time is, above all, political. It is sustained, moreover, on divers literary-theoretical predicates, including psychoanalysis and French theory as propounded by such structuralist and post-structuralist *enfants terribles* and imposters as Michel Foucault, Jacques Derrida, Jacques Lacan, Hélène Cixous, and career-capitalizing gender theorist *formidable,* Judith Butler— voices that have dominated discussion and critical study of the arts. Equally responsible for this state of affairs has been the more traditional feminism, e.g., of Virginia Woolf's signature *A Room of One's Own* (1929). Calling the work out as one "shot through with enfeebling contradictions," Ruth Vanita notes that "Largely as a result of the red herring Woolf started, the acknowl- edgment of Sappho's pervasive influence on male writers has been muted, even in feminist criticism, in the late twentieth century. Sappho has been read more as an influence on women writers, specifically lesbian writers."

My earlier work sought to disclaim this scholarly misappropriation. The essay that follows advances the inquiry into the arts themselves. A clear distinction between the sexes is a predicate of civilization, but not of the art or artistic impulse that helps sustain it.

The Lesbian Lyre further sought to establish an aesthetic for the trans- lation of Greek lyric poetry (7th–5th centuries BC) and, by extension, for classical poetry overall, Greek and Latin. I urge that translation for any au- dience must—in its own way and by its own means—be as compelling as was the original for *its* audiences, the original poet and the translator "coau- thors," perhaps "synergists," of a single appreciation. I highlighted the singu- lar example of John Dryden (1631–1700), whose monumental fame rested more on his translations than on his original poetry, his translated output exceeding that of his original verse. I also noted that a great translation— e.g., Dryden's *Aeneid*—gives the impression that a great original lies behind it; that the best translation often surpasses the quality of putatively more praiseworthy original verse.

To illustrate these principles, I provided close to one hundred transla- tions of five archaic Greek lyric poets: the incomparable woman-enamored Sappho of Lesbos (thus "Lesbian Sappho," and eventually "lesbian"), the vehement Archilochus, the recondite Alcman, the playful Anacreon, and the impassioned Ibycus. These pieces are here again offered, this time in the greater interest of poetry than of aesthetic illustration (PART II). In addition, the pieces are now annotated, not only with background and interpretive materials but with literal renderings, where advised, of what has been paraphrased or variously "reworked" in the service of literary translation. Such paraphrase is dictated by the requirements of meter, rhyme, and other incidents of poetry as traditionally understood and appreciated. It is here the *sense*, not the literal meaning, that matters. Or, as Sir John Denham, Milton's contemporary, put it,

> ... for it is not [the translator's] business alone to translate Language into Language, but Poesie into Poesie; and Poesie is of so subtle a spirit, that in pouring out of one Language into another, it will all evaporate; and if a new spirit be not added in the transfusion, there will remain nothing but a *Caput mortuum* [lit., 'dead head', i.e., 'worthless remains'], there being certain Graces and Happinesses peculiar to every Language, which give life and energy to the words. ...

The literal renderings of certain words and phrases thus illustrate the transformative process involved in the translations here offered, what Dryden—distinguishing metaphrase, paraphrase, and imitation—called "paraphrase," and we call "literary translation." Indeed, the literal renderings (or "metaphrase") show what is or can be *gained* in translation. For example, what I translate in Sappho as "Be on your way, yet remember me now / and again" reads literally in Greek, "Go, and farewell, and be mindful of me." The paraphrase, here as elsewhere, is again dictated by the translation's meter, rhyme, and alliterative or assonantal reach, i.e., by the *formal qualities we associate with traditional poetry in English*, by the translation's *aesthetic*. Where no metaphrase is offered, the reader is assured of translation that closely reflects the original, aesthetic and all.

An addendum to PART II provides a number of "classic," but now unknown, mid-nineteenth to mid-twentieth century Greek lyric translations—the cream of a bygone sensibility. They yet remain, by their formal control and diction, models of fidelity and finesse. My own translations hark back to these, seeking to revive their quality and once universally appreciated manner.

I include my translations of Latin Beuern Songs (11th–13th centuries AD) (PART III). These are more commonly identified with Carl Orff's scenic cantata *Carmina Burana* (1936), the most popular and only regularly performed of Orff's numerous works. The 254-poem collection was discovered in 1803 in Bavaria, at the Benedictine monastery of Benediktbeuern—hence Beuern/*Burana*. Orff selected 24 of this number for his work. These, in the witty and fanciful spirit of Anacreon, focus on "wine, women, and song," themes invariably charged with the idea of changeable fortune. Orff's *Fortuna* is depicted as an orb—filling or fading—or a turning wheel, as in the opening poem's first two stanzas:

> O Fortune, like the moon,
> you ever wane,
> but to regain
> your former circumstance;
> life's equally fain
> to decimate
> as reinstate
> the mind with games of chance,
> prosperity
> and penury
> reversing with a glance.
>
> Immense and futile Fate,
> uneasy ground,
> safety unsound,
> mistakenly awaited,
> to your wheel I'm bound;
> you've hidden your face
> denied your grace,
> for sorrow was I slated;
> I've lost the knack
> this barren back
> shows what you've perpetrated.

Carmina Burana itself comes full circle, beginning and ending with the same poem, the work itself thus emblematic of Fortune's every turn, and of its ever returning.

Primarily in Latin, *Carmina Burana* contains occasional Middle High German and Provençal verse. The original poems, as typical of Latin poetry of the Middle Ages, are all consistently rhymed and metered—as are my translations, though I significantly paraphrase to convey sense and spirit rather than literal meaning. The Beuern songs selected and arranged for this volume were once part of my translation of Carl Orff's *Carmina Burana*, commissioned by conductor Robert Shaw (1916–1999) for the Atlanta Symphony Orchestra's concerts and subsequent Telarc recording. The poems provide a sustained and playfully Anacreontic counterpart to the amatory verse of the volume's initial Greek offerings.

There follow a number of translations from the first century BC to the first AD by the Roman poets Catullus, Petronius, and Lucretius, and by the nineteenth-century French poet Charles Baudelaire (PART IV). These works strike erotic themes derived from, reminiscent of, or consonant with those of Sappho. The seven selections bear introductions explaining the poems' relevance to this work and, as may happen, to one another. For instance, Catullus was the first love poet of Rome, as was Sappho the first of Greece. Though separated from her by some five hundred years, Catullus knew Sappho's poetry, even adapting one of her poems. He names his beloved "Lesbia"—in real life the notorious "Claudia"—meaning "the Lesbian," i.e., "the girl/woman from Lesbos" (not meaning "lesbian" at this early point). Which is also to say Catullus acknowledges Sappho's poetic supremacy, regardless her sexual attentions. The inclusion of Lucretius and Petronius will be apparent in context and from the introductions there offered. Baudelaire, for his part, composed a fifteen-stanza, seventy-five-line poem titled "Lesbos," the first five stanzas of which, here translated, suffice for illustration and comment. "Lesbos" is followed by Baudelaire's formally similar—stanza, meter, rhyme, and invocational *Mère* 'Mother'—but thematically contrastive "Le Balcon" ("The Balcony"). The contrast turns on fever versus calm, on love irremediably lost versus love recollected and reassuring.

Akin to the distress of love lost, and little reassuring for all its multitudes, is the Catullan count of kisses given or desired, their hundreds of thousands measured out against the one lasting night and sleep of death. "Le Balcon" is perhaps the best, the most contemplative, and most soulfully inspiriting of all Baudelaire's poems. His "Lesbos," by contrast, tends toward the steamy, the libidinous, the lurid—of a kind in that respect with other contemporaneous depictions of Sappho, notably those of artist Gustave Moreau (1826–1898) and English poet Algernon Charles Swinburne (1837–1909), himself the English poetic incarnation of Sappho, adapting her formalism and fervor as no poet before or since. Of similar disposition is Pierre Louÿs's (1870–1925) *Les Chansons de Bilitis* (*The Songs of Bilitis*).

PART V offers a new translation and detailed analysis of one of antiquity's most famous and frequently translated poems. The chapter titled, "Safe and Sound Ashore: Horace's *Odes* 1.5, 'To Pyrrha'" is, so to speak, the book's anchor, "weighted" with the theme of "shipwreck sea" as depicted in the book's cover art and in prominent poetic selections. The poem deals with the anticipated consequences of that most disastrously recurring of sexual encounters—libertine lover and her naive and inexperienced partner.

These works have in part inspired my own original poems (PART VI): some of a literary inspiration, including *Les Chansons de Bilitis* and the *Greek Anthology*; others, of Sapphic metric inspiration. These, like my translations, are formalist, which is to say form-driven—exhibiting various meters, rhymes schemes, stanzaic formations, and other such traditional incidences of poetry. If formally structured translation succeeds in its own right as English-language poetry, then one's original poetry hopefully does the same. My own poems over the years are thus both integral to and formally indistinguishable from my translations, the line often thin between translated and original verse. "If I am interested in a certain kind of translation, it is because I am invested in a certain kind of poetry."

I mention in closing that five of my poems—herein §§129, 130, 131, 132, 133—were set to music by Greek-Canadian composer Constantine Caravassilis (b. 1979). The resulting work titled *Five Duban Songs* received its world premiere (and was recorded for future release) at the famed House of the Blackheads, in Tallinn, Estonia, May 19, 2018. The soloist was mezzo-soprano Ariana Chris, with Kaisa Roose conducting the Tallinn Chamber Orchestra (Tallinna Kammerorkester). The work is being readied for CD release together with other Caravassilis Sappho-inspired compositions, including *Sappho de Mytilène* (2008); *My Life a Lyric Cry* (2017), based on Sara Teasdale's "Sappho"; and *From Sappho's Lyre* (2019), based on my translations (from *The Lesbian Lyre*) of "The Hymn to Aphrodite," "He Appears to Me," and Sappho "On Old Age."

– JMD, NEW YORK CITY, 2019

---

*All translations are my own, except those appearing on p. 38 and p. 235, two appearing on p. 298, and those of Homer, for which I rely on Richmond Lattimore, *The Iliad of Homer* (Chicago: Univ. of Chicago Press, 1951), 60th anniversary edition: Univ. of Chicago Press, 2011, introduction and notes by Richard Martin.

Introduction

Five Archaic Greek Lyric Poets

I OFFER AN OVERVIEW of the Greek lyric poets appearing in this volume. As my focus is the poetry and its translation, I de-emphasize biographical minutiae. That Archilochus lived from 680–640 BC and was the son of a slave woman and an aristocrat from the island of Paros, or that Alcman is sometimes thought to have been a Lydian from Sardis, sometimes a Laconian from Messoa, is information as often mentioned as forgotten— though larger elements of biography decidedly contribute to an overview. What follows, then, are brief summaries to the extent relevant to the poetry or poetic persona. Section marks indicate the poems as numbered herein.

SAPPHO

Sappho is the first love poet of the West and arguably the greatest poet of all time. As the English poet Algernon Charles Swinburne (1837–1909) proclaimed, Sappho is "simply nothing less—as she is certainly nothing more—than the greatest poet who ever was at all." Swinburne, for his part, and with his impeccable Greek, is the English poetic embodiment of Sappho, both metrically and emotionally. He is, in fact, preferable to any translation for those wanting to experience the essence of Sappho in English.

Sappho's Lesbos—well wooded, well cultivated, and well populated— lay within several hours of Sardis, the capital of the wealthy kingdom of Lydia in Asia Minor (§§4, 8, 27, 48). The island was active in seventh-century

BC trade and colonization; it was torn by bouts of factionalism and political upheaval to which the aristocratic Sappho was sometimes prey (§28), although her poetry reflects little of this. As Aphrodite is Sappho's special goddess and herself apolitical among the contentious gods, so is Sappho's poetry apolitical. The women of Lesbos were famed for their beauty no less than for their sophistication. Beauty contests were a yearly event.

Ancient criticism of Sappho both reflects and assures an unrivaled poetic supremacy among her contemporaries. In epigrams from the *Palatine Anthology* she is regularly counted as the tenth of the Muses: "Memory [mother of the Muses] herself was astonished when she heard the honey-sweet Sappho, wondering whether mankind possessed a tenth Muse." Sappho is deemed "the equal of any god" and the ultimate in her craft: "You have established the beginning and end of all lyric song." Also counting Sappho among the Muses, the Greek historian and biographer Plutarch (46–120 AD) elaborates: "Sappho utters words truly mingled with fire and gives vent through her song to the heat that consumes her heart." In so doing, she is said to "heal the pain of love with the Muses' melody." Again, in the *Palatine Anthology*, she is considered the "sweetest of love-pillows to the burning young"; a companion to Hymen, god of weddings at the bridal bed, and to Aphrodite, who laments Adonis in the sacred grove of the blessed.

Sappho was praised as well as derided in antiquity, when critics focused on her sexuality rather than on her poetry. The Greek comic playwrights of the fourth century BC were particularly unsparing (and influential), notwithstanding their works are known in mere fragments or by title alone. A key source is Ovid, who espouses both sides of the issue, thus doing little to resolve it. Ovid asks, "What did Sappho of Lesbos teach but how to love maidens? Yet Sappho herself was safe." By 'safe' (*tuta*) Ovid apparently means that Sappho condoned, without herself practicing, homosexuality. Ovid's position here appears to contradict the view taken in his famed "Sappho-Phaon Epistle":

> Not Pyrrha's coterie nor Methymna's girls beguile me now, nor any Lesbian maiden. Dazzling Cydro's of no account—Anactoria and Atthis, once embraced, are now disdained; and the hundred others, loved to my reproach, relinquished this their claim to callous you [Phaon] alone.

2

The rhetorician-philosopher Maximus of Tyre (2nd century AD), in an equally famous statement, takes a more edifying view:

> But is not love of the Lesbian poetess (if one can compare older with more recent) in fact identical with Socrates' amatory art? It seems to me that each of them pursued a particular kind of affection, for women in the one case and men in the other. Both claimed to have many beloveds, and to be captivated by anyone who was beautiful. What Alcibiades, Charmides, and Phaedrus were to the one, Gyrinna, Atthis, and Anactoria were to the poetess of Lesbos.

Forests have fallen for the paper spent on this comparison. We may for the present note that much of Sappho's surviving work is ambiguous about the type of love involved, and for that reason the more interesting. The love that Sappho's Aphrodite controls may be heterosexual or lesbian. Both types find expression in Sappho's work and life (see pp. 13–15). Sapphic love may have been initiatory, the preparation for marriage in a sexually segregated society; it may have been celebratory of Aphrodite and the Muses; it may have been ritually bonding or expressive; it may have been dreamily languid; it may have been fevered, torrid. The nineteenth-century French poet Charles Baudelaire, for one, depicts it just so:

> Lesbos, where balmy nighttimes langu'rously reign,
> That—in mirror's view, infelicitous gain!—
> Goad vacant-eyed girls to self-pleasured disdain,
> Their ripened fruits gladdened where no man has lain.
> Lesbos, where balmy nighttimes langu'rously reign.

[Baudelaire, *Lesbos* (see further pp. 198–201)]

An unrivaled female poet and lover of women in a man's world (where male poets also typically wrote of homoerotic loves), Sappho has in turn been admired, derided, moralized, analogized, and—in her despair of a heterosexual rebuff—allegedly driven to suicide on an obscure island cliff. The analogy to Socrates intellectualizes, even as it seeks to redeem, Sappho's love of women. It further places that love on a par with the love of men for men as propounded and practiced by the wisest man of all. This is surely the firmest ground.

ARCHILOCHUS

❦

Archilochus of Paros—an island in the southern Aegean midway between Athens and Crete—is among the earliest Greek lyric poets. Though his diction is largely Homeric, he often deviates from the conventional epic outlook (e.g., §§82–83). Archilochus's poems span a broad emotional range. He seeks to understand and adjust to the vagaries of life (§81). He expresses the genuine emotion of the soldier–poet (§§78–80) in poems as much from the heart in their way as is his erotic verse. He is the most explicitly sexual of the archaic Greek lyric poets (§§84–88). For all its constraint and veiled allusion, the lengthy Neoboulē fragment (§75) is without parallel. I omit two of Archilochus's poems only because they are coarse in a way that finds no parallel in this volume.

As concerns poetic meter, Archilochus was the literary founder of the iamb—the repeated alternation of short and long syllables (⌣ —) conspicuous in English iambic pentameter. He was also the first extant Greek poet to use the trochee—an alternation of long and short syllables (— ⌣)—less prominent in English, but found, for example, in Henry Wadsworth Longfellow's *Song of Hiawatha.* Iambic meter is considered by poet-critic George Will (b. 1928) "one of the most 'heavily sensuous' of Greek meters," distinguished in its suggestiveness from the more stately dactylic hexameter of Homer, marked by the varied alternation of dactyls (— ⌣ ⌣) and spondees (— —). Archilochus's use and mixture of iambic and trochaic meter impart an "aural sensuousness [that] duplicates sensuous meaning." Notwithstanding the origin of iambic in early Greek religious invective (Gr. *iambo* 'assail'), the meter's adaptation to erotic ends exhibits a quality central to the appreciation of poetry as discussed herein: *decorum*, understood as "the proper harmony between manner and matter," i.e., between form and content.

The intrinsic qualities of his verse aside, a central event in the poet's life—reflected both in his work and in references by later writers—was his betrothal to one Neoboulē ('she of the new plan,' 'recently minded,' or 'new scheme'); and her subsequent dispossession by her father, Lycambes, who married her off to a wealthier suitor (§§74–75). The event is thought to have imparted the vehemence so characteristic of Archilochus's poetry. The

4

legend, developed long after the poet's time, was that he so raged against Lycambes and his daughters that they hanged themselves in desperation.

Direct evidence of Lycambes or his daughters is, however, so scant as to call the event into question. Thus, if the verses do not reflect the poet's *own* person and situation, they serve an invective function, which in turn determines both narrative and narrative persona. By *persona*, we understand the poet's assumed or traditional role in a given genre. A piece like the Neoboulē fragment confirms what we also infer from other fragments, namely, an inherited tradition of vituperative poetry with stylized characters and themes. The issue is one of "assumed personality and the imaginary situation." Invective and its praise counterpart found social expression through the prime medium of verse. The genre's stylized characters include, as in the Neoboulē fragment, the betrayed or thwarted suitor, the wanton or wayward beloved, and the controlling father. The development of literary archetypes is in fact traceable to archaic Greek lyric, beginning with the conceits of vituperation and praise. We note that the relationship between invective and satire is often one of degree. Invective is aggravated satire, the difference between railing against and merely ridiculing. Invective is thus personalized, seeking to "search and destroy," while satire is generalized in its blanketing of current foibles. In either case, however, the character types have enjoyed a rich literary and performance afterlife.

Archilochean in its invective is the Old Comedy of the Athenian Aristophanes (5th century BC), singling out, in fantastical plots, the politicos and sundry reprobates of his day. The New Comedy of Menander (4th and 3rd centuries BC), as shown by the title of his one surviving play—*Dyskolos* (*The Curmudgeon* or *Misanthrope*)—dealt not so much with individualized characters as with types. As types act in predictable ways, the genre is known as "comedy of manners." It, in turn, influenced the Roman playwrights Plautus and Terence (3rd century BC). Roman comedy, e.g., *Menaechmi* (*The Menaechmus Brothers)* and *Miles Gloriosus* (*The Braggart Soldier*), further conventionalized Menandrean plot lines, even while recalling Archilochean themes of adultery, jealousy, and old age—the plots typically involving lovers pitted against disapproving elders. We have the "boor" of the Roman poet Horace (1st century BC), forever hallowed as the unflinching type he is; while the satirist Juvenal (1st and 2nd centuries AD) turns from Horace's gentle derisions to the pointed denunciations of his own more profligate times.

The literary type is also a feature of Greek tragedy—a community-based religious experience in fifth-century Athens. Tragic characters often represent fixed ideas and positions: Creon, inflexible state authority and law; Hippolytus, steadfast and disdainful chastity; Ajax, insuperable and suicidal grievance; Philoctetes, inconsolable and isolating physical injury. Though tragic types helped to universalize the theater-going experience, they did not monopolize the stage. In marked contrast to the Creons and Ajaxes is Orestes, uniquely and intractably duty-bound to slay his mother, thus avenging his father, whom she had murdered. As types are unchanging human nature writ large, their portrayals endure, which is to say, *they are always modern*; that they are *classic*—never "old" or outdated. Distinguished as types, they are necessarily exaggerated, caricatured. A primary vehicle of type-portrayal was sixteenth-century Commedia dell'Arte, its highly popular characters including Harlequin, Columbine, Pierrot, Scaramouch, and Pulcinella; "Pulcinella"—anglicized to "Punchinello"—begetting "Punch" of "Punch and Judy," with regional variants throughout Europe, including the principal character of Stravinsky's *Petrushka*.

Satire and vituperation seek to bruit a complaint to the world. What makes Archilochus's Neoboulē poem atypical, no less than significant in this respect, "is the [unusual] absence of any attempt to give the narrator's experience a permanent or general significance, or to pass on a message to society. Even Archilochus, the archetypal misfit, usually felt moved to involve the community as a whole in his complaints and insults, and to give it the benefit of his advice." Such a view, urging a predominantly emotional response, is contrary to the idea, above stated, of the "poet's assumed or traditional role in a given genre." In fact, the issue of private versus public permeates archaic Greek lyric. Sappho's poetry is what a later age would deem predominantly private. Yet Sappho too is thought to offer a predetermined public persona, dictated by the assumed social context and function of her verse. Thus, when Sappho invokes Aphrodite or other gods, or mentions altars or religious festivities, her poems may have been taken as cult performances—real or imagined—her circle of friends the celebrants. In such a case, the personal is not only amplified through divine affiliation but made communicable as ritual in which others may share. "Quickly [you] arrived," says Sappho in the great "Hymn to Aphrodite" (§1), "a smile on your immortal face." The divine is thus summoned, as if by spell or incantation—the incantatory language and structure of Sappho's very poetry—to intercede in human events. The goddess arrives, the ally of her summoning supplicant, even as she provides a sense of presence and reassurance to all.

Some urge that Sappho is "a feminine counterpart of Archilochus." However, Archilochus is more demonstrative and excoriating, whereas Sappho is contemplative and allusive. Archilochus shares his opinions forthrightly with his fellows; Sappho remains elusive in her emotions, and in language often symbolic. Archilochus is more overtly sensual and self-centered, more autobiographical. He is at times unhinged. The perspective is unlike anything else in archaic Greek lyric, for example:

> Ever short of what she's lusting for,
> she's shown it all, the girl's a whore! (§75)

> And on that skin, insatiable, alight,
> hurling belly on belly, thigh on thigh. (§88)

Sappho, by contrast, reveals an awareness of her ability "to comfort and anchor others." Archilochus's "first remarkable intuition of self" is ultimately self-limiting as he relentlessly squares off against others, unaware of the give and take, the emotional interdependence that resides in human relationships. Aware of the rhythm that governs life (§81), he is yet incapable of emotional control. Sappho's voice, by contrast, is vulnerable and introspective, albeit confirmed in its pride. The audience suddenly shrinks from an entire city to a few close friends, whose problems and qualities she registers. Archilochus's intensity, whether of pleasure or pain, is instead his own rather than ours, and always suffered *alone*. He excels in the use of autobiography to make himself as distinct from everybody else as possible.

ALCMAN

Alcman of Sparta is the earliest choral composer whose work survives in substantial fragments. The grace and gaiety of the scenes Alcman portrays accord with what archaeology and literary references tell of Sparta in the seventh and sixth centuries BC: "Youth's mettle and the clear-tuned Muse bloom there." The phrase is ascribed to the musician and poet Terpander of Lesbos (7th century BC), believed active in Sparta at the time. For all their geographical remove, mid-seventh-century Lesbos and Sparta vied as "centers of musical excellence." Only later, in the fifth century BC, did Sparta become a byword for severity and privation, leaving its *Spartan* namesake to our vocabulary. Where Archilochus addresses his fellow citizens, Alcman composes, more than any other, for his own city; and such as to give his work a "strong, provincial, almost parochial" flavor. He is also fond of reference to obscure foreign tribes, both real and fabulous—to the puzzlement of scholars both ancient and modern.

The longest of Alcman's surviving poems is his *Partheneion* (*Maiden Song*), discovered in 1885 in an Egyptian tomb (§46). The most problematic text of the Greek lyric period, it is riddled with uncertainties, from the smallest to greatest points of interpretation. As Greek lyric scholar-editor David Gerber has lamented, "No poem in Greek choral lyric has been the subject of so many different interpretations as Alcman's 'Partheneion,' and if the following commentary presents no clear or consistent view, the reason is very simply that I am seldom certain in my own mind of the correct solution to many of the problems involved. I have, therefore, often presented various interpretations without stating any preference."

Despite such diffidence, the poem has been tackled and translated anew by Gloria Ferrari in her intriguing, and quite technical, *Alcman and the Cosmos of Sparta* (2008). Ferrari argues that the *Partheneion* chorus members portray archetypal dancers in the form of an astral chorus: "Although it is performed by maidens, 'Partheneion' is not about maidens but about *kosmos*, both in the sense of political order—the constitution of the state—and in the order of the universe." The argument is persuasively couched in "music of the spheres" theory, first articulated by the Greek philosopher Pythagoras (570–495 BC). Ferrari's advancement of the poem's cosmic import, however, does not lessen its ostensible appeal: "Here several female chorus members acclaim . . . one another's outstanding physical qualities graphically and lavishly; here too, they avow in sexually charged language an emotional investment in each other." I do not myself venture a new translation, instead reproducing Ferrari's, in her literal "bracketed" version, and Mary Lefkowitz's in fluid prose rendition.

ANACREON

۶ؖ

According to Pausanias, the Greek traveler and geographer (2nd century AD), Anacreon of Teos—a peninsula off the central coast of Asia Minor—was "the first poet after Sappho of Lesbos to write mostly love poems." For Sappho, love is a matter of recurrent helplessness. She calls repeatedly on Aphrodite for support (§1), though never viewing herself diminished on that account. Like Archilochus in his calmer moments, Sappho appreciates the rhythm, the iterations, of emotional life (§§1, 81). For Anacreon, love's recurrences—the game of it all—are less perturbing. Posterity assessed Anacreon as a drunkard and libertine. When one thinks of wine, women (or boys), and song, one recalls Anacreon. A court poet, like Ibycus, he composed at royal behest, with little recourse to historical, religious, or philosophic concerns. Anacreon's influence on later poets has been the greatest of any archaic Greek lyricist. A substantial body of poems known as *Anacreontics* was composed by various unknown authors from the period of the Roman Empire to Byzantine times. The poems are exquisite, as only elegant trifles can be. Their publication has often been the occasion for tasteful bookmaking.

IBYCUS

۶ؖ

Ibycus came from Rhegium—at the southeastern extreme of Italy, across from the Straits of Messina and Sicily—in the Greek-colonized south of Italy (Magna Graecia). He was active at the court of the tyrant Polycrates of Samos (an island off the southern coast of Asia Minor). There are only two surviving examples of Ibycus's love poetry (§§91–92). Their rich language, vivid imagery, and searing intensity set them off as among the finest examples of Greek poetry in any age. The poet, according to Cicero, excelled in this genre, surpassing Anacreon and Alcaeus (Sappho's contemporary). Indeed, Ibycus quite outdoes his compeers in conveying love's frightfulness.

Sappho describes love, unnervingly enough, as (an) *orpeton* 'crawler/slith-erer': "dissolver of limbs, bittersweet, irresistible, creeping in" (§36); again, she compares her love-smitten soul to mountain oaks "wracked ... by winds above" (§35). Anacreon figures love as a blacksmith, "again . . . striking the hammer's blow / plunging me / in Winter's torrent as I glow" (§46). For Ibycus, love's likeness to a "northern Thracian blast" is but the start: love's blast is "ablaze with flash of lightning, black . . ." (§91). For the archaic lyricists, Love, or *Eros,* is a primordial force, of a kind early recognized by Hesiod in his *Theogony*:

> Foremost of all then was Chaos born, followed by
> Broad-breasted Earth, the ever steadfast seat of all
> The gods, atop snowy Olympus resident;
> Then murky Tartarus, creviced in spacious earth,
> And Eros, fairest among the immortal gods,
> Looser of limbs, crushing in gods and humankind
> Within their breasts all sturdy thought and mindfulness.

The Greeks of the archaic period had thus not yet imagined Love as the winged Cupid—what would come to be known as the quiver- and arrow-bearing child of Venus (the Roman Aphrodite). The malicious night visitant or elfish babe asleep in rosebuds, quick to his mother Venus's bidding, was the creation of Hellenistic and Roman times. Though we have numerous references to Ibycus's narrative poetry, only a single fragmentary example survives, some forty-five verses. In this piece, Ibycus appears to have han-dled epic and mythological themes—Heracles, the Argonauts, the Trojan War—with a peculiarity perhaps owing to Stesichorus. Contemporary with Sappho and Alcaeus, Stesichorus was the first great poet of Magna Graecia (from which also Ibycus). Though considered in antiquity the "most Homeric" of poets, Stesichorus often departed from Homer and Hesiod in the details of his mythology. Ibycus was the second great poet of Magna Graecia and appears to have flourished some twenty-five years after Stesichorus's death.

Having surveyed the poets at issue and seen the variety of their circum-stances and predispositions, we look now, in PART I, to Homer (mid-8th century BC) at the forefront of the Greek literary tradition. Fully known to Sappho, her lyric contemporaries and followers, he is a touchstone, no less then they, of the gender issues by which our own twentieth- and twenty-first centuries are so politically—and pointlessly—divided. PART I looks not only to Homer and the lyric poets but also to key elements of Western culture that developed in their wake. It shows that *gender*—a too facile dictional substitute for *sex* (and its "primal notions of masculinity and femininity")—was as nearly irrelevant to antiquity as it surely is to us.

Part I

Female Homer and the Fallacy
of Gendered Sensibility

And will virtue, as virtue, differ at all whether it
be in a child or in an elderly person, in a woman
or in a man?

– PLATO, *Meno (73a)*

The beauty of Cordelia is neither male nor fe-
male; it is the beauty of virtue.

– MARGARET FULLER, *Woman in the Nineteenth
Century* (1845)

Genius is of no sex.

– HENRY CHORLEY, *Memorials of Mrs. Hemans*
(1836)

Introduction: On Male or Female Attributes,
Genres, and Appropriations

EPIC AND LYRIC POETRY are the bedrock of classical Greek literature
and of the Western literary tradition to which it gave rise—Homer,
antiquity's Poet; Sappho, its Poetess (8th through 6th centuries BC). It is
for a distinction of this kind that the term *poetess* is especially meaningful
and endures. The occasional uncertainty of distinguishing male and female
in poetry, or generally in the arts, is as early as Homer and Sappho both—
for reasons having little to do with their respective genders. As the topic of
gender and gendered creation is relevant to any discussion of Sappho, of her
poetry, and of the lyric genre she has ever dominated, I elaborate.

Though Sappho is known primarily as a female poet enamored of and writing poems for and about women, both her surviving works and the legends surrounding her life are ambiguous about the love she espoused. At the symbolic level, Sappho showed herself, and was equally shown, to be enamored of the moon (feminine) *and* sun (masculine) and, by extension, all things both feminine and masculine. In the poem containing her most extended surviving simile, moon, flowered eroticism, and the yearning for a female companion predominate (§8):

> She thought you a goddess,
> your song her special joy.
>
> Among Lydian women
> she now has her praise—
> as the rosy-fingered moon,
>
> shaming heaven's stars from sight
> shines, ocean-enthroned,
> over flowers in the night,
>
> over fields where chervil grows lush,
> where melilot and roses thrill
> to evening's dewy touch;
> ever wandering there, yearning
>
> for tender Atthis, she languishes—
> her gentle spirit crushed . . .

A quieter, more female-inspired setting and mood are difficult to imagine. This and similar Sapphic verse lend credence to the belief that "Lesbos may have been the most distinguished in what . . . was an early pan-Hellenic 'woman's culture' of colloquial poetry whose brilliance is hinted at in our evidence." At the same time, Sappho is quoted by the Greek rhetorician and grammarian Athenaeus (2nd–3rd centuries AD) as saying, "I love the exquisite—that and yearning for the sun have won me brightness and beauty." The statement marks as both feminine and masculine: feminine, to the extent "the exquisite" (Gr. *abros* [adj.]; *abrosunē* [n.]) symbolizes the delicate texture of sound manifest in Sappho's poetry (by contrast to more traditionally formulaic epic). Such

13

texture has been described as "a sort of phonic icon of the values of delicacy and refinement in [Sappho's] vision of love." Athenaeus's Sapphic attribution is masculine insofar as sun and sunlight, by contrast to the moon and its reflected glow, are direct, assertive, and revelatory. Sunlight pierces and penetrates, moonlight embraces and envelops.

These contrasts are artistically no more apparent than in Bernini's *The Ecstasy of St. Teresa* and Girodet's *Endymion* (discussed below). In another of her poems, Sappho longs for Anactoria, saying she would rather see her "face sparkling radiant with light than / Lydian charioteers and outfitted / infantry" (§4). No pale or muted glow here, but dazzling radiance. The male military image conjures a changing or variegated brilliance in the beloved's face, superior to the panoplied sun-reflected blaze of Lydian infantry. Through this resplendent and decidedly masculine lens, one woman, awestruck, surveys another's peerless beauty. Sappho is a devotee of sun and moon, of dazzling and muted brilliance alike, as person, occasion, and mood ordain.

By the same token, Aphrodite, Sappho's special goddess, controls both heterosexual and lesbian love, both types finding expression in Sappho's work and life. The goddess is responsible for Helen's adultery with Paris (§4), Sappho viewing this instance of heterosexual compulsion (between the world's most beautiful woman and beautiful man) as irresistible. At the time, Aphrodite is responsible for the departure of Sappho's own beloved girl to Lydia (§6). Virginity is a cherished state (§17), but not to be cultivated (§20). Though its loss may be painful (§§18, 19, 21), marriage and the handsomeness of the groom find ready praise (§§22, 23, 24, 25) and sometimes ribald treatment (§§29, 30). One Sapphic fragment (§27), in its use of the indeterminate *pais* 'child, companion, (sexual) plaything' would appear to call Sappho's sexual preference into question, though the reference is likely to her (putative) daughter (arguing Sappho's bisexuality). Sappho's longest surviving work is an epic narrative, in near-Homeric style (i.e., meter), celebrating the wedding of Hector and Andromache (§26), an event not treated, though mentioned in the *Iliad*. According to Ovid (our primary source for the legend), Sappho ended her life in a suicidal leap for unrequited love of the ferryman Phaon, which is another testament to Sappho's heterosexuality. This supposedly occurred from the Leucadian Cliff, on the island of Lefkas, off the western coast of Greece (near Ithaca in the Ionian Sea). The sum of these references makes Sappho an avowed and possibly married lesbian (and mother), dying of heterosexual despair. Shall we conclude from any of this that the masculine and feminine in art, or in life, are necessarily or at all recognizable as such? "It is rare for a woman poet," says acclaimed Australian author Germaine Greer, "to be at ease moving between masculine and feminine, aggressive and passive postures, especially when the subject matter is love." Perhaps not.

However we think to allocate the masculine and feminine in Sappho, she genders as *masculine* at the institutional level by virtue of the male-centric singing and transmission of her poetry. As Laurel Bowman reminds us,

> All poetry remaining to us from the ancient world was disseminated through the almost entirely male-authored public tradition. To survive, female-authored poetry must somehow have become part of this 'mainstream' public tradition. Poetry that was heard only by the segregated female audience would not have been transmitted....

And as Gregory Nagy elaborates, there were two basic social contexts for the singing of Sappho's poetry by men: the symposium and the public festival (eventually including the Panathenaia, the major public festival of the Athenians). The tradition of performing Sappho's songs, which required virtuoso singing leading into choral singing and dancing, became professionalized as a tradition of monadic, or solo, singing as performed by men at symposia in Lesbos and other islands, and later in Athens, as of the early sixth and throughout the fifth century. This, Nagy calls the "professionalization by way of masculinization" of Sappho's poetry—a phenomenon in antiquity not unique to Sappho's poetry, conceptually the most female of all archaic poetries.

There are women's concerns and sensibilities voiced by men—whether as composers or transmitters—and men's concerns and sensibilities voiced by women. The two sexes know, readily reflect and create from, and appreciate each other's perspectives, however subordinate women have been in the process. Absent overt compositional indications, it is the rare reader who distinguishes author gender. The case for a gendered style, treatment, or even subject matter—i.e., "female perspective" or "women's tradition"—is tenuous, the male having traditionally, convincingly, and undifferentiatedly not only portrayed but also popularized and transmitted the female.

"Male perspective" can also, though less often, be tenuous—as anonymous or pseudonymous woman has often written, painted, or sculpted the equal of any man, with no one the wiser. With nothing comparable in the Greek tradition, we look to the Old Testament for female-voiced "male perspectives." The Songs of Miriam and Deborah are militant and militaristic compositions, praising God at length in highly poetic form for the destruction of Israelite enemies—Miriam (Moses's sister) and Deborah both prophets; Deborah also a military leader. But for the Bible's identification of the singers, neither song remotely suggests female authorship. Looking to "perspective," we would instinctively assume male authorship, the male voice superseding the female singer.

The Greek genre of *parthéneia* 'maiden songs'—of which Alcman's *Partheneion* (§46), however fragmentary, is the fullest surviving example—focuses on the beauty, innocence, and engagingly diffident eagerness of young girls. In such songs "the personality of the male author is completely submerged in the female voice"—which is to say, gender-marked authorship is largely a fiction, be the author male or female. Allowing for dictional changes reflecting change in subject matter over time, we further observe that the eventually attested female-authored poetry of antiquity was composed in the same style—i.e., the same traditional meters—as poetry composed by men or, we should say, poetry composed in a male-dominated oral poetic tradition originating in martial narratives. There was no overtly identifiable female poetry, only themes (and at times imagery) possibly more female-than male-associated: e.g., lament, love lyric, and lullaby (this last consisting of protective magical incantations with few surviving examples).

The "lament," as a subgenre of epic, though female-associated, tells an ultimately masculine tale. Prominent Homeric examples appear in the lament over the slain Patroclus (Achilles's companion) by Briseis (Achilles's concubine), and the laments over Hector by Andromache (wife), Hecuba (mother), and Helen (sister-in-law). There are the singularly anticipatory laments over Achilles by his sea-goddess mother, Thetis; while Hector, too, is lamented "though still living." The lament is largely female-marked because women—outwardly at least—tend to be more emotional than men, since closer to life and death processes. These include childbirth and women's intrinsic dependence on ever mortal man for well-being and survival—men in warrior societies daily called upon to slay or be slain.

Their martial preoccupations do not, however, at all exempt men from lament, as seen in the poignant example of Achilles lamenting his beloved Patroclus (although we read only of his role in leading the lament) or as when the entire community, women and men alike, join in the lament begun by King Priam of Troy over his son Hector. It is emphasized that Homer's men are not without emotion, weeping in many and various situations, and that a principal Homeric descriptive, or epithet, of *dakruon* 'tear' (the tears of men and women alike) is *thaleron* 'swelling, blooming, tender'. The longest and most penetrating laments, however, are by the *Iliad*'s female characters.

Further, though the *Iliad* distinguishes between the professional male lead singer of *thrēnos* 'lament', and non-professional male or female lead singer of *góos* 'lament', the distinction is slim. The lamentation for the slain Hector begins with *thrēnoi* (pl.). These are performed by *aoidoi* 'bards', who are the acknowledged performers and purveyors of epic poetry. It is the *Iliad*'s only mention of a *thrēnos*. As the bards lament, the women join in, and Andromache commences the *góos* among Hector's kinswomen. Otherwise, *góos* is the operative gender-neutral term and activity. *Thrēnos*, be it noted, is the exception rather than the rule, found only once in the *Odyssey* as well. There, it is the Muses themselves who antiphonally *thrēneon* 'lamented' the dead Achilles (as told by the ghost of Agamemnon), an event not recounted in the *Iliad*. Not insignificantly, then, are the *Iliad*'s two greatest heroes recipients of *thrēnos*, sung either by the Muses (female) or Muse-inspired bards (masculine). And it is Achilles alone who warrants lamentation by the Muses—he the *Iliad*'s sole warrior-musician and himself the subject matter and embodiment of Muse-inspired epic: "Sing, goddess [Muse], the rage of Achilles, Peleus's son (*Il.* 1.1)." The death of Achilles is the death of Homeric poetry itself and the supremacy it achieved through its singular embodiment of Achilles. The Muses indeed have cause to lament. Their lament—its moment, its monumentality—is such as contravenes Sappho's stricture that sorrow has no place in the house of those who serve the Muses. It has even less place among the Muses themselves; their theme *not* death, but creation and the immortal gods.

Where epic merely relates or tells of lament within its uniform hexametric meter, Greek tragedy *enacts* lament—its song, antiphonal responses, instrumentation, and dance—in its various meters and associated physical movements. In this setting, whether *thrēnos* or *góos* is male- or female-intoned is ultimately moot, because "the definitive form of lament is male by virtue of its being performed in the all-male genre of tragedy" (including the male performances of female roles). Female lament in tragedy is thus essentially *masculinized* "in an act of male appropriation," an act "so realistic that it becomes barely noticeable." Male appropriation comes with mythic/primordial antecedents in the form of the female Muses' empowerment of the male poet. "Male appropriation," as though something recently discovered or disclosed, has nowadays become a censorious feminist rallying cry.

Accordingly, *parthéneia* 'maiden songs' and tragic *thrēnoi/góoi* 'laments', to say nothing of Sappho's own poetry, all masculinize the female voice, imprinting female conduct and concern with male agency. Indeed, if the argument for female authorship or literary tradition cannot be made from these instances, it is little made at all. The case of lament was of concern to the Athenian state, in which tragedy was a civic, communally absorbing, and state-reaffirming enterprise. The fear was that "men who represent the laments of women in tragedy will start to talk and think and even feel like women, not like the men they really are."

Male lament, coming full circle, is readily feminized. The concern was eventually muted with the development from epic lament of the independent genre of elegiac poetry (Gr. *elegos* 'song of mourning'), in couplets of alternating dactylic hexameter and pentameter. As Nagy has noted,

> [t]he sensuality [Gr. *terpsis* 'pleasure'] of lament is passed on, from one lamenting woman to the next. Men hear their song of lament, and they too pass it on, singing elegy. That sensuality gives pleasure, [which] is an elegiac pleasure, derived from the pleasure women take in passing on their own sorrows. Such are the delights of elegy.

Elegy came to be sung primarily by male participants at symposia. It embraced a broad range of topics and emotions, from poems on the transience of life (expressing fear, anger, or hatred) to those of civic pride and allegiance.

The difference then between "lament" and "elegy," in broad outline, was eventually one of focus: lament, on the loss of life; elegy, also on the loss (or shortness) of life, but also the loss (or frustration) of love—love and life the absolutes. Love elegy, as later developed in Rome, would evolve to embrace the frustration of love through the loss or *unobtainability* of the beloved—call it a love lament. Elegy no less than lament became masculin-ized. Of the Roman poets, Ovid especially masculinized the female voice in his *Heroides* (*Heroines*)—elegies written in the voices of fourteen mytho-logical and one historic woman (Sappho) lamenting abandonment by their lovers. For this, Ovid is pejoratively considered the "male appropriator" par excellence, Sappho having failed to find a poetess to embrace her, her situa-tion, and most poignant complaint.

For the larger purposes of this essay, we see, in the above examples, poetry composed by men in so persuasive a female voice, and reflecting so pervasive a female concern, as to equate with female persona. Such poetry manifests *the woman in the man*—the same poetry in due course "masculin-ized" (the precursor of "male appropriation"). At the same time, the "femi-nization" or female appropriation of male persona has been pronounced in various creative epochs. *The man in the woman* presents more frequently, either via pseudonymity—women lacking the creative license of men—or intrinsically to the artistic act itself, the created work in no way gender-marked. The *man in the woman* is also a matter of historical bias, because women who create other than by procreation are often deemed to have embarked upon a male prerogative and, in the process, *become* male. Thus did the Roman poet Horace designate *mascula Sappho* 'masculine Sappho'. Male and female are intrinsically too much of a kind to be resolved one way or the other. Should we expect or want them to be?

There are no Miriams or Deborahs in the Greek tradition and, if there were, their singing (as in the Old Testament) would be indistinguishable from that of their male compeers. Their roles are those of strong, heroic, and initiative-taking women—not of singers performing from a "woman's perspective" or requiring the like analysis or label. They exhibit no female compositional style, any more than does Sappho. Indeed, even the so-called Sapphic meter does not necessarily originate with Sappho, though she makes arresting use of it, ultimately affording it her name. The meter sur-vived into Roman times. More than half a millennium later, it was used to great and quite different effect, among others, by Catullus and Horace (with clear nods to Sappho) and by Ovid, as noted.

Meter is of the essence of classical poetry; it is what makes classical poetry *poetry*. As such, its concern is not with performance gender, but with "rhythmic stylization." By this is meant the ongoing regularization—the formalization and idealization—of poetic language independent of the spoken language from which it derived. Poetic "style" thus concerns, irrespective of gender, the development and refinement of poetic language—its meter and dictional components. There is what has been identified as the "language of Achilles" and the "language of Hector," but such language reflects the development of epic character in unprecedented (Achilles) or recurring (Hector) situations—Achilles grappling with the new epic reality thrust upon him (bravest but most dishonored of the Greeks); Hector ever urging, admonishing, and "hectoring" the Trojans. We further note that in the *Iliad's* "Embassy scene," where Ajax, Odysseus, and Phoenix seek to persuade Achilles to reconcile with Agamemnon and rejoin the fighting, each speaks in a manner indicative of his character and relationship to Achilles. Doing so, they "verge on allegorical figures": Ajax as comrade-in-arms, second only to Achilles in might; Odysseus, craftily, as the famed wily man he is (the brain to Achilles's brawn); and the aged Phoenix, father-like, as the caretaker he was to Achilles, first arrived as a youth to Troy. Andromache, for her part, intones the concerns and sympathies of Hector's loving wife (the "Meeting of Hector and Andromache"); and other women, characteristically, and as noted, intone laments for the dearly fallen. In each case, the "language" associated with a particular male or female actor reflects character, relationship, and situation—not gender as such, or at all.

Says one critic, "A female author, if she chose to compose in such traditionally masculine genres as epic, had to assert the value of her own experience as a woman within poetic forms that, through customary usage, denied the independent worth of that usage." (The same, in light of the above discussion, would apply to a female composer of tragedy.) The hypothetical is a red herring because female authors did *not* compose in the epic genre (as noted by Euripides) and, if they did, would have been unable to express gender-reflective or revelatory concerns within the long-developed metric, thematic, and linguistic framework of epic. Nor did epic "deny the independent worth" of a woman's experience, though dwelling on it less vis-à-vis the heroic matter intrinsic to the genre. As detailed below, there are ample appreciations of women's value and experience in Homer and subsequent poets; while Sappho, expectedly harking to a gentler, more personal lyric muse, is no less male than Homer in her one surviving epic fragment (§26). In fact, the case is made for Sappho's subsequent performance masculinization via the singing of her songs at male symposia and public festivals. The masculinization of her poetry is ultimately what assured its survival.

Thus, and with *parthéneia*, *thrēnoi*, and *góoi*, gender-identified artistry in ancient Greece goes more to performance mode and situational or institutional expectation than to author gender or author-gender associations. Even where Sappho strikes a particularly female stance, exalting the object of one's love, whatever it be, over the putative male delight in sun-reflecting infantry (§4), the composition genders as masculine, if recited predominantly by men, and as female, given a tradition of female performance. Indeed, more than once does Sappho highlight female concerns, in contradistinction to epic concerns. Such instances provide intrinsic or possibly thematic indications of female authorship. In the Greek performance tradition, however, such authorship is certainly not a matter of poetic style—defined *as* and *by* meter—and is eventually subject to male "appropriation."

Three to four hundred years following Sappho, the Hellenistic female poet Nossis (3rd century BC) expressly posits her connection to Sappho, and the poet Erinna (4th century BC) writes verse (however limited) apparently bearing comparison to Homer. Erinna's partially surviving *Distaff*, in hexameters, mourns the death of a young female friend. The *Distaff* is reminiscent of Sappho's laments for the "loss"—through departure—of beloved friends, one of them, as we know, from Lesbos to Lydia (§§6, 8). The *Distaff*, of *known* female authorship, is further novel as a separately composed, a *freestanding*, lament—uprooted, as it were, from the male epic poet's epic-embedded female lament for a fallen hero. This change is argued to have "had the result . . . of eliminating the ventriloquization of the grieving woman by the epic narrator. The mourner now speaks for herself, not as the male narrator imagines her to speak."

Perhaps so, but the male narrator's imagination in such matters is no less compelling, however epic-oriented. Moreover, whatever the object of male- or female-authored lament, it has no bearing on poetic form, Homer and Erinna both composing in epic hexameters. Erinna's reputation rests almost entirely on the 300-line *Distaff*, of which only a papyrus-preserved portion survives. It is yet telling that in effecting a stance independent of epic, Erinna resorts to lament, an epic subgenre traditionally associated with women—albeit in the *Distaff* it's the lament of a young girlfriend rather than of a fallen hero. This but tweaks a traditional theme. Sappho, by contrast, quite upends an epic theme, substituting the love of military display, and its concomitant *kleos* 'glory', with the love for the object of one's desire. Yet even that theme, under Greek performance norms, becomes "masculinized" (unless Sappho or her coterie were performing it). The poem, in its commanding Sapphic meter, nonetheless is and ever remains exquisite, which is all that ultimately matters.

According to "Suidas," author of a tenth-century AD Byzantine encyclopedia, Erinna "wrote the *Distaff*, a poem in the Aeolic and Dorian dialect in 300 epic verses. She composed epigrams as well. She died a maiden at age nineteen. Her verses were deemed the equal of Homer." In other words, she was worthy of Homeric comparison in her composition of a lament, the epic subgenre most associated with women. She doubtless, and equally well, could have lamented a fallen hero in epic style. Comparison of Erinna to Homer, in any event, strikes hollow, being the comparison of a nineteen-year-old, with a single verse composition, to Homer, composing in and as the summation of a centuries-old oral tradition.

Assuming the validity of Suidas's assessment, Erinna, had she lived longer, might conceivably have rivaled Homer as a composer of epic. However, even this would not have made her a female epic poet of comparable stature. By Erinna's time, the oral age of Homeric epic had long passed, written (orally transcribed) texts of Homer were being edited in Alexandria, and what epic we have from the Alexandrian period, i.e., Apollonius's *Argonautica*, though still in hexameters, was written quite in reaction to, not conformity with, Homer. Homer was considered antiquated to the period's avant-garde preferences (even, perhaps, as Bach, toward the end of his life, was considered dated by his own sons). Poetry of the Alexandrian period, in whatever form, exhibits a *neoteric*, or modernist, affect—a precocity—far removed from Homer's innate accessibility, naturalism, and expanse. Erinna, moreover, composed in a combined Aeolic/Doric dialect, while Homeric poetry is primarily Ionic with Aeolic and Doric admixtures. "Erinnic" epic would ultimately have borne little comparison to the Homeric epic with which her *Distaff* is passingly—and seventeen hundred years later—compared. Suidas's direct comparison of Erinna to Homer is both strained and unhelpful.

§▲

Greer elaborates on artistic gendering vis-à-vis poetic inspiration itself. With apparent reference to the 115-line invocation to Hesiod's *Theogony* (*Birth of the Gods*), Greer speaks of "a mystic union with the Muses who enter [the poet], as it were, fertilizing his imagination and making possible the development of the living poem"—"living" because fertilization is generative. The act, Greer further explains, is "penetrative"; positing a *female* fecundator (i.e., infuser of reproductive matter)—a notion yet challenging the traditional view of *male* fecundator and female begetter/genetrix. The muse as fecundator, she continues, is inaccurate, as the Muses do not merely fertilize but are themselves productive—"active artificers" of poetry in their own right. They thus visit the poet, as in the *Theogony*, themselves singing the very song of creation they "breathe into" him. However, though the nature of inspiration bespeaks a female-associated in-taking or receptivity, the male-gendering of poets persists, resisting correction. This hinders women's self-perception as poets and others' perceptions of them as poets. Greer further suggests that women poets, by their idolization of male poets, have themselves largely to blame for their own artistic devaluation and are otherwise devalued by social conventions and expectations.

Deeming the poet–muse construct "oppressive," Greer proposes that the female poet view herself as a "creature of a different kind, not a poet but a poet-ess" (a term perhaps less pejorative or "sexist" when Greer wrote). The nomenclature leads Greer to consider the qualities of expression and sentiment associated with a female poet. These variously, and little surprisingly, include "delicacy, modesty, charm, domesticity, hypersensitivity and piety, as well as filial, sororal, and maternal affections"; and further, "gracefulness, purity, civility, compliancy, reticence, chastity, affability, and politeness." The list by no means forecloses male experience or depiction of the same. Greer, moreover, notes that the poetess "does not aspire to . . . the revelation of gut truths of womanhood, or any negative feelings of rage, contempt, protest, despair or disbelief." This too is arguable. If the poetess does not aspire to such revelations, the poet, in his depictions of women—e.g., Medea, Phaedra, the Bacchantes—surely does; while the poetess, for all her ability, grasp, experience, or intuitive sense of such matter, may equally do so, but rarely does. We recall that the "Madwoman in the Attic" trope originated in Victorian women's literature in Charlotte Brontë's *Jane Eyre* (1847) as a way of depicting unsympathetic female villains. There is surely nothing in the poet/poetess divide, or in the inherent quality of femaleness in any art, delimiting such depiction.

Thus, and as the following discussion urges, there is little in male or female artistic endeavor—be it poetry, the novel, painting, sculpture, or music—that is intrinsically male or female or identifiable as such. Highlighting the femaleness of artists—and subjecting them to feminist analysis—typically proceeds from initial knowledge of the artist's female identity. The analytical premise is for that reason flawed. So too are the theoretical approaches, like narratology, built around "narratives by women." Who is necessarily to know, absent foreknowledge, that the narrative is female-authored? The morass thickens when feminism (an "explicitly political criticism") and narratology (a "largely formal poetics") keep company. The male artist's impulse *and* ability to represent the female have long been apparent, and the result never so marked or successful as when he depicts the female vis-à-vis the male. The same is true of the female author's depiction of the male vis-à-vis the female. In the hope of showing the trees and forest both, I propose that artistic creation is not only non-gendered but also intrinsically unconcerned with gender, that humanity and human nature are sooner the concerns. In practice, however, there is subject matter traditionally associated with each gender, and style is itself sometimes argued—erroneously—to be gendered, the notion being that a female manner of expression is somehow identifiable. Again, *character* may be linguistically conveyed, but not gender. At the same time, and more hypothetically, there is that which each artist does as a gendered artist, whether or not reflecting his or her own gender, and whether or not by design.

1. The Case for the Odyssey's Female Authorship

Though best known for his posthumously published *The Way of All Flesh*, Samuel Butler (1835–1902), iconoclast author, critic, and prose translator of Homer, was also known for *The Authoress of the Odyssey* (1897), ambitiously subtitled: "where and when she wrote, who she was, the use she made of the Iliad & how the poem grew under her hands" (hereinafter *Authoress*). The work retains its vogue, in the words of classicist Mary Beard, "because [it] so consistently symbolizes what we now all agree *we do not think*." Scholars and public intellectuals, following its original publication, viewed it with sarcasm and mirth, or deemed it parody, some speculating the irascible Butler had *himself* intended it as such, however elaborate and learned. As Butler's biographer notes, "The theory did little for his reputation in Britain. As so often, he ruffled the feathers of the orthodox and failed to convince the more radical." More recently, feminist scholars have adverted to it not so much for its authority as to establish a "genealogy" for their own perspectives. I offer that all great art is essentially gender-neutral, by which I mean *indifferent* in both motivation and result to male or female authorship. I say so having earlier "acknowledged an entire literature to the contrary."

That the *Odyssey* was, to a virtual certainty, composed by a male, or through the medium of a male-dominated epic storytelling tradition, did not, in Butler's time at least, foreclose the case for female authorship. Sappho, as noted, was a female poet enamored of and writing poetry for and about women, even while aspects of her life and work (to the extent known) were demonstrably heterosexual. Her male-poet compeers also wrote erotic poetry inspired by the love of young men, yet wrote as well of women and heterosexual attraction. Gender, seen from even such limited examples as these, no sooner prescribes than proscribes artistic impulse or result; the obverse being that art is rarely gender marked.

Butler himself opined that his views would be rejected by the classical mainstream. Some see the self-disavowal as a reverse-psychological ploy intended to heighten interest. Butler has been criticized, among other things, for his anachronistic assumption that Homeric characters should be acting like proper Victorians. Proceeding by way of detailed passage analysis—he read Greek as easily as he did English—Butler explores the compositional development and interrelation of the *Iliad* and *Odyssey*, a continued topic of scholarly interest. In the end, however, his learnedly ingenious arguments had little impact when published and have since been rendered moot by what we now know of oral composition.

Butler's thesis developed from the perception that parts of the *Odyssey* (a domestic poem versus the martial *Iliad*) are of such exquisite sensibility that only a woman could have written them, to say nothing of consummate female portrayals throughout the poem itself; while other, more technical parts are so clumsily handled that *no man* could have written them. To be sure, at the core of both the *Iliad* and *Odyssey* are extraordinary women; and their relationship to men—men the fighters, women the motivation— is critical to epic poetry and its perpetuation. Yet, for all its reverence of Sappho, antiquity never surmised a female Homer. Indeed, the distinction drawn by the Greek literary critic Longinus (1st century AD), the preserver of Sappho's famed "Hymn to Aphrodite," is that Homer composed the more dramatic *Iliad* in the heyday of his genius, and the more narrative *Odyssey* in his declining years. Butler had ultimately to concede that while nothing in the *Odyssey* foreclosed the possibility of female authorship, received opinion, rejecting an *Odyssey* by any *male* other than Homer, would be "dead set" (Butler's words) against female authorship.

Butler had bucked the tide and found it bracing. His premise was misguided from the outset: that only a woman could have created the *Odyssey's* varied and ever felicitous female characters. Shakespeare created Amanda, Beatrice, Cordelia, Desdemona, Imogen, Lady Macbeth, Ophelia, Portia, Rosalind, and Viola. He knew women, it is said, better than any woman—even as the male actors of his day played female characters; these, in the course of the play, sometimes in disguise as men, wooed by unsuspecting male-impostering women (Rosalind/Ganymede; Viola/Cesario). Let postmodernists and gender theorists make of this what they will. And "Mme. Bovary, the immortal Mme. Bovary," said August Emile Faguet (1847–1916), author, critic, and French Academy member, "is the most complete woman's portrait I know in the whole of literature, including Shakespeare and including Balzac." "*Emma Bovary, c'est moi.*" Looking into himself, Flaubert found his heroine. Goethe ended his monumental *Faust* with the redemptive affirmation, *das ewig-Weibliche zieht uns hinan* 'the eternal feminine draws us upward'. By "eternal feminine" he meant the nurturing dominion of woman over man and the willingness of man's surrender to it; the ensign she plants in his plaintive being, claiming both him and his betterment as her own; the awareness that comprises his ideal and ideally heartened and enlightened state—toward which he strives, against which he measures himself, and a primary purpose of which is protection of the biologically weaker and desired female; and the *attraction* that both incites and subdues him, that complements him, that makes woman his proverbial better half, that makes life without her impossible.

This, however, little contents those who disdain the intrusion of male regard or need, finding it better to be and have it all than be another's better half. "Fools," says Hesiod, "who know not how much better the half is than the whole." The disdain finds voice in feminist scholars who begrudge either male depiction of the female, or male handling of putatively female topics— Sappho, for instance. Whereas "male appropriation" has thus far been apparent as quasi-acquisition through performance and performance sponsorship, male appropriation more recently surfaces as male scholarly endeavor. With the entrenchment of Women's Studies, men dealing with matters female are disparaged as "appropriators." Their status is a subset of the larger phenomenon that is "cultural appropriation"—the cornerstone nowadays of grievance-and-complaint fueled by political correctness and multicultural thinking. Cultural appropriation occurs when the dominant culture (or gender) adopts elements of the minority culture (or opportunely minority-associated *gender*, e.g., "women and minorities") in a way suggesting colonialism and imbalance of power (*read*: oppression). The totality of this impulse typically pits everyone against the white male (and occasionally, against the white female).

The classicist author of *Sappho*, Thomas McEvilley (1939–2013), refers to "a contemporary academic *thiasos*," i.e., "band" or "coterie" of Sappho scholars (by analogy to the coterie postulated for the "Sapphic circle" itself). The resultant field, he says, "has almost become what it studies, a new female initiatory discourse. . . ." The message is *no men allowed*, but for the invited sympathetic few to create the appearance of affirmative-action, equal-opportunity scholarship.

The sisterhood seeks to establish the primacy of women's scholarship vis-à-vis Sappho and, within the rubric of "Gender Studies," other female-related areas of interest. Sappho is the centerpiece of its case for "The Women's Tradition in Greek Poetry" (2004)—this the title of a thorough and well-balanced appraisal by the aforementioned classicist Laurel Bowman. Bowman, however, looks to a predominance of female classicists on whose often feminist and psycho-theoretical views she elaborates (e.g., "[Marilyn] Skinner's Lacanian model is the most radical construction of a woman's poetic tradition," p. 7). Bowman in fact cites eight of Skinner's articles, more than twice the number of any other bibliography-listed scholar. The referenced Jacques Lacan (1901–1981), the most controversial psychoanalyst since Freud, is offered as the anointed *male* lighting our understanding of women and poetry. The reliance of gender studies/feminist scholarship on French (and German) theory, "opening so many new possibilities," either manufactures issues and approaches—"problematizing" the inquiry (in theoryspeak)—or dresses up the basics at which any male or female scholar might handily arrive without the slag. Gone is the beauty in simplicity, and gone Sappho's translucence most of all, the discussion masked in the initiate's impenetrable parlance. "The perfection of the Greek style is fine simplicity . . ." asserts T. G. Tucker (1913), "illustrated by Sappho in that region of verse which preeminently demands it, the lyric of personal emotion." But no. One sooner concludes these days that ancient authors wrote encoding their works for decipherment by latter-day theorists—that grab bag of now predominantly Gallic semioticians, structuralists, post-structuralists, deconstructuralists, postmodernists, psychologists, psychoanalysts, and the rest. The most frequently referenced are Bataille, Cixous (p. 269), Deleuze, Derrida, Foucault, Irigaray, Kristeva, and Lacan—with the long-since discredited Marx invariably at their heels.

In sum, the common sense and self-probing sufficiency (*read*: honesty, integrity) of an earlier time no longer serve. Accordingly, a "purely positivist approach does not help us go further," says Andromache Karanika (2014). "Theory is needed to open new vistas for discussion of more complex scenarios." A "positivist approach"—to define our terms—is one reliant on sensory experience reasonably or logically interpreted (nowadays passé). And a scenario is "complex" (nowadays its ideal state) when "problematized"—i.e., seen of a sudden to resemble nothing it had long been thought to be. Complex scenarios derive from tensor-lamp cross-examinations of the commonplace, from the vivisection of rational predicate and empirical fact. "Problematics" is the resultant problem-set now borne by every meaningful issue when "deconstructed" and rendered shambles, to be *reconstructed* in the service of *la cause du jour*. The cause these days is a triumphalist "women and minorities" narrative (though the benefits go by and large to women, being more numerous and not in the least a minority). The haters (as they are sometimes called) believe that the proverbial Blessings of Democracy, with their long and largely sustaining values and outcomes, and the most fostering regard and treatment of women anywhere on earth, have all along been skewed and unfair. From the prattle of this misandry and male-disposability come the conference panels, articles, and books lavishing ongoing academic accolades on the long aggrieved, thereby sustaining their illusions of progress and legitimacy. "Feminist theory," as Camille Paglia most recently notes, "is a lucrative industry generating academic employment in America, where for every competent feminist book, there are twenty others shot through with inaccuracies, distortions, and propaganda."

The times are deliciously confused. During a recent trip to Quebec City the author happened upon the following bookstore title: *Les Hommes Sont-ils Obsolètes? Enquête sur la nouvelle inégalité des sexes* (*Are Men Obsolete? An inquiry on the sexes' new inequality*) (Fayard, 2018), by the young conservative essayist-editor (and Roger Scruton translator) Laetitia Strauch-Bonart (b. 1985). Positioned immediately adjacent to it, by alphabetical happenstance, was the title *Slut Ever: Dispatches from a Sexually Autonomous Woman in a Post-Shame World*. Yes, confused. Do women want virile autonomy or a *Sex and the City* redux? *Of course* equal pay for equal work and, in the workplace and elsewhere, women's equal dignity and personhood (the legacy of Christianity). But there is a natural limit to equality between things intrinsically and empirically *unequal*, by which we mean only *not the same*. Notes Paglia, "Feminism has exceeded its proper mission of seeking political equality and has ended by rejecting contingency, that is, human limitation be it nature or fate." This, the theorists and utopianists are loath to understand, even as they are ultimately content to want and have it all (rather than be the desired or delectable *half* alone).

By "theory" is meant "Critical Theory"—call it the theory that is critical of accepted norms and values. This norm- and normative-exploding outgrowth of the 1930s Marxist-infused Frankfurt School signals Marx still alive and well, if nowhere else than on the college campus. Of Lacan, Deleuze, and others, English political philosopher and aesthetician Robert Scruton (b. 1944) notes as follows:

> And when in the works of Lacan, Deleuze, [and others] . . . the nonsense machine began to crank out its impenetrable sentences, of which nothing could be understood except that they all had 'capi-

talism' as their target, it looked as though Nothing had at last found its voice. Henceforth the bourgeois order would be vaporized and mankind would march victorious into the void.

It is a world in which nothing and anything alike mean anything; a world of meaning annulled. These are the empresses' new clothes, and such is fortress feminist scholarship—on, by, and for women—on women's theoretically determined grounds. The scholarship is cipher for the initiate. Polarizing and protectivist, it is (for purposes of this discussion) based on the identity-political assumption that women best know or understand women and can best teach what is authored by or about women (analogous assumptions underscoring a range of minority interests). The partisanship is apparent in Rosie Wyles and Edith Hall's *Women Classical Scholars: Unsealing the Fountain from the Renaissance to Jacqueline de Romilly* (2016), with its all-female cast of contributors, and an acknowledgment nod to certain helpful "individuals with a Y chromosome."

The sisterhood has thus acquired, to paraphrase Virginia Woolf, "a realm of its own," making political capital of proprietary claims. The male intruder beware—as I would myself learn in a scurrilous review and blog (Lat. *scurra* 'buffoon') by the above British classicist Edith Hall of my *The Lesbian Lyre: Reclaiming Sappho for the 21st Century* (2016). Hall is the self-styled and self-aggrandizing Sappho and classics authority of British TV and lecture circuit, and, by her "Edithorial" (blog), so very self-important. One may compare the imposter Ezra Pound's self-acclaiming "Ezruversity" as showcase for his own multitudinous pronouncements (see *TLL* 350–351). Hall's review was the more callous, the more imperviously calculated, for the book's naming of names and adherence to traditional aesthetics over the modernist twaddle on which she vociferously held forth, faulting this author for his avowed indifference to the same. That Hall was herself nowhere mentioned in the book gave her a censorious carte blanche, were it not itself the goad to her animus (see further note, p. 283).

§**

If the issue is not subject-matter protectivism, it is misguided or insufficient understanding. Peggy Ullman Bell, author of yet another Sappho "autobiography," has Sappho register the following complaint in conversation with her contemporary Lesbian poet Alcaeus:

> Homer was a man, or men, no one is sure. What can a man know of a woman's mind? Can you claim to comprehend the many facets of mine? No. Of course you can't. Nor I yours, but I ask you, [Alkaios,] how might the story read if written by a woman's hand? How would the years of battle sound as told by Helen or Klytemnestra? What might Penelope have had to say about Odysseus' adventures? In her version, might not her troubles exceed his in import? History is written, and oft revised by men, Alkaios, and men, when it comes to their precious honor, are unmitigated fools.

The issue is not one of "comprehending the many facets" of a single mind. We care not what Helen or Clytemnestra thought outside Greek epic or tragedy. Though like Odysseus they may be "many-minded," it is not their facets of mind that matter, but their *mind-set* within a given story and situation, *situation* the key. We look to their *dramatic* dispositions, which are the aggregate of inherited mythological pasts applied to the narrative moment. Helen and Clytemnestra, be it remembered, are half sisters, each perfidious in her way. Yet we have no conversations between them or other information concerning what they thought of each other or thought outside the stories in which they figure. Nor does it matter, insofar as concerns their *own* stories and situations. Clytemnestra, as noted, provides a cautionary tale for Penelope, but that is the extent of it. Such characters (both male and female) are archetypes, larger than and illustrative of life. Realistic detail or incidental elaboration only diminishes their universal stature. It is their mythic-historical dimension, not personal circumstance, that matters.

An *Odyssey* might have been composed from any one character's perspective, male or female, by either male or female author—and we would be none the wiser. Consider Euripides's depiction of a "woman scorned" in *Medea*, including strategic references to the pains of childbirth, or his portrayal of Phaedra's suicidal love for a stepson in *Hippolytus*. Would these have improved or substantially differed by female authorship? Or Virgil's depiction of the betrayal, lament, and suicide of Dido, which the likes of Saint Augustine and Hector Berlioz confess reduced them to tears. Did Dido's own suffering in any way suffer for want of female authorship? Most

31

recently we have the example of Madeline Miller, acclaimed for her 2012 novel *The Song of Achilles* (translated into twenty-five languages). She has now published the novel *Circe*, of which she says, "Epic has been so traditionally male. All these stories are composed by men, and I really wanted a female perspective." But has she discernibly delivered one? By the criteria to follow, I imagine not. It took a male to expound the thesis of the *Odyssey's* female authorship. Why, if the poem so abounds in the possibility, did a woman at least not raise the issue?

"The growth of Man," says women's rights advocate Margaret Fuller (1810–1850), "is twofold, masculine and feminine. . . . [T]he faculties have not been given pure to either, but only in preponderance." Similarly, the Sapphic poet (and metrist) extraordinaire Charles Algernon Swinburne (1837–1909): "The lineaments of woman and of man seem blended as the lines of sky and landscape melt in burning mist of heat and light"—what he called "supersexual beauty." Though progressive thinking and the increasing alphabet of sexual self-identities would have it otherwise, the two sexes are all there is—being, by the grace of God, complementary (though treated vastly differently). They are thus capable of poignant and mutually sympathetic portrayal. Assuming the individual authorship of Homer, or *a* Homer, it is doubtful whether an archaic woman poet's depiction of Penelope would be recognizable as such, or different from, or superior to, a male Homer's depiction. Whether its register would differ in *any* genre, epic or otherwise, is also doubtful. Granted, Coleridge, in an avuncular tribute to English poet Mary Matilda Betham (1776–1852), comparing her to Sappho and hoping she might be the like to Britain, wrote, "There's a natural bond / Between the female mind and measured sounds." Such "bond" was specific to Coleridge's then frame of mind vis-à-vis his poem's subject. It is an understatement to say that English poetry to an audience of Coleridge's time sooner discloses a virtually conclusive bond between the male mind and metered poetry. Conversely, Edna St. Vincent Millay's 1936 translations of Baudelaire were savaged by one reviewer as not achieving "a closer approach to an acceptable rendering . . . partly because she is a woman."

2. The Novel Ungendered

A continuous prose narrative with origins in epic, the novel has resisted gendered identity from the time women became novelists. Coleridge's contemporary Jane Austen (1775–1817) pseudonymously published her first two novels, *Sense and Sensibility* (1811) and *Pride and Prejudice* (1813), under the teasing tag "A Lady," apparently wishing to convey the *impression* of female authorship absent self-disclosure. One wonders the reception had she published under a male pseudonym or, as the Brontës (below), under gender-non-determinative pseudonyms. Only would the then 78-year-old author V. S. Naipul (1932–2018) have been the wiser, noting, "I read a piece of writing, and within a paragraph or two, I know whether it is by a woman or not," owing to women's "sentimentality [and] their narrow view of the world," and particularly chiding Austen's sentimentality. George Eliot (Mary Anne Evans) (1819–1880) adopted a male pen name both to be taken seriously as a writer and to conceal her scandalous extramarital affairs. To be taken seriously meant disassociation from female authorship of the high-spirited romances of the day. The romance novel, then as now, was a markedly female endeavor. So identifiably female was the romance that Eliot feared being "pigeonholed" as a romance author by virtue of gender alone. The pseudonymous Eliot quite succeeded in evading the risk. Her female authorship was never suspected and, when finally disclosed, without effect on her professional reputation, despite societal opprobrium over her personal life.

Eliot's famed contemporary George Sand (Lucile Aurore Dupin) (1804–1876) brazenly adopted a male name *and* outward male persona— hers a singular case and accomplishment from which generalizations cannot be made. She chummed with her publishers as "one of the guys," and became involved in celebrity love affairs—her most famous with Frédéric Chopin. She was admired for her "manliness" by Flaubert and Henry James. Sand's first novel, *Indiana* (1832), pseudonymously written following her divorce, rails against the oppressiveness of marriage. Its heroine, suffering with exquisite intensity and self-absorption, is for the first time of any literary moment a *female* romantic hero. Yet for all that, the novel's female authorship was never suspected. In 1847, Charlotte Brontë published *Jane Eyre: An Autobiography* under the pen name Currer Bell. Here was female autobiography purportedly written by a male—and again was no one the wiser. Its runaway success marked the end of Brontë's pseudonymous authorship. Twenty-five years after *Indiana* came Flaubert's *Madame Bovary*

(1857), treating a similar theme; and twenty years later Tolstoy's *Anna Karenina* (1877). This was shortly followed by Guy de Maupassant's *A Woman's Life* (*Une Vie*) (1883), a novel describing the increasing disillusionment and despair of an aging divorcée with a mother's manic love for her gambling debt-ridden son. It bears emphasizing that Lawrence Durrell's *Alexandria Quartet* (1957–1960), with its multi-perspective depictions of women—Justine (*Justine* and *Balthazar*), Leila (*Mountolive*), and Clea (*Clea*)—has entered the canon as an unparalleled exploration of love in the twentieth century. None of these works, probing women's lives, motives, and passions, is in any way less true or conceivably different on account of male authorship. Women would have so told us, or rewritten them, were that the case.

The progenitor of the Brontë type—the "man in a woman," as we shall come to know the phenomenon—is the scandalous and equally prolific Mary Wollstonecraft Shelley (1797–1851), wife of Percy Bysshe Shelley. Wollstonecraft famously created *Frankenstein* (1818), a work of singularly male inspiration and import (though not without its feminist supporters). Subtitled "The Modern Prometheus," with its classical associations of male defiance and indignation, the work is allegorically read as a caveat to hubris in the Industrial Revolution. Prior to the publication of *Frankenstein*, however, Wollstonecraft was best known for *A Vindication of the Rights of Woman* (1792), arguing sexual equality based on equality of education. Describing women in highly negative terms even as it seeks to assert their value, *A Vindication* is considered the founding text of modern feminism. Wollstonecraft was artistically *ungendered*, as capable of male as of female portrayal and concern.

It was not only Charlotte but all three Brontës who wrote pseudonymously: Charlotte, b. 1816 (aka Currer Bell); Emily, b. 1818 (aka Ellis Bell); and Anne, b. 1820 (aka Acton Bell), each preserving her real-name initials. So critical was the semblance of male authorship to Charlotte that she maintained the charade even when corresponding with her publisher and used masculine pronouns when referring to her sisters. The sisters' sheltered upbringing reflected then reigning prescriptions for female education and nurture. Nonetheless, the ingrained ferocity and spiritual dissolution of their male literary characters, and the brutality not only of those characters' fates but of those around them, astounds. Contemporary reviewers, when the sisters' identities at last stood revealed, were amazed at the gulf between the sisters' uneventful lives and the violence, passion, and sometimes coarseness of their novels. Minds so powered in lives so scant, unbridled imaginations in lives so sheltered.

In the United States, Harriet Beecher Stowe published *Uncle Tom's Cabin* (1852), apparently under her own name. It was a book in its own time second in sales only to the Bible. According to legend, Stowe was greeted by President Lincoln with the remark, "So you're the little woman who authored the book that started this great war" (1862). She then wrote, among other works, *The Chimney Corner* (1868), a book dealing with women's issues, under the name "Christopher Crowfield." Stowe came from a well-to-do religious background, receiving the kind of classics and mathematical education traditionally reserved for men. An upper-crust litterata from the start (a magazine editor no less), she required no pseudonym, even in an age that frowned upon female authorship. During the same period Louisa May Alcott published her best-known novel, *Little Women* (1868/1869, in two parts), under her *own* name while also writing fiction under the non-designative pseudonym "A. M. Barnard." Also worth noting is that George Eliot was no less literarily accomplished in her time than Stowe, and equally at liberty to write under her own name. Eliot yet decided on pseudonymity owing to various circumstances—including the lightweight "romance" associations of female authorship of her day (as noted above; see also p. 284, note) and her living openly and scandalously with philosopher and literary critic George Henry Lewes.

3. The Brontës: Male and Female Merged

The Brontës were women possessed of extreme male sensibility—a sensibility acquired from the dashing, dissolute, and entirely excessive Lord Byron (1788–1824). Byron was the neck-glamorized swoon of Victorian ladies, both proper and improper; the delicious depravity of his day; and in appearance and effect an Elvis Presley-type precursor. Byron's first major publication, his autobiographical and singularly successful *Childe Harold's Pilgrimage* (a narrative poem published in four parts from 1812–1818), brought the archetypal Byronic hero to life: the disaffected, self-conflicted, world-weary, seductive, and sexually voracious sophisticate. Such, in significant part, was the model for Rochester in Charlotte's *Jane Eyre* (1847); for

Heathcliff in Emily's *Wuthering Heights* (1847); and for Captain Wentworth in Jane Austen's *Persuasion* (1817) (though Austen had earlier satirized gothic conventions in *Northanger Abbey*, 1803). Byron was an irresistible illness, famously described by his fanatical lover Lady Caroline Lamb as "mad, bad and dangerous to know."

The Brontës, however sheltered as women, readily grasped and replicated the alpha male of their day: Rochester and Heathcliff quintessentially male portraitures conceived in Byron's image. Their gothic portrayals include isolated and depressive surroundings, manic behavior, secretive pasts, debilitating physical injury, assorted physical and psychological cruelties, and the madness of those about them, including skeletons in the closet and mad women in the attic. A review of Emily's *Wuthering Heights* read in part as follows:

> In *Wuthering Heights*, the reader is shocked, disgusted, almost sickened by the details of cruelty, inhumanity and the most diabolical hate and vengeance, and even some passages of powerful testimony to the supreme power of love—even over demons in the human form. The women in the book are of a strange fiendish-angelic nature, tantalising and terrible, and the men are indescribable out of the book itself.... We strongly recommend all our readers who love novelty to get this story, for we can promise them they never read anything like it before. It is very puzzling and very interesting...

On the other hand, our dear heroine Jane Eyre is a model of persevering, self-awakening, and increasingly self-sufficient womanhood. Shunned and mistreated as a child, she attains the increased maturity of adolescence, benefiting from education at a charity school for girls. She then becomes a salaried governess at Thornfield Hall, and from there the beloved of its owner, Mr. Rochester (though refuses to be his illicit lover). She finally becomes the angelically ministering wife of the maimed and blinded protagonist—still the proverbial man of her dreams. *Jane Eyre* offers a famously compelling first-person account from the inner depths of a female character, oppressed not by men (as is Hardy's Tess) but by circumstances—all overcome, at least once within an inch of her life. Considered ahead of its time for its stalwart portrayal, the novel is now considered proto-feminist, even one of the first feminist novels. For all of that, it was believed written by a man.

No one at the time doubted the pseudonymous Currer Bell's ability to create so staunch and sympathetic a character as Jane Eyre, though Thackeray divined a woman's pen. Conversely, nothing of Charlotte's true gender foreclosed the male-gothic sensationalist aspects of her writing, including in *Jane Eyre* the "madwoman in the attic" trope. In these respects, Charlotte Brontë shared much with the creator of *Frankenstein*. Also characteristically gendered are Heathcliff and the passionate Catherine Earnshaw (both symbolically named) in Emily Brontë's *Wuthering Heights* (1847). Catherine, soon driven mad, is torn between nature and culture in the persons of Heathcliff and Edgar Linton. She is "earnestly" beset with woman's perennial dilemma: choosing between men of dramatically opposed natures. It was not until 1850, in Charlotte's posthumous "Preface" and "Biographical Notice" to editions of her sisters' works, that the sisters' true identities surfaced. No one had been the wiser between times. Responding to a critic who would praise her *Jane Eyre* if written by a man, and condemn it if written by a woman, Charlotte famously wrote to her publisher, "To you [i.e., my critics] I am neither man nor woman. I come before you as an author only. It is the sole standard by which you have a right to judge me—the sole ground on which I accept your judgment." What we have in Charlotte, then, is a pseudonymous author, writing as much like a man as like a woman, and rejecting gendered designation.

Which is to say that great art is unconcerned with male or female authorship, with gender-identifiable portraiture, and least of all with gender-based revisionism or territoriality, but with the totality of human nature and experience and—to the extent involving gender—gender *complementarity*. If there is any one passage a male *or* female author could equally have penned it is Catherine's confession in *Wuthering Heights*:

> What were the use of my creation, if I were entirely contained here? My great miseries in this world have been Heathcliff's miseries, and I watched and felt each from the beginning: my great thought in living is himself. If all else perished and he remained, *I* should still continue to be; and if all else remained and he were annihilated, the universe would turn to a mighty stranger: I should not seem a part of it. My love for Linton is like the foliage in the woods. Time will change it, I'm well aware, as winter changes the trees—my love for Heathcliff resembles the eternal rocks beneath—a source

of little visible delight, but necessary. Nelly, I am Heathcliff—he's always, always in my mind—not as a pleasure, any more than I am always a pleasure to myself—but as my own being—so, don't talk of our separation again—it is impracticable.

Notes de Beauvoir, "This is the cry of all women in love; [Catherine] is another incarnation of the beloved, his reflection, his double: she is *he*. She lets her world founder in contingence: she lives his universe."

The totalizing unification of "Nelly, I am Heathcliff" has a literary pedigree with marked religious overtones which we do well to consider. The quotation resonates with, and is part of the same trope as, Flaubert's "Madame Bovary, c'est moi," positing ungendered assimilation. The same is apparent in Wagner's searing love story, *Tristan und Isolde*, Is. *Herz an Herz dir, Mund an Mund*; Tr. *eines Atems /ein'ger Bund* 'heart to heart, lips to lips; the single bond of a single breath'. So too Abelard and Heloise throughout their letters, disavowing distinction one from the other. While other examples could be adduced, we especially note Michelangelo's Sonnet XXX, to a male beloved (Tommaso Cavalieri), assimilating his own sight and—as in the Wagnerian example—*breath*, to his (Cavalieri's):

> With your fair eyes a charming light I see,
>   For which my own blind eyes would peer in vain; ...
> Wingless upon your pinions forth I fly;
>   Heavenward your spirit forces me to strain; ...
> Your will includes and is the lord of mine;
>   Life to my thoughts within your heart is given;
>   My words begin to breathe upon your breath:
>
> (John Addington Symonds, tr.)

> [Veggio co' bei vostr'occhi un dolce lume,
>   Che co' miei ciechi già veder non posso; ...
> Volo con le vostr' ale senza piume;
>   Col vostr' ingegno al ciel sempre son mosso; ...
> Nel voler vostro è sol la voglia mia,
>   I mie' pensier nel vostro cor si fanno,
>   Nel vostro fiato son le mia parole:]

Michelangelo concludes, protesting he shines, as the moon, only with the reflected light of his beloved's sun—a reverse-gendering image, whether the beloved be male or female.

Positing complete union and identity with one's beloved, and adoration of one's by-the-other-possessed image within, is of a kind with religious striving for the internalization of God's presence, and adoration of one's by-God-possessed image within. This, to be sure, is aspirational rather than actualized union. For the latter, or its likeness, we look to Gian Lorenzo Bernini's masterpiece *The Ecstasy of St. Teresa* (1647–1652) (see plate 1). The sculpted and voluptuously beautiful Teresa of Ávila (1515–1582) is here convulsed in rippling habit, the arrow-brandishing cupid-like seraph poised above her having just struck and soon to strike again—whether with sacred or profane love, we wonder. The figures are illuminated by light from a dome-inset window above, reinforced by gilded stucco rays extending downward the length of the tableau. The erotically convulsed Teresa is depicted consistently with her own oft-quoted diary entry:

> I saw in his hand a long spear of gold, and at the iron's point there seemed to be a little fire. He appeared to me to be thrusting it at times into my heart, and to pierce my very entrails; when he drew it out, he seemed to draw them out also, and to leave me all on fire with a great love of God. The pain was so great, that it made me moan; and yet so surpassing was the sweetness of this excessive pain that I could not wish to be rid of it. The soul is satisfied now with nothing less than God. The pain is not bodily, but spiritual; though the body has its share in it. It is a caressing of love so sweet which now takes place between the soul and God, that I pray God of His goodness to make him experience it who may think that I am lying.

This is one manner of possession, call it invasive. Its counterpart appears in Anne-Louis Girodet's hauntingly quiescent *The Sleep of Endymion* (1791) (plate 2), a painting, by way of contrast, seemingly Bernini-inspired. In Girodet's depiction of a perennially rendered theme, the slumbering shepherd is as quintessentially beautiful as is Teresa voluptuous. Beloved by the moon goddess Diana, Endymion, in a comparable albeit relaxed posture, absorbs her suffusing rays, while Eros, positioned as Bernini's Eros-like seraph (both of them "mercurial and malicious") assists by parting the brambles to allow the rays entry. Teresa's languid left foot (see p. 138) has its counterpart in Endymion's languid left arm. Teresa is completely clothed, as Endymion is nude. Teresa is the female-possessed, convulsed beneath the rays of a male-gendering sun. Endymion is the male-possessed, reposed beneath the beams of a female-gendering moon. The antitheses are marked. Historian Barbara Stafford incisively explains the Girodet as follows:

> The wonder of the unio mystica [divine union] is the descent of the divine into *the receptive soul that has finally become still.* . . . Girodet painted the human soul "open" to the "influence" of a god. Serenity, passivity, absence of all sense of self—an inert state very reminiscent of sleep—are the external indications for this moment of greatest receptivity. Translated into visual terms, Girodet renders the absorbing and reflecting of light, the dissolving of the ego in slumber; in short, he creates a state favorable for the influx of the divine, now scientifically shown to be immanent in the physical energies of nature (emphasis added).

This description might equally apply to Teresa, insofar as receptiveness to divinity is concerned, though receptiveness of a different kind. Perhaps "the receptive soul that has finally become still" (above) is the post-convulsive repose to which the initial intensity of divine possession ultimately yields— rest following restlessness, as night follows day.

The assimilation of godliness is in any event not instantaneous, but sequential, via lower forms of eventually relinquished physical attraction or intellectual perception. Plato's *Symposium* (5th century BC) posits a hierarchical ascent: from love of individual physical beauty, to love of all physical beauty as a single form of beauty, to love of all forms of beauty as the ideal of beauty— i.e., *to kalon* 'the beautiful'—to love of that supreme beauty that is wisdom and its acquisition through philosophy—philosophy the ultimate desideratum.

Neoplatonism, starting with Plotinus (3rd century AD), also posits a hierarchy, not with philosophy but with immaterial divinity as its goal—divinity of a kind manifest in the depictions by Bernini and Girodet, above. This is "the One," the god or godliness become one within us, which we seek to know and assimilate. It is the divine/universal realization of which earthbound gendered union is a mere simulation or particular instance. This monotheistically anticipatory goal has antecedents in Plato's Form of the Good—the ultimate Good of which all others forms of good are merely facsimiles—and in Aristotle's prime mover, that which moves (i.e., causes movement) without itself being moved. Such antecedents anticipate and are assimilated into the Judeo-Christian belief in a supreme being, and into the (initially Puritan) belief of marital union as an earthly counterpart to union with Christ—divine espousal a model for its human equivalent; marriage in Christ as analogue to, or sublimation of, human marriage.

Incorporating his creatures and all creation, God is "the One," the Unity from which all issues and into which all returns reconciled and undifferentiated. This notion is reflected in Rodin's iconic *Hand of God* (1907) (plate 3), a large right hand, itself emerging from a rough-hewn block of marble holding a clod of earth. Modeled within the earth, either emergent or returned, either active or quiescent—are the inchoate figures of Adam and Eve. In this work, Rodin, as his "master" Michelangelo before him, equates artistic and divine creation as forms of emergence, here from the selfsame hand of God and artist, God as artist. The analogy recalls the creational "hands-on" intercession of God in the Book of Jeremiah. Instructed by God to "go down to the potter's house," the prophet observes the give-and-take of the potter's method "as it seemed best to him." Then was the parable annouced:

> O house of Israel, cannot I do with you as this potter? saith the Lord. Behold, as the clay in the potter's hand, so are ye in my hand, O house of Israel.

Further to the biblical account, man originally incorporates woman, or the rib from which she is taken, and is "lord" over her. At the same time, however, man is thereafter ever emergent from woman, seeks to return to her, wants again to be with her, within her, *one* with her, reconciled and undifferentiated. But their biblical *basár achád* 'one flesh' is not merely a matter of physical union, but of personhood, as theologian Jay Adams explains (within the marital context) apropos of the argument herein: Male and female marriage partners don't merely make an exact "fit" sexually, "their maleness and femaleness 'fill out' or 'complete' one another in every respect. The two constitute a 'whole'. In a proper marriage, men have the opportunity to see the world through their wives' feminine eyes, and women through their husband's masculine eyes." The union is thus ideally total: physical, physiological, sensory, spiritual, and intellectual.

❧

Returning, then, to Brontë, Catherine's biblically resonant declaration be-speaks sacred love. She does not *seek* ultimate union with Heathcliff but posits it as already *given*, harking back to a condition of primordial elemental unity and deeming her and Heathcliff's corporalities earthbound-merged. She is the bedrock, the strength, of Heathcliff's earthen being (the "cliff" of his namesake, as it were), as in Rodin's depiction of Adam and Eve, the two earthbound, emerging from stone. Catherine and Heathcliff's condition is, in fact, not merely biblically resonant but recapitulatory: *Adam* from Heb. *adamah* 'earth', and the Adam-latent Eve (Heb. *chavah* 'source of life, living one'). Adam called Eve "woman, because she was taken out of man" (Heb. *īsh* 'man'; *īshah* 'woman'): "Therefore shall a man depart his father and mother, and shall cleave unto his wife, and they shall be one flesh." As bedrock to his soil, Catherine is the superior and more enduring element, not submerged and forgotten within him but his *constituent* element, no less than that which constitutes them both. The negation of sexual partisanship or priority, this is a pre-gendered figuration, even as humankind emerges from, is constituted of, and returns to its earthly element. Brontë here gives us a primordially and prenatally cleaving Catherine, a still-Heathcliff-embedded element, one with and within him. Their union is decidedly ungendered; they are a sexu-ally undifferentiated *One*. Tennyson strikes the same chord in *Fatima*:

> I will possess him or will die.
> I will grow round him in his place,
> Grow, live, die looking on his face,
> Die, dying clasp'd in his embrace.

Extreme though such formulations may seem, they urge an antecedent truth. Notes Germaine Greer, "At first when love was seen as the force that ruled all creation and the beloved emissary of divine love made flesh, it tran-scended gender." Transcendence of both gender and flesh is the hallmark of sexual union among angels (all nominally male) in Milton's *Paradise Lost*:

> Whatever pure thou in the body enjoyest,
> (And pure thou wert created) we enjoy
> In eminence; and obstacle find none

Of membrane, joint, or limb, exclusive bars;
Easier than air with air, if Spirits embrace,
Total they mix, union of pure with pure
Desiring, nor restrained conveyance need,
As flesh to mix with flesh, or soul with soul. . . .

Catherine's stance has nonetheless been criticized as a sellout of her identity—a defensible argument under the narrowest possible reading. What we have in Catherine's devotion is the lover's sense of an undifferentiated beloved, an "all in all"—in life, preceding life, and throughout eternity. Prototypical examples include Abelard and Heloise, Tristan and Isolde, Romeo and Juliet, Robert and Elizabeth Barrett Browning, and perhaps even Brahms and Clara Schumann. In sum, the characters of Brontë novels, male or female, are equally forceful, despite author gender or gender charade. As women, and however sheltered as women, the Brontës intuitively understand and flawlessly depict the extreme male, ever mindful of its inescapable female complement. A male author could have done no better—nor would the Brontës themselves, however better traveled or more experienced of the world.

৯▲

Again in the United States, Nathaniel Hawthorne's *The Scarlet Letter* (1850), published three years after *Jane Eyre*, provides a forceful example of ungendered imagination in a consummate storyteller. This "quintessentially American Novel," focusing on the shameful plight of Hester Prynne, a young Puritan woman in seventeenth-century Massachusetts, is its male author's singular exploration of a woman's mind and heart. Hawthorne minutely probes Hester's shame and isolation, and a mother's love for her daughter, Pearl ("little Pearl"), the product of adultery. The exploration's female quality is suggested by the smooth and lilting cadences of Hawthorne's prose (versus the Brontës' often regimented formality). For all that, Hester exhibits a "manly" and more-than-manly resolve and defiance in the face of impossibility. Hawthorne keeps his heroine strong, refusing to have her debased by opprobrious society. The manliness of Hester's resolve increases by contrast to the guilt, fear, and irresolution (approaching "lunacy") of the Reverend Arthur Dimmesdale, the child's undisclosed father.

Hawthorne also describes the flowered beauty and innocence of Pearl. He aligns her with nature. He soulfully tracks her growth and youthful impressions, admiring her precocity, and portraying her as physical perfection. It is not only their distinctive female natures that this male author consummately conveys, but the special nature of their bond. In a feminist-progressive vein, Hawthorne has Hester disavow society as a woman, looking past it all to a more egalitarian future:

> As a first step, the whole system of society is to be torn down, and built up anew. Then, the very nature of the opposite sex, or its long hereditary habit, which has become like nature, is to be essentially modified, before woman can be allowed to assume what seems a fair and suitable position. Finally, all other difficulties being obviated, woman cannot take advantage of these preliminary reforms, until she herself shall have undergone a still mightier change; in which, perhaps, the ethereal essence, wherein she has her truest life, will be found to have evaporated.

This is as forceful a statement as any female author and/or women's rights advocate of the time might make. We value and accept it no less coming from a male author. Before the nineteenth century was out, another great novelist would scrutinize the lives of women. Henry James's *Daisy Miller* (1878), *A Portrait of a Lady* (1881), and *The Bostonians* (1886) are further testament to the artist's defiance of gender expectation or stereotyping. We marvel that a male author's psyche and imagination lie behind the probing of a young woman's mind in *Daisy Miller* and inspirit the independent Isabel Archer and feminist Olive Chancellor. Or perhaps we do not, any more than we marvel at the inspirations of Rochester and Heathcliff.

4. Elizabeth Barrett Browning as Epic Author on Female Themes

We take but passing note of the then renowned, now largely forgotten Victorian poets Felicia Hemans (1793–1835) and Letitia Elizabeth Landon (1802–1838), as well as poet-critic Matthew Arnold's (1822–1888) conflicted and inveterately misogynistic response to them and all female poets, including Elizabeth Barrett Browning (1806–1861). Hemans and Landon are credited with founding a new "poetry of sensibility," a sentimental poetry significantly gender-marked. However, if emotion and love's inevitable disillusionment are the criteria, many a male poet—Arnold included—come up in the net. Widely read and known in her day, Landon fell from favor until the late twentieth century, when Germaine Greer included a one-hundred-page chapter in her *Slip-Shod Sibyls* (1995) titled "Success and the Single Poet: The Sad Tale of L. E. L." Greer notes at the chapter's outset that "The problem that confronts the student of women's creativity is not that there is no poetry by women, but that there is so much bad poetry by women." In this regard, women are quite the equal of men.

Poetic beacon of her day was Elizabeth Barrett Browning, Landon's longer-lived contemporary. Browning wished to be not like Hemans and Landon, but "the feminine of Homer," for which her then most popular epic poem, *Aurora Leigh* (1856), would be the calling card, "authoritatively rewriting the masculine genre of epic from a woman's point of view." If since forgotten, it is because this long and unprecedented work was excessively autobiographical and topical, which is to say, lacking in epic scope and concern. The sonnet cycle traditionally a *male* endeavor, *Sonnets from the Portuguese* distinguished Elizabeth as the only female sonnet cyclist in the more than six and one-half centuries between Dante (b. 1265) and Rilke (b. 1926). Her husband, fellow poet Robert Browning, believed it the best sonnet cycle since Shakespeare. The title conveys the fiction that the poems were translations from the Portuguese, an artifice adopted to insulate the author against the excessively personal nature of the poetry. Browning thus curiously sought, in lieu of pseudonym, concealment of the poems' status as originals. Sonnet cycles typically treat love (most often unrequited) as a condition equally known to both sexes. Elizabeth sought the *assertive* role, wanting in her poetic persona at least, to be lover rather than beloved. However, the couple's singular relationship defies generalization.

5. Rebecca West as Epic Author on Female Themes

We further mention two titans of prose epic, Ayn Rand (1905–1982) and Rebecca West (1892–1983). With her devotion to Nietzschian individualism and aspirational entrepreneurship, and hatred of groupthink (for her, communism), Rand was unrepentantly male in outlook, generating feminist apologists aplenty. West, for her part, is widely known for her feminist-deflating definition of feminism: "I myself have never been able to find out precisely what feminism is. I only know that people call me a feminist when I express sentiments that differentiate me from a doormat or a prostitute."

West and Rand were writing when male pseudonyms for female authors were long passé, though West (Cicely Isabel Fairfield) used a pen name. Citing a consensus definition of epic as "an extended narrative poem, exalted in style and heroic in theme," Bernard Schweizer suggests that "epics are narrative texts of superior literary merit that typically tell of signal exploits and acts of bravery, of collective destinies, and of superhuman interventions, all of which are embedded in an authoritative moral, social, and religious framework." As concerns West in particular, says Schweizer, a "misotheistic [god-hating] outlook bespeaks the inclusion of spiritual, supernatural, and mythic elements in her world of ideas . . . the *sine qua non* of epic composition."

Thus seeking to designate West a female author of epic, through criteria developed over millennia by an exclusively male-dominated enclave, Schweizer focuses on her *Black Lamb, Grey Falcon* (1941). The book, of more than epic proportions at 1,100 pages, was written in the aftermath of West's six-week trip to Yugoslavia in 1937. In it she recounts Balkan history and ethnography, while delving the significance of Nazism—the book's publication coinciding with the Nazi invasion of Yugoslavia. West's objective was "to show the past side by side with the present it created." The work, in Schweizer's analysis, exhibits an

> extraordinarily capacious cultural vision and an authoritative spiritual outlook, together with a prose style of the highest order. . . justify[ing] this invocation of the modern epic in connection with a historically inspired text. . . . [It] should figure in any treatment of the modern epic, not only because of its magisterial prose style, but also because it conveys an epic scope and furnishes a timeless analysis of Western civilization.

By such criteria, West is decidedly a female writer of epic, a woman in a traditionally male genre.

Schweizer yet injects a feminist take, quite spoiling the simple truth.

Having identified the formal elements of the book's epic framework, Schweizer proposes

> how the ideologically charged elements of heroism, quest, and cultural critique are given a distinctively feminist coloring. . . . Specifically, West argues that spiritual and philosophical knowledge, as well as the pursuit of beauty, are true objects of the female quest, thereby expressing her preference for brains over brawn. Moreover, she elevates suffrage, emancipation, and the attainment of women's rights to the status of legitimate objects of heroism, considering any success in these areas as evidence of women's epic calling.

The claim is disputable. Brains over brawn is no less paradigmatically male than female, as evidenced by such conniving characters as the wily Odysseus, the Greek trickster Hermes, the Welsh trickster and magician Gwydion, and the cross-cultural panoply of the cunning and crafty, both human and divine. As we learn at the start of the *Odyssey*, Odysseus

πολλῶν δ᾽ ἀνθρώπων ἴδεν ἄστεα καὶ νόον ἔγνω
saw/knew the towns of many men and grasped their minds.

For which reason, among others, he is *andra . . . polutropon* 'the man of many turns'. The Trojan Horse, effecting the fall of Troy, was Odysseus's idea—the quintessential display of brains over brawn (though its taking ten years to figure out is another matter).

Moreover, "spiritual and philosophic knowledge, as well as the pursuit of beauty," being collectively integral to classical thought, is not properly given to gendered parsing or differentiation. Consider Plato's *Symposium* for starters, which ends with Socrates's discourse concerning what he learned of wisdom and beauty from the priestess Diotima. Philosophic inquiry, we thus learn, is a male pursuit—all the dialogue's interlocutors are of course male—though its summation is female. The dialogue thus culminates in Diotima's peroration, signaling that while men might strive to comprehend the nature of wisdom and acquire it, *sophrosyne* 'wisdom' is woman's principal virtue, *intrinsically*. The primary case is none other than Odysseus's long-suffering Penelope, protector of her husband's domain and prerogatives during the twenty years of his absence. What the Greek state was ultimately deemed to need most, in a line of examples descended from Penelope, was "citizens who excel in qualities that, in Greek society, are most often seen in women." Following the perfection of Homer, believed to have occurred in the mid-eighth century BC, both the Old Comedy of fifth-century Athens (Aristophanes) and the philosophical writings of the fourth (Plato) "commended as essential to the well-being of the state the virtues that were familiar . . . as the qualities proper to women—self-restraint, cooperation, lack of aggressiveness." Such qualities, however, do not bespeak the preference of brain over brawn, nor are they objects of the female quest.

Diotoma, however persuasive, is a relatively small player in the Greek scheme of things, a scheme requiring no special pleading. Athena, the goddess of both wisdom and warcraft, is at the forefront of Greek "brains," though hardly lacking brawn. Parthenogenetically born from the forehead of her father, Zeus, Athena is the fully armed and insulated female sprung from the seat of cosmic wisdom. She is thus in her own wisdom supreme, her thoughts coextensive with Zeus's own. She is patron goddess of Athens, the heart of Western civilization. Virgin in life as in birth, Athena has no mate or sexual partners (she is too wise for that), bypassing the passions destructive of reason and armed in reason's defense.

6. Epic and the Questing Hero: Knowing One's Gendered Place

Wisdom is ultimately a matter of self-understanding; of the improvement of self and the community or civilization in which one prospers. The Greeks enshrined the belief in one of two inscriptions above the Delphic Oracle: *gnōthi seauton* 'Know thyself'; the other, complementary inscription, *mēden agan* 'nothing to excess'. Self-understanding and its civilizational benefits are ultimately the objective of *any* quest, whether by brain or brawn. Brain or intellectual quest, though rarer, is no less fraught with journeying, peril, revelation, and acquisition (see note). The derivation of the word *quest* is Lat. *quaero/ quaesitum* 'ask, inquire'/'asked, inquired' and, by extension, 'strive for, seek to obtain' (Eng. query, question, inquest); cf. Lat. *acquiro* (*ad* + *quaero*) 'acquire'. An archetypically male endeavor, the quest involves immense journeying (e.g., *Gilgamesh, Odyssey, Aeneid, Beowulf, Divine Comedy*) or cataclysmic clash under divine auspices, far from home (*Iliad, Mahabharata*). It demands extraordinary strength and endurance. The notion of travel is itself semantically associated with toil and exertion; cf. Fr. *travailler* 'to work'; *travail* 'work';

Eng. travail, travel. The further and more dangerous the travel, and the more overcome, the greater the acquisition—of understanding, self-understanding, redemption. Travail, both physical and spiritual, is the essence of quest travel. Rarely accomplished by brain alone, but by brawn, *quest*, if one may so put it, is the *acquisition* of brain (so the scarecrow in Oz). "Human 'nature' is a nature continually in search of itself, obliged at every moment to transcend what it was a moment before."

Brain alone, however, is the revisionist means to the feminist quest, for the inescapable reason that women are not biologically brawny. Male death in combat aside, women tend to outlive men. And despite the strength and good health required for childbearing, the dangers and mortality concerns of giving birth, especially in preindustrial society, were significant; as much so as the dangers and mortality concerns confronting men in the defense and support of women in combat and otherwise. One might think of propagation and protection as the most demanding of labors assigned the sexes, both peril-ous—protection the stuff of epic, childbearing not.

In preindustrial society, agriculture as the dominant mode of sub-sistence necessarily kept *both* sexes close to home, with the means and comfort of travel in any event limited. The quest, and other forms of male initiation and self-validation, taking the male far from home, was danger-ous, admirable, and enthralling. Were women to quest, the undertaking would significantly lessen not only the protective appeal of men to women but also the safety and repose required for civilized existence—existence *at home*; the home returned to, enshrining woman, graced and made livable by woman's presence. "Getting the girl"—or keeping or returning to her—is, after all, the quest concomitant, typically its ultimate reward or objective, since she often inspires or dictates the hero's challenge. If, in the quest en-deavor that is combat, fighting women are butchered and dying alongside men, what is there to fight for, return home to? Man's female-focused home-coming from combat emerges from the iconic "V-J Day in Times Square" photograph by Alfred Eisenstaedt, portraying a U.S. Navy sailor "grabbing" and kissing a nurse on Victory Over Japan Day, August 14, 1945 ("kissing the girl" preliminary to "getting the girl," or getting her *back*). The nurse, in a swooning pose, is wearing white (a symbol of healing, nurture, and good-ness), in the center of Times Square, New York City, the metropolis of the West and, by extension, of civilization and the world.

The female as restorative post-chaotic goal is evident in the various modes of quest endeavor: physical, artistic, and redemptive. Thus, in the physical, most conventional scenario, the *Odyssey*'s adventure-quest results, after long absence, in the wayward hero's reunion with his faithful wife, Penelope, and resumption of the domestic/civilized life she struggled to safeguard in his absence. The *Iliad*'s battle-quest results in Menelaus's recapture of his errant wife, Helen, and return home to Sparta, where the pair resumes a regularized, if fidgety, domestic life (*Odyssey*, Book 4). This is an instance of "getting the girl *back*." In the *Aeneid*, the hero, losing his wife, home, and hearth in the destruction of Troy, ventures to Italy and founds Rome, the "New Troy," after a combative quest against the native Italians. The hero Aeneas marries the Italian princess Lavinia. En route, he disastrously "gets" Dido, widowed Queen of Carthage, in what might have been an abortive "New Troy" in Africa.

For artistic quest, we have Wagner's *Die Meistersinger von Nürnberg* (*The Master Singers of Nuremberg*), in which the knight-errant Walther von Stolzing wins Eva, the marital prize of a communal singing contest. He does so by innovatively and controversially "questing" his way through the thicket, as it were, of the master-guild's rigid rules and conventions. For artistic *anti-quest* we look to Wagner's *Tannhäuser und der Sängerkrieg auf Wartburg* (*Tannhäuser and the Minnesingers' Contest at Wartburg*) (Ger. *Minnesang* 'love song'). No knight-errant in courtly quest (see below) or seeking love's redemption, Tannhäuser is an amorously crusading musician, a voluptuary who has indulged the orgiastic pleasures of *Venusberg* 'the Mountain of Venus' in Venus's own company. For this, upon subsequent pilgrimage to Rome, Tannhäuser is not absolved but *damned* by the Pope. Next seeking return to the source of his former pleasures, he is denied reentry to Venusberg for having left it in the first place. Only in the death of his beloved and long-suffering Elisabeth does he find redemption, the only redemption suited to such travail: death at Elisabeth's bier.

For the redemptive quest, we look to Wagner's *Parsifal* and *Der Fliegende Holländer* (*The Flying Dutchman*). In *Dutchman*, the accursed sea captain (having once invoked Satan) endlessly roams the sea, putting ashore only once every seven years until he finds a wife who will be faithful to him. And Parsifal is the prophesied fool come to serve the Grail Guild by reuniting the Grail and Holy Lance (originally separated by their prior owner's sexual self-indulgence;

cf. *Tannhäuser*). Parsifal learns compassion while resisting sexual temptation. The power of the Grail is decisive in the mastering of human passions; the Grail its own reward. Otherwise, Siegfried, in Wagner's opera of the same name, gets the sleeping Brünnhilde, passing through a ring of fire (and other trials) to do so. He is the semi-divine Achilles-like prototypically adrenalized hero who quite "gets" his equal in this particular "girl."

The female expects heroism or manliness, resourcefulness, and means (if she deign expect anything at all in a post-modern world) as an assurance of male protective ability, and heroism is paradigmatically shown through the quest. The successful quester can endure, overcome, and protect against anything. He is the master and perfect mate in a dangerous and perilously mortal world. The quest has its rewards, sex foremost among them. Not simply sex for its own sake or self-gratification, but for the amorous and/or propagative potential it provides the species. Never does the quest-rescued female object to sex with her rescuer (though great is the complaint upon subsequent abandonment). Nor does the *con*quest-rescued female shun the liberator's "deserved sexual prerogative"—answering to the want felt and comfort sought by both. Deserved sexual prerogative bypasses wooing, being a direct connection to the life force itself and to life-sustaining pleasure and hope. Rape and rapine, by contrast, are the unmerited sexual prerogative of the occupier (the villain). As the antihero is dispossessed of his taking—or initially barred from taking at all—it is the hero's sexual prerogative that realigns the sexes' essential normative expectations; also realigning social structure, world order, and cosmic stability. The paradigm, however, is not without its failings.

Emblematic of these vicissitudes is the myth of Perseus and Andromeda. Andromeda is the daughter of the Aethiopian king Cepheus and his wife, Cassiopeia. When Cassiopeia boasts her daughter is more beautiful than the Nereids (sea nymphs, daughters of Nereus), Poseidon sends the sea monster Cetus to ravage her as divine punishment. Stripped and chained naked to a rock as a sacrifice to sate the beast, Andromeda is saved by Perseus, who gets/takes/marries her—the beast's prerogative frustrated; the hero's asserted.

This "princess and the dragon" or "damsel in distress" motif is central to the quest, with broad social and psychological implications for male validation vis-à-vis woman and the perils confronting woman in an age of rampant predation. The damsel in distress gives rise to the medieval figure of the knight-errant (Lat. *erro* 'wander')—growing out of Arthurian romance

(Gawain, Lancelot, Percival) and culminating in the paradigmatic, if trav-estied, Don Quixote (becoming insane through excessive absorption of chivalric romances). The knight-errant wanders in search of adventure to prove his chivalric virtues. These are often realized in the service of "courtly love," i.e., the knight's ennobling—because typically unconsummated—passion for his lady. The endeavor is thus at once erotic and spiritual, "illicit and morally elevating, passionate and disciplined, humiliating and exalting, human and transcendent"—a maddeningly impossible mandate, prone to disaster (as in the cases of Tristan and Lancelot). Victorian representations reprise the Perseus and Andromeda theme by showing the "damsel," in vari-ous states of undress, tied to a tree as her "hero" slays or otherwise routs the foeman (e.g., *The Knight Errant* by Sir John Everett Millais [1829–1896]; *Chivalry* by Frank Bernard Dicksee [1853–1928]). The aftermath is often depicted by the knight's carrying off the rescued damsel on horseback (e.g., *The Rescue* by Vereker Monteith Hamilton [1856–1931]).

The restorative post-rescue "marriage" reenacts and confers the security and blessings of the *hieros gamos* 'divine marriage', i.e., the sublime and ben-eficial union of the gods themselves. Conspicuous by way of example is the lovemaking, described in the *Iliad*, of Zeus and Hera, king and queen of the gods. It is they who dominate the Olympian dispensation and "set the tone" for mankind's lot below:

> So speaking, the son of Kronos caught his wife in his arms. There
> underneath them the divine earth broke into young, fresh
> grass, and into dewy clover, crocus and hyacinth
> so thick and soft it held the hard ground deep away from them.
> There they lay down together and drew about them a golden
> wonderful cloud, and from it the glimmering dew descended.
> So the father slept unshaken on the peak of Gargaron
> with his wife in his arms, when sleep and passion had stilled him . . .

"The glimmering dew" is lovemaking's effluence—fertilizing and quick-ening. Effluence and essence alike, it is the by-product and effective cause of vigor and bounty, and their concomitant: beauty. Earthbound union in the aftermath of deliverance shares in the restorative "divine." It is wom-an's beauty—the need and want of it—that inspires the rescue. As the principal incitement to sexual fulfillment, it is beauty that both incites and sanctions post-rescue sexual prerogative. Beauty, standing conspicuously forth in its perfected assurance, is the will to life itself versus threatening anomalous nature. The obverse of anomaly, beauty of itself all but subdues anomalous and diabolical nature. We look, by way of prominent example, to the serpent's (momentary) stupefaction before Eve:

> She most, and in her look summs all Delight.
> Such Pleasure took the Serpent to behold
> This Flourie Plat*, the sweet recess of *Eve*
> Thus earlie, thus alone; her Heav'nly forme
> Angelic, but more soft, and Feminine,
> Her graceful Innocence, her every Aire
> Of gesture or lest action overawd
> His Malice, and with rapine sweet bereav'd
> His fierceness of the fierce intent it brought:
> That space the Evil one abstracted stood
> From his own evil, and for the time remaind
> Stupidly good, of enmitie disarm'd,
> Of guile, of hate, of envie, of revenge;

*flowered plot of ground

Satan's proximity to Eve is the prototype of evil's or the grotesque's obsession with unsuspecting beauty, of beauty's indiscriminately attractive power, of the taming of the savage(d) breast—from the grossly deformed Quasimodo's love of Esmeralda to King Kong's docile fascination with Ann Darrow (Vina Fay Wray), what Michael Walsh calls Kong's "interspecies affection for the silky, slinky Ann Darrow." Beauty tames the beast—literally and figuratively—which verily perishes on its account. Quasimodo, having tried to protect and save the falsely accused Esmeralda (who is executed), finds her discarded corpse and, entwined within it, dies of starvation. When later found, the disintegrated dust of their remains is indistinguishable (Katherine and Heathcliff, if you will, in death). Kong, as is known, falls to his death from the Empire State Building, but not before elevating Darrow to a last magnificent paw-held view of Manhattan. *That* is his most triumphant moment, if not the steroidal hypostatization of the Eternal Feminine. Indeed, the dizzying heights from which Kong and Quasimodo work (the latter from Notre Dame's parapet) give curious point to the notion that the Eternal Feminine "draws us upward" (*zieht uns hinauf*).

There, as in the quest paradigm, it is the damsel's allure that predominates. The scores of Andromeda paintings throughout the centuries linger on her mutually reinforcing voluptuousness and vulnerability, chained and *displayed*, immobily nude upon her jagged crag for Perseus to see, desire, and risk his life for. "Smooth and unblemished, figures like *The Greek Slave* [below] and *Andromeda* asserted the moral virtue of the subjected woman, while affirming the pure gaze of the beholder." Does the variously depicted Andromeda bespeak a male perspective, or do women also dream to be so ideally alluring and desired? Sex for the male is ultimate pleasure and self-validation. It restores his equilibrium and, under the appropriate circumstances, social and world order. The female partakes of comparable satisfactions. While Rome's conquering generals received triumphal parades, classical and subsequent questers were rewarded with sex—meaning they "got the girl"—obtaining both reward and the will to carry on, i.e., to quest another day.

The combat hero quests/fights for life, for a way of life and its protection. The goal is typically woman and all she stands for, including home, hearth, and family, i.e., the orderings and amenities of civilized life. Civilization is hewn and must be protected from barbarism. It necessarily abides fixed in place and purpose (there have been no nomadic civilizations). While a male endeavor, it prospers beneath the domesticizing and further civilizing influence of woman. For what does the hero fight and return to, if all is uprooted in the perils of *female* combat and quest? The feminist argument that women are "denied" the quest or other forms of self-empowering narrative is head-on-backwards (akin to the notion of quest by brain alone). The quest, however much dependent on woman, is simply *not* a woman's narrative to be had.

The analogy between woman's body and nurturing earth is primordial (Gr. *Gaia* 'Mother Earth'), making the post-combat return to woman equally a return to and repossession of the land itself—woman's sex, like land, a territory to be recovered; sexual possession of the female's body inextricable from national sovereignty. The liberation and repossession of woman is thus the paradigmatic accompaniment to the liberation and repossession of the land she both occupies and signifies. Having wagered his brawn on the salvation of both, the hero will cultivate them, begetting progeny, and for its survival, produce. In the epic-literary sphere, however, feminist thought seeks to circumvent reality by recourse to brain over brawn, and by the resolute censure and correction of social wrongs. Thus does it "consider any success in these areas as evidence of women's epic calling" (Schweizer, *supra*).

Other circumventions involve a proposed change in subject matter. Elizabeth Barrett Browning may have aspired to epic standing: "As Homer was among men," she says of one of her female characters, "so [would] she be among women—she [would] be the feminine of Homer." Barrett Browning herself, as seen, never attained that status through *Aurora Leigh*, the most ambitious of her "epic" undertakings.

The aspiration toward openly female "Homericism" on matters of female concern was, in any event, impeded for the very reason female authors of Barrett Browning's time took pseudonyms—to escape the disapproval and perception of sentimentality associated with female authorship. And with what might the "feminine of Homer" regale her audience? Had comparably enduring women's themes existed, they would doubtless have been exploited before Barrett Browning's time. Or, a woman might at any time have composed an *Iliad* or *Odyssey*—a woman writing as a man, writing a man's work of interest primarily to men. No, of interest to *humanity*, as Homer necessarily is.

Says Isobel Hurst:

> The most obvious way to rival Homer was to write an epic, but 'the feminine of Homer' would *perhaps wish* to highlight the position of women in a society of heroes, to *redefine heroism* in a way that would allow women to achieve this ideal, and to condemn and *perhaps replace* stories of war and violence [emphasis added].

The statement concedes that one best rivals Homer by writing Homeric epic. Had a woman ever done so, there would be little or no talk of "redefining" heroism as a means to female epic authorship, because the "feminine of Homer"—or a feminine Homer—would have met Homer on his own terms. Absent the same, there surfaces the *notion alone*—"*perhaps wish . . . redefine . . . perhaps replace*"—of a woman's feminizing Homer. Redefining heroism is, however, not the answer. One does not meet a standard by changing it (nor does one logically wish otherwise of ingrained sexual dichotomies). There is no such thing as "affirmative-action equal-opportunity" epic. As van Creveld has argued in his *The Privileged Sex* (2013), women have often been granted gendered concessions. These are ill-advisedly jeopardized or exchanged for parity with men and with what men endure on woman's account and otherwise.

7. Does Homer Require Feminization?

Epic reflects an age when life was short, uncertain, subject to predations, and little helped by medical interventions. It was a largely lawless warrior society, in which men taken captive, if not first slain, became the enslaved workforce of their captors. There was no indigenous workforce or sustaining economy. It was an age in which livelihood and the means of survival were largely acquired by *taking*, by war waged for plunder. War was then the norm; the times of peace between merely breathing spaces. The Trojan War was itself a *taking* war—Troy the wealthiest city of antiquity, strategically located at the mouth of the Hellespont, and thus a prime target for plunder—the causal tale of Helen's abduction a likely later invention. From there, through repeated tellings, the tale grew in proportion (epic proportion), vastly exceeding its workaday inception.

The *taker* in such brutal and recurring enterprise is as likely to be slain as not—*and knows it*. So he fights for the *kleos aphthiton* 'undying fame' which, through lasting song, will compensate for pitifully transient life. You may well die, but the song about you won't. It will immortalize you, make *you* undying, as *it* is undying. For the sensibility of the time and culture, the offer is irresistible. One thus transcends death by readily yielding to it as inevitable. Such readiness renders paramount the danger and grandeur of the enterprise, the extent to which one has paradoxically helped others achieve *their* immortality (by killing them), and the manner of the telling thereafter. The more elaborate (and elaborated on) the enterprise, and the more expertly told, the more undying the fame. This occurs only with the paramount prize—life itself—in the balance, a situation traditionally, if necessarily, encountered by men as destroyers (Achilles), protectors (Hector), or founders (Aeneas) of civilization. Civilization is the most enduring and purposeful of human enterprises, and the fame associated with it the most lasting. But in the feminist argument, with no mention of civilization and its benefits, however imperfect, "gendered writing [is no] more evident than in the traditional epic, the *heroic* poem that 'fathers' the peoples and nations and values that give birth to western patriarchy and male hegemony."

As "man is a history-making creature," civilization is anchored in the *city* (or settled community) where history is made and first and ever recorded. *City* and *civilization* both derive from the same verbal root (cf. Lat. *civis* 'citizen'; *civitas* 'city'), be it Troy, Carthage, Rome, or—for that matter—the Emerald City. The quest, often departing from the city, leaves or returns to the city, even as it benefits the city. As in the expansive case of Rome, it may become a *metropolis* ('mother city'; Gr. *polis* 'city'), tantamount to civilization itself. We thus speak alike of the city of Rome and of Roman civilization. Civilization is an epic undertaking, as rooted and continuous as the epic impulse itself, as regularized and constant as epic poetry. Civilization ideally endures; if destroyed, taking root elsewhere. As epic is continuous, so is the civilizational enterprise, again exemplified by paradigmatic Rome: founded from the ashes of Troy by the questing Trojan survivor, Aeneas—himself (as he later learns) with preexisting Italic roots. After defeating the indigenous Rutulians, Aeneas further wins Lavinia, Latinus's daughter.

Dido, who commits suicide because of her abandonment by a destiny-bound Aeneas, failed in her nation-building quest. As one critic notes, "a long view of the ancient genre suggests that epic is at odds with women's authority, since triumphant womanhood so often appears insignificant or *threatening* to the glory of nation and empire classically sung by men for Man" (emphasis added). The operative term here is *threatening*, especially so in the case of Rome, which for over a century waged three monumental wars with Carthage for control of the Mediterranean (the Punic Wars, 264–146 BC). By Virgil's time, the wars were, of course, long past. The *Aeneid*, however, explains the conflict in terms of contending power claims dating back to city foundings on opposing sides of the Mediterranean. Dido—Carthage—was a *threat* to Aeneas's founding Rome, the thwarting of his destiny and, by retrospective implication, the thwarting of Rome itself. Carthage would yet threaten Rome's hegemony, once the two potentially nation cities began their expansions (hence the Punic Wars). Triumphant up to a point, Dido was thus necessarily, if tragically, sacrificed—according to script.

A "feminine of Homer" that might (according to Hurst, *supra*) "condemn and perhaps replace stories of war and violence" is not the answer. Given the Homeric ethos, and the quality and duration of the poetry it generated, the idea is both facile and counterintuitive as a means toward providing female access to Homeric repute. But why replace at all? Homeric poetry bears its own inherent condemnation of war and violence—part of its humanistic appeal—seen in the numerous pitiful vignettes of fallen heroes, in counterpoised recollections of peacetime, and in the wistful peacetime activities conjured forth in Homeric similes. The *Iliad* is not bloodshed and killing for their own sakes, as supposed by the "feminine of Homer" seeking malleable substitutes.

Morever, the *Iliad* is the anguished story of Achilles, as irresistible as is Achilles himself. Achilles likely developed from, or was assimilated to, epic-combat narratives not containing him. As such and other narratives were embellished over centuries of recitation, Achilles grew with them—his dilemma and its consequences, his anguish, his thoughts and actions—making his a singularly compelling tale, and the work containing it one of unique genius and perennial appeal. We actually see Achilles *fighting the epic tradition itself*, fighting its norms as he ponders, proclaims, and objects his way through them. In a sense, the epic tradition, with the introduction and development of Achilles, strains to contain him, even while subordinating everything to him. All this in the first work of the Western literary tradition. The story being to this day unparalleled, the tradition that created it is poorly tampered with, modified, or redefined. Does Homer really require *feminizing* beyond what strikingly feminine concerns he already conveys? To those we may add that Achilles, for all his anguished blood-lusting, is epic's biggest "mama's boy." His semidivine mother, Thetis, frequently frets for his fate, is at his side weeping, and mourns his death in advance. Achilles sheds his own abundance of tears. Thetis is epic's singular *mater dolorosa*, humanizing the barbaric hero that is her son. Every mom worries about her son, and boys never outgrow their mothers. What more is needed?

In the same vein, the "feminine of Homer" need not make her point through more scenes like the tearful leave-taking of Hector and Andromache (*Iliad*, Book 6). The epic's most memorably domestic scene—and our only look inside the walls of Troy—is a scene traditionally most relished by female readers. An increase in scenes depicting the love of husband and wife, and the fate of women and children in heroic society, would not sustain a Homeric enterprise. Homer's one entirely memorable scene alone *universalizes* the case, makes it a touchstone, an archetype, as does, in *its* way, the lamentable death of the young Greek warrior Simoeisios (discussed below). In fact, such concision is the essence of Homer's art. Though seemingly long at over 15,600 lines, the poem covers some fifty days in the tenth and final year of the war, presenting a single dramatic situation, or plot. It was for its dramatic unity that Aristotle praised Homer above other, decidedly more discursive, tales of the "epic cycle." Yet through one artistic device or another, the *Iliad* manages to convey a sense of the war in its entirety. Need Homer, then, describe—as he does—one battlefield killing after another to make his point? *Nunc leti mille repente viae* 'now suddenly a thousand ways to die'. Homer's detailed and varied descriptions of recurring battlefield wounding and slaughter underscore the pathos of war, and implicitly condemn it.

There is, in short, no "relative, gendered version of [Homer's] greatness." The values underlying Homer are *absolute*—necessity, fate, and death; their acceptance; fame outlasting death; forthrightness and its expectation (Achilles); absolute valor (Achilles); and absolute beauty (Helen). Helen and Achilles, as cause and driving force of the war, are *themselves* absolutes, as conceived and acting within the poem. The *Iliad*, as it developed, became an absolutely superior poem with and because of the absolutes of its subject matter. These more broadly include the absolute pity of war, the absolute transience of life, the absolutes themselves of death, love, hate, honor, pity, friendship, revenge, forgiveness, and redemption (the last sought by Achilles but never quite achieved). Life *as lived* does not consist in absolutes but in compromise. The *Iliad* in essence emphasizes the extreme whereby to enjoin the mean, paradigmatically showing how difficult and costly the accommodation can be. The need for, and draw of, this paradigm resides in human nature—again, in *humanity*—not in the one or the other gender. Absolutes are not relativized.

Women, as the source of life and nurture, are instinctively more protective of life—theirs and others'. Men, as the protectors of those who generate and nurture life, of those who, in return, care for them as men, necessarily see things differently. It is thus a male outlook that informs epic and its appreciation. And though there may have been female bards, it was male bards that brought epic to light and consummate perfection. This is not male chauvinism but the fact of the matter. A "relative, gendered version of Homer" is revisionist, an adulteration of inherent civilization-sustaining dichotomies from time immemorial and for as long as storytelling and recorded history have existed. Such dichotomies, as cannily noted, are of Darwinian import, as is the clear division between the sexes. The duties and responsibilities of each, as set forth in the "Parting of Hector and Andromache" are essential to the survival of the state. That is the way Homer must be read and appreciated: *on his own terms*. That the present age thinks differently of gender alters neither the facts nor circumstances from which epic, its truths, and perennial appeal emerged.

8. Competing for the Female

The male sex, both human and animal, competes for the female, as for most everything else—livelihood most of all—in a world of finite resources. Competition for the female comes with the male's expectation of refuge and comfort (he need no longer quest nor prove himself) and the female's expectation of protection and support. The quest, of whatever kind, with its trials of strength, intelligence, or faith, is one such manner of competition—winner take all. Being inherently attractive to and wanted by men, women need not compete for men; rather, they are wooed by them. The impracticality of women's questing or self-validation through demanding and self-endangering forms of competition thus coincides with their lack of need to do so. Again, the prospect of two questing sexes is not only curious but biologically unnecessary vis-à-vis who gets what and why; who survives and how.

Lacking the need to quest in the traditional epic manner, women have been spared the perils that questing men encounter in proving worth. It is nonetheless telling that Virgil, for his high-questing and city-founding Aeneas, holds up Dido, Queen of Carthage, as a city-founding paradigm (though we know little of the travails she encounters in her passage from Phoenicia to Carthage). Aeneas is further counseled and guided by the Cumaean Sybil in his descent to the underworld, even as Odysseus is counseled by Athena throughout the *Odyssey*; Achilles by Thetis in the *Iliad*; and Dante by Beatrice in Heaven. Though never herself questing, the female is rarely physically distant as guide or advisor or, as in the case of Diotoma, never intellectually distant. For the uncertainties of Hell and (the beginning of) Purgatory, Dante enlists the ghost of the experienced Hell-harrowing Virgil.

There is to be sure something heroic in Rebecca West's repeated calls for the improvement of women's lot; heroic in the manner of Prometheus's seeking the improvement of downtrodden humanity by the gift of fire (for which he suffers grievous punishment from Zeus). The same is reminiscent of Virginia Woolf's "conspicuous 'heroism' . . . reserved for the characters—male and female—who possess an 'ordinary mind on the ordinary day' . . . and who attempt to cope and survive in an increasingly painful world." Such characters have epic dimensions outside of epic proper; which is to say, epic dimensions within the narrower scope of drama. We recall in this connection that epic dialogue is strikingly dramatic; and drama, an outgrowth of epic. However, quest is properly concerned with "justify[ing] the ways of God to men"—not with the justice (social or otherwise) of man toward man or woman; not with the sympathetic betterment of humankind; and not with the struggles of daily life. Epic is the Will to Power (*Kraft* versus *Macht*). Its concern is self- and world mastery, self-control, self-understanding, and self-betterment. Composed in and reflecting *-ism*-less society, epic is impervious to transient concerns. Rather, focusing on absolutes, the quest is transcendent and redemptive, as supremely embodied in the archetype of the Holy Grail. Its focus is divine will, destiny, and necessity. Its means are cataclysmic warfare, the all but impossible return home, and the founding and nurture of civilization with its inherent imperfections. If Rebecca West elevates suffrage and related women's causes to heroic status, it is, in a manner of speaking, as the worthy and compelling matters they are, but not as transcendent means to the heroism that is *epic*.

The urge to co-opt an author such as West is, of course, irresistible, though West would herself have none of it (as seen in her rejection of feminist labeling). People of West's stature defy labels and glad-handing. Nonetheless, whereas West was "guided by ideals of social justice, fellow feeling and emancipation," Ayn Rand, author of the epic-length *Atlas Shrugged* and *The Fountainhead* "not only attacked altruism at every turn but also propagated capitalism as a 'miraculous productive system.'" She professed a rigid "Objectivism." Nonetheless, in both West and Rand we have woman doing man's work—"a man in a woman"—an Artemisia or Vittoria.

9. Gender and Gentileschi: Man in a Woman

In late-Renaissance painting one strains to differentiate the seventeenth-century painters Orazio (*père*) and Artemisia (*fille*) Gentileschi. Artemisia's best-known picture, *Judith Slaying Holofernes* (1611–1612) (plate 4), depicts the agonistically horrific decapitation of the general Holofernes: Judith doing a man's work. Although Judith's courage may have made her attractive as a female subject from the Old Testament, and despite Artemisia's then prominence as the painting's author, there is nothing discernibly female about the execution (in either sense). Judith leans slightly back, her head turned sideways, and is hardly squeamish as she beheads Holofernes with her blade. If her pose or facial expression show a touch of female reserve, a male painter would as likely have depicted it thus. The image was in fact deemed repellent at the time and for upward of two hundred years (into the early nineteenth century). Its militancy too rich to relinquish, the picture was appropriated and iconicized by the feminist movement of the 1970s and its subsequent revision of art history. The revision pervasively sought to overlay considerations of artistic merit with those of gender and biography. For example, "An unresolved tension between violence and decorum lies at [the painting's] core—and at the heart of Artemisia Gentileschi's life," and "The Judith story takes on different layers of meaning when its author is a woman artist"—the anti-patriarchal "layers" of often numbing theory. That Artemisia typically painted threatened female characters "genders," if at all, as *masculine* (not the opposite); that "she knew quite well what female hands are supposed to do" is without gendered trait. Any artist worth the paint knows what hands, *any* hands, are supposed to do. Special pleading vis-à-vis the depiction of female anatomy or matters of a putatively feminine bent—as, for example, Vigée Le Brun's depictions of lace (p. 77)—is a dead end. Why argue that Artemisia knew what female hands were supposed to do when male artists have forever quite knowingly rendered the female form in its every part, posture, and nuance?

Caravaggio's Judith is believed to be the inspiration for Artemisia's. But *his* Judith looks as though she is neither certain of what she is doing nor necessarily committed to doing it. She stands strangely aloof from the act, which is not in the least agonistic and is thus unpersuasively conveyed. The maidservant adds nothing to the wanted sense of vigor (be the artist male or female). But for the spurting of Holofernes's blood, Caravaggio's Judith could as easily be slicing turkey. It is an effort needing the overhaul Artemisia gave it. Her father Orazio Gentileschi's several depictions of Judith and maidservant are all *following* the decapitation—the concealing or bearing off of Holofernes's head—and thus provide little comparison to Artemisia's or Caravaggio's versions.

Artists being extraordinary people, their lives are thus often of interest to critics and biographers alike. Such interest is irrelevant to the art itself, the impression it makes, and the assessment made of it *as art*—art coming from a deeper place than life as lived. Artemisia returned to the story, painting *Judith Slaying Holofernes* a second time some ten years later, and twice painting *Judith and her Maidservant* (the latter with Holofernes's head). It was the theme *as theme* that governed, absent speculation concerning Artemisia's personal need to exorcize the demons of her own rape (see note, p. 294). Nor do Artemisia's more sedate depictions, like *David and Bathsheba,* reveal a female perspective, notwithstanding Germaine Greer's discerning in it "something . . . of Artemisia's insight into magnanimous womanhood." This is but special pleading for an artist known to be female—"magnanimous womanhood" as much the province of a male as female artist. Rather, Artemisia painted forcefully, as any man *or woman* might; in fact, no less forcefully, and in the case of Judith, even more so, than her father. The intent of art—what lies beneath its execution and what we are intended to take away from it—is unknowable. Ten different critics will differently answer the same question. However finite or markedly realistic the art, the artist is yet interpreted.

In the perennially painted *Susanna and the Elders* (1610) (plate 5), which Artemisia herself undertook on three occasions, it is impossible to gauge the extent to which the depicted sexual approach or proposition by two older men is a traumatic event, as most often proposed by feminist interpreters. The Susannas of Rubens (four times), Allori (plate 6), Van Dyck, Batoni (twice), Tiepolo, and even Millet—the last demonically rendered for all Millet's pastoralism and softened female forms—depict comparable Susannas, with whatever variations. Greer makes but a single reference to Artemisia's *Susanna* of 1610, concluding, "Only she could paint female figures which had a skeleton as well as flesh and skin texture. Susanna's pelvis is not the invention of voluptuous fantasy, but something observed and understood." *All* the Susannas are equally "observed and understood," and their male depicters not voluptuaries for being male. Greer elsewhere writes (at odds with her appraisal here) that Artemisia's "women are unconsciously voluptuous, engrossed as they are in their own activities."

There is considerable overstatement in the interpretation of *Susanna and the Elders* as an assault by sexually intemperate men. Few of the Susannas display actual violence being done to the subject; it is sooner the possibility of violence and its impending nature that compels. For rape or assault, actual or imminent, we look to *The Rape of the Sabine Women, The Rape of Proserpina, The Rape of the Daughters of Leucippus, The Abduction of Hippodameia,* or *Death of Lucretia* (Lucretia choosing suicide over defilement). What we typically have in the Susannas are two voyeuristic septuagenarians. According to the apocryphal story—as variously reflected in the paintings—the elders do not actually attack Susanna but proposition her, threatening accusations of sex with a young lover if she refuse them. As the opportunists are old men, and repellent as such, Susanna's steadfastness comes as no surprise. In fact, the elders by their very nature are at odds with Susanna's virtue. Such suitors could little tempt Susanna to stray. As the adage goes, virtue untried is virtue unproven. As these paintings more reasonably suggest, Susanna is sooner surprised or importuned than fearful or horrified, even when the elders tug at her garment or towel, as in some depictions. Noted feminist art historian Mary D. Garrard observes that Susanna's "expressive range runs from protest of a largely rhetorical nature to the hint of outright acquiescence"; and further (of Artemisia's 1622 *Susanna*), "She does not resist but engages her assailants, her uplifted eyes expressing only mild anxiety, and even this seems merely a baroque rhetorical convention." Indeed, in the depiction of Ebenezer Crawford (1830–1873), Susanna is a totally nude self-preening seductress; and in the work of the "Orientalizing" sensualist Eugene Ansen Hofmann (1862–1955), she strikes an unreservedly seductive pose, as if beckoning.

Rape? Attack? In two of the four Susannas by Tintoretto (1519–1594), the elders are so distant as to be hardly noted on the canvas; in a third (c. 1557, the most famous), they are near enough, but as yet unrevealed to the idly voluptuous bather. The fourth (c. 1555) (plate 7) tells another—and little told—story: it is one of the few in which an elder actually makes intimate contact with Susanna (as also in Allori's depiction). The elder's hand extends across her chest to take hold of her breast. From this Susanna does not recoil, seeming instead to lean into the hold. At the same time, a rocky outcropping between the two suggests that neither will move any further toward the other. From the beatific look on *this* elder's face, he seems to have all he might want or be capable of. The other elder stands opposite, bending deeply at the waist, right hand to his heart, left extended in a sweeping courtly gesture. This is all very peculiar for the meaning typically assigned Artemisia's *Susanna and the*

Elders, namely, that, as painted by Artemisia or any male artist, it depicts the terrifying assault on an unsuspecting and unwilling woman.

The painting by Claude Vignon (c. 1640) is another in which an elder takes hold of Susanna's breast, but such depictions are in a clear minority. There is a sixteenth-century piece of Flemish statuary depicting a hand to the breast, and a vivid early-seventeenth-century engraving by René Boyvin in which Susanna seeks to restrain the arm about her waist of the elder leaning inward, as it appears, to kiss or nestle the side of her breast. In various other depictions, there is a "taking hold" of one kind or another, with varying degrees of response from Susanna. The most striking portrayal of forcible taking—judging from Susanna's panicked face and body position, and the elders' own dastardly looks; one of them tearing off her cover—is that of the Flemish Francis van Bossuit's ivory-carved relief, c. 1690 (Getty Museum). It is unparalleled in this respect by any painting on the subject.

There is also the elders' chutzpah as part of the story. Local judges, knowing the dire consequences to whichever party is proven false (the accused or accuser), they are friends of Joachim, Susanna's husband. Do they imagine they will have their way with Joachim's wife in his very backyard, and depart scot-free? Should she refuse them, they intend to blackmail her by accusations of sexual assignation with a young lover. Do they expect her thus simply to acquiesce? Somehow resisting or escaping, she would have accused the elders of inappropriate conduct, a lewd and indecent proposal, unwanted touching, attempted rape, and blackmail. Whom would Joachim believe?

Susanna depictions are thus shot through with ambiguity, each and collectively. One wonders why the lovely Susanna is so lushly and self-displayingly nude, and often bejeweled, thus inviting attention. Margarita Stocker, author of *Judith Sexual Warrior*, calls Susanna a "bathing beauty," comparing her to Bathsheba, "the Bible's striptease artist and concubine"—both of whose toilettes belong to the moralistic *Vanitas* genre, the warning to women against the sin of self-love. Our attention, as viewers, is one thing: we wish to see beauty beautifully displayed. But the work's artistically finessed nudity within an amorous garden setting is at cross-purposes with the story's moral of triumphant female virtue. Which is to say, the assiduously virtuous tend *not* to be thus displayed or thus taken with themselves when they are. Why does Susanna bathe unattended, outdoors on her husband's estate, at a predictable hour each day? That her attendants may have left to fetch the bathing oils is no explanation; they might have brought them in the first place. And what did the elders assume could be done during the brief interval of the attendants' absence? The elders, knowing Susanna's beauty, might seek advantage, regardless the state of her dress or undress. Such considerations challenge *Susanna and the Elders* interpretation, which is as it should be. Indeterminateness inheres in great art, and a certain suspension of disbelief is part of it. The artist's gender, however, is not.

Outstanding in this connection is Artemisia's conception of *Aurora* (*Dawn*). The theme typically elicits figureless atmospherics capturing the hour's rosy hue—Homer's *rhododaktulos ēōs* 'rosy-fingered dawn'—and other muted shades. If rarely showing figures, the paintings depict boats at harbor or sea, fields, isolated buildings, or even townscapes; on occasion, some goddess-like figure, dreamily afloat, bringing on the day. More often, however, the paintings simply portray the sky and its dawn-associative colors, with landfall or reference points nowhere in sight. Enter Artemisia with her singular *Aurora* (1627) (plate 8), showing a tall, firmly striding goddess of dawn, scantily rose-color draped. Arms outstretched to either side, fingers splayed and Homerically rose-tinted, she pushes back recalcitrant night to bid enter a backgrounded emergent dawn. The figure recalls nothing so much as the mannerist elongations of El Greco (1541–1614) or Henry Fuseli (aka Johann Heinrich Füssli) (1741–1825). This markedly muscular *Aurora*—by a female artist—the first Aurora of its kind, is virtually without parallel. Artemisia's is a male depiction by a female artist. Subsequent depictions include: *Aurora and Zephyr* (1845) by William Etty (a chariot-disembarked dawn strides forth, rosy-cheeked, appareled in dawn's fiery colors; arm raised above bared breast; embraced by a cloud-seated Zephyr); *Dawn* (1881) by William-Adolphe Bouguereau (white-draped nearly nude figure on toe, lily-enraptured, harbinger of day's freshness and possibilities); *Dawn* (1895) by Evelyn Pickering De Morgan (standing, elaborately gowned winged figure, pouring light onto the horizon from a shouldered jug); *Gates of Dawn* (1900) by Herbert James Draper (Dawn an anatomically enrapturing, if somewhat severe, gate-opening beauty); and *Angel of Dawn* (1919) by William Abbott Thayer (firmly positioned angel, wings outspread; right arm positioned upward, left downward).

Predominant though they be, such examples are inconclusive of gendered authorship, female or male. By contrast as markedly female are the irretrievably sweet children's depictions of Louise Elisabeth Vigée Le Brun (1755–1842), her own daughter among them; and the obsessive mother-and-child singularity of Mary Cassatt (1844–1926). At the same time, a vein of lush female portraiture emanates from Thomas Lawrence (1769–1830) and Thomas Sully (1783–1872). And what of the multitudinous ballerinas, in sculpture and paint, of Edward Degas (1834–1917)? Though male artists are generally obsessed with the nude female form and accompanying beauty of visage, we would not necessarily expect workaday ballerinas from a male artist, but for the idealized poise of which they are capable. Viscerally female are the many self-portraits of Frida Kahlo (1907–1954), depicting her miscarriages and the frequent operations she underwent following a catastrophic accident at age eighteen.

More recently, the work of artist Florine Stettheimer (1871–1944) was on exhibit at New York's Jewish Museum (May 5–September 24, 2017), with her four *Cathedral* canvases part of the New York Metropolitan's permanent collection. For all her delicacy—her artifice and stylization, her high camp sensibility—she is not an identifiably female artist. Her work shares Fauve, naïve, or abstract qualities with the likes of Matisse, Dufy, and Redon, and otherwise "exist[s] apart from the major currents of her time." Her four *Cathedrals*, as her paintings, are suffused with fey and whimsical figures, often randomly disposed. The canvases have nonetheless evoked male-artist comparisons: first, to the mural artistry of Diego Rivera (though, given Rivera's vigor, the comparison is tenuous); and, for her figures' random spatial dispositions, to the work of Marc Chagall (Chagall, perhaps more a "woman in the man"). Stettheimer's personal life and poetry, however, tell a different story. "She was a determined feminist, yet equally determined to be feminine in the most conventional sense of the term." The work of her younger contemporary, the French painter Marie Laurencin (1883–1956), appears, in its "elfin" style, reminiscent of Stettheimer's—Laurencin typically considered, in her art and life, a feminine aesthete.

10. Judy Chicago: The Faux-Gendering of Genre Art

Transcendence is the goal of high or fine art—the idealization of form, condition, or state of mind. Short of transcendence, of course, there is a range of art-elicited emotions. These include the sweet reverie induced by superior depictions of everyday things, places, and situations, the art form known as genre art. A premier example is Jean-Baptiste-Siméon Chardin (1699–1779). His kitchen maids amid domestic scenes evoke the beauty of still life at home, with its family members and workday activities—grace before meals, the water woman, the larder, the peeling of turnips. Such scenes, superiorly portrayed, capture a moment's serenity with its often subdued or muted beauty. Such scenes seek not to be riveting, but centered, equable. Genre representation also exists outside the household: at the inn or market, in the street—scenes brimming with people, produce and other comestibles, and frequent commotion. The Flemish Baroque (16th and 17th centuries) excelled in genre painting (Jean-François Millet, the Bruegels, the Teniers). Similarly excelling was the Dutch Golden Age (17th century) (Vermeer, Hals, Steen, de Hooch). Vermeer was so accomplished in the haunting and often refined intimacy of his interiors and their subjects—and his surviving works so few—as to have sustained particular veneration to this day. And the Bruegels' boisterous wedding feasts delight, in all their minutiae, to this day. At the same time, however, genre art was deemed the lowliest of painterly pursuits; history painting, with its heroic and outsize actors and events, the most esteemed.

Genre art of the twentieth century witnessed an unlikely upending in the person of Judy Chicago (b. 1939), whose *The Dinner Party* (1979) at once sexualized and politicized this typically quiescent art form (the work, a floor installation, now on permanent exhibition at the Brooklyn Museum). Paintings of elaborately staged dinner tables beset with diners of any and all social classes have been a staple of genre art, even elaborately set tables without diners, simply showing themselves off. However, Chicago's *The Dinner Party* is a suggestively triangular banquet-table, set with 39 plates that depict floral labial and vulvar designs "celebrating women," a Sappho plate included. The work is widely regarded as the first feminist artwork on an epic scale, functioning as a symbolic marker of women's experience in Western cultures. At the same time, it is the predominant example of what has been called "cunt art" and, as with the misguided notion of epic on female themes, is deemed to heroicize female achievement on a scale traditionally reserved for men. But can this really be how women wish their commemoration?

Such art is no more inviting from a female than male artist, as we surmise upon first viewing Gustave Courbet's *L'Origine du Monde* (*The Origin of the World*) (1866). This oil-on-canvas—unique in an age of extreme sexual reserve and hypocrisy both—is a close-up depiction of the pubic-hair covered genitals and abdomen of a woman lying on a bed, legs spread (its most recent owner none other than the feminist-theory-congenial Jacques Lacan). The painting hails from a time when men, some of them at least, might have little known that women had pubic hair. The case in point is John Ruskin (1819–1900), the leading English art critic of his day. In 1848 he married Effie Gray, the beautiful and intelligent nineteen-year-old socialite, only to have the marriage annulled, unconsummated—as some speculate, because repulsed by the wedding-night revelation of Effie's pubic hair (Ruskin better acquainted with the smoothness of the classical nude statuary that was his métier). Rodin may have been influenced by *L'Origine* when drawing his similarly positioned nude (pubic hair shaven) in *Avant la Création* (*Before the Creation* or *Prior to Creation*) (1900). The *art* in art, Horace famously notes, is *concealment,* or—to quote Swinburne—the "pure artist never asserts, he suggests, leaving the reader to work out suggestions." Adults little need to see such actualities so deliciously up close. At the same time, however, Courbet presents a compelling idea—that of erotic and generative concinnity: the pleasure, even lust, that induces reproduction and thus assures its occurrence. This is a far cry from Chicago's prandial pussies.

Indeed, Courbet's painting has been taken as a metonymically essential representation of woman herself; of man's ineluctable longing for woman at, and as represented by, the crux of her being and source of his own; and of man's need, in woman's absence, for the creation of that art which is woman herself. The painting is further taken to indicate woman as the original inspiration of the very first artwork. Renowned art historian Linda Nochlin (1931–2017) succinctly summarizes the effort to

> 'trace back' historically the origin of art to the engraving of crude but recognizable vulvas on the walls of caves in southern France during the Aurignacian period, about 33,000 to 28,000 BC. According to this scenario, masculine desire literally led lusting but frustrated Aurignacian males to represent in stone the desired, absent object—the female sex organ—and thereby to create the very first artwork. In light of this assumption, all other artwork ought to be considered simulacra of the originating male act, and representation must itself be considered a simulacrum of that desired original.

This is further to say that art in the first instance is coextensive with man's desire for woman and that man's recurring depictions of the female nude are themselves reproductive reenactments of primal desire (Hesiod's cosmic pre-Aphroditic Eros). Courbet's is a unique, daring, and ultimately profound artistic message that would ill sustain imitation or repeated conveyance— the pleasuring and generative womb instead of more genial breast, the latter signifying what arouses, nurtures, and inspires (rather than generates).

While Courbet depicts it, his *L'Origine du Monde* is not cunt art, but "the forbidden site of specularity and the ultimate object of male desire ... construed as the very source of artistic creation itself." It is unembellished and matter-of-fact in its *givenness*. Chicago, by contrast, is mere spectacle, subverting the instinctive depiction of male desire from one of generative and erotic compulsion to a belaboredly decorative feminist banner. Its ultimate irony is that *The Dinner Party* adopts an absolute male object of female identification to assert female independence and accomplishment, casting the female—as in no other case—through a male envisioned rep-resentation. Chicago, moreover, has said that she wished to "make butterfly images that are hard, strong, soft, passive, opaque, transparent—all different states—& I wanted them to all have cunts so they'll be female butterflies & at the same time be shells, flowers, flesh, forest—all kinds of things simulta-neously." Courbet at least had and made a point. Chicago merely exempli-fies the adage that "a point in every direction is no point at all," even as the etymologically rooted purpose of art (as noted) is to *fix, position*, or *make clear*; not confuse, disperse, or proliferate; to make a statement or urge a possibility, not proffer multitudinous tropes (cf. *concinnity* [above], "fitness, suitableness, connectedness, harmony" [Merriam-Webster]). *The Dinner Party* is overwrought in its too purposeful symbolism: "twenty-five women who were eaten alive" [or just "eaten"]; an illustrious women's "Last Supper," which is to say, women sacrificed on the altar—or dinner plate—of male voracity.

The stack of dishes, before being set about the table, might indicate the odds are stacked against women by the patriarchy. But Chicago de-cided she "would like the plate images to physically rise up as a symbol of women's struggle for freedom." This rather trivializes established and intuitively compelling notions of striving, metaphorically conveyed by sun and stars, mountain peaks, and birds in flight. Writes Nochlin, "The growing power of women in the politics of both sex and art is bound to revolutionize the realm of erotic representation." In Chicago's words, "Feminist art is that art which illuminates women's life experience. You know a woman did it." *The Dinner Party* allegorizes rather than illumines, but that "a woman did it" is sadly certain. Its failure resides first in its feminist, and thus political, browbeating; and then in its ultimately seeking to do too much and trying too hard.

11. Markedly Male Eroticism

Female nudes are often voyeuristically painted in a way that reflects male fascination, with those of Pierre-Auguste Renoir (1841–1919) largely excepted. Renoir's often less-provocative and rosily plump ladies look as though they've just stepped out of the sauna. Quite otherwise is Antoine Watteau's (1684–1721) highly voyeuristic *Secret Toilet* and *The Remedy* (side-recumbent nude being administered a clyster by her maid) (plate 9). At the same time, however, Watteau's *femmes-en-fête* are of a seemingly more female inspiration for their wistful sense of love's transience and the passing of earthly delights. Obsessively male is the Rococo whimsy of François Boucher (1703–1770) and Jean-Honoré Fragonard (1732–1806): Fragonard's frisky hide-and-seek demoiselles; Boucher's fleshy recumbents, including the backside-receptive odalisque (the more scandalous for being his own wife). There are Jean-Baptiste Greuze's (1725–1805) models—including his wife, *The Milkmaid*—ever on the verge of a "wardrobe malfunction."

As for William Etty (1787–1849),

> he was the first and only English painter before the [20th] century for whom nude painting was essential to his artistic creation. Indeed, his interest became obsessional: nudes were to him, in Browning's words, "Mistresses with great smooth marble limbs."

Etty devoted himself to painting, "finding . . . God's most glorious work to be WOMAN, that all human beauty had been concentrated in her." Be it said of Etty that his depictions of the female breast have a singularly voluptuous quality, difficult to comprehend as rendered by a female artist. While no one begrudges female artists female nude depictions, it is more the exception than the rule, and never an "obsession." Etty, moreover, was one of the few painters of his day, to depict (however modestly) female pubic hair and (somewhat more forwardly) male genitalia (preceded in both practices by French Pierre-Paul Prud'hon [1758–1823]). A female artist had never done so. If frequent painters of nudes typically gender as male, Etty is the extreme case.

William-Adolphe Bouguereau (1825–1905) captivates with his chaste and statuesquely posed and polished nudes, each worth a Pygmalion's rapture. More pruriently male are: Bouguereau-influenced Henri Gervex's (1852–1929) *Rolla*, the lovely and languid post-coital prostitute being abandoned by her handsome lover (plate 10); Léon François Comerre's (1850–1916) *Golden Rain*, with Danae writhing on her bed, legs sheet-entangled as Zeus rains down in a mist of gold; and Guillaume Seignac's (1870–1924) *The Jewel Box*, a prone languid nude—arm draped about the head of a lion skin—trifling with jewels spilled before her as she invites on-lookers with a sultry self-confident glance. All are wishfully, emphatically male, while Renoir, again—his models frequently clothed—offers a more demure sensibility in his Cassatt-like *La Promenade* (mother and two children), *The Bath* (mother and child), *Girl with a Watering Can, Children on the Seashore*, and the iconic *Young Girls at the Piano*.

One allows for qualification as concerns Boucher, Fragonard, Watteau, and the rococo (18th century). That rococo whimsy was "obsessively male" indicates only that, by professional dominance and gendered predisposition, one would expect such painting from a male rather than a female. The period, in fact, was one witnessing the feminization of men—especially in elite society—and of cultural production alike, one in which sexual difference was deemphasized and opposite-sex affectation not uncommon. In this atmosphere, Boucher, for one, became popular with women, who were largely responsible for his enormous success. While moralists of the day, Diderot foremost among them, inveighed against Boucher for his "prettification" of art and moral bankruptcy, Boucher's appeal to both genders, despite or regardless his own, was unquestionable. To speak of his documented or rumored sexism, trivialization of women, or the like is to speak anachronistically—judging, rather than evaluating, the past. Accepted on its own terms, love in the eighteenth century was synonymous with entertainment and forthright pleasure.

12. The Masculine in Female Artist Depictions

Angelica Kauffman (1741–1807), a woman artist not again equaled in Europe until Vigée Le Brun, depicts an appropriately feminized Paris in her *Hector Accuses Paris of Effeminacy*, as she does to even greater effect in her *Paris and Helen Flee the Court of Menelaus*. Kauffman's contemporaries disingenuously criticized her "inimitable femininity" and inability to depict heroes as men. The judgment likely issued from knowledge of the painter's gender and reluctance to concede her prodigious abilities. The appraisals were misdirected both because Paris *is* effeminate in dress, manner, and anti-heroics as depicted throughout by Homer; *and* as readily reflected by mid-eighteenth-century rococo sensibility, one of aristocratic foppishness—society portraits of men in fur-lined capes, ruffled blouses, wigs atop exposed foreheads, etc. The notion of inimitable femininity is thus overstated. There is nothing markedly feminine in Kauffman's work aside from the purposefully feminized Paris and other such intentional portrayals. One may compare Canova's celebrated *Paris* (1810) and David's *The Loves of Paris and Helen* (1788) (both in *galante* style). The former was praised for its "truth to nature [and] character appropriate to the subject [*carattere cosi proprio del soggetto*]; the ideal of Paris." It was also commended for its "light grace . . . which responds agreeably to the subject" (*un sentiment de grace legère . . . qui respond agréablement au sujet*). It was praised, in a word, for its *decorum*, defined as the proper harmony between manner and matter, or what is aptly called imitative harmony.

Paris is the most beautiful man alive, as is Helen the most beautiful woman. His career begins as judge in a beauty contest, deciding who of Hera, Athena, and Aphrodite is most beautiful. Paris's first appearance (*Iliad*, Book 3) is in showy leopard skin rather than traditional battle gear. It would be odd were he *not* effeminately portrayed. In the end, one would not know from Kauffman's work that this child prodigy and most cultivated personage of Europe was a woman.

Moving briefly to the twentieth century, we note Polish-born painter Theresa Bernstein (1890–2002), whose work and century-plus life were the subject of a wondrous retrospective at Philadelphia's Woodmere Art Museum (July 26–October 26, 2014). Noting that Bernstein was a founding member of a group of women artists, The Philadelphia Ten, and belonged to several women's rights organizations, reviewer Pamela J. Forsythe adds, "While women's issues are sometimes explicit . . . even when they are not, Bernstein often placed women prominently, relegating men to the shadowy perimeter and rendering them in less detail." One may, however, trust that it takes no woman to "place women prominently" and render ancillary figures, male or female, in lesser detail. Nor does Bernstein's placement of women "front and center in her canvases . . . defy stereotype" (as Forsythe further states).

Special pleading aside, the exhibit itself connects Bernstein to the male painterly tradition, close colleague and fellow-exhibitor that she was to urban realist painters John Sloan and Robert Henri, and with Henri protégés Edward Hopper and Stuart Davis (all major contributors to the development of American art). In fact, the exhibition greets the viewer as follows:

> Her work was frequently described as 'masculine' for its bold qualities and it was said she 'painted like a man.' She depicted urban subjects and the social phenomena of her time, and possessed a prodigious talent for capturing humanity in her figures.

However, "bold qualities" are hardly the province of male artists alone, while greatness in art is always "prodigious." At the same time, "capturing humanity" is any great artist's stock in trade. None of this signals gender specificity or crossover. Bernstein's paintings stand, as they must, on their non-gendered merits and are wondrous each.

13. From Painting to Sculpture

The Woodmere Art Museum also owns a splendidly draped portrait bust of Abraham Lincoln (plate 11) which may serve to extend our discussion of gendered art to sculpture. The sculptor was the little-known Sarah Fisher Ames (1817–1901). Of the five Lincoln busts Ames executed, one was purchased by the government in 1868 and placed in the Senate wing of the U.S. Capitol Building, where it remains to this day, an iconic work. Another Ames Lincoln bust (in a different style) graces the Williams College Museum of Art. Also warranting mention in this connection is Vinnie Ream Hoxie (1847–1914). Hoxie, in her late teens, was the first woman to receive a sculpture commission from the U.S. government. Her nearly seven-foot-high Lincoln (1871) (plate 12) stands to this day in the Capitol Rotunda (her portrait bust of Lincoln the competition entry piece). Also noted is Anne Whitney (1821–1915), among whose prominent works in both bronze and marble is the seated bronze of Charles Sumner (Harvard Yard).

Warranting special note is Harriet Goodhue Hosmer (1830–1908), whose stunning and elaborately draperied marble *Zenobia in Chains* (1859) (plate 13) was deemed a near-impossible marvel of female workmanship in its time. It is the rival of anything by Hosmer's older contemporary, the famed Hiram Powers (1805–1873). Powers's chained standing nude *The Greek Slave* (1843) (plate 14) was his most famous sculpture; as *Zenobia* was Hosmer's—granted that Powers's work is the more graceful and done to human scale, whereas Hosmer's is rather stolid and "bigger than life." Comparison none-theless abounds between these sculptors, female and male, whose reputations largely reside in a similar concept, differently executed: an enslaved female in chains. The one is nude, the other elaborately draped. The one is chained at the wrists, the other more loosely bound and appearing to hold her chains (thus seeming more empowered). The one is any captive woman, the other a famed warrior queen (on a par with Cleopatra). Either statue could none-theless have been executed by the one or other sculptor. That Hosmer, as we know from her writing, represented Zenobia's strength and bearing consis-tently with her own feminist beliefs is nothing apparent on the face of Zenobia herself, though of interest as background.

Nor is Powers's *The Greek Slave* more "titillating" for being nude; rather, it is "pure because . . . innocent of shame." The force of arousal goes to various painters of the period, including Jean-Léon Gérôme's (1824–1904) *Phryne Before the Judges* (1861) (Kunsthalle, Hamburg), *Slavemarket* (1866) (Clark Art Institute); and Jean-Auguste-Dominique Ingre's (1780–1867) *Grand Odalisque* (1814) (Louvre), and more so to his *Odalisque with Slave* (1839) (Harvard Art Museum). Such and earlier works bespeak European, and particularly imperialist French, nineteenth-century reverie in the per-ceived sensuality of North Africa and the Levant, not that a female artist was incapable of the same putatively male subject matter. Zenobia, Queen of (Syrian) Palmyra under the Roman emperor Aurelius (121–180 AD), was also of Near Eastern extraction, and her artistic handling by a male sculp-tor might on that account have differed from Hosmer's. Of scores of female sculptors, the one most masculinely enamored of exultantly youthful female form was Rodin student Harriet Whitney Frismuth (1880–1980). *The Vine* (1923) (plate 15), embodying the pliancy of the nubile ecstatic female form, is Frismuth's signature work. She disavowed the label *sculptress*.

The Greek Slave (1843), for all its nudity, woeful beauty, and attractive fascination, became an abolitionist icon—occasioning not leering looks but aspirations of freedom for America's slave population—a statuary *Uncle Tom's Cabin* (1852), as it were. *The Greek Slave* inspired John Bell's (1811–1895) bronze and silver *The American Slave* (1853) (plate 16). Bell presented a chained Negress, facially and anatomically more realistic than Powers's stone-smoothened figure—and daringly beautiful for the times—awaiting transport to the United States. Bell sought to convey that Powers's slave figure, neoclassically idealized and thus corporeally remote, not be seen to soften the visceral anguish that was slavery. However, in the ten years preceding Bell's "revision," Powers's original had made its mark. One may compare Jean-Baptiste Carpeaux's portrait bust *La Négresse* (1868) (Ny Carlsberg Glyptotek, Copenhagen, and in other media elsewhere). The roped bust with agonized features and backward-straining shoulders (suggesting wrists bound) is titled *Pourquoi naître esclave?* 'Why (be) born a slave?'

Gendered predilections, artistic temperament, and public reception aside, the sculptor of the most sheerly beautiful female nudes of our time has been Frederick Hart (1943–1999). His figures in *Creation of Mankind* (plate 17), Washington National Cathedral, West Portal, evoke (as elsewhere in his work) what one imagines to have been the beauty of Eve herself. In his depictions, Hart, in the footsteps of Rodin, not merely conveys but does God's work.

14. Falsely Signaling the Female

An exhibit at the National Museum of Women in the Arts, Washington DC, titled "Royalists to Romantics: Women Artists from the Louvre, Versailles, and Other French National Galleries" (February 24–May 27, 2012), featured more than seventy paintings, prints, and drawings by revolutionary-era French women artists. Yet nothing in these consistently superior and often breathtaking works signaled female artistry, though the same was urged in descriptive tags alongside the various paintings. It is of course significant that women painters—as women artists of all kinds—have struggled for independence and recognition, with some, like their literary peers, selling paintings under male pseudonyms; or again like their literary peers, seeing their works "reattributed" to male artists when their own gender was known. Others have used the names of masters with whom they studied to obtain prices comparable to their male counterparts. The individual stories inspire admiration no less than sympathy.

Aside Vigée Le Brun's *The Princess Belozersky* (1798) we read: "The swirling drapery shows Vigée Le Brun's artistic virtuosity," as though the depiction of elaborate clothwork were a uniquely female skill. Rather, the painting of period attire, down to the finest gauzes and lace, is so much the painter's medium as to barely warrant mention. Le Brun's *Head of a Young Girl* (aka *Girl Wearing a Veil*) (1785) references the "piled on, formalized coif" and the "deep-bodiced attire"—as things, again, of intrinsically female expertise, when the like was comparably done by a Fragonard, Van Dyck, Rubens, Gainsborough, and any number of others. It was in fact Le Brun's short-lived contemporary Peter Toms (1748–1777), a founding member of the Royal Academy, who excelled as a "drapery painter," employed for that purpose by the painting elite, including Sir Joshua Reynolds (first Royal Academy president), Benjamin West, Francis Cotes, and Johan Zoffany. Vigée Le Brun's superior abilities, neither enabled nor hampered by her sex, made her the most sought-after portraitist of her day throughout France, all of Europe, and Russia (where she was initially exiled during the French Revolution). As much may be said of her likely influence and predecessor in the genre, the Venetian-born Rosalba Carriera (1673–1757).

Of particular interest was Angélique Mongez's *Mars and Venus* (1841). A student of David, Mongez was the first Frenchwoman to lay full claim to the title of history painter, the male painter's domain par excellence. It is a horizontally imposing, stunningly executed canvas, of which we read, "The artist has divided the composition into two gendered halves, with muscular chestnut steeds and the robust warrior Mars on the left, in contrast to the wispy clouds, delicate flowers, and a graceful, seductive Venus and Cupid on the right." "Two gendered halves"? The depiction is *as it must necessarily be*, regardless the painter's gender. Any number of male painters would have rendered it the same.

Also exhibited was Adrienne Grandpierre-Deverzy's *The Studio of Abel de Pujol* (1822), showing the master instructing a class of female students. The tag anachronistically informs us that "gender-appropriate symbols abound." These consist of fully clothed female students, an elegantly dressed female model, and a male torso—shelved overhead and judiciously turned to the wall. The painting's "gender-appropriate symbolism" merely reflects period and class sensibility, and as Nochlin urges, the then shortcomings of social situation, structure, and institutions. Similarly, but not part of the exhibition, Angelica Kauffman's *Zeuxis Selecting Models for His Painting of Helen of Troy* (c. 1764) (Annmary Brown Memorial, Brown Univ.), in which the artist especially considers one of five female beauties, all shown in clavicle-to-ankle Greek-style attire. The picture was nonetheless inspired by the *Venus Kallipygos* 'Venus of the Beautiful Buttocks' (Museo Nazionale, Naples)—an exhibitionist backside-emphatic nude (cf. Bradley Ives Chauncey, *Pandora* 1858, the Huntington and elsewhere). The *Zeuxis* further recalls numerous renderings of the Judgment of Paris (of which Helen was the prize), depicting—within the parameters of period taste—a nude Hera, Aphrodite, and Athena.

However, the then traditional license for painting nude mythological figures did not generally apply to the painting of real-life models, whether by male or female artist. Inspired by artistic nudity at every turn, Kauffman could have painted nudes with the best of her male counterparts, but was constrained (as was Grandpierre-Deverzy) by the conventions of her time. As the former could not render Helen-as-prospective-model in the nude, the latter could not render an actual studio model in the nude. Whereas male artists of course had nude female models stand for them in private, a nude male model so engaged by a lone female artist (or in any studio) would have then been unthinkable. It was the pervasive and endemic double standard of the time—women lacking full rights and freedoms, and more than a century removed from women's liberation and feminist waves that followed. However, constraint was called for in works by male painters as well. John Singer Sargent's *Madame X* (1884) (Metropolitan Museum) scandalized fin de siècle French society (and drove Sargent to exile in London) for the hint of impropriety in the subject's fallen shoulder strap. We have, by extreme contrast, already considered Courbet's *L'Origine du Monde* (1866). For all its implications, *The Studio of Abel de*

Pujol is a resonant reminder of the female painter's lack of essential foundation in Western art training: the nude model.

Finally, though other examples abound, the exhibit showed Rosa Bonheur's *Highland Raid* (1860). Bonheur, consummate *peintre animalier*, is known for her spirited equines, inspired by subject-matter predecessors George Stubbs, Théodore Gericault, Eugène Delacroix, and Greek sculpture, to be sure. Bonheur's signature canvas is the huge *The Horse Fair* (1852–1855) (Metropolitan Museum) modeled on Géricault's *The Race of the Riderless Horses* (1817) (the Getty). Bonheur—wearing trousers in the manner of George Sand and living with a longtime same-sex partner—is incontrovertibly masculine in style. More recently, the aluminum sculpted equines of Anna Hyatt Huntington (1876–1973), such as *Fighting Stallions* (1950) (Brookgreen Gardens, SC), are the equal of Bonheur's on canvas.

Highland Raid, however, depicts a herd of onrushing bulls, shaggy and in rut, on the verge, it seems, of bounding forth from the canvas, with testosterone enough to take the paint with it. This professional and personal anomaly of a female painter was ignored by the exhibition, Bonheur's body of work here turned to the wall, as it were—the male torso in Pujol's studio. The suggestion finds support in omission of *Highland Raid* from the exhibition catalogue and the absence of Bonheur herself from the alphabetic "Exhibition Checklist." Rutting bulls are apparently ill at home with lace and ruffle. Thus, when a female painter handles a generic though putatively female subject or scene, female critics treat it as though it were a particularly female endeavor (e.g., depicting lace). But when a female painter handles a male-gendering subject (e.g., stampeding bulls), the response tends to be muted, so as to obviate male intrusion, especially in an exhibit of woman painters at the National Museum of Women in the Arts.

However much of a knockout this exhibition, it suffered badly from sequestration in the Museum of Women in the Arts—the result of seeking to make it the special property or interest of women. Had the exhibit been shown at the nearby National Gallery, or in any other mainstream metropolitan museum, it would have been seen, as deserved, by multitudes. The exhibition's self-imposed gendering was markedly self-defeating.

15. Vittoria Colonna: The Male in an Impeccably Female Poet

Returning to poetry and the poets most exemplifying the premise of ungendered artistic creation, the Renaissance offers the exceptional instance of the poet Vittoria Colonna (1490–1547). A beauty in her time, and referred to in publications of her own works as *la divina Vittoria Colonna*, she was drawn by Michelangelo (plate 18) and believed to have been the model of several of his Mary depictions. She was the first woman to have a volume of poetry published in Italy. Admired by contemporary luminaries Pietro Bembo and Baldassare Castiglione for her literary acumen, she was painted throughout subsequent ages; stunningly, and as in no other case, by Jules Joseph Lefebvre, *Diva Vittoria Colonna* (1861). Colonna was characterized in a poem by Michelangelo as *un uomo in una donna* 'a man in a woman' and was "frequently praised for the *gravità* 'weightiness' of her poetry. This quality genders as masculine in the poetic of Colonna's fellow Petrarchist and Tuscan/early Italian language scholar Pietro Bembo, forming a dialectic with its opposing feminine quality of *piacevolezza* 'charm.'" In her Sonnet LXXVII, Colonna combines *gravità* with an acute—with a sacrificial—female sensibility. Man in a woman, she is yet woman through and through:

> What lavish offering, what sainted pious will,
> What humble benediction made in purest faith
> Can one present, if but in part alone, equal
> To your worth, my lord, insofar as I deem it?

> Already on your altar have I placed my heart,
> Who undergoes a thousand wounds on your account;
> Perceive you this my heart, both open and exposed,
> Fatigued in lamentation, burning with desire:

> Because its verdant hope to drywood is transformed,
> Full nourishing itself ablaze precisely so,
> To burn at every hour unreduced to ash.

> And even were such sacrifice unprincipled,
> Rejoice I yet the more in you, O saintly one,
> Since with my soul's full mastery it honors you.

[Qual ricco don, qual voler santo e pio,
Qual prego umíl con pura fede offerto,
Potrà mostrarsi uguale al vostro merto,
Signor, in parte, o almeno al pensier mio?

Già' l proprio core a voi sacro fec'io,
Che mille piaghe ha già per voi sofferto;
Ed or pur lo vedete e nudo e aperto,
Molle del pianto e caldo del desio:

Chè la sua verde speme in secco legno
Mutassi, e in fiamme si nodrisce in modo,
Che senza incenerirsi arde ad ogn'ora.

E benchè sia tal sacraficio indegno
Di voi, spirto divino, io pur mi godo;
Chè con quanto più può l'alma v'onora.]

Colonna and her poetic colleague Veronica Gambara are noted as "the ineluctable starting point for all listings of 'modern Sapphos.'" They are peculiarly progenitors of the previously mentioned Victorian Felicia Hemans and Letitia Elizabeth Landon, Landon the "English Sappho" of her own day. Unlike Sappho, however, or the imputations surrounding her, Colonna and Gambara were acknowledged for their moral character as well as consummate poetic skill, thus "establishing the respectability of literature as an appropriate activity for women." Stylistically, Colonna's verse impressed contemporaries for its remarkable formal mastery and the weightiness and grandeur of its register; on first acquaintance with her poetry in 1530, Bembo described one of her sonnets as "finer and more ingenious and graver than one would expect from a woman."

The masculine imprint of Colonna's poetry would mark her as male, defying, but for initial knowledge of her sex, the notion of gendered creativity. Horace refers to *mascula Sappho* 'male Sappho', referencing, as most sensibly understood, Sappho's engagement in an art traditionally associated with men. Known, like Colonna, for her exemplary virtue, Katherine Philips (1632–1664), "the English Sappho" of her day, was also "a man in a woman." The characterization reflected the literary tradition of heterosexual platonism and male friendship within which she expressed her affections for women. Conveyed through the conventions of a male poetic discourse, Philips's affections, however unconventional for her day, were yet considered as ennobling as those of the male model.

Of further note is Colonna's name, with its male resonances of victory (*vittoria*) and steadfastness (*colonna* 'column'). The resonance reflects the prodigious military traditions of the Colonna family—father Fabrizio Colonna the esteemed general of Machiavelli's *Dell'arte della guerra*, her maternal grandfather the legendary *condottiero* ('mercenary captain') Federico da Montefeltro. Against this background, Michelangelo's drawing depicts a sexually ambiguous Vittoria. She is, first, beautifully coiffed and visaged: large eyes; broad, arching eyebrows; and forehead generously exposed from beneath hair parted to either side (the hair as in Lefebvre's painting). At the same time, however, the seated Colonna is masculinized in a way reminiscent of Michelangelo's Medici Chapel sculptures of Lorenzo and the assassinated Giuliano (plate 19), completed twenty years earlier. The brothers are seated above their respective sepulchers: Lorenzo introspective, even as Michelangelo's Colonna stares vacantly into space. Giuliano's chest armor, suspended from ornate straps, is sculpted skin-tight (indeed, skin-like), his abdomen taut and rippling. Michelangelo portrays Vittoria to comparable effect: her breasts overlaid with protective gear suspended from shoulder strapping, and her abdomen, set off by a breast cincture, anatomically flexed.

Michelangelo, as often observed, painted as he sculpted: *muscularly*, his painting two-dimensional sculpture. His masculinized Vittoria yet highlights the woman. Her hair, high on her head and helmet-like, presents a quasi-armored figure in the likeness of Athena, goddess of wisdom and battle. As Athena was parthenogenetically born from the forehead of Zeus, standing ever apart from sexual relations, Michelangelo's Vittoria offers a singularly virile model of feminine virtue.

The fate of other Renaissance (and medieval) women poets has been examined by longtime professor of conducting and choral music Joan Catoni Conlon, in an essay titled "Must We Sing of Women Only as Men Have Sung." The essay, which appears in *Wisdom, Wit, and Will: Women Choral Conductors on Their Art* (2009), provides a sampling of valuable and little-known poetry (original texts with translation), including its social milieu and significance as women's statements of their condition. The essay's conclusion is especially instructive for our revisionist and quite iconoclastic times, urging that one cannot erase biased or misogynistic history, but only understand it in context.

Conlon's essay, however, answers its own question concerning why such female poets are not better known, notwithstanding their wit, ability, and discernment. As with Barrett Browning's personal and domestic *Aurora Leigh*, or the feminist take in Rebecca West's *Black Lamb, Grey Falcon*, the subject matter never soars. "The rich palette of women's worldly observations," says Conlon, explores, among other things, "modesty and vulnerability; arranged marriage; a longing for love; unhappiness in a convent; equality among lovers; oppression; writing, spinning and weaving (endeavors women could respectably pursue); jealous men; freedom; and occasionally, passionate defenses of good women who were scorned, unappreciated, or punished."

Most of these topics are sadly humdrum. Oppression and defenses against poor treatment—the "poetry of complaint"—are not the stuff of the best and most often read poetry. It is not modesty and vulnerability that impress but assertiveness. Curiously, and nowhere noting their preeminence, Conlon begins by asking whether poems by Vittoria Colonna, Veronica Gambara, and other female poets of the era, were the "artistic and technical equivalents" of named male poets of the day. Had Conlon simply weighed Colonna and Gambara against their female contemporaries, the reason for their contemporaries' obscurity would have been apparent.

16. Gendered and Gender-Exclusive Texts

Colonna and Gambara's poetry found ready acceptance because of both women's superior abilities. They had no need to conceal their identity as women, and readers had no need to determine or second-guess it. Their genders were readily known and accepted as a manifestation of the extraordinary times of the Renaissance. But that has been the exception, not the rule—an optimal exception in the best of times. Where the artist's gender is undetermined, it often remains so vis-à-vis the work created. To the extent it is of interest, it must be teased from the work itself. Even then, the determination is difficult.

Not to belabor the obvious, Sappho's poetry is most often discernible as female-authored (e.g., §§1–4, 6, 8, 28, 34) with other such examples throughout literature and into our time, much of it neglected. Significant parts of *Sonnets from the Portuguese* (1850) reveal female authorship—apparent in certain forms of address, "Unlike are we, unlike, O princely heart!" (III); in gender-specific allusion, "I lift my heavy heart up solemnly, / As once Electra her sepulchral urn" (V); or in self-reference, "Nay, let the silence of my womanhood / Commend my woman-love to thy belief, – / Seeing that I stand unwon, however wooed" (XIII). Otherwise, the collection's superb opening sonnet, "I thought once how Theocritus had sung," is gender-neutral; and the theme, poignantly equating love and death, universally attuned. Also gender-neutral is the collection's best-known poem: "How do I love thee? Let me count the ways" (XLIII). The lines "I love thee freely, as men strive for Right; / I love thee purely, as they turn from Praise" nonetheless suggest a male point of reference and authorship.

Poet Sara Teasdale's (1884–1933) anthology of love lyrics by women lacks a specifically female voice in any number of poems. We further note the possibility of "crossover" poetry: male or female writing from the other's perspective. Against this Teasdale was herself on guard: "I have included no long poems, and no translations, and I have avoided poems in which the poet dramatized a man's feelings rather than her own." Conversely, Teasdale would have excluded poems in which a male speaker conveyed a woman's feelings or wrote from a woman's perspective. She would thus have rejected Tennyson's stunning Sappho-influenced "Fatima" (1833), with stanzas such as these:

> Last night, when some one spoke his name,
> From my swift blood that went and came
> A thousand little shafts of flame
> Were shiver'd in my narrow frame.
> O Love, O fire! once he drew
> With one long kiss my whole soul thro'
> My lips, as sunlight drinketh dew....

> ◆

> My whole soul waiting silently,
> All naked in a sultry sky,
> Droops blinded with his shining eye:

I will possess him or will die.
I will grow round him in his place,
Grow, live, die looking on his face,
Die, dying clasp'd in his embrace.

Teasdale would have rejected so impassioned a woman's plea had she known it was written by a man. So, what is the gain, and what the compelling interest? The sexes clearly speak and were meant to speak each other's hearts. Consider Auden's "Stop all the clocks," an elegy upon the death of his homosexual lover:

He was my North, my South, my East and West,
My working week and my Sunday rest,
My noon, my midnight, my talk, my song;
I thought that love would last forever: I was wrong.
The stars are not wanted now; put out every one,
Pack up the moon and dismantle the sun,
Pour away the ocean and sweep up the wood;
For nothing now can ever come to any good.

If not for Auden's known authorship and homosexuality, could one reasonably doubt female authorship? In the end, gender-specific predilections are misguided in the valuation of works of art. Gender neither trumps nor determines merit.

17. Gendered Hoaxes: No One the Wiser

Poet, translator, and essayist Kenneth Rexroth (1905–1982) claimed in *The Love Poems of Marichiko* to have translated the poetry of a contemporary "young Japanese woman poet." When later revealed as the author, he was nonetheless critically acclaimed not only for having so authentically conveyed the feelings of the opposite sex but also for having thus captured a different culture. His biographer claims that "in the Marichiko poems, he [Rexroth] explored every aspect of what he imagined to be one woman's psyche in order to come to terms with how he as a man who had professed great love for women could at last acquire a rudimentary understanding of woman's nature." If the ruse succeeded, then perhaps he could be sure of having achieved a deeper empathy with women. A highly sympathetic impulse precedes, indeed dictates, such self-involvement. "Madame Bovary, c'est moi." Again, looking into himself, Flaubert found his heroine.

Highlighting the available examples is the greatest fin de siècle gender hoax of them all, Pierre Louÿs' *Les Chansons de Bilitis* (*The Songs of Bilitis*) (1894), discussed above (p. xxi–xxii). This work of faux prose-poem translations—the originals ascribed to one Bilitis, a courtesan contemporary with Sappho—caused a sensation persisting long after the hoax had been revealed; the poems, in one way or another, exquisite. The work was actually Louÿs's own, "the uniquely potent brew of [his] recondite classicism, febrile imagination, and decadent sensitivity." The work bespoke the female heart: "[Bilitis] knows herself to be at once Sappho and more than Sappho. One can at least know Bilitis, whereas Sappho will remain ever at a distance." Readers were none the wiser for the work's male inspiration, and no less approving after it was known.

18. The Odyssey's Female Authorship: Iliadic Conclusions

We return, in ring-compositional manner, to Samuel Butler's ultimately misdirected but ever engaging thesis that a woman authored the *Odyssey*. There were certain parts so sympathetic, as he thought, that only a woman could have authored them; and others so inept in their understanding of the world and its workaday technicalities, that surely no man could have authored them. And yet, we encounter in the *Odyssey*, for all its exquisitely drawn female characters, an essentially masculine text mostly concerned with Odysseus's wayward journeying and "encod[ing] the traveller as a male who crosses boundaries and penetrates spaces." Even that view has of late been upended. In her *Sappho's Leap* (2003), Erica Jong propels the fearless Sappho about the Mediterranean on divers voyages, including the rescue of her brother, enslaved in Egypt. Though favorably reviewed, the book's facile substitution of Sappho for Odysseus, and the utter transparency of its Homeric patterning, make it little more than feminist angling. There's more bang for the bard in reading the *Odyssey*, whether male- or female-authored.

Nor for its hardened martial core does the *Iliad* want for riveting female portrayal and sensibility, as was clear even in an age of male-dominated scholarship:

There is no good quality that [the Homeric poems] lack ... [Homer] has to write of battles; and he delights in the joy of battle, and in all the movement of war. Yet he delights not less, but more, in peace: in prosperous cities, hearths secure, in the tender beauty of children, in the love of wedded wives, in the frank nobility of maidens, in the beauty of earth and sky and sea, and seaward murmuring river, in sun and snow, frost and mist and rain, in the whispered talk of boy and girl beneath oak and pine tree.

Helen, despising herself as only one can whose identity is sexually determined, also despises—even as she makes love to him—the sexually astute but useless Paris. By contrast, Andromache, Hector's wife, that shimmering but woesome paragon of womanly virtue, laughs through her tears, confessing Hector her all-in-all—"father, reverent mother, kinsman, and bounteous husband." The scene is rife with emotion, with what one would deem female sensibility. We see Hector departing for battle, while Andromache—her name meaning "fighting like a man"—pleads that he fight only defensively. Hector follows by prophesying both his own death and Andromache's subsequent servitude. Their little boy, Astyanax, frightened by his father's high-cresting helmet plume, seeks refuge in his mother's "fragrant bosom." Shall we conclude that only a woman could have fashioned such a scene, any more than exempt a man from the wrenching emotion of Priam's ransoming Hector's body, of Priam's doing what no man had ever done: "raising his lips to the hands of the man who slew [his] son"?

There are tears enough in the *Iliad* to suggest a female sensibility, while the poet's instinctive recourse to domestic settings or analogies is nothing if not female. Menelaus, dodging the Trojan Pandarus's arrow, escapes with a flesh wound. Marvelously domesticating, or interiorizing, the near-death encounter, Homer says that Athena, standing alongside Menelaus, "brushed the arrow away, as a mother brushes a fly from her sleeping child." Focusing on the coloration of Menelaus's wound, Homer compares it to a Phoenician (i.e., purple) dye that some Maionian or Carian woman might use to stain a horse's ivory cheek piece. The ornament

... lies away in an inner room, and many a rider
longs to have it, but it is laid up to be a king's treasure,
two things, to be the beauty to the horse, the pride of the horseman:

so, Menelaus, your shapely thighs were stained with the color
of blood, and your legs also, and the ankles beneath them.

The inward turn is, again, instructive: from battlefield mayhem to domestic
tranquility, from the disfigurement of war to decorative preoccupation; the
ornament stored in the *thalamos*, the bed or bridal chamber, the household's
inner and peaceful sanctum.

The description of Menelaus's wound thus has a markedly female-as-
sociative element. So also the extended simile at the start of *Iliad*, Book 16,
where Patroclus implores Achilles to relent and rejoin the battle. Achilles
compares Patroclus to "a girl who runs to her mother, tugging at her gown
and begging to be held, weeping until her mother relents." Similarly Hector,
facing doom at Achilles's hands, acknowledges in feminizing terms that the
time for prattle is over: "There is no / way anymore from a tree or a rock to
talk to him gently / whispering like a young man and a young girl, in a way /
a young man and young maiden whisper together."

There is, further, a feminizing element even in the description of battle-
field death and its effect on others, as first—strategically—described toward
the start of *Iliad*, Book 4:

> ... Telemonian Aias struck down Anthemiōn
> Simoeisios in his stripling's beauty, whom once his mother
> descending from Ida bore beside the banks of Simoeis
> when she had followed her father and mother to tend
> > the sheep flocks.
> Therefore they called him Simoeisios; but he could not
> render again the care of his dear parents, he was short-lived,
> beaten down beneath the spear of high-hearted Aias,
> who struck him as he first came forward beside the nipple
> of the right breast, and the bronze spearhead drove right
> > through the shoulder.
> He dropped to the ground in the dust, like some black poplar,
> which in the land low-lying about a great marsh grows
> smooth trimmed yet with branches growing at the uttermost
> > tree-top.

This length of description for an otherwise unknown underscores Homer's
awareness of the pathos of death in war—any death. It is as much the

unknown and unsung, as it is the hero, who mean the world to those left mourning them, who instill sorrow and regret for life cut brutally short. Such Iliadic tableaux resonate with female sensibility, as does the *Odyssey*, for that matter. As with any essential artistic insight, however, the heart is itself ungendered. The scene's pathos is first apparent in the initial reference to Simoeisios (*sih-mō-áye-see-os*) as the "son of *Anthemion*" (Gr. *anthos* 'flower'; Eng. anthem, anthology). True to his *flowering* parentage, Simoeisios falls like a "black poplar," smooth-trimmed in the marshlands—a stagnant, decaying site. He is still "in his stripling's beauty," unmarried—yet old enough for all his youth to die and die brutally. The spear's entry point at the nipple feminizes his vulnerability. The irrevocably severed family bond is the frequent concomitant of Homeric battlefield-death descriptions. Three generations are here evoked. Simoeisios's mother was with her parents when he was born, and his own parents' love for him will now go unrequited as the family line expires. The pathos is further pronounced as the lad falls before Ajax, the second mightiest of the Greeks after Achilles (and the mightiest in his Iliadic absence). It is all of a highly emotional register, recalling nothing so much as the fate of women and children when a city is sacked and taken. The first extended battlefield death of the *Iliad*, it sounds the knell for the fallen all. In fact, one scholar opines that "If either Homeric poem were written by a woman, it would be the *Iliad*, with its keen awareness of the victims of war" (Q.E.D.).

Such vignettes, on a smaller scale throughout the *Iliad*, belie the notion of its necessarily male authorship and glorification of war. Their poignancy has had an influence on subsequent ages, finding a vivid afterlife, e.g., in Victor Hugo's elaborated and highly noteworthy reflection on the Battle of Waterloo:

> If anything is terrifying, if there is a reality that surpasses dream, it is this: to live, to see the sun, to be in full possession of manly vigor, to be full of health and joy, to laugh valiantly, to run toward the glory in front of you, dazzling, to feel in your chest lungs that breathe, a heart that beats, a will that reasons, to speak, to think, to love, to have a mother, to have a wife, to have children, to have the light, and all of a sudden, in the time it takes to let out a cry, in less than one minute flat, to tumble into an abyss, to fall, to roll, to crush, to be crushed, to see the blades of wheat, flowers, leaves, branches, and yet not be able to stop yourself by grabbing any of them, to feel your saber useless, men underneath you, horses on

89

top of you, to flail about in vain, your bones broken by some kick in the dark, to feel a heel making your eyes pop out of your head, to bite into horseshoes with rage, to suffocate, to howl, to twist yourself in knots, to be at the bottom of all this and tell yourself: Just now I was one of the living!

Except as earlier noted, Butler's *The Authoress of the Odyssey* is largely ignored by feminist scholars and is rarely, if ever, cited in support of the *Odyssey*'s female sensibility (Butler's assumptions, by today's standards, sexist). Butler's daring has made him little more than a fondly patronized oddity. Even so, and as David Grene notes in his introduction to a more recently published version of *Authoress* (Phoenix Books, 1967), "the correctness of Butler is so interesting because it is so significantly combined with his wrongness." *Authoress*, in sum, is the grand failure that comes from getting it all wrong, while never once being dull. "As regards the mind of the writer of the *Odyssey*," remarks Butler, "there is nothing that impresses me more profoundly than the undercurrent of melancholy which I find throughout it . . . . Now that I know the writer to have been a woman, I am ashamed of myself for not having been guided to my conclusions by the exquisitely subtle sense of weakness as well as strength that pervades the poem, rather than by the considerations that actually guided me."

Butler thus haplessly ends with the conviction that he was right for the wrong reasons. It is a telling insight. Referring to the "Slaying of the Suitors," with which the *Odyssey* climaxes, Butler notes "a woman can kill a man on paper as well as a man can." She can, as seen, kill him equally well on canvas. And as Garry Wills notes of Sarah Ruden, referring respectively to her translations of Virgil and Petronius, "she is as good with the gore as she was with the raunch."

Conclusion: From Sex in Art to the Sexes' Art

As noted from the outset, the sexes are complementary, and thus capable of poignant and mutually sympathetic portrayal. In popular parlance, the sexes are yin and yang, congenial opposing forces whose whole is greater than their parts. The sexes' ideally sympathetic posture is intimate, amorous—conveyed in such works as Canova's *Eros and Psyche* (1793); Rodin's *The Kiss* (1889) and *Eternal Spring* (1907); Claudel's *La Valse* (1895); Sinding's *Man and*

Woman (1893) (Nasjonalmuseet); and other such ideally stylized erotic-devotional figurations.

The sexes' perpetual antagonism was popularized by John Gray's relationship guide, *Men Are From Mars, Women Are From Venus: The Classic Guide to Understanding the Opposite Sex* (1992). The work, however, ignores the factual significance of the two planets' location within the same solar system, with Earth, the sexes' habitat and cohabitational realm, in between. It further neglects that the mythological Venus and Mars are decidedly purposeful lovers. Yes, Venus and Mars on one level represent the polarities of human existence: Venus, female/love/peace/creation; Mars, male/hate/war/destruction. The polarities, however, dissolve within the protagonists' sexual union which—in the first instance—is the primordial love/hate relationship itself. In that union, female and male, love and hate, life and death, creation and destruction, surrender to and become each other.

Sexual union—life's ultimate pleasure and steadfast self-preservational pursuit, life's own pulse and source—simultaneously destroys and creates (see further pp. 193–198). It destroys by merging individuality, identity, and sexual differentiation; and the will and equilibrium on which these are premised. In that sense, sex levels and eradicates—as does its equally potent counterpart, death, which love/sex seeks ever to nullify. At the same time, sex restores and regenerates, creating more sentient and, potentially, more creative being; granting preservational release; creating new being itself (sex as *recreation* having its own restorative effect). Sex, to paraphrase philosopher-aesthetician Roger Scruton (b. 1944) is or can be self-revelatory incandescence. As elaborated by music critic and author Michael Walsh (b. 1949), sex is

> the most powerful engine in human existence, the one thing that brings us closest to the Godhead, a force of such overwhelming power that it can change the course of our lives, bringing death or transcendence in its wake. Children are the primary issue, but also transformative insight, bravery, courage, altruism, self-sacrifice; great works of art are born from the union, lives sacrificed and won, everything ventured, worlds gained.

Sex, as does the relationship between Venus and Mars, variously signals the simultaneity of opposites. The sexes' antagonisms—the agonistic nature of sex itself—and the conflicts and accords to which these give rise, occur in alternation, which is to say they are cyclical, if not cyclically predetermined. The contrarieties are inscribed in the sexual act itself, seeming at once pleasurable and painful, loving and hostile, creative and destructive, and having long-term potentials for creation and destruction alike.

The sexes can and do know each other. In their physical union they *are*—and *know* each other as—*one*. It is the sexes' steadfast sexual engagement that (in heterosexual union) signals not only their purpose but also the vitality and continuance they lend to life. It is the female that gives birth, but the process is not parthenogenetic. And while the male's physiological role is fleeting, the sexes do ultimately share in continuing creation—as pro-creators, co-creators. The process, ideally deliberative and soul-searching, invests each sex with its own greater sense of purpose and awareness of the other. Creating with and for each other, the sexes know each other's minds; partaking of an empathetic relationship, they are one in mind as well as body. Sex, to the extent possible, and under ideal conditions, is a biological paraphrase for a meeting of the minds. This is but a contemporary formulation of the French-originating *querelle des femmes* 'the woman question'—the literary debate concerning the nature and status of woman that ranged from the early sixteenth century onward. Supporters of women emphasized that the sexes, created in God's image, were essentially one—God being androgynous—differentiated solely for procreative purposes. As God is also incorporeal, the sexes imitate only God's spirituality, rendering physical differences of sex irrelevant. In the same vein, man and woman's reason, understanding, and virtue are equal; disparity in education (reflecting societal biases) alone responsible for disparity in woman's treatment.

For whatever biological, social, or institutional reasons, artistic creation is typically male creation, often appearing male-oriented. This is especially so in the male artist's perennial depiction of the female nude. The nude's co-creator is the female as muse. Female artists did not traditionally use, or even have access to, nude female models. They certainly had no access to male nudes. Male artists typically painted the female nude because the female (and all she represents) has ever been an *instinctive* object of male attraction and inspiration, "an embodiment of universal beauty, the paradigmatic metaphor for the artist's power to create perfect form"—in a way the male form would never be to a male artist. In sum, man's muse is woman, and woman's muse is, well, *not man*. In gendered terms, woman's muse is *none*. If inspired by man, the female artist will sooner look to man's—to *a* man's—intangible rather than physical attributes. A woman, it is said, wants the one man who fulfills her every desire; a man, every woman who fulfills his one desire. "What does a woman *really want*?" The question is never posed of men. What men *want* is women. What they ever *do* is consummately render and venerate—Lat. *Venus*—woman's image and being.

The veneration to which women accede is puzzling. In some societies, it calls for lipstick, nail polish, eyeliner, and heels. These are real-time enhancements, seeking the perfection *here and now* of woman's form and idealized likeness; a temporal or interim means by which to *artifact*, i.e., "make art of," woman, preserving her as something ever beautiful, ideal, and unchanging. Such enhancement is apparent in the connection between rococo color and women's cosmetics, in "painting as makeup." As for the beauty and elaboration of women's attire, it is said that the success of a woman's dress is measured by a man's desire to remove it.

In Greek mythology, the sculptor Pygmalion falls in love with the statue of the sea-nymph, Galatea, that he has created. The statue is then brought to life, art not imitating life but coming alive. The aspirational force of art, of art's need for and rapture with woman as its focus, is so compelling as to have occasioned countless artistic representations of the Pygmalion myth. The myth's cornerstone is *devotion* (rapture's constituent element), represented by man's complete and needful subservience to woman, as conveyed in such works as Rodin's *Eternal Spring* (and his own *Pygmalion*); in Viegland's *Man and Woman, Devotion* (Ekbergparken, Oslo) (1908); and Sinding's *Adoratio* (Ny Carlsberg Glyptotek, Copenhagen) (1910). It is all wondrously circular, whole, and self-fulfilling: the perfected statue come to life; the perfected form *statuized*. As the Renoir-contemporary sculptor-painter Aristide Maillol (1861–1944) is quoted as saying: "When I see a girl pass by, I undress her with my eyes and I see marble under her skirt."

We earlier noted that woman need not quest to "get the boy" (as it were); it is hers to be wooed, to withdraw from the fray and its dangers. There is a biological imperative for women's withdrawal, for her constraint. The female, as she must be for her own survival, is sexually self-protective (whether in the human or nature's realm) and thus more inward, private, and retiring. Her anatomy dictates, her vulnerability requires, and her disposition reflects that reality. Artistically, woman's survivalism is reflected, by contrast to man, in her treatment of conflict, "with a preference for harmony over revolt (see Jacques-Louis David's *The Intervention of the Sabine Women* [1799]). Were the male equally so disposed, the species would be imperiled. In other words, one of the sexes *must be sexually more assertive*—more anatomically and dispositionally *forward*—for species survival, among other reasons. The excess of male sexuality comes at a cost, of course. But it is by nature's generative excess in all realms that survival is assured.

It is the excess or *surplus of male sexual and dispositional forwardness* that manifests as the male creative impulse, the artistic impulse included (*homo faber* 'man the maker'). Sexual surplus in the male beast manifests in horns; hence, "horny" with reference to erection as horn-like protrusion. What incites male machismo is *woman's bodily surplus*: her malleable, silken, and suggestible parts. Their superfluity, in de Beauvoir's words, is alluring: "breasts and buttocks . . . prized . . . because of the gratuitousness and contingency of their development." Also desirable is the pear-shaped aspect to the hips and the length and luxuriance of hair—its flow and forest-imagined fragrance; its amplitude, glamour, and peril- and entanglement-laden fascination. The male artist's impulse to render woman immutable seeks, among other things, to annul the transience of what is gratuitous and contingent, mutable and subject to decay, as are all things in generative-and-moribund nature. The artist's ultimate goal is not the temporal pleasure taken in any one woman, but the Platonic pleasure taken in idealized woman and womankind; the universally rather than the particularly embraced woman.

As earlier seen, Plato's *Symposium,* conceives a hierarchy in terms of ascent (p. 40). The progression is one from love of the physical (the body) to love of the intellectual (ideas). Fitting the ascent's second stage—love of all physical beauty as a single form of beauty—is du Maurier's formulation: "All beauty is sexless in the eyes of the artist at his work—the beauty of man, the beauty of woman, the heavenly beauty of the child, which is the sweetest and best of all." At this stage, both the artist's *and* subject's genders are irrelevant. Indeed, the child is valued not only for its innocence but for the as yet unrealized sexual consciousness, activity, and partisanship that innocence entails. The condition is not of this earth but "heavenly."

The male artist's obsession with the perfected female form has its temporal aspect in the need of her physical person *here and now* (in whatever state of undress), in the purposefulness of attracting, joining with, and *having* her. However, making *art* of woman, *fixing* or depicting her in one place and time for all time remains the imperative; capturing and venerating *das ewig-Weibliche* 'the Eternal Feminine.'

At the same time, woman's beauty is not simply manifest—"there" to be recognized and appreciated for what it is—but is initially *communed* through individual, even invasive, encounter reminiscent of the Muse's inspirational visitation (e.g., to Hesiod). From such *in-breathing* emerges the concept itself of beauty; the empathetic awareness of its presence, requisite to its conveyance through art: woman's beauty, first impressed upon one's being, as initiatory-transformative appreciation. Says author Wilkie Collins (1824–1889):

> The woman who first gives life, light, and form to our shadowy conceptions of beauty, fills a void in our spiritual nature that has remained unknown to us till she appeared. Sympathies that lie too deep for words, too deep almost for thoughts, are touched, at such times, by other charms than those which the senses feel and which the resources of expression can realise. The mystery which underlies the beauty of women is never raised above the reach of all expression until it has claimed kindred with the deeper mystery in our own souls. Then, and only then, has it passed beyond the narrow region on which light falls, in this world, from the pencil and the pen.

The process by which man's deepest sympathies are first "touched," and artistically enabled, is described by Marcel Proust (1871–1922), in his famed account of first hearing the name Gilberte:

> And so was wafted to my ears the name of Gilberte, bestowed on me like a talisman which might, perhaps, enable me some day to rediscover her whom its syllables had just endowed with a definite personality, whereas, a moment earlier, she had been only something vaguely seen. So it came to me, uttered across the heads of the stocks and jasmines, pungent and cool as the drops which fell from the green watering-pipe; impregnating and irradiating the zone of pure air through which it had passed, which it set apart and isolated from all other air, with the mystery of the life of her whom its syllables designated to the happy creatures that lived and walked and travelled in her company; unfolding through the arch of the pink hawthorn, which opened at the height of my

shoulder, the quintessence of their familiarity—so exquisitely painful to myself—with her, and with all that unknown world of her existence, into which I should never penetrate.

Proust then describes how the sense of woman's beauty, wakening in his soul, emanates outward, suffusing all creation:

> I loved her. . . . I walked away, carrying with me, then and for ever afterwards, as the first illustration of a type of happiness rendered inaccessible to a little boy of my kind by certain laws of nature which it was impossible to transgress, the picture of a little girl with reddish hair, and a skin freckled with tiny pink marks, who held a trowel in her hand, and smiled as she directed towards me a long and subtle and inexpressive stare. And already the charm with which her name, like a cloud of incense, had filled that archway in the pink hawthorn through which she and I had, together, heard its sound, was beginning to conquer, to cover, to embalm, to beautify everything with which it had any association.

Proust's revelatory awakening, a child's in response to a child, has a famed antecedent in Dante's (1265–1321) astounded awakening, described in his *Vita Nova*, upon first being greeted by the beautiful and angelic Beatrice, the two of them at the time under age ten—both Proust's and Dante's awakenings partaking of the "heavenly beauty of the child" (du Maurier, above). Faust too, magically transformed into a young man, is beguiled by the child in Gretchen. The Beatrice of *Vita Nova* is believed to be the same who later guided Dante, in his *Divina Commedia*, through Purgatory (starting in Canto XXX, upon Virgil's leave-taking) and onward to Heaven. So doing, she brings Dante ever closer to the divine, vouchsafing neither physical nor even spiritual love, but the essential consummation that is love of God. So also in its way, Faust's Gretchen-fostered redemption—she leading him through the higher spheres of heaven; and in *Dutchman*, the village girl Senta's freeing the Dutchman from ship and curse alike, and by her suicide ascending heaven with him. Dante and Beatrice, no less than Proust and Gilberte, are neighbors. The two revelations occur outdoors, as the young girls walk with their elders. Beatrice wears white, and Gilberte is bid "come along" by a woman wearing white. The Wilkie Collins insight is from his novel *The Woman in White* (1859). It is the iconically restorative color, as in the Times Square nurse's uniform (above).

All three revelations are past-tense conveyed, refining insight through retrospection. Collins bids the reader think of protagonist Laura Fairlie

> as you thought of the first woman who quickened the pulses within you that the rest of her sex had no art to stir. . . . Let her footstep, as she comes and goes, in these pages, be like that other footstep to whose airy fall your own heart once beat time. Take her as the visionary nursling of your own fancy; and she will grow upon you, all the more clearly, as the living woman who dwells in mine.

One rarely, if ever, finds such probing or revelatory discoveries of *men* by female artists, focused, as they are, neither on the male (nor female) form per se, nor on its perfected representation, nor on what it represents. Even in an age abounding with female artists no longer subject to either social restriction or taboo, the nude is rarely paramount, its rarefaction beside the point. One suspects the contemporary mandates of feminism, feminist art, and feminist theory have to do with this: that modernist preoccupations, political position, and gendered-vindication—versus the necessary effacement from bonafide art of self, group, and *-ism*—here trump perennial concerns. Indeed, the transformation of Linda Nochlin over a thirty-year period from sagacious art critic to feminist combatant (see note, p. 278) suggests as much, even as French women artists from the eighteenth and nineteenth centuries, when exhibited at the National Museum of Women in the Arts, garnered no audience.

One cannot generalize from instances of female art that might convey a female perspective. A putatively female perspective does not necessarily result in a truer, better, or more representative work of art, whatever the subject depicted. Will the unknowing viewer necessarily surmise the artist's gender? That the result may somehow differ does not make it better. A biographical approach to art denies what art is and is meant to be: a comment or reflection on the human condition.

A recently politicized area of female endeavor is the translation of epic poetry, with results leaving much to be desired. In 2008 Sarah Ruden became the first woman to translate Virgil's *Aeneid*. The translation was heralded by one prominent critic as the best translation since Dryden (Dryden's *Aeneid* the signature work of his lifetime and since). In fact, it was nothing of the kind, as I have earlier demonstrated (2016), its marked monosyllabism quite depriving it of rhythm, forward movement, and interest. More recently, Emily R. Wilson's 2017 translation of the *Odyssey*, the first by a woman, was similarly heralded by the *New York Times,* among other media. The result is more lacking yet. Here are the opening monosyllabic lines, *deadening* even as concerns the words' appearance on the page:

> Tell me about a complicated man.
> Muse, tell me how he wandered and was lost
> when he had wrecked the holy town of Troy,
> and where he went, and who he met, the pain
> he suffered in the storms at sea, and how
> he worked to save his life and bring his men
> back home. He failed to keep them safe; poor fools,
> they ate the Sun God's cattle, and the god
> kept them from home. Now goddess, child of Zeus,
> tell the old story for our modern times.
> Find the beginning.

Where in these lines are the rhythm, forward movement, and sense of engagement? Of the ninety-two quoted words, all but nine are monosyllabic. "Complicated man" for Gr. *andra . . . polutropon* 'the man of many turns' is mere modernist affect, here reinforced by the gratuitous "for our modern times," etc. Homer's audience twenty-seven hundred years ago surely considered itself every bit as "modern" as we consider ourselves modern today—and so it is with every audience in every generation. As I have maintained, "When judging translation, especially epic, we begin not *in medias res,* but *ab initio,* since the beginning usually tells all"—and here it surely does. Ultimately, all that can be said, for all that women have translated them, is that Ruden's *Aeneid* is better than Wilson's *Odyssey*, and neither a close second to their betters.

There is finally the case of John Fowles's novel *The French Lieutenant's Woman* (1969) and its protagonist, Sarah Woodruff. This is a reputedly feminist work set in Victorian times. In a variation of the usual opprobrium, the portrayal of Sarah is questioned not for being male-authored (though that is necessarily part of it) but for being entirely articulated by the novel's male characters. Says one feminist critique, "The ideological nature of any perspective is undeniable and in this case the male perspective, which has been and still is dominant in western culture, brings to the novel all sorts of preconceptions and myths about women."

The imputed male perspective—here, the perspective of a male author's male characters—thus becomes an ideological indictment of the author's portrayal not only of a female character but of all Western culture. Among other shortcomings, its *own* ideological bias included, such critique fails to consider that the female portrayal of female characters will be identifiable as such only by degree, if at all. Such discernments require not the saber, but the scalpel.

The truest art in all genres is that which signals the artist's humanity, not gender. It is an art that proceeds from a gender-neutral understanding of life as broadly constituted, an understanding of the "human condition"—an art which, given that condition, comforts with some manner of fixity, if not transcendence. For the heterosexual male artist, it is *woman*, through the constant reprise of her idealized form. To know the art that sustains and makes life livable—art "extract[ing] equipoise and permanence from chaos"—is to apprehend the irrelevance of gender to its creation or consideration, if it aspires to greatness as art. Art does not categorize or lay claim by gender. Gender is itself a category, and nowadays an ever specially (and speciously) pleaded, and militant, claim. Gender as category and claim did not concern the foundational art which, like it or not, supremely concerned itself with sex, sexual depiction, and sexual realities. "Gender" was not its frame of reference, any more than "sexuality" (today-speak for love). From the mid-twentieth century to date, however, gender and other categorizing concerns have skewed not only art but the arts in general, giving us gendered antagonism rather than sexual complementarity and equipoise. Gender and other self-centered or specially pleaded concerns should be put aside going forward. Said women's rights advocate and Hawthorne-contemporary Margaret Fuller:

> By Man I mean both man and woman. These are the two halves of one thought. I lay no especial stress on the welfare of either. I believe that the development of the one cannot be effected without that of the other. My highest wish is that this truth should be distinctly and rationally apprehended, and the conditions of life and freedom recognized as the same for the daughters and the sons of time; twin exponents of a divine thought.

We leave the last word to a wise woman.

Part II

Archaic Greek Lyric Poets:

Sappho, Archilochus, Alcman, Anacreon, and Ibycus

THE FOLLOWING TRANSLATIONS are essentially found in my previous work, *The Lesbian Lyre* (*TLL*). In 2014, I retranslated an earlier version of §2 *phainetai moi* 'He appears to me', to provide a *TLL* version closer to the line length of the Greek. The "New Sappho" refers to the poem on love and old age, first discovered in 2004 (§39). Yet "newer Sappho," discovered as recently as 2016—the "Brothers Poem"—is not included here, as it is unrelated to the subject matter of this volume. Translators often use brackets (to excess) when the Greek is either missing (as on a papyrus), corrupt (mistranscribed), or otherwise illegible. I use brackets sparingly, either to indicate a brief gap in an otherwise readable text or to venture a translation where the text is uncertain.

The bolded parentheses following each numbered translation designate the authoritative Greek edition for the original text. Thus, **§1 (1LP)** indicates that the Greek for translation §1 is text 1 in the edition of Lobel and Page. A short bibliography of referenced Greek editions appears at p. 327. Asterisked parentheses—e.g., §1 (1LP)*—indicate noteworthy earlier translations included in an Addendum to this PART II. Cross-references to poems §§1–94 of this PART II are given by section symbol and number alone; to poems §§95 and higher, by page number as well. Also included is a Glossary of the sources here cited to which we owe the preservation of each Greek text.

A Word on Athenaeus

Greek grammarian and rhetorician, Athenaeus (2nd and 3rd centuries AD), was from the Egyptian city of Naucratis (45 miles southeast of Alexandria), Egypt's first Greek colony. Athenaeus's *Doctors at Dinner*—Gr. *Deipnosophistae*, also *Dinner-Table Philosophers* or *Learned Banqueters*—survives in fifteen books. The first two—and parts of the third, eleventh, and fifteenth—exist only in summary. The work warrants mention, among other reasons, as a primary source for the preservation of the poems and poem excerpts herein. Many of the following notes thus indicate, "preserved by Athenaeus," followed by book and section number of his *Deipnosophistae*. A vast compendium of information on matters of dining, the work contains remarks on music, dance, games, courtesans, and luxury. Athenaeus refers to nearly 800 writers and 2,500 separate works; one of his characters boasting to have read 800 plays of Athenian Middle Comedy (4th and 3rd centuries BC). Athenaeus is our sole source for much valuable information about the ancient world, many authors whom he mentions being otherwise unknown. Book 13 is essential to the study of sexuality in classical and Hellenistic Greece (see McClure [2003] and Jacob [2013]). The entirety of what remains of Athenaeus is available in the dual-language Loeb Classical Library (Harvard Univ. Press).

Other poems or poem fragments here included are preserved by literary critics, grammarians, rhetoricians, and others, sometimes citing poems or individual lines or phrases for their poetic value, sometimes for workaday grammatical reasons or to illustrate figures of speech. Poem fragments are also preserved on papyrus, often in the form of mummy cartonnage, or on parchment, and in one case an unearthed piece of ceramic. Those specializing in the decipherment and reconstruction of papyri are known as papyrologists. Papyrological finds are regularly published in discipline journals. The vagaries of such preservation provide pause over just how close we have come to having nothing at all.

THE HYMN TO APHRODITE

Ποικιλόθρον', ἀθάνατ' Ἀφρόδιτα,
παῖ Δίος, δολόπλοκε, λίσσομαί σε
μή μ' ἄσαισι μήτ' ὀνίαισι δάμνα,
  πότνια, θῦμον·

ἀλλὰ τυῖδ' ἔλθ', αἴποτα κἀτέρωτα
τᾶς ἔμας αὔδας ἀΐοισα πήλοι
ἔκλυες, πάτρος δὲ δόμον λίποισα
  χρύσιον ἦλθες

ἄρμ' ὑποζεύξαισα· κάλοι δέ σ' ἆγον
ὤκεες στροῦθοι περὶ γᾶς μελαίνας
πύκνα δινεῦντες πτέρ' ἀπ' ὠράνωἴθε-
  ρας διὰ μέσσω.

αἶψα δ' ἐξίκοντο· σὺ δ', ὦ μάκαιρα,
μειδιάσαισ' ἀθανάτῳ προσώπῳ,
ἤρε', ὄττι δηὖτε πέπονθα κὤττι
  δηὖτε κάλημι,

κὤττι μοι μάλιστα θέλω γένεσθαι
μαινόλᾳ θύμῳ· τίνα δηὖτε Πείθω
ἄψ σ' ἄγην ἐς σὰν φιλότατα, τίς σ', ὦ
  Ψάπφ', ἀδικήει;

καὶ γὰρ αἰ φεύγει, ταχέως διώξει,
αἰ δὲ δῶρα μὴ δέκετ', ἀλλὰ δώσει,
αἰ δὲ μὴ φίλει, ταχέως φιλήσει
  κωὐκ ἐθέλοισα.

ἔλθε μοι καὶ νῦν, χαλεπᾶν δὲ λῦσον
ἐκ μερμίναν, ὄσσα δέ μοι τελέσσαι
θῦμος ἰμέρρει, τέλεσον· σὺ δ' αὔτα
  σύμμαχος ἔσσο.

§1 (1LP)* Our source for the "Hymn to Aphrodite," the opening of Sappho's nine books of verse, is the Greek rhetorician and historian Dionysius of Halicarnassus, teaching in Rome (1st century BC). Dionysius, in his lengthy treatise *On Literary Composition*, quotes the poem in full as an example of the polished and exuberant style. The poem is discussed at length in *TLL*, Chapter 24. Says Dionysius,

> The finished and brilliant style of composition . . . has the following characteristics . . . it would not be out of place for me to enumerate here the finest exponents of it. Among epic writers I should give the first place in this style to Hesiod, among lyrists to Sappho, with Anacreon and Simonides next to her; among tragic poets there is only one example, Euripides. . . . I will now give illustrations of this style, taking Sappho to represent the poets.

◆

> Appareled in flowered allure, deathless,
> Deceiver, daughter of Zeus, Aphrodite!
> Subdue not nor destroy this heart, my lady,
>   with distress.

But come to my side, if ever before
while listening alert from afar as I cried
you attended, and came leaving your father's
    golden door,

Coupling lovely sparrows to the chariot's rein
that swiftly drew you down to darkened earth,
their wings awhirr along the way through aether's
    middle main.

Quickly they arrived, and you, O blessed one,
a smile on your immortal face, were asking
what I suffered this time, why this time did
    I summon;

And what it was my maddened heart did long
for most. "Whom this time shall persuasion lead
as captive to your love? Who, O Sappho,
    does you wrong?

For if she flees at first, she'll soon pursue;
the gifts she has spurned, she'll shortly bestow;
the love she flouts, she'll soon long languish for
    not wanting to."

Come even now to my side and free me
from crushing concern. Fulfill whatever
yearnings my own heart would fulfill, yourself
    my ally be.

Appareled in flowered allure: In rendering the opening epithet *poikilo-thron'* I have followed (among others) Putnam (79–83): "Aphrodite is invoked by Sappho as the goddess whose robe is richly-dight with the charms of love, perhaps in the form of flowers." The epithet occurs only here and is usually rendered to convey the notion of Aphrodite as seated on a decorated throne. This meaning, while supported by a number of literary and artistic representations, is not as fully congenial to the nature of the goddess nor to the tone of the poem, overall—an idea I was pleased to find early corroborated in Farnell's commentary of 1891: "The epithet in this sense ['goddess of the spangled flowers'] would be particularly appropriate from the lips of Sappho, whose love of flowers is conspicuous." The controversy is summarized by Stanley (309–310), stating "it would be unwise ... to exclude either translation." In a recent work, duBois (17) matter-of-factly urges both meanings at once: "The goddess is remote, on her highly wrought throne or garlanded with flowers."

Subdue not, nor . . . lady: lit., "Do not, I implore you, break my spirit, lady, with *heartache* or *anguish*." The italicized words, similar in both sound and meaning in Greek (*asaisi* / *oniaisi*), are hardly distinguishable. They are used by medical writers in reference to physical distress.

if ever before: This is not the first time Sappho has had to call on Aphrodite for help with unrequited love, though it is the only time in Greek literature that Aphrodite is called on to champion a same-sex love—Aphrodite in her own loves being entirely heterosexual. The thrice repeated "this time" (lit., "again") indicates Aphrodite's appreciation of the situation and shows her response to be one of playful and sympathetic reproach (though some believe it outright reproach). "If ever before" is further humorous in context. In traditional prayer requests, the suppliant expects a favor in return for services rendered. So with Homer's priest Chryses: "if ever it pleased your heart that I built your temple, / if ever it pleased you that I burnt all the rich thigh pieces / of bulls, of goats, then bring to pass this wish I pray for: / let your arrows make the Danaans pay for my tears shed" (*Il.* 1.39–42, R. Lattimore, tr.). Sappho's *quid pro quo* is one not of reciprocity but of precedent on the goddess's part: *You've done it before, so do it again.*

father's golden door: Aphrodite is here depicted as daughter of Zeus (by the goddess Dionē). It is in Hesiod (*Th.* 176–200) that Aphrodite is born from the sea, more specifically, from the seas's *aphros* 'foam'—hence *Aphro*dite. The birth results from the castration of Ouranos and the casting of his genitals into the sea. Thus, for *foam* one understands *semen*. Dionē, the mother of Aphrodite in Homer and elsewhere, is an obscure goddess—*Dionē* being a feminized derivative of the verbal root **di-* —nominative, *Zeus* 'Zeus'; genitive, *Di-os* 'of Zeus'. The goddess briefly appears at *Il.* 5.370.

sparrows: Sparrows have long been proverbial for their lasciviousness and fecundity. Their flesh and eggs might be eaten as aphrodisiacs. It is natural, then, that they draw the love-goddess's chariot. The only known depiction, by an anonymous artist, is reproduced at p. 103. Sparrows appear in the erotic contexts of Poems 2 and 3—to "Lesbia"—of the Roman poet Catullus (see p. 187). It seems less natural, however, that Aphrodite should at all descend in a (war-) chariot. Aphrodite is, in fact, characterized by a mock militancy throughout the poem ("subdue not . . . my ally be"), the analogy of amatory to military encounter being commonplace. That the horses, expected both by context and diction, appear as sparrows, replaces the expected combat with no small measure of charm. For the epic influences in this poem and their implications for lyric as a whole, see Beye, 124.

smile . . . immortal face: One of Aphrodite's traditional epic epithets is "smile-(or laughter-) loving." Hesiod (*Th.* 205–206) lists her domains as "the whispering together of girls, smiles, deceits, delight, and the sweetness of love and flattery."

why this time (see note, above, "if ever before"): The word is often used in erotic verse of love's ever renewed assault (see §48). Sappho begins by indirectly quoting Aphrodite in the first three of five questions and then quoting the goddess directly. She thus provides stylistic variety to what might otherwise prove a cumbersome number of questions if all asked the same way. The indirectness of the first three questions is further significant for Sappho's allowing her most direct and compelling concerns to be indirectly voiced by Aphrodite. One thus senses Sappho's own awareness of how routine the goddess views such concerns. In the end, Sappho *knows* what Aphrodite will ask and moves the inquiry along, as it were, sparing Aphrodite the effort by framing her very questions.

For if she flees . . . pursue: Sappho's conquest is of an *unwilling* lover, the chase archetype being the grim pursuit and death of Hector by Achilles (*Il.* 22.199–201). The stanza invites varying interpretation. Aphrodite's statements, be it noted, contain no direct object. She does not say that the girl will pursue *Sappho*, i.e, "For if she flees at first, she'll soon pursue *you*." Thus the girl's punishment might be one entirely independent of Sappho.

not wanting to: The feminine singular participle *etheloisa* 'wishing, wanting' is the only indication in the poem that Sappho's love is for one of the same sex. The other gendered indications in English (i.e., "she") are not reflected in the Greek; recall Lat. *portat 'he, she or it carries'*. Indeed, the masculine participial form *ethelān* (three syllables versus *etheloisa*, four) would not fit the meter. The beloved's female gender is thus metrically no less than psychologically determined. Translators had long found it convenient to "overlook" the feminine participle, rendering the love interest as masculine. The turning point came in the 1925 translation by Marion Mills Miller and David Moore Robinson. Writes E. Govett: "His [Miller's] translation of this hymn is unquestionably the best in our language, though this is perhaps partly due to the fact that he is almost the only translator who has adhered to the text in regard to the sex of the loved person" (Miller-Robinson, 10–11). Aphrodite's power is such that it can force the recalcitrant lover to a passion of which she remains disdainful. This heightens both Aphrodite and Sappho's victory, as the girl's loving "not wanting to" makes her undergo the opposite of Sappho's loving without being wanted. The result would be far less commanding if the two "loved happily ever after." Sappho's anguish is instead transferred to the girl who, disdainful all the while, yet yields.

Come ... free ... Fulfill ... be: All direct commands in Greek. Sappho is no less reluctant to call upon Aphrodite continually than she is to make her demands outright. So also "subdue not ... But come."

ally: Gr. *summachos* 'fellow-fighter'. A common metaphor in love contexts. Aphrodite is expectedly ineffective in battle as seen, for instance, by the wound she suffers at Diomedes's hands in *Iliad*, Book 5. Her efficacy in the battles of love is also questionable, given her frequent inability to effect a permanent result. Such is love, and such Aphrodite—as symbolized by her only *some-time* control over the god of war himself, Ares/Mars; see Lucretius Prologue (§§116–117; pp. 193–198).

§2 (31LP)* Our source for *phainetai moi* 'He appears to me' is the rhetorician and literary critic Longinus (1st century AD). In his sole surviving work, *Peri (h)upsous* (*On the Sublime*), Longinus quotes the poem for its consummate marshaling of the emotions accompanying delirious passion. The poem is discussed at length in *TLL*, Chapter 22. The second of the two translations is closer in line length to Sappho's original. It is informed by Sappho's words to Anactoria in Swinburne's poem of the same name (lines 74–75): "But thou— thy body is the song, / Thy mouth the music. . . ." Sappho's poem was freely adapted, to quite different effect, by Catullus, Poem 51 (see *TLL* 319–322). Longinus (*On the Sublime* 10.1–3) prefaces his quotations of the poem with the following remark:

> For instance, Sappho everywhere chooses the emotions that attend delirious passion from its accompaniments in actual life. Wherein does she demonstrate her supreme excellence? In the skill with which she selects and binds together the most striking and vehement circumstances of passion.

After quoting the poem, he goes on to comment:

> Are you not amazed how at one instant she summons, as though they were all alien from herself and dispersed, soul body, ears, tongue, eyes, color? Uniting contradictions, she is, at one and the same time, hot and cold, in her senses and out of her mind, for she is either terrified or at the point of death. The effect desired is that not one passion only should be seen, but a concourse of passions. All such things occur in the case of lovers, but it is, as I said, the selection of the most striking of them and their combination into a single whole that has produced the singular excellence of the passage.

The assessment was once criticized on the ground that the poem's comprehensive inclusion of symptoms does not properly constitute a "selection." Whether containing a selection or not, the poem quite overwhelms by its intensity. The view, now outmoded, long prevailed that the poem was sung at a wedding and that the man in the opening verses was a bridegroom. The view seeks, as does the gender "cover-up" in §1, to mitigate the poem's intensity.

(2014)

Equal to the gods, or so he seems,
that man sitting opposite and near
to you, beguiled by your lyric voice
    upon his ear

and blissful in your laughter. My heart,
at that sight, I do swear, is distraught,
and of a sudden am I undone;
    my tongue untaught,

forgotten its skill; excruciate
flame enters racing beneath my skin,
recognition gone, and sight, and naught
    but deaf'ning din—

a cold sweat commands me, a tremor
takes hold; more pallid than grass am I,
needing only, or so I seem, but
    little to die.

(1983)

Equal to the gods does he appear
to me, that man who sits close by you,
hears the sound of your sweet voice
   —intently near—

and your delightful laughter. That sight,
I do swear, does unsettle my heart;
The slightest glance at you puts my
    speech to flight!

My tongue unhinges, a delicate
flame slips racing neath my skin,
I see nothing, am blinded, my ears
    ring, pulsate,

a cold sweat commands me, fear
grasps at my heart. More pallid
than grass, nearly dead to myself
    I appear.

This is ultimately a poem about appearances. To Sappho, the man "appears equal to the gods"; to herself, she "appears nearly dead"—in a striking contrast between divine prerogative and human limitation. This is not a poem about jealousy. Jealousy requires a realistic sense of competition or attainment—here impossible, as Sappho cannot compete with her beloved's male admirer. No, this is a poem about the choking rage and desperation that come with sexual exclusion. To Sappho, the man appears equal to the gods because he can endure the beloved's presence at close range and thrive in it. But for Sappho, the sight of him—of them—eviscerates her being.

For a riveting contemporary analogy to the breakup of Sappho's physical, emotional, and artistic life, one may look to the apoplectic scene in *Hilary and Jackie* (2003), where the multiple sclerosis that cruelly claims cellist extraordinaire Jacqueline Du Pré takes hold as she concertizes. Though she impassionedly finishes the Dvořák Concerto, the film conveys, grippingly and in slow motion, the breaking asunder of her world: the screech of the strings beneath her fingers (like chalk on a blackboard), the thunder within her brain, the perspiration, the vacant stare and dilation as she seems to be playing by reflex alone; in short, the inner seizure and incipient paralysis. She finishes bow in hand, head lowered, arms parted to the cello's either side, as if nailed to her instrument or experiencing the stigmata. For those familiar with *phainetai moi*, the scene is necessarily reminiscent of Sappho's own, crippling seizure.

Equal to the gods: Or, "like the gods"—a frequent description of Homeric battle heroes here transferred to an amatory context. The man, in any event, is of heroic proportions for his ability to withstand and thrive in the beloved's presence, as noted above.

hears the sound . . . laughter: The intonations of speech and laughter, appearing to betray an unexpected intimacy between two other people, act as "detonator of intolerable emotional stress" (Dover [1978], 178).

the slightest glance: lit., "for whenever I look at you briefly."

My tongue unhinges: lit., "My tongue breaks to silence." Sappho's helplessness is complete. For a poet in an essentially oral culture, to lose the power of articulation is to lose the core of identity.

More pallid / than grass: Gr. *clōrotera de poias* (*chlōrotera* 'greener'; feminine comparative of *chlōra* 'green'). A lyric adaptation of Homeric *chlōron* [neuter] *deos* 'green fear' (e.g., *Il.* 8.77; *Od.* 11.43). In Homer, the phrase "traditionally connotes *supernaturally induced fear* . . . convey[ing] the involvement of a deity" (Foley, 29; emphasis in text). In the Sapphic context, it is pallid or pale, i.e., unwatered and withered, grass that is at issue, a possible instance of "harmoniz[ing] the color-value and the emotion within English usage" (Foley, 29).

nearly dead to myself / I appear: At the start of the poem, Sappho relates how the man "appears" to her. In reacting, she comes full circle to how she "appears" to herself—the Greek "appear" being the first word of lines 1 and 16. The English "I appear to myself nearly dead" is idiomatic; in Greek, lit., "I appear to my very self needing of little to die." The near finality of death and the reiterative "appear" would seem to bring the poem to a close at line 16. But this is not necessarily the case. Longinus continues with an only partially comprehensible verse: "But everything is endurable, since even a poor man . . ." Longinus might have stopped when he realized the stanza no longer illustrated his reason for quoting (Gerber, 170). The line, needless to say, has occasioned much speculation. In truth, so decidedly does the poem end without it, we would be none the wiser for its omission.

§3 (2LP)* This poem, written on a potsherd in a hand assigned to the third century BC, is one of the two oldest surviving remnants of a text by Sappho. The only lyric fragment thus preserved, it was first published in 1937. The stanzas lack line divisions. At the ends of the stanzas themselves, a small space is left vacant. The text is highly corrupt, though the hand is quite legible. The copyist may have been less than fully comprehending of the Greek. Lines of this poem are quoted in essentially the same form by subsequent authors. Lines 5–8 are known from Hermogenes (2nd century AD), author of *On Forms*. Lines 13–16 are known from a version in Athenaeus (11.463e). Aphrodite is thought to be among the poem's invited celebrants: "The earthly occasion has a divine significance" (Bowra, 198). The poem most likely did not end here, as Athenaeus continues with words that are likely a prose paraphrase of the beginning of another stanza. We should expect Sappho to give some reason for her invocation of the goddess (Page, 39).

> Leaving Crete for this sacred enclosure
> arrive! Here your pleasing grove
> of apple trees, here altars breathing
>   scents of myrrh.
>
> Roses and shadows in this place abound;
> cold water babbles neath apple bough
> branches whose shuddering leaves sprinkle
>   sleep to the ground.
>
> Here a spring-flowered meadow
> with horses agraze, where breezes
> gently blow [   ]
>   [   ]
>
> Here then [   ] taking, Aphrodite,
> with your exquisite touch admix
> the nectar golden-cupped to blend with
>   our festivity.

Leaving Crete: Sappho summons Aphrodite to a temple to join her and her companions in some public festivity. In §1, Sappho summons the goddess for purely personal reasons. Though linked to Crete, Aphrodite, according to the prominent Hesiodic legend (*Th.* 188–200), is more firmly connected to Cyprus. Ancient authorities believe that Aphrodite, upon birth from the sea, stepped first onto Paphos (southwestern coast of Cyprus). In this connection, see Baudelaire, "Lesbos" (§118, pp. 198–201).

grove / of apple trees: The apple, being ruddy and round, has erotic associations and is one of Aphrodite's emblems (see §17). At Magnesia, within Thessaly (northeastern coast of Greece), Aphrodite was worshiped as "Aphrodite of the Apples" (Bowra, 197, n. 4). The fruit in question may equally be a quince (see §91). In one of his elegies, the Roman Propertius, after a late-night debauch, famously returns to his beloved Cynthia's bedroom and stands tipsily over her slumbering form. He fusses with her fallen hair and places furtive *poma* 'apples' in her open hands, watching them drop across her pendant breasts to the floor (*El.* I.3.23–26).

sleep: Not just sleep (Gr. *hupnos*), but deep sleep (*kōma*) induced by enchantment or other supernatural means—here by the bubbling water and rustling leaves (Campbell, 267–268).

with horses agraze: Because of their vitality and grace, horses often have erotic significance. Thus, the detailed comparison of Paris to a horse, after a sexual encounter with Helen (*Il.* 6.503–514; cf. §§49, 54). In §94, the horse is decrepit and broken down, exhausted from his many runnings of love's course (see also pp. 163–164).

exquisite: Gr. *abros*, a favorite word of Sappho's; the essence and process of Aphrodite (see §§26, 45, and p. 138). For the range of the word, see Nagy (1974), 56–57, and Verdenius, 392–393 (noting the underlying sense of "ripeness," of "being in the flower of youth"; hence the adverb "luxuriantly"); more recently Kurke (1992), with exhaustive bibliography. Kurke connects the term with the luxuriant aristocratic, and surely sensual, Lydian lifestyle emulated by the East Greeks—i.e., Lesbos and other Greek islands off the coast of Asia Minor. In this context, see further Gorman and Gorman, 30–31, 262–268. F. Ferrari, 66–70, provides a helpful list of (*h*)*abrosúnē* 'exquisiteness' contexts, noting the "precise ideological context" given the term by Sappho, as "a choice of lifestyle founded on art and elegance." One may compare Voltaire over two millennia later, with reference to *le luxe / la mollesse* 'luxury / indolence':

These times profane delight my wonts precisely,
Luxury love I, and indolence* the more,
All pleasures and the Arts do quite entice me,
Finesse, good taste, decorum—these I adore:
Such preferences prove men well bred not slightly.

*lit., *la mollesse* 'softness', and by extension, an exertionless life.

[Ce temps profane est tout pour mes moeurs
J'aime le luxe, et même la mollesse,
Tous les plaisirs, les Arts de tout espèce,
La propreté, le goût, les ornements:
Tout honnête homme a de tels sentiments.]

[Voltaire, *Le Mondain*, 1736]

Le Mondain (*The Worldling* or *The Man of the World*) is Voltaire's highly controversial philosophical poem (he was forced to flee Paris after writing it), advocating hedonism over Christian doctrine. The work is consonant with the "fashionable" and "emancipated and cultured" attitude toward eroticism during the French Enlightenment, exemplified, e.g., by Voltaire's younger contemporary, Boucher, and the rococo emphasis on "entertainment and forthright pleasure" (p. 72). "Love becomes the outstanding myth of the eighteenth century. In the form of the impertinent flying Eros, he summons people not to the tragedy of grand passions, but to entertainment. Love in the eighteenth century is pleasure." Althaus, ed., 11–12 (quoting, Philip Stewart, *Le Masque et La Parole: Le Language De L'Amour Au XVIII Siècle* [Paris: Librairie Jose Courti, 1973]), 13.

§4 (16LP) Preserved on papyrus. Sappho marks her own feminine ideal against those who delight in military display. Her view is absolutist, insofar as sanctioning passion, no matter the outcome—including the Trojan War itself, resulting from Helen's runaway adultery with Paris. Being the most beautiful, Helen naturally determines what is most beautiful.

Some claim that infantry, cavalry corps,
or seas decked with fleets are the dark earth's
fairest sight. But I claim whatever
you adore.

The fact is apparent, self-evident,
for Helen, far surpassing all mortals
in beauty, leaving a husband
  unmatched, went

sailing to Troy nor showed any remorse
for dear parents or child. [Aphrodite]
drove her to follow [obeying love's
  greater force]

[   ]
[   ] lightly [   ]
that makes me think of Anactoria
  though distant,

whose lovely step I would sooner see
and face gleaming radiant with light, than
Lydian charioteers or outfitted
  infantry.

whatever / you adore: lit., "that, whatever it be, which one loves." The Greek conveys a comprehensive range of possibilities.

Helen, far surpassing: For other poets, Helen serves as a warning, or object of condemnation, even as she condemns herself in the *Iliad* (Greeks and Trojans unable to do so, lest it decrease her value as contested object). For Sappho, "the story of Helen is not . . . a warning, but an example, readily understood, of the power of love to break familiar bonds and force its victims to risk everything for it. Sappho makes it the center of her life, because it is not only radiant and enthralling but in the end irresistible" (Bowra, 181).

a husband/unmatched: The reference is to Menelaus who—truth be told—is largely a mediocrity. Menelaus's adulterous wife is stolen away. His brother, Agamemnon, is leader of the Greek host, though it is Menelaus's wife for whom the Greeks fight. Menelaus fares ridiculously in single combat with Paris (*Iliad*, Book 3). When Helen and Menelaus appear together, returned to Sparta after the war (*Odyssey*, Book 4), Menelaus is decidedly upstaged and made to look the dullard by his entrancing wife. As we learn from the Hesiodic *Catalogue of Helen's Suitors*, Menelaus won Helen by offering the most gifts (see Evelyn-White, 199).

nor showed any remorse: At *Il.* 3.139–140 and 15.662–663, however,

Helen is filled with self-reproach and longing for her family and native Sparta. Helen and Menelaus's children are Hermione (see §16) and Megapenthes ("great suffering") (see *Od.* 4.1–14).

think of Anactoria / . . . distant: Sappho's beloved Anactoria has become the byword for the distant and longed-for lesbian beloved (see pp. 201–202). Edna St. Vincent Millay (1892–1950), herself often compared to Sappho, wrote to her (much older) publisher and lover, Arthur Hooley, invoking Anactoria(s) as follows:

> It really isn't necessary that I should be a man, Arthur, in order to know what the word *girl* means to you—What do you suppose the word *man* sometimes means to me?—In a place like this? . . . This is a strange place. I had known, but I had not realized, until I came here, how greatly one girl's beauty & presence can disturb another's peace of mind,—more still, sometimes, her beauty & absence.— There are Anacatorias here for any Sappho. . . .

And Hooley, with extreme empathy and altruism, responded:

> Even if you had cared for a girl, & even if you had given yourself (so far as you could), I do not think I should care, greatly. No, I should not. For everything would have been beautiful, to you. As to Sappho. And so, to me [quoted in Milford, 132].

lovely step . . . charioteers: Anactoria's radiant face and *eraton . . . bama* 'lovely step'—i.e., step with the force of Eros—exalt her above the ranks of *pesdomachentas* 'infantry, foot fighters' (Gr. *bama* 'step' from *bainō* 'go'; Gr. *pes-* 'foot'). On foot/feet, see further §43.

face radiant with light: The key to Sappho's poetry, in the optical as well as aesthetic sense, is surely *radiance*: light, luster, brilliance—their increase and intensity. Sappho is quoted as saying, "I love the exquisite—that and yearning for the sun have won me brightness and beauty" (Athenaeus, 687b). In the poem, Sappho longs for her beloved Anactoria, saying she would sooner see Anactoria's "face sparkling radiant with light, than / Lydian charioteers and outfitted / infantry." The idea may be adapted from the *Iliad*'s depiction of the Greeks' bronze-armored sunlit advance— Homer focusing on the panoply of Greeks; Sappho on a single face:

As obliterating fire lights up a vast forest
along the crests of a mountain, and the flare shows far off,
so as they marched, from the magnificent bronze the glare went
dazzling all about through the upper air to heaven.

[*Il.* 2.455–458 (R. Lattimore, tr.)]

Sappho's image conjures forth a variegated brilliance in the beloved's face, superior by comparison to the panoplied resplendence of Lydian infantry. A dazzling image, to be sure: the sun-reflected luster of a beloved's face, outshining—and yet more awesome and commanding than—myriad infantry ranged against the sun. The point is easily missed: "The idea may seem a little fanciful: but this stanza was either a little fanciful or a little dull" (Page, 57). The Lydians were known as a particularly powerful and splendid race (see §§8 and 27).

Lydian charioteers: Lesbos, off the northwest coast of Asia Minor, directly faced the wealthy kingdom of Lydia—where Troy too was located. Greek culture before the classical period, as earlier noted, was essentially an East Aegean culture, enmeshed in Asian refinements and decadence.

§5 (95LP) Preserved on papyrus as lines 11–14 of a sixteen-line fragment. In the beginning, Sappho apparently relates that her life has become unhappy, whereupon the god Hermes appears. Sappho, notes one scholar,

> clearly recalls well-known epic motifs concerning death and the afterlife, and then reverses her audience's expectations. . . . the narrator *refuses* the offer of Hermes [of "exaltation"], *desires* rather than fears a transition to the world of death, and imagines a Hades of fertility and tranquility. The poem becomes a new, personal statement of values, a denial and reshaping of epic-heroic ideals. The end result is one that only she could envision: a death that nurtures, an Elysian Acheron.

See Boedeker, 52. On Sappho's reshaping of epic-heroic ideals, see §4; on her reversal of audience expectations, see §26; on her repeated wish to die, see §§2, 6.

> I'm filled with desire to die,
> see the dewy lotused shore
> of Acheron [flow by . . .

dewy lotused shore: "Lotus, first, implies the fertile beauty of flowers and the easy nurture of fruit effortlessly gathered. . . . The *lethe* ['forgetfulness'] induced by the Odyssean lotus [*Od.* 9.83–103] may well have influenced Sappho's choice of plant in this setting: not only is her Acheron floral and fertile, perhaps it also nurtures oblivion to the cares which motivate the desire for death" (Boedeker, 48). The symbolism is ambivalent, as dew signals the revival of day. The lotus, for its part, is associated with birth, sun, and life (Grigson, 197).

§6 (94LP) Preserved on parchment and published for the first time in Berlin, 1907. The same parchment contains §8 and several other scraps. Sappho's theme is the departure of a friend whom Sappho reminds of happy days spent together. "The poem preserves the moment when Sappho transmutes the old physical closeness into a new purely emotional connection. So the poem becomes the container of shared memories, hence itself the private space . . . [where] either can enter and find the other imaginatively" (Stigers [1981], 59). See p. 202.

> "Honestly, I wish I were dead"!
> She was leaving me, tears in her eyes.
> Much she said, this most of all:
> "Ah, Sappho, what we've suffered through;
> I swear, I leave not wanting to."
>
> And I made this reply:
> "Go then, yet remember me now
> and again. You know how
>
> we have cared for you.
> If not, I'd remind you [   ]
> of joyous times which we once knew:
> of rose wreaths and crocus,
> of violets arrayed at my side,
> necklaces flower-tied
>
> [tossed] round your gentle neck;
> how you anointed yourself
> with [   ] a queen's costly scent

and on yielding beds
gentle [   ]
desire [of maidens] spent
and no dance [
no shrine [   ] where
we two were not found

No precinct [
                    ] sound
                    ] . . ."

Honestly, I wish: "Honestly," lit., 'undeceitfully' (Gr. *adolōs*). 'Deceit' (*dolos*) is one of Aphrodite's attributes, as when Sappho addresses her as "Deceiver" (§1, Gr. *doloploke* 'weaver of deceit'). Thus understood, the term conveys more than the everyday notion of "honestly"; it communicates the sincerest love from which that most treacherous quality of deceit is absent. The first verse is assumed to be Sappho's, though it could be that of the departing friend.

I wish I were dead: "The wish to die, as elsewhere in Sappho, seems to be a metaphor for the rejection of present time, and memory, that tomb where the present lies when it has died, may serve as a surrogate for physical death" (McEvilley, 59).

Ah . . . suffered through: lit., "how terribly we've suffered." The Greek verb *paschō* 'suffer', always indicating a negative, here injects a retrospective note of pain into joys previously shared, as the joys are contemplated at the moment of termination. "The loss now gripping both women . . . cannot be separated from the loss and suffering which cling to all sweet and satisfying moments" (Bagg, 58.) The same ambivalence is evident in lines 10–11: lit., "if not, I would remind you of such lovely things as we have suffered."

Go then, yet remember: lit., "go, and farewell, and be mindful of me." The Greek phrasing recalls situations in epic where a female is forced to reconcile herself to a lover's, or would-be lover's, departure, e.g., *Od.* 5.204–205 (Calypso to Odysseus) and *Od.* 8.461–462 (Nausicaa to Odysseus).

desire [of maidens] spent: The restoration "of maidens," however agreeable, is contested. See Bowra, 191 (restoring the bracketed word), and Page, 80 ("all we can say is that it [the word] is not 'maidens'"). Otherwise, "The appealing restoration" strengthens a suggestion which, even without it, is amply strong, since Sappho uses *apalos* 'gentle' (lines 16 and 19) elsewhere, predominately to describe girls in erotic situations (McEvilley, 3). That the girl, to judge from the verb form, appears to be satisfying *someone else's* desire is a moot distinction (Stigers [1979], 468; Dover [1987], 176). The passage appears to refer to a homosexual act and is the only such reference in Sappho's surviving poetry. A fragmentary lyric sometimes ascribed to Sappho, sometimes to Alcaeus, is argued to contain part of the word *olisbos* 'dildo' (but see *TLL* 403–404).

§7 (34LP) Quoted by Eustathius in his commentary to *Il.* 8.555. The moon, as depicted in both this and the following poem, has been taken to signal Sappho's connecting women with "the mysterious rhythms of the moon as separate from the sharp, bright male world of sun and stars" (Stigers [1979], 470), but Sappho finds equal attraction in the sun and, as noted above, in all things bright.

> The stars about the radiant moon
> consider their brilliant orbs unsightly
> when in her fullness she burns brightly
> upon the earth . . .

§8 (96LP)* From the same parchment as §6. Both are poems of departure or absence. Sappho comforts Atthis (see also §§9, 10) by assuring her that another girl, now in Lydia, has not forgotten her. Containing Sappho's most expansive surviving simile, the poem begins after three broken lines and trails off into some nineteen lines of fragments.

> She thought you a goddess,
> your song her special joy.
>
> Among Lydian women
> she now has her praise—
> as the rosy-fingered moon,
> shaming heaven's stars from sight
> shines, ocean-enthroned,
> over flowers in the night,
>
> over fields where chervil grows lush,
> where melilot and roses thrill
> to evening's dewy touch;

> ever wandering there, yearning
> for tender Atthis, she languishes—
> her gentle spirit crushed . . .

rosy-fingered moon: The phrase has occasioned puzzlement. Homer often speaks of "rosy-fingered dawn"—the rising sun streaking the sky with rosy rays, or "fingers" (see further p. 66 and plate 8). The rosy-fingered moon, however, is "an extraordinary symbol that combines a reddish dusk, a transformation of a setting sun into a rising moon, an erotic condensation of Lesbian love play, and perhaps, an experiment with a new, woman's language" (Friedrich, 113–114).

as the rosy- . . . dewy: lit., "like the rosy-fingered moon after sunset, surpassing all the stars, its light spreads over the salty sea and the flower fields; and the dew descends abroad in beauty—the roses, tender chervil, and flowery melilot bloom."

Ever wandering . . . crushed: "Wandering," lit., "going to and fro." We return to the girl after a simile that "has gone so far beyond its starting point, that the girl is, for the moment forgotten" (Page, 94–95). It is, however, noted that "the moon is both a mental image of comparison and a sight to behold: and the longed-for girl's essence flows easily from the one into the other. . . . Her beauty and far-off-ness and presence are implicitly emanating from the moon. . . . Their friend's personality is spreading toward them through the medium of moonlight, encourages the dew to make flowers blossom and will have a reviving effect upon Atthis" (Bagg, 61–62). The papyrus contains eighteen additional highly fragmentary verses. Of these only several yield any sense: "for us, it is not easy to rival goddesses in beauty of form, but you (?) . . ." and ". . . Aphrodite poured nectar from a golden [bowl]."

§9 (49LP) The first line is quoted by Hephaistion; the second line by Plutarch. Terentianus Maurus suggests by his version that the verses were consecutive, though "one would never have guessed as much" (Campbell, 276). Sappho seems to be saying either that she loved the girl before the girl merited the affection, or that the girl's awkward exterior did not veil her inner qualities or their potential.

> I loved you, Atthis, once long ago;
> a child to me then with little to show.

child . . . with little to show: lit., "graceless, immature." It is for the sake of this word (Gr. *acharis*) that Plutarch quotes the verse. Ancient sources understood the Greek word to designate an age too young for marriage: "The outward quality of grace thus becomes the mark of marriageability. In being a member of Sappho's circle, the young girl acquires not only the grace which makes her a beautiful woman, but the acquisition of this quality opens the door to marriage" (Calame I, 401).

§10 (131LP) Quoted by Hephaistion with the preceding, and likely to be grouped with it (LP, 92–93). Andromeda did not, however, always win out. In a verse also quoted by Hephaistion, "Andromeda has her just deserts."

> Atthis, now you regard me hatefully;
> running off to Andromeda you flee.

§11 (57LP) Quoted apropos of Andromeda by Athenaeus (1.21b-c). The social standing of the girl in question would be much the opposite of the girl who spurns Anacreon (§49) (see further *TLL* 399–401).

> What country girl
> dressed in country style
> has turned your head around,
> unable to keep
> her hemline raised
> from sweeping up the ground?

§12 (137LP) The quotation is introduced by Aristotle (*Rhetoric* 1367a) as follows: "They reproach what is shameful in what they speak, do, and intend, as even Sappho composed when Alcaeus said, 'There's something I'd tell you.'" On Alcaeus, see *TLL* 35–36, 60–64. On the nature and circumstances of the exchange as quoted by Aristotle, see Bowra, 224–227, Page, 106–109, and F. Ferrari, 75–78. Sappho and Alcaeus likely lived part of their lives in the same city, at the same time, while members of the same aristocratic circle. Though they probably never met, they may have performed at the same festivals. They have nonetheless been depicted together in ancient vase paintings, canvas paintings, and fiction from antiquity onward. Much more of Alcaeus's than Sappho's poetry survives. But whereas Sappho's poetry (or what we know of it) was largely and intensely personal, Alcaeus's was largely political and inciting. Marcus Holland (Taylor Caldwell), *Sappho: A Drama in Verse* (1948), depicts Sappho and Alcaeus as adversaries.

> *Alcaeus to Sappho:*
>
> "There is something I'd tell you
> but shame [won't allow . . ."
>
> *Sappho to Alcaeus:*
>
> "If you had a desire for the noble and true,
> and weren't stirring your tongue in some
>   scurrilous brew,
> then shame would depart your lowered brow,
> not dawdling you'd speak your mind somehow."

weren't stirring your tongue: lit., "and your tongue were not concocting something base to say." The Greek phrase is both colorful and colloquial, *ekuka kakon* 'cooking, concocting, stirring evil'. Commentators have been overconcerned about what is probably a mock-abusive tone; "Her [Sappho's] words are certainly chilly, if not harsh and disapproving, and the metaphor in *ekuka* . . . is more colloquial than we should expect from her in such company" (Bowra, 125); "an unusual metaphor, and more forcible than the context requires; but not necessarily offensive or ill-humored" (Page, 105).

§13 (15bLP) Preserved on papyrus, first eight lines illegible, interpretation uncertain, Doricha unknown. Athenaeus (13.596b-c) says Doricha was reviled by Sappho. The situation may be as follows. An unspecified suitor has suffered Doricha's rebuff; Doricha then has a change of heart. Sappho hopes Doricha will be denied the satisfaction of the suitor's renewed interest.

> Be yet more severe with Doricha,
> let her not boast thus in her pride,
> that he came once again for the love
> which at first he was denied.

§14 (22LP) Preserved on papyrus as lines 11–14 of a nineteen-line fragment.

Longing floats round
the beautiful girl,
aflutter beholding the gown,
to my delight . . .

§15 (21bLP) Quoted by Athenaeus (15.674e). Two verses follow the quotation, appearing to indicate that the Graces prefer what is garlanded.

Dica, wreathe your hair, weaving garlands
of supple anise with tender hands.

§16 (23LP) Preserved on papyrus as lines 3–6 (restored) of a twelve-line fragment. Hermione is Helen's daughter (see *TLL* 218–223).

Such brilliant beauty as you possess
does make Hermione's seem the less.
Rightly are you compared
to Helen golden-haired.

§17 (105aLP)* Quoted by Syrianus in his commentary on Hermogenes. Himerius says that Sappho compared the bride to an apple, the groom to Achilles. The fragment, then, formed part of an epithalamium, or marriage song: as the apple atop the tree escapes being picked, so the girl avoids marriage until the proper time (Grigson, 177). Conversely, "because the girl who values her position is hard to win she may be left hanging for want of a worthy man to pick her" (Stigers [1977], 91). The fragment may also connote "sour grapes": the rarest beauty is often the most inaccessible; failure to obtain it may result in pretended unconcern. The erotic symbolism of apples has been noted. The best contemporary discussion is by Anne Carson, who notes of this tantalizing three-line fragment, "The poem is incomplete, perfectly" (Carson, 26–29). This sentiment underscores the wistful belief that Sapphic fragments are so exquisite as to seem *composed* as fragments.

As the sweet apple reddens atop of the bough
by the tip at the furthest height,
the pickers forgot it, no, they didn't, not quite,
but just couldn't reach it somehow.

§18 (105cLP)* Quoted by Demetrius, but without specific attribution of authorship.

> As the hyacinth
> on the mountain top,
> trampling shepherds did
> not see the purple flower drop.

Similarity to the preceding poem suggests the lines may have formed part of a wedding song. There is, in the contrast between §§17 and 18, "flower and vulnerability on the one hand and fruit and inaccessibility on the other. These are two modes of coming into a relationship with men" (Stigers [1977], 91). Catullus is clearly indebted to the image.

> As a flower grows, hidden in a walled-off plot,
> Undetected by herds, uprooted by no plow,
> Which breezes nurture, sun and showers train— many
> The boys, many the girls desiring it—which wilts
> When shorn by the slender blade, and none the boys, none
> The girls desiring it—so a maiden adored
> Remains the while inviolate. When, once defiled,
> She's lost her flow'r, boys no longer find her lovely;
> Girls, no longer dear. . . .
>
> Poem 62.39–47

§19 (114LP) Quoted by Demetrius. Two verses in the Greek, the second uncertain.

> "Maidenhood, maidenhood,
> where go you leaving me?"
>
> "I leave you for good,
> you've outgrown my company."

§20 (107LP) Quoted by Apollonius Dyscolus.

> Do I yet long for virginity?

§21(104aLP)* Quoted by Demetrius, who finds charm in the repetition of the word, "(you) bring."

Hesperus, restoring all that shining Dawn
has scattered far and wide,
You bring the sheep, bring the goat, bring
  every fawn
back to its mother's side.
  [Not so the bride—
who leaving home is forever gone.]

As in the case of the Sappho-inspired §18, Catullus again has Sappho in mind:

Hesperus, what crueler star traverses heaven?
You sunder the daughter from a mother's embrace,
You sunder her clinging from her mother's embrace,
Bestow her maiden's favor on an ardent youth.
What crueler does the foe in laying cities waste?

Poem 62.20–25

As Sappho's verses are sometimes considered part of a wedding song, she may have continued as follows: "But evening does not bring the bride back to her parents' home" or "so evening brings the bride to her husband's home" (Campbell, 282). I have supplied a couplet in the spirit of these suggestions (see further F. Ferrari, 119–123).

Hesperus: *Esperos* in Sappho's Aeolic dialect, and understood as deriving from *es, eis* 'into' + *p(h)er* 'bring'; i.e., the Evening Star marks an ingathering, and the couplet develops in accordance with this etymology. The Greek *phereis* 'you bring' reverses *Es-p(h)er(-os)* in the name of the Evening Star; and the poem, as a whole, is intended as a counterpart to Hesiod's description of centrifugal dawn (see J. Clay, 302–305; *WD* 578–581).

§22 (141LP) Quoted by Athenaeus (10.425d).

A bowl of ambrosia had
there been blended,
for the gods Hermes poured,
all were attended.
They all raised their cups,
poured a libation,
wishing the bridegroom
his heart's elation.

§23 (115LP) Quoted by the Hephaistion. Although the author's name is not given, the lines are believed to be Sappho's. Subjecting the groom to multiple comparisons seems to have been a well-known parlor game (Campbell, 284). The most eligible bachelor and maiden in Homer are compared to saplings: Achilles at *Il.* 18.56, and Nausicaa at *Od.* 6.163.

> What likeness, O bridegroom, do you most bear?
> To a tender sapling you best compare.

§24 (30LP) Preserved on the same papyrus as §4 (papyri sometimes containing the remains of more than one poem). My rendering follows the restoration by Bowra, 221.

> May unwed maidens
> the entire night long
> make of you and your
> violet-girt bride their song.
> Awake, spread the call,
> to your companions all,
> that we such hours keep
> as put the nightingale asleep.

violet-girt bride: Gr. *kolpos* 'bosom, fold, garment'; cf. §39, Μοίcαν ἰ]ọκ[ό] λπων '[of the] violet-bodiced Muses' (brackets indicating a missing or conjectured letter; dot, a faint but likely papyrus or parchment letter).
nightingale asleep: The nightingale is known for insomnia. The most evocative of all the surviving words ascribed to Sappho—the epitome of her lyric voice—are: Ἦρος ἄγγελος ἱμερόφωνος ἀήδων 'Spring's messenger, the longingly-voicèd nightingale'. Quoted by the scholiast on Sophocles, *Electra* 149: "the nightingale is the messenger of Zeus, because it is the sign of spring." There is an extensive literature on the nightingale's song/singing and poetry.

§25 (112LP) Quoted by Hephaistion (see §23).

> O blessed groom, now your wedding's complete
> as you prayed; yours is the girl you've adored
> as you prayed; her generous beauty, yours.

And the eyes of your bride are honey-sweet,
love's smile on the beautiful face, outpoured;
you are graced with the Cyprian's honors.

with the Cyprian's honors: lit., "Aphrodite has honored you surpassingly." The first half of the Greek line is missing. "The Cyprian" refers to Aphrodite, born, according to Hesiod, from sea-foam onto the island of Cyprus (*Th.* 188–200).

§26 (44LP) Preserved on papyrus. The poem differs from Sappho's remaining poetry, being narrative rather than personal; and exhibiting the characteristics of epic dialect, meter, and style. Such features are best explained by the poem's epic theme. See detailed discussion in *TLL*, Chapter 17. The first line in translation condenses three fragmentary lines of Greek. A one-line gap precedes line 2. Though Homer nowhere depicts the marriage of Hector and Andromache, Sappho's treatment might have had its origin in a reference to Andromache's home (*Il.* 6.394–395). Homer's silence about the tale does not necessarily make it "Sappho's own invention" (Bowra, 231). The story was instead extraneous to Homer's subject matter, as Homer chose, modified, and invented to suit his immediate needs—and in such way as to impart Panhellenic appeal to his synthesis. On Panhellenism see *TLL* 70, 177–178 (and sources cited). Sappho brings her own distinctive emphases and flavor to the marriage tale, some of which are bitterly ironic. Among other such features is Sappho's description of the martial pair as "godlike," a term reserved in the *Iliad* for Achilles, Hector's slayer (see Nagy [1973], 137–139). Similarly, the wedding couple's cart-drawn entrance into Troy, to the accompaniment of shouts, bitterly anticipates the entrance into Troy of Hector's ransomed corpse in *Iliad*, Book 24. Sappho's wedding poem comes close to being a funeral dirge in disguise, the poem a pronounced instance of theme developed contrary to expectation.

Came the herald, Idaeus, swift messenger [
" . . . and of the rest of Asia, imperishable fame
Hector and his comrades bring a bright-eyed girl
from holy Thebes, in ships on the salty sea,
from Placea's streams—exquisite Andromache.
Bringing purple robes, ivory, bracelets of gold,
oddly-tooled trinkets, silver cups untold."

Thus the messenger. His father quickly rose;
to his friends, through streets well paved, the tiding goes.
Trojan sons bend mules to rapid carriages,
the crowd surges, ascends; women, girls unmarried [
Priam's daughters, apart [and men unwed lead
horses to their carts, and greatly charioteers
[unknown number of missing verses]
                     ] like to the gods
                     ] holy, all together
set forth [   ] to Ilium,
the sweet-sounding flute [and lyre] blend.
Castanets clash; clear sacred maiden songs ascend,
the wondrous echo reaches the skies [
throughout the streets [
chalices, bowls, [
mingled frankincense, cassia and myrrh
elder women calling clamorously,
men's thrilling melody, shouted aloud
summons Paon, great archer, great lord of the lyre,
they sang of Hector, Andromache, like to the gods.

Idaeus, swift messenger: Idaeus, the chief herald of Troy. In the *Iliad*'s ransoming of Hector's body, Hermes (the messenger god), disguised as Idaeus, drives Priam across the plain and battleground of Troy—that no man's land and Hades above ground—to Achilles's camp and back. Sappho's audience would immediately make the ironic connection.

imperishable fame: Gr. *kleos aphthiton*—language used by Achilles alone in the *Iliad*'s sole instance (*Il.* 9.413). *Kleos aphthiton* is nonetheless the ultimate desideratum; and *kleos* 'fame, glory', plain and simple, the goal of every epic warrior/hero. More generically, there is *kleos* 'report, news'. All meanings derive from Gr. *kluo* 'hear' (fame [Lat. *fama*] being what is heard or reported). See *TLL* 185–205, 211–212, 608–620; Nagy (1974), 27–149; Redfield, 31–39.

exquisite Andromache: Gr. *abran* (see §3).

Bringing purple robes: Illustrative of the view that the poem's appeal is "not so much dramatic as pictorial" (Bowra, 231).

His father . . . rose: Hector's father, Priam, King of Troy.

to rapid carriages: Gr. *satinai*, a rare word designating 'women's conveyance' as opposed to *arma* 'chariot'.

like to the gods: Gr. *ikeloi theois*. The final words of the poem occasion pause, being an inversion of epic *theoeikelois*.

[and lyre]: Supplied by Campbell in his printing of the Greek text.

Castanets clash, clear: Of the instruments included, castanets alone are unmentioned in Homer.

the wondrous echo ... skies: Reminiscent of the stanza by Alcaeus (on the beauty contest in Lesbos):

> Where yearly the girls range about making show
> of their beauty in sweeping gowns;
> where the sacred shout and its wondrous echo
> from the women aside them resounds.

frankincense ... and myrrh: Sappho is the earliest writer to mention these (see also §3).

Paon: A Homeric epithet: The Paean seems originally to have been a hymn addressed to Apollo in his role as Healer (see Campbell, xix, and *TLL* 64, 69).

§27 (132LP)* Quoted by Hephaistion (see §23). A papyrus line reads, "She [Sappho] had a daughter Cleïs, named after her mother." The poem is three lines in Greek, the last of which requires a verb, such as "I would not take." The rhythm of the words *chrusioisin anthemoisin* ['with] golden flowers' is especially appropriate with its girlish lilt. Homer achieves a similar effect in the name of the Phaeacian princess Nausicaa with its repeated final vowel.

> A flower, golden-petaled, is my child,
> Precious Cleïs, for whom all Lydia . . .

§28 (98LP) Preserved in fragmentary form on a papyrus dated to the third century BC. Among the oldest extant papyri of Sappho or Alcaeus (Page, 98). Sappho discusses a subject suitable to a young girl—most likely her daughter, Cleïs—the type of headband she should wear. If an expensive headband is unavailable, flowers will suit Cleïs equally well. From the yet more fragmentary lines that follow, the harsh circumstances of Sappho's exile may have placed so fine an item beyond her means. The following is decipherable from about ten lines: "Lately . . . a decorated headband from Sardis [capital of Lydia] . . . for you, Cleïs, I have no headband, and know not where I shall get one." Sappho then makes several political allusions—unusual in her poetry—and a mention of exile. On the social implications of the referenced headband and of Lydian apparel generally, see F. Ferrari, Chapter I, "Song of the Headband."

> She who bore me used to say
> that in her youth a splendid sight
> was hair adorned in a purple band,
> but even better the strands
> yet yellower than torch's light
> wreathed in chapleted flower display.

§29 (110LP) Quoted by Hephaistion. At issue here and in §30 is exaggerated size; risqué banter (or ribald humor) being a common feature of archaic Greek wedding songs. Commentators refer to the traditional attempted "rescue" of the bride by her friends, after the couple has entered the bridal chamber. A friend of the groom who "protected" the chamber entrance is here the object of Sappho's mock ridicule.

> The doorkeeper's feet are fourteen yards long,
> his sandals are stitched five oxhides strong,
> ten cobblers labored at fitting the thong.

§30 (111LP) Quoted by Demetrius. The opening line is the inspiration for J. D. Salinger's novella *Raise High the Roof Beam, Carpenters* (1955, 1963). The poem has generated its share of apologists: "This is neither bawdy or exalted, but playful. If the humor is a bit primitive, that is due to tradition, which expected jokes at this level" (Bowra, 216); "the fun may be childish, as in the preceding piece" (Campell, 284, also noting possible indecency). "If . . . the bridegroom is so described 'because he is fantastically ithyphallic' (hence the order to raise the roof), this is the only example in Sappho of the ritual obscenity common in wedding-songs" (Gerber, 179, quoting source). The piece reflects its meaning. Notes Demetrius: "The style in which she [Sappho] mocks the awkward bridegroom or the keeper of the wedding door is very different. It is quite commonplace, and the words are better suited to prose than to poetry. Indeed, these poems of hers can be better spoken than sung, and would not be suitable for the chorus or the lyre, unless for a kind of talking chorus" (see further F. Ferrari, 123–125).

> Raise the roof higher
> —sing joy to the groom—
> carpenters, raise it,
> give him more room.
> Rivaling Ares he enters the door,
> more duly endowed than you built it for.

sing joy to the groom: Gr. *umenaōn* 'Hail Hymen' (the god of marriage), a one-word exclamation in Greek, traditional for the wedding ceremony.

give him more room: The idea exists by implication in the original. The erect bridegroom is having a door-clearance problem.

Rivaling Ares . . . door: A touch of the mock-heroic meant to recall such references as *Il.* 11.604, where the phrase "he came forth equal to Ares" describes Patroclus as he enters the battle, clad in Achilles's armor. The precise reading of the verb *enters* is uncertain in the preserved version of Sappho's text. It is likely adverbial indicating a rush forward, as in battle, but here stressing the bridegroom's impetuosity (Gerber, 179).

more duly endowed . . . for: lit., "much bigger than a big man." Demetrius quoted the poem for the way in which this final line gracefully modified the hyperbole of the line before.

§31 (51LP) Quoted by Chrysippus.

> I know not what I want,
> My every thought's a taunt.

§32 (50LP) Quoted by Galen.

> Beauty is beauty as far as it goes,
> a good man's beauty immediately shows.

§33 (126LP) Quoted in the Etymologicum Magnum.

> May you find rest
> on a maiden's soft breast.

§34 (102LP)* Quoted by Hephaistion.

> Mother dear, no longer
> does the loom delight—
> sweet Love commands,
> desire conquers me quite.

§35 (47LP) Lobel's reconstruction of the paraphrase found in Maximus of Tyre. Maximus writes: "Love wracked her [Sappho's] heart, as a wind falling on oaks throughout the mountain." For the comparison of love's violence to wind, see also §93.

> My heart
> was wracked by Love—
> like mountain oaks
> by winds above.

§36 (130LP) Quoted by Hephaistion. "In a very few words Sappho conveys the turmoil of her state which is both physical and mental and which she both welcomes and hates" (Bowra, 184) (see also §§47, 73).

> Love undoes me again—
> dissolver of limbs
> bittersweet irresistible
> creeping in.

again: The iterations of love, however variously expressed, are common to lyric poetry (cf. §§1, 6, 13, 36, 42, 48–50, 69).

dissolver of limbs: Gr. *lusimelēs*, a traditional epithet of love. See §73 and *Th.* 120–122 for description of Eros, the primordial power (not "Cupid"): "And [there was at first] Eros, the loveliest among the deathless gods, who dissolves the limbs and overpowers the mind and wise planning within them of all gods and all men." Sappho, however, gives the traditional term new force in context (Bowra, 184).

bittersweet: Gr. *glukupikron* 'sweet bitter', an original compound in Sappho, not occurring in other authors until Hellenistic times. One notes the freshness of the paradox first conveyed by the term (Snell, 60), a paradox akin to that of §§46, 47.

irresistible: Gr. *amachanon* 'not to be devised against'.

creeping in: Gr. *orpeton* 'a crawler' (Eng., serpent, herpes), a neuter noun modified by the two preceding adjectives. The word, intentionally vague, can designate almost anything that creeps, slithers, or moves on all fours (Bowra, 184). It is for this reason that Eros is *amachanon*. The serpentine metaphor is decidedly phallic.

§37 (48LP) Quoted by Julian, thought to be Sappho's.

> You came, calmed my desire,
> for you I raged;
> my breast, a burning pyre,
> is now assuaged.

§38 (Fr. Adesp. 976P)* Quoted by Hephaistion, without attribution to Sappho.

> The moon departs the sky,
> the Pleiads pass from sight,
> midnight's hour slips by,
> and I lie alone tonight.

Sappho's authorship, once doubted on grounds of dialect, is now beyond question. Arguably not a fragment, but a complete poem, the work has inspired many translations, including the tremor-inducing versions by classicist-poet A. E. Housman (1859–1936), reproduced at pp. 171–172. Also see Gomme, 265–266, and D. Clay, 119–129. Clay surveys the history of scholarship on the poem (not a fragment, but with §1, one of Sappho's two then surely complete poems). The moon, personified in the poem as *Selanna*, was enamored of the handsome shepherd Endymion, believed to be the first human to observe the moon. For the mythological context, see Boardman & LaRocca, 128; A. Weigall, 287–290; and pp. 39–40.

Pleiad(e)s: The seven daughters of Atlas and the ocean nymph Pleionē. Zeus transformed them into a constellation to save them from the advances of the giant slayer Orion. Their pursuer was set beside them in the skies (as in Housman's second version, above).

hour: Gr. *ora*, used in Homer to indicate the proper time or season for a thing—most commonly for sleep or bed, and understood by D. Clay as "the season of the night" in Sappho's poem. Significant in this connection is that the notably pale and wavering Pleiads "served the whole ancient world as heralds of seasonal change"; see Burnett, 30–31 (apropos of Alcman's *Partheneion*).

§39 (58V) The text of the "New Sappho" was first published in 2004 by Michael Gronewald and Robert W. Daniel in *Zeitschrift für Papyrologie und Epigraphik* (*Journal of Papyrology and Epigraphy*), a University of Cologne publication announcing the identification of a University of Cologne papyrus (see also §78) that contained poems of Sappho. The papyrus was recovered from Egyptian mummy cartonnage dated to the third century BC. Copied approximately three hundred years after Sappho's lifetime, the work is not only one of the earliest manuscripts of Sappho's poetry but also the longest after the "Hymn to Aphrodite" (§1). It is likely a complete poem, making it, again with the "Hymn," one of only two or three completely surviving poems by Sappho (with §§2 and 38; see further *TLL* 146–148).

Dealing with the incapacities of advancing age, the poem makes telling reference to the myth of Tithonus, a beautiful Trojan youth beloved by the goddess Dawn (Gr. *Ēōs*, Lat. *Aurora*), who claimed and swept him away. Tithonus here shares the fate of the Trojan Ganymede, beloved and taken by Zeus. Asking Zeus to grant Tithonus immortality, Dawn forgets to request eternal youth as well. Tithonus was thus fated to live forever, growing older and more debilitated as he did. It is an untenable situation for "rosy Dawn"—forever young and fresh, without existence or thought past morning—who must rid herself of the increasingly oppressive Tithonus. Dawn is here referred to as "rosy armed," recalling the Homeric epithet, "rosy-fingered" Dawn, which, as noted above, conjures the pinkish streaks of the early morning sky. See further p. 66 and plate 8.

The account is also related in the *Homeric Hymn to Aphrodite* (that goddess too wedding a mortal, Anchises, father of Aeneas). As the *Homeric Hymn to Aphrodite* relates, "But when loathsome old age pressed full on [Tithonus], and he could neither move nor lift his limbs, this seemed to [Dawn] in her heart the best plan: to lay him in a room and fasten the shining doors. There he babbles endlessly, and no more has strength at all, such as once he had in his supple limbs." As Tithonus bears the weight of advancing years, so, Sappho feels, does she.

The poem bears a marked resemblance to Anacreon §72. Gr. *eis eschata gās* 'to the ends of the earth'—here translated (line 10) "to earth's furthest bourn"—indicates an idealized location by the earth-surrounding streams of Ocean, associated with wonders, special felicity, and prosperity denied mere mortals (see Brown, 21–25).

> To the violet-bodiced Muses' gifts aspire,
> children dear, to the gentle song-loving lyre.
>
> But as for me, advancing years torment me quite,
> skin earlier taut now slack, black hair turned to white.
>
> Now is my heart all heaviness, now fail the knees
> erstwhile to dalliance startled with fawn-like ease.
>
> As fully futile, then, as bitter, my lament,
> that toiling life expires in youthful beauty spent;
>
> And once, as told, enamored rosy-armèd Dawn
> was to earth's furthest bourn with her Tithonus gone,
>
> then young and trim. But hoary age did nonetheless
> encompass him—though with mate immortal blessed.

ALCMAN

§40 (59D) The Riphēan mountains, a far-northern legendary range unvisited by the sun. Sometimes associated with the Urals, the Riphēan mountains were said to be beyond Scythia in the North on the boundary of the fabulous Hyperboreans, a fabled race of Apollo worshipers among whom the god, according to Delphic legend, spends his winters. For the genre concerning marvels, wonders, and strange beings at the world's end, to which this fragment might have belonged, see Bowra, 26–27.

Forest
flowered
mountain,
Riphē,
evening's
breast

evening's breast: Because Riphē was never visited by the sun.

§41 (3D) Preserved on papyrus dating to the end of the first century BC; first published in 1957. The poem had at least one hundred and twenty-six lines, some sixty of which preceded the present segment. Of the sixty, only lines 1–10 provide any sense, literally as follows: "(the song) will at once scatter sweet sleep from my eyes / and desire drives me to go to the contest / where especially I will toss my golden hair." The singers focus on the praises of another girl, Astymeloisa, who may be leading the worship. The text again becomes fragmentary. The sense following line 76 appears to be, "If she took me by the soft hand, I should at once become her suppliant." The content, style, dialect, and meter of this fragment are reminiscent of Alcman's *Partheneion*. Comparison of the two pieces occupies the better part of Calame, Vol. II, with a summary of results at 144–146.

With longing that dissolves the limbs
Casting glances more melting than sleep and death
Her sweetness serves no idle whim;

Astymeloisa makes me no reply
but holding a garland
like a glittering star
or golden shoot
or tender down
[   ]
    ] she has come on luxuriant stride
] the moist charm of Cinyras
which settles on maidens' hair

] Astymeloisa in the host
] people's darling
] winning praise

casting glances more melting: See §94.

her sweetness serves ... whim: The reading is uncertain. Otherwise translated "not at random is she sweet" (Page), "not at all in vain is she sweet" (Bowra).

holding a garland: The Greek word indicates a garland of the variety used in the worship of Hera. The girls (led by Astymeloisa) appear to be making an offering to Hera in her capacity as goddess of birth and protectress of children, over whom Hera watches until they wed (see further Bowra, 34). The first two lines describe the rapidity and ease of Astymeloisa's movement. Comparison to a star is frequent in archaic Greek poetry. The third line appears to describe her supple form and downy softness of skin, perceived a'close. The context, however, remains uncertain.

the moist charm of Cinyras: A circumlocution for Cyprian perfume or hair oil. Cinyras was a king of Cyprus, the island famous for its scents.

Astymeloisa in the host: The name means "Concern of the Town."

in the host / people's darling: "People's darling" may be a punning reference to Astymeloisa's name, and her appearance in male society may have marked a debut, a wedding, or some other kind of public occasion (Hallett [1979], 463; see further §54).

§42(101D) Quoted by Athenaeus (13.600).

> Again sweet love
> through Aphrodite's will
> does melt and distill
> my heart.

§43 (36D) Quoted by Hephaistion.

> It isn't Aphrodite
> but Eros, wild
> as a child at play,
> down over the flower tops
> heading this way—
> don't touch them, I pray.

It isn't Aphrodite / but Eros: The contrast is between a waggish Eros and a more demure Aphrodite. Eros's traipsing over the flower tops is the precursor to love's onslaught, the proverbial calm before the storm (cf. §48).

Down over the flower . . . way: lit., "coming down over the topmost flowers of the clover." Lightness or delicacy of foot is a frequent attribute of Love or of the beloved. Plato speaks of Eros's most gentle step: "He [Love, Erōs] proceeds not upon land nor upon summits—these are in no way delicate—but amid the softest of all things existing does he both proceed and reside" (*Symposium* 195e). So also Aphrodite's delicate step: "There came forth [from the sea] a lovely and revered goddess, and grass grew up about her from beneath her tender feet" (*Th.* 194–195). Sara Teasdale (1884–1933) (see pp. 84–85) poignantly conveys the same idea in her narrative poem *Sappho* (III, 42–46): "Ah, Love, there is no fleeing from thy might, / No desert thou has left uncarpeted / With flowers that spring beneath thy perfect feet." So also Bliss Carman (1861–1929): "In this garden all the hot noon / I await thy fluttering footfall / Through the twilight." So Sappho herself: "Whose lovely step I would sooner see / and face gleaming radiant with light, than / Lydian charioteers or outfitted / Infantry" (§3). In Euripides, delicacy of step is associated with (*h*)*abrosúnē* 'elegance, gracefulness, luxuriance' (see §3): αἰεὶ διὰ λαμπροτάτου βαίνοντες ἁβρῶς αἰθέρος 'ever stepping gracefully [adv. (*h*)*abrós*] through the bright air', and ἁβρὸν βαίνουσα παλλεύκῳ ποδί 'on purely white foot stepping gracefully' [adv. (*h*)*abron*] (*Medea* 830, 1164); ἄγετε τὸν ἁβρὸν δήποτ' ἐν Τροίᾳ πόδα 'guide the foot aforetime graceful [adj. (*h*)*abron*] in Troy' (*Trojan Women* 506).

The foot is also a starting point for seduction, from the bottom up, as it were—each bodily part appreciated and praised en route. The sequence is vividly apparent in the biblical Song of Songs 7:2–7, beginning: "How lovely your sandaled step, O daughter of opulence," and ending with praise of the beloved's head and hair. The Heb. *mah yaphu* 'how lovely' is elsewhere used to designate the beloved's own lovemaking, 4:10: *mah yaphu dōdayich achōtī kalah* 'how lovely your embraces, my sister, my bride' (see further Ariel Bloch and Chanah Bloch, 200 at 7:2).

Botticelli everywhere highlights the foot's erotic appeal (canvases and Sistine Chapel alike), while the most erotically charged foot of the late Renaissance or any period is that of Bernini's *The Ecstasy of St. Teresa* (aka the "spiritual orgasm" of St. Teresa) (1652). See further pp. 39–40 and plate 1. On the statue's marked eroticism, see Schama, 78–80, 111–121, 125.

More recently, the beloved's foot—her beloved foot—is nowhere more exalted than in George Du Maurier's novel, *Trilby* (1894). The foot is a "wondrous thing," says a Du Maurier character, "perhaps even more so than the hand, but is hidden away, discolored, and deformed by the heel and boot for fashion's sake" (18). Having thus been suppressed since its Greek sandaled day,

> . . . The sudden sight of [the foot], uncovered, comes as a very rare and singularly pleasing surprise to the eye that has learned how to see!

> Nothing else that Mother Nature has to show, not even the human face divine, has more subtle power to suggest high physical distinction, happy evolution, and supreme development; the lordship of man over beast, the lordship of man over man, the lordship of woman over all! [19–20].

"The lordship of woman over all!" The recognition returns us to Sappho's beloved Anactoria (§4), whose glowing face and *eraton . . . bama* 'lovely step'— i.e., step suffused with Eros—exalt her above the ranks of *pesdomachentas* 'infantry, foot fighters' (Gr. *bama* 'step' from *bainō* 'go'; Gr. *pes-* 'foot'). We note in passing the "well turned ankle"—the entirety seen as perfected in the part observed.

There is Charles Algernon Swinburne (1837–1909), the Greek-learned Victorian for whom Sappho is "simply nothing less—as she is certainly nothing more—than the greatest poet who ever was at all." Swinburne, himself the English poetic incarnation of Sappho, eroticizes the foot in his Sapphically metered poem "Sapphics," relating how he saw Aphrodite's "feet unsandalled / Shine as fire of sunset on Western waters; / Saw the reluctant / Feet. . . ." and "Heard the flying feet of the Loves behind her." See also author Wilkie Collins (pp. 95–96), equating the pulse of footstep and heart.

Swinburne is imitated to fair effect by American attorney-poet John Myers O'Hara (1870–1944) in his "The Daughter of Cyprus" (i.e., Aphrodite, born onto the island of Cyprus). O'Hara's foot-and-ankle-focused stanza— with impressive Homeric detail—reads as follows:

> Saw the gleaming foot, and the golden sandal
> Held by straps of Lydian work thrice doubled
> Over the instep's arch, and up to the rounded
> Dazzling ankle.

O'Hara's own vision is impressive, though meter and phrasing falter, here and elsewhere in his poem's seven stanzas (e.g., a second-syllable-accented "insteps" in the third line; trisyllabic "dazzling" in the last). The poem is yet admirable. I track its sequence in my adaptation, "Epiphany" (§144, p. 258), with occasionally borrowed phrasing.

§44 (94D) Quoted by Antigonus of Carystus. Antigonus explains that when male halcyons grow old and can no longer fly, they are borne on the wings of the female birds. So Alcman, weak with age, and no longer able to join in the maidens' dance, wishes to be borne aloft.

> Maidens with honey tones
> and voices of desire,
> my limbs no more can
> carry me. Ah, but to be
> above the flowering wave—
> a halcyon, a fearless flier
> aloft on wingèd span,
> a sprightly bird blue as the sea.

honey tones, voices of desire: Gr. *meligarues*, (*h*)*iarophonoi*, the compound adjectives translated by each of the two English phrases.
blue as the sea: Gr. (*h*)*aliporphuros*, also a compound adjective, used in the *Odyssey* of purple wool and robes (see also §§48, 60).

§45 (58D) Quoted by Apollonius the Sophist to show that Alcman used the word *knōdalon* 'seamonster'. The theme of the sleep of nature, while common in Greek literature, is rarely described in such detail. If, as commentators suggest, a contrast is intended between the peaceful sleep of nature and, e.g., the poet's feverish love, the piece may have developed similarly to §91. The visual quality of Alcman's description has been elaborated as follows:

> We travel down from the mountain peaks, step by step, via the river beds to the foothill promontories and gulfs at the seacoast; the animal world is broken down and shown in detail, from a general picture to animals of the mountains, creatures of the lower slopes and of the sea, all beneath the birds of the air. It is a conducted tour, of whose progress one might almost draw a picture [Dawson, 60].

◆

Mountain peaks and gullies sleep,
ravines and headlands silence keep,
sleep forests and each quadruped
that dusky earth has ever bred,
sleep mountain breasts and swarming bees,
monsters in blue-chasmed seas,
birds that soar on wingèd spread.

§46 (1P) *Partheneion* (*Maiden Song*) The poem is preserved on papyrus datable to the mid-first century AD, and was first published in 1863. The papyrus was discovered in 1855 by a French Egyptologist at Saqqara, the burial ground serving as necropolis of the city of Memphis. For the Greek text, see Page, 1951. The poem's pervasive textual uncertainties do not warrant another translation. Those here provided are by Mary Lefkowitz and Gloria Ferrari. The first is a polished prose version; the second, a line-by-line translation. As concerns the poem's setting,

> A chorus of young girls describe themselves and their ceremonial role in a special song. . . . Emphasis on the beauty of face and hair suggests that they are involved in a ritual that marks the transition (hence perhaps the references to battle) from girlhood to womanhood: the running of races is also a feature of puberty rites. . . . Comparison to horses may suggest the imminence of marriage, which is often described in metaphors of taming and yoking [Lefkowitz (1982), 119; see also §51].

◆

(Mary R. Lefkowitz, 1982, 119)

I sing of Agido's light. I see her as the sun; Agido calls him to testify to us that he is shining. But our famous leader will not let me either praise or criticize her; for our leader seems to us to be supreme, as if one set a horse among the herds, strong, prize-winning, with thundering hooves— a horse of the world of dreams.

And don't you see: the race-horse is Venetic; but my cousin Hagesichora's hair blooms like unmixed gold. And her silver face—why should

I spell it out? Here is Hagesichora. And she who is second to Agido in looks, runs like a Colaxian horse to an Ibenian. For the Doves bring the robe to the Goddess of the Dawn for us; they rise like the dog star through the immortal night and fight for us.

There is not enough purple to protect us, nor jewelled snake of solid gold, nor Lydian cap-adornment of girls with their dark eyes; nor Nanno's hair, no nor Areta who is like the gods; not Sylakis and Cleeisera. You wouldn't go to Aenesimbrota's house and say: let me have Astaphis; may Philylla look at me, and lovely Damareta and Vianthemis—no, it's Hagesichora who excites me.

For Hagesichora of the fair ankles is near her; close to Agido . . . she praises our festival. Yes, gods, receive [their prayer]. From the gods [come] accomplishment and fulfilment. Leader, I could say—a young girl that I am; I shriek in vain from my roof like an owl, and I will say what will please Dawn most, for she has been healer of our troubles; but it is through Hagesichora that girls have reached the peace they long for . . .

◆

(Gloria Ferrari, 2008, 155–157)

   . . . I sing
the light of Agido. I see it
like the sun, whom
Agido summons to appear and
witness for us. But the glorious chorus mistress
forbids me to either praise
or blame her. For she appears to be
outstanding as if
  one placed among a grazing herd
a perfect horse, a prize-winner with resounding hooves,
  one of the dreams that dwell below the rock.

Don't you see? That one is an Enetic
courser, while the mane
of my cousin
Hagesichora shines forth
like unalloyed gold.
Her face is of silver,
Why do I tell you explicitly?
There is Hagesichora herself.

Next will run Agido, her appearance
that of a Colaxian horse following an Ibenian.
For against us the Pleiades contend
   at daybreak, carried aloft
like Sirius across immortal Night,
   as we bring the season of the plow.
For surfeit of purple
does not help,
nor chased golden
snake-bracelet, nor Lydian
tiara, pride
of violet-eyed maids,
nor Nanno's tresses,
not even godlike Areta
or Thylacis and Cleesithera,
nor will you go to Ainesimbrota's house and say:
"let Astaphis stand by me,
   and let Philylla and Damareta
and lovely Hianthemis look upon me,
   but Hagesichora effaces me."

Nor does Hagesichora
of the beautiful ankles remain in place
to Agido. . .
and lauds our festival.
But [
accept. To the gods belong the fulfillment
and the end. Mistress of the chorus
I would say I myself
a maiden wail in vain from the sky,
an owl. But most of all I long
to please Aotis for she is ever
   the healer of our labors.
Away from Hagesichora, maidens
   enter upon delightful peace.
To the trace-horse
in the same way
to the steerman must
on a ship too [
the song of the Sirens
indeed more harmonious,
for they are goddesses, instead of [eleven]
children ten [

143

sings . . . on the streams of Xanthus
the swan. She of the lovely golden hair
[
[
[
   [

ANACREON

§47 (37G) Quoted by Clement of Alexandria.

Exquisite Eros I'll not neglect,
I'll praise him, garlanded, flower-decked,
who over gods maintains his sway,
as over creatures of a day.

Exquisite Eros: See §§3, 26.
who over gods: See *Th.* 120–124.

§48 (25G) Quoted by Hephaistion. This vivid description of love's assault
derives from *Od.* 9.391–393: "As when a smith plunges an axe or an adz,
hissing greatly, in cold water, and tempers it—for therein is the strength of
iron . . . ." Few images could better convey the rigors of Love. The burning
lover is first hammered into submission, forced to yield will and substance
beneath Love's incessant pounding. But a renewed and better-tempered
substance emerges after he is plunged, as if baptismally, into freezing tor-
rents. The power of the image has been either understated or misunder-
stood: "Love has struck Anacreon a nasty blow and left him in trouble . . .
Anacreon is not killed [as an ox struck by a similar blow at *Od.* 3.442–450],
but he sees himself as at least stunned" (Bowra, 290).

Like a smith—
again Love strikes the hammer's blow,
plunging me
in winter's torrent as I glow.

§49 (46G) Quoted by Hephaistion.

> Again do I love, again love not,
> this moment sane, the next distraught.

Compare Catullus, Poem 85.

> Odi et amo. Quare id faciam fortasse requiris.
> nescio, sed fieri sentio et excrucior.

> I love and I hate. Wherefore you might inquire.
> I know not, but feel it, tormented entire.

§50 (13G) This complete poem is quoted by Athenaeus (13.599c) apropos of the untenable view that Sappho and Anacreon were contemporaries: "Chamaeleon in his *Concerning Sappho* declares that, according to some, Sappho was the subject of Anacreon's verses 'Again . . . agree.'" Athenaeus then quotes, to disclaim, Sappho's supposed reply. This is the only archaic text showing an express link between Lesbos and homosexuality.

> Again tossing his purple ball my way
> blond Eros strikes calling me out to play
> with a gaily sandaled girl.
> But she's of Lesbian pedigree
> and won't have any part of me
> because my hair is grey,
> and gapes that some other girl agree.

Again tossing: For the repeated assaults of love, see §§1, 18, 36, 46–48, 67. It is possible that Anacreon's repeated use of the word, unlike Sappho's, indicates a certain lack of seriousness (cf. §65).

purple ball: Eros in later literature is depicted as a ballplayer. The ball is at times associated with the lover's heart as it is associated with the apple (see Gerber, 229–230, and §3).

purple / blond / gaily: The three adjectives in consecutive verses strike a vivid color contrast with the poet's gray hair in the final line (cf. §§68–70).

calling me . . . play: The play, here as elsewhere, is amorous (cf. §60).

with a gaily sandaled girl: For the erotic significance of feet (fascination and fixation) in antiquity, see §43 and Glenn, 113–116.

But she's of Lesbian pedigreee: lit., "But she is from well-built Lesbos." The term "well-built" is used in epic of fine or impressive cities, though its use here is mock-heroic. The present rendering emphasizes the girl's cosmopolitan credentials.

gapes that some other girl agree: Gr. *chaskei* (Eng., chasm) shares a coarseness with its translation "gapes," indicating eager anticipation and a certain overall lack of refinement. Only here does the Greek word appear in an amatory context. The phrase is literally rendered, "gapes toward another" (in hopes of a response). "Another" is feminine singular, indicating, without the use of "girl" in Greek, the gender of the person in question (so also §1, *etheloisa* 'wanting'). According to other more sexually "protective" interpretations, the girl, gaping toward *another head of hair*—i.e., a younger man, not another female—is heterosexually inclined (see Woodbury, 277–287; cf. Gomme, 259, n. 13; Dover, 183).

§51 (78G) Quoted by Heraclitus as an example of allegory: "Anacreon, abusing the meretricious spirit and arrogance of a haughty woman, used the allegory of a horse to describe her frisky disposition." The poem, apparently complete, has a light-hearted air and charms by the aptitude of its risqué metaphor. As concerns the poem's place in Greek poetry:

> This strikes a new note in Greek poetry; for it is both lyrical and witty, both passionate and fanciful. . . . The comparison of the girl with a filly recalls Alcman's treatment of Hagesichora and her friends [§46] but the skill and precision with which the image is developed and completed shows that Anacreon has found his own individual voice. The wit comes in the amatory undertones . . . he faces the facts, and smiles while he sings of his desire, and a note of sly mockery is audible among words which are perfectly apt and delicate. . . . Anacreon enjoys the situation and knows that others will enjoy it too. His head understands his heart, but refuses to make too many overt concessions to it [Bowra, 272].

◆

Thracian filly, why cast sidelong glances,
why flee as if I'd lost my senses?

> I could easily bridle your head in place,
> rein you in, run you round the race.
>
> now grazing in meadows you lightly skip
> with no nimble horseman to hug your hip.

Thracian filly: Thrace, in northeastern Greece, is associated with what is wild, unsubdued (cf. §93). Thracian horses were famous from Homer's time onward. For references in ancient literature, see Campbell, 328–329, Gerber, 236–237. Hesychius glosses "filly" as "courtesan."
you lightly skip: lit., "lightly skipping you play." For the erotic connotation of "play," see §48.
hug your hip: lit., "mount you," with the same connotation in Greek as in English. The association between women and horses would develop more sinister connotations (see Chadwick, 95–97).

§52 (22G) Quoted by Maximus of Tyre.

> Boys by my words would be disarmed,
> what I say, what I sing is charmed.

§53 (15G) Quoted by Athenaeus (13.564d) to illustrate the attention given by lovers to the eyes of their beloved.

> Lad with the maiden's glance,
> I wish only to have you near;
> you give me not a chance—
> my soul's unwitting charioteer.

my soul's . . . charioteer: lit., "not knowing you drive the chariot of my soul," the metaphor nicely realized as the last word of the stanza (cf. §96).

§54 (83G) Quoted by a scholiast to Aristophanes's *Birds*. Anacreon proposes to remedy a young boy's rejection of his advances by appealing directly to Eros.

> To Olympus I wing my fragile way
> to plead with Eros there,

that a lad no longer will delay
his youth with me to share.

§55 (96G) Quoted several times by Athenaeus (14.634a, 635c), vis-à-vis
the precise type of lyre designated by the rare Gr. *magis*.

I pluck this lyre's twenty strings;
Ah, Leucaspis,
each with your youthful freshness sings.

§56 (96G) Preserved on papyrus, four fragmentary stanzas in the Greek.
The "Cyprian" refers to Aphrodite, associated by birth with the island of
Cyprus. The opening vocative phrase "O most beautifully-visaged of chil-
dren" leaves the gender in question, as do the subsequent Greek pronouns.
The poem's extant lines fall into three stages: the child's shy restricted life
at home, his discovery of Aphrodite, and his appearance in public (Bowra,
289). For the erotic significance of horses and meadows, see §§3, 51, 53.

O lad with the lovely face,
another's look makes your heart race.
Your caring mother thinks that she

at home will nurse you constantly,
but you [   ] the meadows
of hyacinth, where the Cyprian

tethers her horses after they're run.
In the midst [   ] you darted down
setting hearts astir throughout the town.

but you . . . they've run: In introducing the meadows of hyacinth, Anacreon
does yet more strikingly what he does in making Eros a blond ball-tossing
youth (§48). He gives substance to a state of mind by making it entirely
visual and concrete and enriching it with mythic associations, i.e., "the
Cyprian," referencing the birth of Aphrodite onto the island of Cyprus
(Bowra, 288–289). The meadow—green, lush, expansive—is symbolic of
desire's awakening (cf. §90).

In the midst . . . darted: The Greek verb "to dart" often appears in Homer
to convey the rapidity of a god's movement, especially when proceeding

from Olympus to Earth. The sense of the first and third stanzas appears to be that the boy's heart beats quickly, i.e., is affrighted, at the awe-filled expressions that his beauty—unbeknownst to him—occasions in the on-looker. But when the boy darts through the streets, oblivious to those he passes, it is the townsfolk whose hearts race. The admiration of a beautiful youth could well have aroused city-wide, not merely personal, admiration (see Robinson and Fluck, 3).

§57 (19G) Quoted by Athenaeus (15.671d). Anacreon takes pride in the part played by Megistes in the worship of Dionysus, whose cult may have been the concern of boys reaching puberty (Bowra, 277).

> The season comes round;
> Megistes, warm of heart,
> is willow-crowned,
> with honeyed wine assumes his part.

the season comes round: lit., "(it is) ten months since."

§58 (99G) Quoted in the *Etymolgicum Magnum*.

> I hate all who rant
> and are given to riot.
> Megistes, you grant
> the repose of the quiet.

I hate ... the quiet: lit., "I hate all who have underground and difficult manners. I have learned that you, O Megistes, are *of those who do not play the Bacchant.*" Gr. **tōn** ('of those') **abach**idzomenōn (**a** 'not', **bachidzō** 'act like Bacchus'); thus, "of those Bacchusizing" (the Greek verb a genitive plural participle). The lines are cited for the occurrence of the word. The Bacchants were the frenzied followers of Dionysus, also known as Bacchus.

§59 (43G) Quoted by the scholiast on Pindar's *Olympian* 7 to illustrate the meaning of Gr. *propinō* 'extend, yield, surrender, bestow'.

>] but extend
> Your tender thigh, my friend.

§60 (28G) Quoted by Athenaeus (9.396d) and others apropos of whether the female deer has horns. Making the mother horned, Anacreon perhaps intends to indicate she is formidable. The issue is not one of zoological precision, however, but of the gentle shyness of a fawn-like boy (Bowra, 294).

> Gently, like a suckling fawn, newborn,
> affrighted in the wood—
> antlered mother gone, and he forlorn.

§61 (76G) Quoted by a scholiast to Sophocles's *Antigone* in explanation of the verb "quivered." A single verse in Greek.

> In dark-leafed bay
> and green olive
> he quivered.

§62 (14G) Quoted by Dio Chrysostom on the unseemliness of a king's calling on a god, as does Anacreon.

> Master, with whom rosy Aphrodite,
> blue-eyed nymphs and conquering Eros play,
> whose mountainous empery
> enthrones you over all that you survey,
> I beseech you: come well disposed to me,
> kind-hearted, attentive, as I pray
> Kleoboulos be well advised
> and the love I bear him not despised.

Master, with whom: The divinity is Dionysus, named in the last verse of the Greek.

whom rosy Aphrodite: Gr. *porphuree* 'purple', the same Greek word as in §50. The appropriateness of the word to Aphrodite is variously explained. She is rosy because of the glow that shines from her (Bowra, 284); the adjective "is spoken in reference to the goddess or her garment which shines as a rainbow with different colors" (Gentili, 13); the word may suggest radiance or dazzle (Gerber, 228). The Greek word is frequent in descriptions of the sea and has thus occasioned interpretation vis-à-vis Aphrodite's birth from the sea (see §§1, 3, 25, 43). Otherwise, Anacreon "imagines the god with his joyous company and . . . makes them vivid not by the stock epithets derived from epic but by new epithets of his own minting" (Bowra, 283). For the association of Aphrodite and Dionysus, see Euripides, *Bacchae* 402–416, and the commentary by Dodds (1960). The Nymphs were Dionysus's nurses.

play: See §§48, 50, 51.

Kleoboulos be well advised: lit., "be a good counselor [Gr. *sumboulos*] to *kleo-boulos*." The wordplay suggests a light tone as Anacreon implores Dionysus's help in winning over Kleoboulos, i.e., that a drunken Kleoboulos yield to the poet's advances.

§63 (5G) Quoted by Herodian to illustrate the figure of speech *poluptoton* 'much falling', i.e., the name *Kleoboulos* repeated, or falling, in different grammatical cases. Cf. Tennyson, *Maud* I, 672: "My own heart's heart, my ownest own, farewell."

> Kleoboulos I adore
> for Kleoboulos I rage
> on Kleoboulos I gaze.

I gaze: Gr. *dioskeō*, a rare verb, explained by Hesychius: "*to gaze*: to look continuously, not altering one's glance. [The word] is used of being swept away in body and soul."

§64 (33G) Quoted by Athenaeus (10.427a) to illustrate the proportion for mixing wine and water. The mixture here is weak by any standard (elsewhere Alcaeus calls for 1:2, a blend four times as potent) and indicates the poet's sense of decorum, even when reveling. Despite moderate drinking, the symposium seems to have gotten out of hand in the last four lines. Giving unmixed wine to the Cyclops, Odysseus gets the Cyclops drunk, blinds him, and escapes with his own men.

> Come, my lad, let the ladle abound
> whose fifteen fathoms no thirst can sound;
> ten measures of water, five of wine,
> reveling yet would I walk a straight line.
>
> Come, again, no longer let us pour
> amid the din's riotous uproar;

no, let us intone sweet hymns instead,
raising our cups as men well bred.

§65 (56G) Quoted by Athenaeus (11.463a) to indicate the correct conduct at a symposium. The translation expands on the four lines of the original.

I do not like the speakers
of strife and tearful war
whenever festive beakers
are filled and hold no more;

I'd rather one who mixes
sweet gifts of love and song
and, wistful, reminisces
of good times all night long.

§66 (38, 65G) Quoted by Athenaeus (11.782a) as evidence that the ancients, when mixing wine, poured water into the bowl first. Demetrius notes that the poem's rhythm is precisely that of a drunkard. As both concerns are remote for readers today, attention focuses on the playfulness of "going a round" with Eros, highlighted by Anacreon's use of the Gr. *puktalizō* in place of the more usual *pukteuō* 'to box'. The same image is used with greater power and solemnity by Sophocles, *Women of Trachis*, 441–442: "Whoever stands up to Eros for a round of fisticuffs has lost his wits" (see further Bowra, 293). That Anacreon did not always leave the ring unscathed is evident from the rejoinder—*I who sparred.*

Bring water, bring wine, my boy,
flowered necklaces bring,
with Love would I enter the ring.

◆

I who sparred so painfully
can finally lift my head and see.

§67 (111G) Quoted by a scholiast on *Il.* 23.88, where the same word *dice* occurs. Eros and the equally young and attractive Ganymede (seized by Zeus to be his "cupbearer") are depicted at play with dice, or knucklebones, by Apollonius of Rhodes and by one Asclepiades in a poem (12.46) pre-served in the *Palatine Anthology* (see Klein). The last word of the poem is Gr. *kudoimoi* 'din of battle, uproar'. The elevated diction thus adds a mock-heroic tone. This touch, combined with the playful meter and frivolous dice imagery, shows how little Anacreon took love's anguish seriously (Campbell, 327).

> Love's dice, fully loaded for
> derangement and din of war.

§68 (108G) Quoted by Athenaeus (10.433ef). Spoken to a woman (*generous* feminine in the Greek).

> Generous to passers-by,
> Let one drink who's languished dry.

§69 (94G) Quoted by Hephaistion. See *TLL*, Chapter 4, for discussion.

> Drunk with love,
> again, up the Leucadian cliff I go
> and leap to the pallid brine below.

Drunk with love: Since Euripides's Cyclops also jumps drunk from the Leucadian cliff (*Cyclops* 166–167), "those who made the leap sometimes comforted or steeled themselves first with drink, and Anacreon may have made use of the idea for his own purpose" (Bowra, 290).
Leucadian cliff: To leap from the high rock on the island's southern tip was to cure unrequited love or, if you survived, to win over a recalcitrant lover (Gerber, 232). There is further a "sexual element inherent in the motif of a white rock" and a latent motif of sexual relief through jumping. See Nagy (1973), 146 (noting the opposite in §54 as symbolic of sexual frustration).

§70 (84G) The restoration is by the nineteenth-century German philolo-gist Theodor Bergk from a prose statement quoted in Lucian.

> Love who has seen my chin grow white
> wings past gold-gilded in his flight.

§71 (74G) Quoted by Hephaistion. The addressee might be a goddess (Gentile, 55), the epithet "gowned in gold" elsewhere used of goddesses.

> Listen to me who am old
> fair-haired maiden, gowned in gold.

§72 (36G) Quoted by Stobaeus. Being of sober bent, Stobaeus considered this the only one of Anacreon's poems worthy of inclusion in his anthology. For Stobaeus and Sappho, see *TLL* 204–205, 406.

> Temples already white,
> gray thinning hair now slight,
> graceless my agèd plight,
> my teeth have lost their bite.
> Of life all but bereft,
> brief is the sweet time left.
>
> This then do I lament
> by dread of Hades rent:
> death is a horrid pit,
> hard the path down to it.
> Descend, and that descent
> is fully infinite.

Commentators, noting the idea is commonplace, do not give Virgil's adaptation its due.

> ... facilis descensus Averno:
> noctes atque dies patet atri ianua Ditis;
> sed revocare gradum superasque evadere ad auras,
> hoc opus, hic labor est.

> ... easy the descent to Hell:
> All night and day its gates unfastened dwell,
> But return regaining the upper air—
> There's the task, therein despair.

Aen. 6.126–129

Artwork

Plate 1. Gian Lorenzo Bernini, *The Ecstasy of Saint Teresa* (1647–1652)

Plate 2. Anne-Louis Girodet de Roussy-Trioson, *The Sleep of Endymion* (1791)

Plate 3. François Auguste Rodin, *The Hand of God* (1907)

Plate 4. Artemisia Gentileschi, *Judith Slaying Holofernes* (1614)

Plate 5. Artemisia Gentileschi, *Susanna and the Elders* (1610)

Plate 6. Alessandro Allori, *Susanna and the Elders* (1561)

Plate 7. Tintoretto, *Susanna and the Elders* (1555)

Plate 8. Artemisia Gentileschi, *Aurora* (c. 1627)

Plate 9. Antoine Watteau, *The Remedy* (1717)

Plate 10. Henri de Gervex, *Rolla* (1878)

Plate 11. Sarah Fischer Ames, *Abraham Lincoln* (1868)

Plate 12. Vinnie Ream Hoxie, *Abraham Lincoln* (1871)

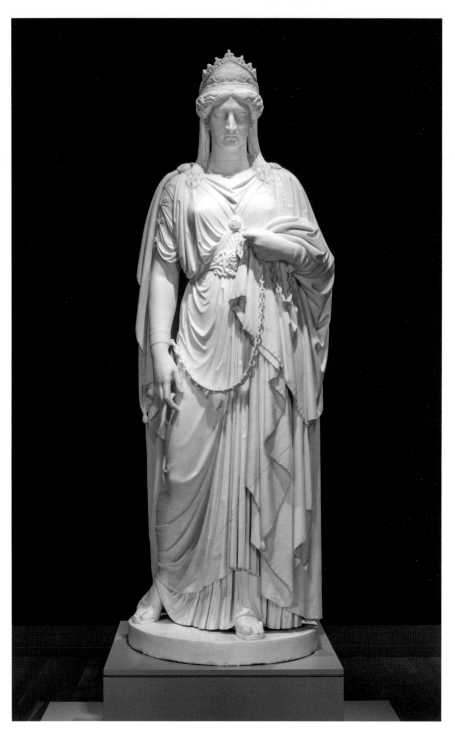

Plate 13. Harriet Goodhue Hosmer, *Zenobia in Chains* (1859)

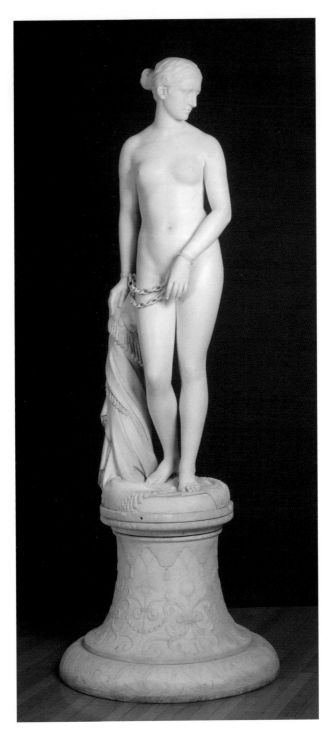

Plate 14. Hiram Powers, *The Greek Slave* (1843)

Plate 15. Harriet Whitney Frismuth, *The Vine* (1923)

Plate 16. John Bell, *The American Slave* (1853)

Plate 17. Frederick Hart, *Creation of Mankind* (1982)

Plate 18. Michelangelo, *Vittoria Colonna* (1540)

Plate 19. Michelangelo, *Giuliano de' Medici* (1553)

Plate 20. Paul Emile Chabas, *September Morn* (1911)

ARCHILOCHUS

❧

§73 (203T) Quoted by Stobaeus.

> I lie wretched, alone,
> lifeless, pierced to the bone,
> mercilessly pained,
> thus the gods have ordained.

§74 (197T) Quoted by Stobaeus.

> By love's desire fast possessed,
> eyes misted, faint, at Love's behest,
> frail spirit stolen from my breast.

eyes misted ... behest: The "misting" of one's eyes is a frequent element in Homeric descriptions of death (cf. §2).

§75 (212T) Quoted by Hephaistion (cf. §36).

> But desire, dissolving my limbs,
> undoes me, my friend.

§76 (111T) Quoted by Plutarch apropos of the formulation for beginning a prayer ("If only I might ..."). That this might be a lover's wish places the poet's feeling toward Neoboulē at variance with that in the following section. Alternatively, the words might express the rejected poet's animus: "Might my hand but lay hold of Neoboulē!" As such, the words suggest "violent revenge or even a savage violation, akin to the coarse and vigorous lines [§90] in the same meter" (Kirkwood, 41).

> Ah, could I but touch Neoboulē's hand ...

§77 (196aW) The longest-surviving fragment of poetry attributed to Archilochus—a poet otherwise only scantily preserved—the work survives on a first- or second-century AD papyrus discovered in the 1960s amid mummy wrappings from the Abusir el-Melek cemetery at the Faiyum Oasis (west of the Nile, just south of Cairo). As the mummy was then held at the University of Cologne, the poem is sometimes called the "Cologne Epode." The poem begins with a dialogue between the poet and an unidentified maiden, perhaps the sister of Neoboulē. It ends with a negotiated erotic consummation—a compromise, as it were. The poem is unique in theme and meter in ancient Greek poetry. First published in 1974, it generated a storm of controversy, most of it focusing on the final verses and nature of the consummation described—though what happens is surely clear enough. On Neoboulē and the conventions of invective poetry, see pp. 4–5.

As the poem opens (following the loss of an undeterminable number of lines), a young girl urges restraint in the face of a would-be lover's advances. Her reluctance seems prompted by the fact that the proposed "sex here and now" includes no plan of marriage. She thus urges his affections on Neoboulē, perhaps her older sister, as one more suited to his designs. "What the girl must be saying, albeit indirectly, is that she herself is willing to be seduced if her seducer first promises marriage. By mentioning another maiden, the girl obliquely offers herself under what she considers the best obtainable conditions" (see Henderson [in Van Sickle, ed.]).

The alternative girl is expectedly unacceptable. The man reverently invokes the young girl's departed mother, as if to suggest that the mother's high ideals ("no sex without marriage") are buried with her. The girl must decide things for herself. In the most enigmatic formulation of the poem (line 13), the man offers a compromise in the form of "a joy aside from [i.e., just outside of] the divine"—an activity which will allow for his sexual release without her violation, an activity brought to completion in the closing lines.

> ". . . totally keeping yourself,
> and in like fashion I'll forbear.
> But if you are so very spurred,
> with bed to all things else preferred,
> we have at home a girl quite fair,
> now most desiring to be wed;
> her looks are quite beyond compare."
> So much she spoke, and this I said:
>
> "Daughter of Amphimedo
> —a knowing mother nobly bred—

whom now dank earth conceals below,
many joys does the goddess grant
young men, aside from the divine;
of these some one will do just fine.
We'll better know the one we want
in parlance hushed, god-sped, lights low.
As you urge, so shall I go.
You think me eager, in a rush?
But by the gated portico
—don't be begrudging, don't say no—
I'll put in where the grass is lush.
Neoboulē!? The likes of such
consign to someone else's bed.
She's overripe, flower-fresh no more,
with grace of girlhood long since shed.
Ever short of what she's lusting for,
she's shown it all, the girl's a whore!

"To hell with her, and far from me!
May never ruler Zeus decree
that I, possessed of such a cur,
become a neighbor's mockery.
It's you whom I do most prefer,
you're not a two-faced liar like her.
She, in a word, is too severe,
and many the man whom she holds 'dear.'
'Haste makes waste,' as often said,
avoid what ill you know is near."

I spoke, she followed as I led
to flowers, where I urged our rest.
Enfolded by my cloak outspread
(my hand positioned neath her head),
she hindered trembling like a fawn,
though I, undaunted, urged her on
and gently took hold of her breast.
Soon after was she all undressed—
Such maiden's charm in that fair skin
I scarce knew where I should begin—
I reconnoitered all her frame
released all my force and fell tame,
just touching on the tawny hair . . .

§78 (109T) Quoted by Athenaeus (10.433e) (cf. §68).

> With you love's battles to engage,
> battle as drink when thirst does rage.

§79 (190T) Quoted by Plutarch.

> Such did she conspire:
> in one hand water; the other, fire.

§80 (1T) Quoted by Athenaeus (14.627c) as evidence of the poet's equal emphasis on civic and poetic activities. There is novelty in the theme: "In the Epic, a man may be as good in speech as in action (*Il.* 9.443), and a great warrior might pass the time singing a song (*Il.* 9.189), but it is inconceivable that the same man could be both soldier and poet. . . . A social revolution is epitomized in this couplet" (Page, 134). Further, "By pairing the two traditionally separate activities, Archilochus is asserting a new role in society, characteristic of the century that followed him and played both by the elegist-politician Solon and by the lyricist-politician Alcaeus—a role that makes the man of the Muses no longer the onlooker" (Kirkwood, 310).

> Enyalius, lord of battles, I attend;
> the Muses' lovely gift I also comprehend.

Enyalius: As in Homer, largely synonymous with Ares, the god of war. Enyalius is considered a son of Ares by the goddess Enyo, herself a war goddess generally synonymous with the goddess Eris 'Strife'. Enyo is often associated with the destruction of cities.

§81 (2T) Quoted by Athenaeus (1.30f). A good soldier's vigilance knows no unpreparedness. The couplet has occasioned various interpretations, depending on the meaning of the thrice-repeated Gr. *en dori* 'in my spear', e.g., "equipped with my spear," or "in or on a tree," or "in my ship" (the Greek root: *tree stem*—hence "shaft, plank, ship"). According to the interpretation based on "in my spear" ("In my spear is my bread, in my spear is my wine," etc.), the poet depends on his weapon for the basics of existence. This is unlikely—not so much for grammatical reasons as for the lack of parallel to wine and bread as the stated objectives of a soldier's fighting. Soldiers fight for *kleos* 'fame'. And while they cannot fight on an empty stomach (*Il.* 19.154–174), the source of their "daily bread" goes unemphasized. Be that as it may, Archilochus likely did not intend *en dori* identically in all three instances. Verbal play may have motivated the Greek couplet.

> I knead my bread with spear in hand,
> pour my wine with spear in hand,
> drinking aside my spear I stand.

§82 (96T) Quoted by Dio Chrysostom. Four verses in the Greek. The poet will have no part of a foppish or affected commander. We here have a soldier's heartfelt commendation of authority rooted in manly camaraderie.

> I hate the general, heavyset,
> standing feet spread wide,
> who most about his beard does fret,
> whose hairdo is his pride;
> I rather one who's spare and smart,
> who walks firm-footed, full of heart.

§83 (105T) Quoted by Stobaeus. One of the more expansive examples of self-exhortation in archaic poetry (see, e.g., *Il.* 22.98; *Od.* 5.407, 20.18). From line 2 ("bearing your chest") onward, the poet transforms his heart (Gr. *thumos*) from the seat of emotion to the individual winner or loser *having* emotion. Moreover, *thumos* in Homer refers to either the emotions, will, or intellect. "Here, however, the meanings implied by *thumos* shift three times—from heart (as seat of emotions), to spirit or courage, to heart again, and finally to mind or soul (as seat of thought)" (Rubin, 6–7).

> Heart, heart, overwhelmed with confusion past cure,
> to adversities bearing yourself, endure.
> Stand safely aside from the snare of a foe,
> don't in victory overexultant grow,
> nor bested, indoors bemoan your overthrow.
> Temper triumph, be not grieving overwrought,
> comprehending the rhythm of mankind's lot.

§84 (8T) Compiled from quotations in several authors; often referred to and imitated. Other famous poets who threw away their shields include Anacreon, Alcaeus, and Horace. It is aptly observed that "the flippant attitude toward warfare revealed in this famous fragment stands in stark contrast to the epic and the Spartan concept of valor which demanded that a warrior return from battle either with his shield or on it" (Gerber, 15).

> In my shield does some Thracian now rejoice,
> which, flawless, I jettisoned, having no choice,
> were I to escape alive. Let it go to Hell!
> Another will serve me just as well.

Let it go to Hell: Quite literally the meaning of Gr. *erreto*.
Another . . . just as well: lit., "I will again purchase one not worse."

§85 (102T) Quoted by Stobaeus. As in the preceding piece, the poet debunks an accepted notion, that glory is undying and worth dying for.

> Deference and fame depart the dead,
> dying is naught but dread;
> let life and living be sought instead.

§86 (16T) Quoted by Athenaeus (13.594d). Figs and fishing were the mainstays of Archilochus's poverty-stricken Paros. So fragment 87T: "Good riddance to Paros, and those figs, and the life of the sea." The fig, known for its cheapness, sometimes designates female genitalia (Aristophanes, *Peace* 1350).

> A fig tree on its rock, feeding many crows,
> accessible, loved by all, to all exposed.

accessible . . . all exposed: lit., "to all dear [Gr. *pasiphilē*], good-natured, receptive to strangers."

§87 (44T) Quoted by a scholiast on Aratus.

> Like a mating crow,
> pleasured, perching low,

> poised on a jutting peak,
> slack pinioned, sleek.

§88 (43T) Quoted in the *Etymologicum Magnum*.

> We have a sturdy ox at home,
> knows how to plow, need not be shown.

§89 (118T) Second verse quoted by Aelian (first verse a reconstruction).

> Gain gathered by long time and labor
> often flows down the gut of a whore.

§90 (112T) Quoted by a scholiast on Euripides's *Medea*. Sometimes thought the sequel to §76 (both in the same Greek meter).

> And on that skin, insatiable, alight,
> hurling belly on belly, thigh on thigh.

skin: Gr. *askos* 'wineskin'.
insatiable: Gr. *drēstēn* 'hardworking' (Gr. *draō* 'do, accomplish'). The word shows contempt and sexual ferocity; cf. "slavish bag" (Kirkwood, 41).

§91 (25, 26T) The first two verses are quoted by Ammonius; the last three (two in the Greek), by Synesius, who says the poet is praising a courtesan's hair. The two fragments are often taken consecutively.

> Her joy is a myrtle sprig
> and a lovely flowering rose,
> the long hair shades her
> shoulders and neck,
> all down her back it flows.

myrtle . . . rose: Symbols of Aphrodite which "would probably not be held so boldly by an entirely respectable maiden" (Rankin, 67; cf. Henderson [1975], 150).

§92 (27T) Preserved on papyrus.

Breast and fragrant hair
to seize an old man with despair.

to seize . . . despair: lit., "to make [him] fall in love."

IBYCUS

§**93 (6D)*** Quoted by Athenaeus (13.601bc) as an example of Ibycus's love poetry. The poem strikes a contrast between the serenity and regularity of spring and the determinedly random onslaughts of the poet's passion. For this and the following poem, see *TLL* xxv–xxix.

In spring the river streams bedew
the quinces in Cydonia,
where sacred stands the Maidens' grove
and shading bough vine-blossomed grows;
this love of mine no season knows
but races—northern Thracian blast
from Aphrodite's shrine outcast
ablaze with flash of lightning, black
with shameless fits of parching rage,
pain unrelenting, unassuaged.

river streams bedew: The rivers are led through the orchards in channels for irrigation.

quinces in Cydonia: The quince trees of Cydonia (northwest Crete) are related to the awakening of love. The lyric poet Stesichorus, writing of the wedding of Menelaus and Helen, describes the throwing of "many Cydonian 'apples'" (= quinces; cf. §3). Ibycus intends the quince as a familiar symbol of love that swells to ripeness as girls grow to maidenhood. More pointedly, "In early Spring, the beginning of the special season of love, the five sepals of each quince flower bend back from a remarkably firm bud, which is pointed, and at first less pink than brown. The bud swells and stands erect, opening to its rose-like shape of tender pink, each petal lightly netted and veined" (Grigson, 200).

sacred (or inviolate) . . . grove: The countryside nymphs are probably intend-ed. Euripides has the virginal Hippolytus offer Artemis a garland of flowers in just such a place (*Hippolytus* 73–78), symbolizing unsoiled innocence.

bough vine-blossomed grows: To quinces and inviolate enclosures, Ibycus adds budding vines with their association of youthful growth. He conveys the natural growth from innocence to love through the figure of grapes swelling to fullness. The first image (quinces) suggests the ripening of girlhood toward love; the second (inviolate meadows), the secure innocence in which it lives; the third (vine blossoms), the moment before it is ready for marriage (Bowra, 260–262).

this love . . . no season knows: lit., "my love is at no time asleep"; Gr. *kata-koitos* (only here), lit., *kata* 'down, down upon' + *koitos* 'bed' (*koitos* Latinized as Eng. *coitus*). To be *katakoitos* thus means to be or go 'down' onto a 'bed', i.e., be abed, asleep. Ibycus actually wishes to be "abed," but *not* asleep—his love never passively "abed," but wanting always to be "bedded." The sense is conveyed in my Petronius translation (§115, pp. 191–192): "but be just so, abed our holiday / thus bound, thus kissing the hours away."

northern Thracian blast: For love as a wind, see §35. Ancient writers considered the Thracians a primitive people consisting mainly of ferocious mountain tribes (cf. §51).

shameless . . . parching rage: In contrast to "river streams bedew."

pain unrelenting, unassuaged: lit., "it violently strikes me from the feet (up)."

§94 (7D) Parmenides, in the Platonic dialogue bearing his name (137a), paraphrases these verses, expressing his reluctance to embark on a lengthy exposition. The scholiast provides the actual poem, believed to be com-plete. The poet feels himself past the age for love and trembles at the prospect of once again being "harnessed." See also §53: "my soul's unwit-ting charioteer" and §122 (p. 246): "Love's glory day is past." No more capable of running love's course than resisting the yoke, he will be forced to stumble through love's paces. That the theme is commonplace with the lyric poets in no way detracts from Ibycus's unique expression of it.

> Love's melting look from eyes dark-browed
> has cast me into Cyprian chains
> unfailing, charmed in every wise.
> How I shake at his approach—
> as a horse once winner of the prize

in later years must bear the reins
and cart, unwilling, past the crowd.

Love's melting look: lit., "eyeing (me) meltingly." On the metaphoric "melt" of love that effaces autonomy, i.e., one's physical and personal borders, and melds two people, see *TLL* 415.

from eyes dark–browed: Compare Hesiod's description of the Graces: "Love flows from their gazing eyes, a limb-loosing love. And beguilingly they gaze from beneath their lids" (*Th.* 910–911).

into Cyprian chains: The chains (lit., "nets") of Aphrodite, the Cyprian goddess, are inescapable. Her boy, Eros, seduces the prey into them. On Aphrodite and Cyprus, see §§3, 25, 41, 56.

as a horse: See §§3, 54.

ADDENDUM

Noteworthy but sadly unknown Greek lyric translations from the late-nineteenth to mid-twentieth centuries.

§1 (above, etc.)

(T. G. Tucker)

Guile-weaving child of Zeus, who art
Immortal, throned in radiance, spare,
O Queen of Love, to break my heart
  With grief and care.

But hither come, as thou of old,
When my voice reached thine ear afar,
Didst leave thy father's hall of gold,
  And yoke thy car,

And through mid air their whirring wing
Thy bonny doves did swiftly ply
O'er the dark earth, and thee did bring
  Down from the sky.

Right soon they came, and thou, blest Queen,
A smile upon thy face divine,
Didst ask what ail'd me, what might mean
  That call of mine.

'What would'st thou have, with heart on fire,
Sappho?' thou saidst. 'Whom pray'st thou me
To win for thee to fond desire?
  Who wrongeth thee?

Soon shall he seek, who now doth shun;
Who scorns thy gifts, shall gifts bestow;
Who loves thee not, shall love anon,
  Wilt thou or no.'

So come thou now, and set me free
From carking cares; bring to full end
My heart's desire; thyself O be
  My stay and friend!

◆

(F. L. Lucas, in Sapphic meter)

Aphrodite, daughter of Zeus, undying
Goddess, throned in glory, of love's beguilements,
Do not now with frenzy and desperation
    Utterly crush me.

Hear and come!—if ever before Thou heardest
Cry of mine, that called from afar Thy succour;
Then, in haste, with chariot swiftly harnessed,
    Forth from the golden

Hall of Zeus, Thy father, to me Thou camest—
Then Thy lovely sparrows from Heaven swept Thee
O'er the dark-loamed earth, through the ether beating
    Swift wings together.

Fast they brought Thee hither; and Thou, most blessed,
With a smile of heavenly lips didst ask me,
What it was I suffered; and why I called Thee
    Hither to aid me.

'Tell me what it is, then, that most thou cravest,
Heart so full of madness?—who is it, Sappho,
Passion must awake to desire and love thee?
    Who is it wrongs thee?

'For, although she shun thee, she soon shall seek thee;
Though she scorn thy presents, herself shall bring them;
Though she love thee not, yet she soon shall love thee!—
    Yea, though she would not.'

Come again today, then, as once Thou camest.
Save my soul from sorrow, that grows too bitter—
Grant my heart's desiring—be Thou my helper,
    Thou, Aphrodite!

◆

(John Addington Symonds, in Sapphic meter)

Star-throned incorruptible Aphrodite,
Child of Zeus, wile-weaving, I supplicate thee,

Tame not me with pangs of the heart, dread mistress,
    Nay, nor with anguish.

But come thou, if erst in the days departed
Thou didst lend thine ear to my lamentation,
And from far, the house of thy sire deserting,
    Camest with golden

Car yoked: thee thy beautiful sparrows hurried
Swift with multitudinous pinions fluttering
Round black earth, adown from the height of heaven
    Through middle ether:

Quickly journey they; and, O thou, blest Lady,
Smiling with those brows of undying lustre,
Asked me what new grief at my heart lay, wherefore
    Now I had called thee,

What I fain would have to assuage the torment
Of my frenzied soul; and whom now, to please thee,
Must persuasion lure to thy love, and who now,
    Sappho, hath wronged thee?

Yea, for though she flies, she shall quickly chase thee;
Yea, though gifts she spurns, she shall soon bestow them;
Yea, though now she loves not, she soon shall love thee,
    Yea, though she will not!

Come, come now too! Come, and from heavy heart-ache
Free my soul, and all that my longing yearns to
Have done, do thou; be thou for me thyself too
    Help in the battle.

§2

(T. G. Tucker)

Blest as the gods, methinks, is he
Who sitteth face to face with thee
And hears thy sweet voice nigh,
Thy winsome laugh, whereat my heart
Doth in my bosom throb and start;

One glimpse of thee, and I
Am speechless, tongue-tied; subtle flame
Steals in a moment through my frame;
My ears ring; to mine eye
All's dark; a cold sweat breaks; all o'er
I tremble, pale as death; nay more,
I seem almost to die.

◆

(F. L. Lucas, in Sapphic meter)

Him I hold as happy as God in Heaven,
Who can sit and gaze on your face before him,
Who can sit and hear from your lips that sweetest
  Music they utter—

Hear your lovely laughter, that sets a-tremble
All my heart with flutterings wild as terror.
For, when I behold you an instant, straightway
  All my words fail me;

Helpless halts my tongue; a devouring fever
Runs in flame through every vein within me;
Darkness veils my vision; my ears are deafened,
  Beating like hammers;

Cold the sweat runs down me; a sudden trembling
Sets my limbs a-quiver; my face grows paler
Than the grass in summer; I see before me
  Death stand, and madness.

§3

(T. G. Tucker, 2nd stanza)

Through apple-boughs, with purling sound,
Cool waters creep;
From quivering leaves descends around
The dew of sleep.

§8

(F. L. Lucas, elaborated)

Atthis, our own loved Anactória
In Sardis dwells afar,
And yet, there too, of us her memories are;

Recalling other days—how once you were,
To her, divinely fair,
And with your song no singing could compare.
Now among Lydia's daughters that dear head
Shines, as when day is fled
The risen moon, with fingers rosy-red,

Outshines the stars, and flings her glory wide
Across the salt sea-tide,
Across the many-flowered countryside,

While fair her dew falls on the flowering rose,
And where soft anthrysc grows,
And where in bloom the melilotus blows.

Yet, Atthis, still of you her memories wake,
Where'er she goes, and make
That gentle heart grow heavy for your sake.

'Come back!' she cries. We know. For many be
The ears of Night; and She
Brings us that cry across the sundering sea.

§17

(T. G. Tucker)

On the top of the topmost spray
The pippin blushes red,
Forgot by the gatherers—nay!
Was it "forgot" we said?
'Twas too far overhead!

◆

(F. L. Lucas)

As the sweet apple reddens, high up against the sky,
High on the highest branch, where the pickers passed it by,
Forgetting—ah, no, not forgetting—they never could reach so
   high.

§18

(T. G. Tucker)

The hyacinth so sweet
On the hills where the herdsmen go
Is trampled 'neath their feet,
And its purple bloom laid low—

◆

(F. L. Lucas)

As the hyacinth high on the mountains under the shepherds'
   tread
Lies trampled, and to earthward bows down its purple head. . . .

§21

(F. L. Lucas)

All things thou bringest, Hesper, that the bright Dawn did
   part—
Sheep and goat to the fold, and the child to the mother's
   heart.

§27

(T. G. Tucker)

I have a maid, a bonny maid,
As dainty as the golden flowers,
My darling Cleis. Were I paid

All Lydia, and the lovely bowers
Of Cyprus, 'twould not buy my maid.

§34

(F. L. Lucas)

I cannot, sweetest mother,
My loom I cannot mind;
Delicate Aphrodite
With longing leaves me blind.

§38

(T. G. Tucker)

Sunk is the moon;
The Pleiades are set;
'Tis midnight; soon
The hour is past; and yet
I lie alone—

◆

(F. L. Lucas)

Moon's set, and Pleiads;
Midnight goes by;
The hours pass onward;
Lonely I lie.

◆

(A. E. Housman, *More Poems*, "XI," 1936)

The rainy Pleiads wester,
Orion Plunges prone,
The stroke of midnight ceases,
And I lie down alone.

The rainy Pleiads wester
And seek beyond the sea
The head that I shall dream of,
And 'twill not dream of me.

♦

(A. E. Housman, *More Poems*, "X," 1936)

The weeping Pleiads wester,
And the moon is under seas;
From bourn to bourn of midnight
Far sighs the rainy breeze;

It sighs from a lost country
To a land I have never known;
The weeping Pleiads wester
And I lie down alone.

§93

(F. L. Lucas)

Only in spring do the quince flowers quiver
Blossoming deep in the garden-close
Sacred to Maidenhood, where from the river
Many a quickening channel flows;
Only in spring do the vine flowers throng
Under the leaves; but all year long
No rest my passion knows.
Sent by the Cyprian (as from the north
Headlong the Thracian tempest breaks,
While from its gloom the lightnings shoot),
Raving it smites me in its wrath,
Shrivelling all—to the very root
My heart it shakes.

Part III

Selected Beuern Song Translations:
From *Carmina Burana*

W<small>E FOLLOW WITH SELECTIONS</small> from Carl Orff's ever engaging *Carmina Burana* (1937), their provenance explained in the Preface. Translation of the full work was originally prepared at the invitation of Conductor Robert Shaw (1916–1999) for the Atlanta Symphony Orchestra. The translation appeared as program notes both for ASO's concerts and subsequent recording for Telarc records.

This is a *literary*, not *literal*, translation. It is guided by two principles:

> I did not think it required to translate word for word, but have retained the spirit and force of the passage. For I saw it my duty not to count but weigh out the words for the reader.

> – CICERO, *De Optimo Genere Oratorum* (*On the Best Kind of Orators*), 4.14

> It is not [the translator's] business to translate Language into Language, but Poesie into Poesie.

> – SIR JOHN DENHAM, *The Destruction of Troy: an essay upon the second book of Virgils Aeneis, written in the year 1636*

Here, for comparison's sake, is a representative example, insofar as concerns *these* pieces, of literary versus literal translation. It is in every instance the poem's *spirit* that prevails, riotous or soulful, as the case may be.

§95

Original	Literary Translation	Literal Translation
O Fortuna	**O Fortune**	**O Fortune**
O Fortuna, velut luna	O Fortune, like the moon,	O Fortune, like the moon
Statu variabilis,	you ever wane,	you are changeable,
Semper crescis	but to regain	ever waxing
Aut decrescis;	your former circumstance;	and waning.
Vita detestabilis	life's equally fain	Hateful life,
Nunc obdurat	to decimate	first oppresses,
Et tunc curat	as reinstate the mind	and then soothes
Ludo mentis aciem,	with games of chance,	as joy overtakes it;
Egestatem,	prosperity	poverty
Potestatem	and penury	and power,
Dissoluit ut glaciem.	reversing with a glance.	it melts them like ice.
Sors immanis et inanis,	Immense and futile Fate,	Fate – monstrous and empty,
Rota tu volubilis,	uneasy ground,	you whirling wheel,
Status malus,	safety unsound,	you are malevolent,
Vana salus	mistakenly awaited,	well-being is in vain and eventually
Sempter dissolubilis,	to your wheel I'm bound;	fades to nothing,
Obumbrata	you've hidden your face	shadowed
Et velata	denied your grace,	and veiled
Mihi quoque niteris,	for sorrow was I slated;	you plague me too;
Nunc per ludum	I've lost the knack,	now, through the game
Dorsum nudum	this barren back	I bring my bare back
Fero tui sceleris.	shows what you've perpetrated.	to your villainy.
In taberna quando sumus	**When we are in the tavern**	**When we are in the tavern**
In taberna quando sumus,	When we order up a round,	When we are in the tavern,
Non curamus quid sit humus,	we disavow six feet of ground,	we do not think how we will go to dust,
Sed ad ludum properamus,	but rush to gaming, place our bet,	but we hurry to gamble,
Cui semper insudamus.	at this you'll find us in a sweat.	which always makes us sweat.
Quid agatur in taberna,	What goes on here in the pub	What happens in the tavern,
Ubi nummus est pincerna,	amid the coin and chug-a-lug,	where money is host,
Hoc est opus ut queratur	be this the scene that you seek out,	you may well ask,
Si quid loquar, audiatur.	it's this that I would speak about.	and hear what I say.
Quidam ludunt, quidam bibunt,	One and all they drink and game,	Some gamble, some drink,
Quidam indiscrete vivunt.	they live a life that knows no shame,	some behave loosely.
Sed in ludo qui morantur	those who trust in a gambler's knack	But of those who gamble,
Ex his quidam denudantur,	depart the game with a barren back.	some are stripped bare,
Quidam ibi vestiuntur.	Some leave the premises very well heeled,	some win their clothes here,
Quidam saccis induuntur.	others leave naked in sack cloth concealed.	some are dressed in sacks.
Ibi nullus timet mortem,	No one there of death thinks twice,	Here no one fears death, but they
Sed pro Baccho mittunt sortem.	when for the drinks they roll the dice.	throw the dice in the name of Bacchus.

§96

O Fortuna, velut luna
Statu variabilis,
Semper crescis
Aut decrescis;
Vita detestabilis
Nunc obdurat
Et tunc curat
Ludo mentis aciem,
Egestatem,
Potestatem,
Dissoluit ut glaciem.

O Fortune, like the moon,
you ever wane,
but to regain
your former circumstance;
life's equally fain
to decimate
as reinstate
the mind with games of chance,
prosperity
and penury
reversing with a glance.

Sors immanis et inanis,
Rota tu volubilis,
Status malus,
Vana salus
Semper dissolubilis,
Obumbrata
Et velata
Mihi quoque niteris,
Nunc per ludum
Dorsum nudum
Fero tui sceleris.

Immense and futile Fate,
uneasy ground,
safety unsound,
mistakenly awaited,
to your wheel I'm bound;
you've hidden your face,
denied your grace,
for sorrow was I slated;
I've lost the knack,
this barren back
shows what you've perpetrated.

Sors salutis
Et virtutis
Mihi nunc contraria,
Est affectus et defectus
Semper in angaria;
Hac in hora
Sine mora
Cordis pulsum tangite,
Quod per sortem
Sternit fortem
Mecum omnes plangite.

Unknown to me remain
salvation's lot,
of virtue aught,
equally loss and gain
await the hangman's knot;
this very hour
fails my power,
my pulse beats on the wane—
fortune's a knave
to impale the brave,
all weep now for my pain.

§97

Fortune plango vulnera	Fortune's blows do I lament,
Stillantibus ocellis,	my eyes, with weeping, red,
Quod sua mihi munera	to find her favors but for rent
Subtrahit rebellis.	and she, the harlot, fled;
Verum est quod legitur,	true to form is her intent
Fronte capillata,	all riches to impart,
Sed plerumque sequitur	and then flee with your every cent
Occasio calvata.	and leave you there to smart.

In Fortune solio	Once I sat aloft, secure,
Sederam elatus,	on Lady Fortune's throne,
Prosperitatis vario	thinking her favors would endure,
Flore coronatus;	but now stripped to the bone;
Quicquid enim florui	once was I full fatly grown,
Felix et beatus,	massaged and manicured.
Nunc a summo corrui	My former self's now overthrown,
Gloria privatus.	my misery assured.

Fortune rota volvitur;	Fortune's wheel slowly turns
Descendo minoratus.	leaving me sorely bowed,
Alter in altum tollitur	since Fortune's warmth increasing burns
Nimis exaltatus.	the thoughtless over proud;
Rex sedet in vertice,	let high-seated potentates
Caveat ruinam!	the wheel's script discern:
Nam sub axe legimus	his royal person and his mate's
Hecubam reginam.	collected in an urn.

§98

Veris leta facies	Of spring's fair-countenanced delight
Mundo propinatur,	the world entire drinks,
Hiemalis acies	harsh winter's frost is put to flight,
Victa iam fugatur.	sharp ice recedes and shrinks.
In vesititu vario	In her gaily pied attire
Flora prinipatur,	Flora now holds reign,
Nemorum dulcisono	praised throughout the world entire
Qui cantu celebratur,	in sweet-canticled refrain.

Flore fusus gremio
Phebus novo more
Risum dat, hoc vario
Iam stipate Flore.
Zephyrus nectareo
Spirans in odore,
Certatim in bravio
Curamus in amore.

Steeped in flowers upon her breast
Phoebus, as befits the hour,
does laugh to find himself caressed
by flower after flower.
Zephyr wafting from the west
breathes fragrance through the bower–
O let us hasten Love's behest,
concede his every power.

Citharizat cantico
Dulcis Philomena,
Flore rident vario
Prata iam serena.
Salit turba avium
Silve per amena,
Chorus promit virginum
Iam gaudia millena.

Now the tuneful nightingale
trills forth her melody,
now the flower-resplendent vale
revels in variety.
The winged flock soars heaven-bound
throughout the pleasant lea,
there maiden songs resound,
there joy reigns constantly.

§99

Omnia Sol temperat,
Purus et subtilis,
Novo mundo reserat
Faciem Aprilis,
Ad amorem properat
Animus herilis,
Et iocundis imperat
Deus puerilis.

The sun rules over everything,
piercing and delicate,
fresh April bids the world to sing
of its renewed estate;
young men's spirits are rallying,
when thoughts are thus elated,
the boyish god is on the wing,
Let one and all be mated.

Rerum tanta novitas
In sollemni vere
Et veris auctoritas
iubet nos gaudere,
Vias prebet solitas,
Et in tuo vere
Fides est et probitas
Tuum retinere.

Spring's exalted renovation
does everywhere reside,
spring commands no jubilation
excluded or denied;
when spring embarks you on the wanton
paths she has supplied,
see that your true and only one
strays not from by your side.

Ama me fideliter,   So cherish me with all your heart,
Fidem meam nota,   such is the love I feel,
De corde totaliter   no greater love could I impart,
Et ex mente tota,   no truer love reveal;
Sum presentialiter   even times when we're apart
Absens in remota: your presence is no less real,
Quisquis amat taliter   who loves and loves with such a heart
Volvitur in rota.   lies wracked upon the wheel.

§100

Ecce gratum   Anticipated,
Et optatum   variegated
Ver reducit gaudia,   spring bursts into sight,
Purpuratum   long desired
Floret pratum,   violet-fired
Sol serenat omnia.   fields abound with light;
Iamiam cedant tristia!   let sorrows take to flight!
Estas redit   summer's heat
Nunc recedit   marks the retreat
Hyemis sevitia.   of winter's barren blight.

Iam liquescit   Flee frost and snow
Et decrescit   away they go
Grando, nix et cetera. together with the rest,
Bruma fugit,   spring's growing thirst
Et iam sugit   e'en now is nursed
Ver estatis ubera;   at fragrant summer's breast;
Illi mens est misera,   his life is dreariest
Qui nec vivit,   who, in restraint
Nec lascivit   resists, a saint
Sub estatis dextera.   to summer's warm behest.

Gloriantur   They rejoice
Et letantur   raise high their voice
In melle dulcedinis,   in love's elated manner,
Qui conantur   whose foremost choice
Ut utantur   it is to hoist
Premio Cupidinis;   Love's decorated banner;
Simus iussu Cypridis be love then our commander,
Gloriantes   that we elated
Et letantes   be equated
Pares esse Paradis.   with princely Alexander.

§101

Floret silva nobilis
Floribus et foliis.
Ubi est antiquus
Meus amicus?
Hinc equitavit.
Eia, quis me amabit?

The noble woods bloom,
scent the air with perfume,
Ah, where shall I find
that old lover of mine?
He has galloped away,
who will love me, now, say?

Floret silva undique
Nah mime gesellen ist mir wê.
Gruonet der walt allenthalben.
Wâ ist min gesele alse lange?
Der ist geriten hinnen.
O wî, wer sol mich minnen?

The forest blossoms far and wide,
and I yearn for my lover.
When woods turn green on every side,
will I my love recover?
He's left as fast as he can ride,
will I of all love be denied?

§102

Estuans interius
Ira vehementi
In amaritudine
Loquor mee menti:
Factus de materia
Levis elementi,
Similis sum folio
De quo ludunt venti.

Storming with indignation,
afflicted past relief,
my sorrow lacks remission,
I question all belief;
this my mortal element,
will one day come to grief,
plaything to the blustering winds,
as brittle as a leaf.

Cum sit enim proprium
Viro sapienti
Supra petram ponere
Sedem fundamenti,
Stultus ego comparor
Fluvio labenti,
Sub eodem tramite
Nunquam permanenti.

When choosing a location,
the wise man will select
a bedrock as foundation,
his interests to protect;
but I, the fool, am washed along,
in my own refuse wrecked,
a firm and solid footing
I everywhere neglect.

Feror ego veluti
Sine nauta navis,
Ut per vias aeris
Vaga fertur avis.
Non me tenent vincula
Non me tenet clavis,
Quero mihi similes
Et adiungor pravis.

To what then do I compare?
To a skipperless craft,
a bird tumbling through air,
blown away by the draft;
no chains are there to bind me,
no keeper holds the key,
I seek such as remind me
of my depravity.

Mihi cordis gravitas
Res videtur gravis,
locus est amabilis
Dulciorque favis.
Quicquid Venus imperat,
Labor est suavis,
Que nunquam in cordibus
Habitat ignavis.

I consider the troubled thought
to sport mal apropos,
sweet dissolution is my lot,
what better way to go?
What Venus bids her favorite rake
(let dullards sleep the day)
I'll not disdain to undertake,
a consummate roué.

Via lata gradior
More iuventutis.
Implicor et vitiis
Immemor virtutis.
Voluptatis avidus
Magis quam salutis,
Mortuus in anima
Curam gero cutis.

The road abounds with ample vice,
each will I sample twice.
Virtue's a chore I've no need for,
I'll pay damnation's price;
to self-indulgence do I turn,
salvation's promise spurn.
Roast my soul, take Satan his toll,
the flesh is my only concern!

§103

Olim lacus colueram,
Olim pulcher extiteram,
Dum cignus ego fueram.
Miser, miser,
Modo niger
Et ustus fortiter.

Once I lived by the river's tide,
formerly most glorified,
while as a swan I did abide—
Alack, alack,
now roasted black
from side to side.

Girat, regirat garcifer,
Me rogus urit fortiter,
Propinat me nunc dapifer.
Miser, miser,
Modo niger
Et ustus fortiter.

Slowly I'm turned by the Maitre d',
I'm scorched as black as I can be,
garnished with slips of greenery—
Alack, alack,
now roasted black,
could anything be sadder?

Nunc in scutella iaceo,
Et volitare nequeo,
Dentes frendentes video:
Miser, miser,
Modo niger
Et ustus fortiter.

Here I lie upon the platter,
that once I flew now doesn't matter,
teeth now greet me at full clatter—
Alack, alack,
no turning back,
could anything be sadder?

§104

Ego sum abbas Cucaniensis
Et consilium meum est cum bibulis,
Et in secta Decii voluntas mea est,
Et qui mane me quesierit in taberna,
Post vesperam nudus egredietur,
Et sic denudatus veste clamabit:

Wafna, wafna!
Quid fecisti sors turpissima?
Nostre vite gaudia
Abstulisti omnia!

I'm tavern abbot of Cucany,
with drinkers keep I company,
a gambler's is my pedigree.
Who seeks me for dice at early morn
will by night of shirt and shorts be shorn,
and thus denuded will he mourn:

O infamous Fate,
I am forlorn,
joy's former estate
is turned to scorn!

§105

In taberna quando sumus,
Non curamus quid sit humus,
Sed ad ludum properamus,
Cui semper insudamus.
Quid agatur in taberna,
Ubi nummus est pincerna,
Hoc est opus ut queratur
Si quid loquar, audiatur.

When we order up a round,
we disavow six feet of ground,
but rush to gaming, place our bet,
at this you'll find us in a sweat.
What goes on here in the pub
amid the coin and chug-a-lug,
be this the scene that you seek out,
it's this that I would speak about.

Quidam ludunt, quidam bibunt,
Quidam indiscrete vivunt,
Sed in ludo qui morantur
Ex his quidam denudantur.
Quidam ibi vestiuntur,
Quidam saccis induuntur,
Ibi nullus timet mortem,
Sed pro Baccho mittunt sortem:

One and all they drink and game,
they live a life that knows no shame,
those who trust in a gambler's knack
depart the game with a barren back.
Some leave the premises very well heeled,
others leave naked in sack cloth concealed.
No one there of death thinks twice,
when for the drinks they roll the dice.

Primo pro nummata vini,
Ex hac bibunt libertini,
Semel bibunt pro captivis,
Post hec bibunt ter pro vivis,
Quater pro Christianis cunctis,
Quinquies pro fidelibus defunctis,
Sexies pro sororibus vanis,
Septies pro militibus silvanis.

First they roll to see who pays,
to that their cups they freely raise;
they drink next to all who captive dwell,
and third to those alive and well,
fourth to their Christian brethren,
fifth to the dearly departed. Amen!
sixth to vain sisters as years take their toll,
seventh to foresters out on patrol,

Octies pro fratribus perversis,
Novies pro monachis dispersis,
Decies pro navigantibus,
Undecies pro discordantibus,
Duodecies pro penitentibus,
Tredecies pro iter agentibus.
Tam pro papa quam pro rege
Bibunt omnes sine lege.

eighth to such brothers as don't give a damn,
ninth to the absentees out on the lam,
tenth to sea captains addicted to sailing,
eleventh to rioters, ranting and railing,
twelfth to the rueful who penance pay,
thirteenth to the backpacking émigré.
As much to the papacy as to the king,
untiringly drink they to everything.

Bibit hera, bibit herus,
Bibit miles, bibit clerus,
Bibit ille, bibit illa,
Bibit servus cum ancilla;
Bibit velox, bibit piger,
Bibit albus, bibit niger,
Bibit constans, bibit vagus,
Bibit rudis, bibit magus.

Host and hostess unstintingly pour,
What could the parson or soldier like more?
They drink one and all, whatever the gender,
the tabletop wiper and sweetmeat vendor,
they drink, the swift and slow of wit,
white or black doesn't matter a bit,
drink the steadfast and dissipated,
the ignorant and doctorated.

Bibit pauper et egrotus,
Bibit exul et ignotus,
Bibit puer, bibit canus,
Bibit presul et decanus,
Bibit soror, bibit frater,
Bibit anus, bibit mater,
Bibit ista, bibit ille,
Bibunt centum, bibunt mille.

Drinks the poor man in failing health,
prodigal son gone to waste with his wealth,
the aging man and pubescent lad
cannot recall how much they've had,
the prelate, deacon, mother, and hag,
sisters and brothers are all in the bag.
They drink irrespective of gender or years
they drink till it gurgles inside of their ears.

Parum sexcente nummate
Durant, cum immoderate
Bibunt omnes sine meta.
Quamvis bibant mente leta.
Sic nos rodunt omnes gentes,
Et sic erimus egentes.
Qui nos rodunt confundantur.
Et cum iustis non scribantur.

Six hundred cups is a meager amount
for those long ago losing track of the count;
and so they imbibe with no limit to set,
as gladly they'd swim in it sans regret.
Thus decent folk do chew us out,
degrade the indigent devout.
Let those who demean us be disgraced,
from the rolls of righteous men erased.

§106

Amor volat undique,
Captus est libidine,
Iuvenes, iuvencule
Coniunguntur merito.

Love flies about the world entire
o'ertaken by his own desire;
young men and women aware of it,
are joined together, as is fit.

182

Siqua sine socio
Caret omni gaudio:
Tenet noctis infima
Sub intimo
Cordis in custodia:
Fit res amarissima.

If any maid lack her companion,
lacks she all her heart to gladden,
enclosed, instead,
within her breast,
she chambers dreaded night's bequest.
This fate is the bitterest.

§107

Stetit puella
Rufa tunica:
Si quis eam tetigit
Tunica crepuit. Eia.

A girl never such
stood in crimson gowned;
the gown, if but touched
breathed a rustling sound. Eia!

Stetit puella
Tanquam rosula;
Facie splenduit,
Os eius floruit. Eia.

A girl never such
exquisitely posed;
her complexion ablush
her mouth red as rose. Eia!

§108

Si puer cum puellula
Moraretur in cellula
Felix coniunctio,
Amore suscrescente,
Pariter e medio
Avulso procul tedio.
Fit ludus ineffabilis
Membris lacertis labiis.

If lad and maid slip away
for a moment's bit of play,
happy is their embrace,
as passion increasing
puts shame to disgrace.
Then is sport past words to tell,
arms, limbs, and lips
and all pell-mell.

§109

In trutina mentis dubia
fluctuant contraria
lascivus amor at pudicitia.
Sed eligo quod video,
Collum iugo prebeo:
Ad iugum tamen suave transeo.

Here's balance of uncertainty
that lays the equal claim to me
of lusty love or chastity.
But what I see, that I select,
and to the yoke submit my neck;
let it my every thought direct.

§110

Tempus est iocundum,
O virgines.
Modo congaudete,
Vos iuvenes.

Dear maidens, the season
now does call,
rejoice young bachelors
one and all.

Oh, oh, oh, totus floreo,
Iam amore virginali
Totus ardeo;
Novus novus amor
Est quo pereo.

Mea me confortat
Promissio,
Mea me deportat
Negatio.

Tempore brumali
Vir patiens,
Animo vernali
Lasciviens.

Mea mecum ludit
Virginitas,
Mea me detrudit
Simplicitas.

Veni, domicella,
Cum gaudio,
Veni, veni, pulchra,
Iam pereo.

Oh, oh, oh—
I flower from head to toe,
with maidens' love
am I aglow,
new love is this,
my overthrow.

I thrill to think his wish I'll grant,
grieve to consider
that I shan't.

All winter long
man perseveres,
by spring his lust
is in arrears.

Virginity
I'd cast away,
but innocence
won't let me stray.

Come joyously
my only one,
come, else am I
this day undone.

Part IV

Expository Translations from the
Latin and Charles Baudelaire:

Kisses Uncounted, Onslaughts, Hardening, Satiety,
Profligacy, Enravishment, and the Infinite Abyss

CATULLUS

Lesbia, kisses uncounted

THE POET SEEKS INNUMERABLE kisses. These contrast with the far-
thing's worth of old men's disapproval, with the final sunset of life
and the single lasting night—*nox . . . perpetua una*—to which life yields.
The demand for kisses quickens in defiance of death, its urgency marked
by line-initial alliterations: *da* 'give', *dein* 'then', *deinde* (twice) 'then again',
dein 'then'. Increasing syllabic elisions—one word ending, the next begin-
ning with a vowel, the adjoining vowels pronounced as a single syllable—
signal the kisses' indistinguishability. Thus, *perpetu[a] una dormienda*;
mill[e] altera; deind[e] usqu[e] altera. The earlier appearing *dormienda*
'must be slept' anticipates the cascade of alliterative "d." Enjambed
polysyllabic *fecerimus* 'we will have completed' / *conturbabimus* 'we will
confound' (the kisses) adds to the multitudinous and run-together effect
(with alliterative "m" throughout). The poem is a masterpiece of compres-
sion, of *multa in parva* 'much within a small scope'—the more intense and
impressive for that.

§111

Vivamus, mea Lesbia, atque amemus,
rumoresque senum severiorum
omnes unius aestimemus assis!
soles occidere et redire possunt:
nobis cum semel occidit brevis lux,
nox est perpetua una dormienda.
da mi basia mille, deinde centum,
dein mille altera, dein secunda centum,
deinde usque altera mille, deinde centum.
dein, cum milia multa fecerimus,
conturbabimus illa, ne sciamus,
aut ne quis malus invidere possit,
cum tantum sciat esse basiorum.

◆

My Lesbia, let us live and love,
a farthing's worth not thinking of
the tales censorious elders tell.
Suns in succession rise and fall,
but our lives set but once withal
e're dwelling mid the asphodel.
Give me kisses a thousand score
these increase by the thousands more,
surpassing surfeit's power to quell.
Confound the reckoning to a blur
upon which count none may concur,
and none the envious to aver
what number these our kisses were.

Lesbia, the nipping onslaught

This is one of Catullus's best-known and most often cited and imitated poems, even in antiquity. Catullus envies the pain-and-pleasure intimacy enjoyed by Lesbia and her pet sparrow. Sparrows—drawing Aphrodite's chariot, §1—were known for their lasciviousness. *Sparrow* in Catullus's poem may also be understood as "the bird"—the word *digitum* 'finger'

prominent in the poem—and by analogy, *penis*. The Roman epigram-
matist Martial (1st century AD) capitalizes on the association which has
otherwise had its vogue, though generally ignored or bypassed by twenti-
eth-century commentators. See Gaisser, ed., 305–340. This gives the little
poem a particularly wicked slant. In a companion piece, Catullus intones
a mock-heroic dirge for the death and descent of his lady's bird—the same
sparrow—into Hades. The sparrow never strayed far, always piping and
fluttering back to its lady's lap. She now laments its passing, which is to say,
Catullus's detumescence.

§112

Passer, deliciae meae puellae,
quicum ludere, quem in sinu tenere,
cui primum digitum dare appetenti
et acris solet incitare morsus,
cum desiderio meo nitenti
carum nescio quid lubet iocari
et solaciolum sui doloris,
credo ut tum gravis acquiescat ardor:
tecum ludere sicut ipsa possem
et tristis animi levare curas!

◆

Sparrow, my darling lady's pet,
to her breast nestled when she frets,
to which she gives her fingertip,
her sorrow easing nip by nip
when some dear whim thus pleases her
its ardent onslaughts to incur.
To my bright love thus does it please
by this her play love's pain to ease.
Oh, would that I at play with you
might have my own pain tended to!

Lesbia, Catullus hardens

See, I'm already getting over you—just look! And while I'm at it, have a rotten life! This is the sum of it, as Catullus determinedly—*destinatus* (last line)—takes his leave of Lesbia. His disdain is driven by the now bitter and ultimately disappointed memory of past sexual delights. Who now, he asks, will provide these? My translation, occasionally paraphrasing or elaborating on the original, preserves the Latin's emphasis on *hardening—obdurat* '[Catullus] hardens', *obdurā* 'harden'! Yes, Catullus has hardened his heart—remaining as hard for Lesbia as ever.

§113

Miser Catulle, desinas ineptire,
et quod vides perisse perditum ducas.
fulsere quondam candidi tibi soles,
cum ventitabas quo puella ducebat
amata nobis quantum amabitur nulla.
ibi illa multa cum iocosa fiebant,
quae tu volebas nec puella nolebat,
fulsere vere candidi tibi soles.
nunc iam illa non vult: tu quoque impotens noli,
nec quae fugit sectare, nec miser vive,
sed obstinata mente perfer, obdura.
vale puella, iam Catullus obdurat,
nec te requiret nec rogabit invitam.
at tu dolebis, cum rogaberis nulla.
scelesta, vae te, quae tibi manet vita?
quis nunc te adibit? cui videberis bella?
quem nunc amabis? cuius esse diceris?
quem basiabis? cui labella mordebis?
at tu, Catulle, destinatus obdura.

◆

Wretched Catullus, forgo your feckless ways,
forget what is finished, cease being amazed.
Once favored of fortune, its fabled delight,
sun's radiant orb in your mistress's sight,

devoutly you loved her, no other could be
better accomplice to your each fantasy,
continuous fucking, no fussing about,
all constraint, all obstacles driven to rout.
But now she's averse, so you, upright, prepare,
live not good for nothing, renounce what's not there.
Your hardness display, be inflexible, firm:
My lovely, farewell, hear Catullus's terms!
He ends his pursuit, he has marked your disdain.
Get on with your life, be it ever your bane.
Who now will approach you, who, thinking you fair?
Whom now will you love, whom reduce to despair?
Whom lavish with kisses? Whose lips will you bite?
No matter, Catullus is hardening quite.

Lesbia, the profligate cursed

One of two Catullan poems in Sapphic meter, this one recalling §1. There, Sappho summons Aphrodite for help in unrequited love, and the goddess hastens by chariot from Olympus, traversing the expanse of "aether's middle main." Here, by embittered mock-heroic contrast, Catullus summons two comrades, themselves ready to traverse with him the world entire, from Egypt to Britain to India—with all their exoticisms, attractions, and mythohistorical associations. Undermining the grandiose itinerary, however, is the friends' summoned purpose—to cross the street, as it were, and curse out the debauched Lesbia. No unrequited love here, as in §1, but love betrayed. *He* has been faithful; she has not. Catullus's bravura, the abrasiveness of his message, the vastness of the world he invokes, all stunningly contrast with his own ultimate vulnerability and isolation. Losing Lesbia, he no longer commands but has lost the world. Now inhabiting the field's furthest edge, he is its solitary flower, lopped by the passing plow—himself deflowered, feminized. The poem in fact works on many levels. Michael Putnam incisively traces Virgil's "refractions" of this poem throughout the latter books of the *Aeneid,* finding allusions in both authors to the recent history of Roman power, and a "scrutiny" (proper to lyric) "spread . . . out as a larger glow over a grand stretch of epic time" (Putnam 1982). The poem is discussed at length and in light of its Sapphic predecessors in *TLL* 330–337.

§114

Furi et Aureli comites Catulli,
sive in extremos penetrabit Indos,
litus ut longe resonante Eoa
    tunditur unda,

sive in Hyrcanos Arabesue molles,
seu Sagas sagittiferosue Parthos,
sive quae septemgeminus colorat
    aequora Nilus,

sive trans altas gradietur Alpes,
Caesaris uisens monumenta magni,
Gallicum Rhenum horribile aequor ulti-
    mosque Britannos,

omnia haec, quaecumque feret uoluntas
caelitum, temptare simul parati,
pauca nuntiate meae puellae
    non bona dicta.

cum suis uiuat valeatque moechis,
quos simul complexa tenet trecentos,
nullum amans vere, sed identidem omnium
    ilia rumpens;

nec meum respectet, ut ante, amorem,
qui illius culpa cecidit velut prati
ultimi flos, praetereunte postquam
    tactus aratro est.

◆

Furius, Aurelius, Catullus' friends—
Should India beckon from earth's far ends
Where thundering Ocean batters the shore,
    Echoing evermore;

Should Persia, Caspia, or soft Araby
Or the Parthians' equine archery
Or waters run brown with Nilotic silt
   From mouths twice-seven spilt—

Should the lofty Alps yield to being crossed,
And battered Britain's shoreline tempest-tossed,
The Rhine engineered and traversed from France,
   And sights within Caesar's glance,

Prepared to bestride the world entire
Wheresoever divinity require
Relate but this to the beloved girl
   Whom I adored erstwhile:

May she live and prosper a practiced whore,
Clutching the three-hundred-strong at her door,
Each derelict drained of his overload
   Till his balls implode—

Nor may she count on my love as before
Which has dropped by her fault like a flower
Once traversed on the distant meadow's floor
   By the passing plow.

PETRONIUS

Love's measure restored

A poem ascribed to Gaius Petronius Arbiter, the *elegentiae arbiter* 'judge of elegance' in the court of the crazed and debauched Nero (1st century AD). His *Satyricon*, a Roman "novel" in a mix of prose and poetry, describes, among other things, the sexual raunchiness of the Roman underclass—the work brilliantly rendered in film by Federico Fellini (1969). Of Petronius the Roman historian Tacitus famously said, "He spent his days in sleep, his nights in attending to his official duties or in amusement, that by his dissolute life he had become as famous as other men by a life of energy, and that he was regarded as no ordinary profligate, but as an accomplished voluptuary" (*Annales* 16.18). Here putting depravity aside, Petronius discloses a decidedly tender and reflective disposition:

§115

Foeda est in coitu et brevis voluptas
et taedet Veneris statim peractae.
non ergo ut pecudes libidinosae
caeci protinus irruamus illuc
(nam languescit amor peritque flamma); –
sed sic sic sine fine feriati
et tecum iaceamus osculantes.
hic nullus labor est ruborque nullus:
hoc iuvat, iuvat et diu iuvabit;
hoc non deficit incipitque semper.

◆

Odious is coition's joy, and brief;
the hurried consummation tiresome.
Thus be we not as rutting beasts undone,
reckless our inclination and relief,
thus falters love and dwindling dies the flame,
but be just so, abed our holiday,
thus bound, thus kissing the hours away.
Here labor none, here banishment of shame,
here bliss entire, beguilement in the chore,
nor deficit, but bounty evermore.

LUCRETIUS, *DE RERUM NATURA* PROLOGUE, BOOK I

❧

Venus, enravishment of gods and men

The opening prologue to Lucretius's epic poem *De Rerum Natura* (*On the Nature of Things*) (1st century BC) takes pride of place in any volume of erotic verse, Venus controlling the realms of physical, emotional, and intellectual attraction and begetting. The prologue's concluding lines alone mark the poet's imagination as one—literally—of breathtaking sensuality, Venus taking Mars's very breath away (cf. §§131–132, pp. 250–251). Lucretius depicts the god of war succumbing to love's eternal wound, in Love's own lap, gaping, breathing his last, as it were. The image bears erotic affinity to Bernini's *The Ecstasy of St. Teresa* (plate 1) no less than to Michelangelo's *Pietà* (Christ having already breathed his last). Erotic and religious transport, the transports of physical love and sacred devotion, the throes of love and death themselves—all ever proximate (see pp. 38–39). Thus, the prologue's conclusion:

§116

> For you alone with limpid peace
> Dispel the pain by man endured,
> Since Mars, renowned in weaponry,
> Takes refuge on your sacred breast,
> Subdued by love's enduring wound;
> And tilting back his tapered neck,
> With gaping parted lips regales
> His eyes ablaze with love on you—
> His breathing lingering round your mouth.
> Pour down a sweet complaint on him
> Reclining on your sacred breast
> To bring, clear goddess, peace for Rome!

Venus's eroticism, as noted, is pervasive in every sphere. As beauty incarnate, Venus dictates *all* attraction—physical, emotional, and intellectual (body, heart, and mind). She is also the generative force of art, the need and striving for beauty that permeates the artistic impulse, which is to say the love of fixed and lasting refinement. Note the word *art*, coming (via Lat. *ars, art-*) from the Greek root **ar-* 'fix, set, make permanent'. It is in her artistically generative capacity that Lucretius bids Venus, quo magis **aeternum** da dictis, diva, **leporem** 'The more so, goddess, grant **charm everlasting** to [my] words'— *charm* the attractive power of love. "Charm everlasting" is thus the enduring, the undying quality represented by the immortal and ever seductive Venus (Lat. *se* 'away, apart' + *duc-* 'lead'). Only with this quality will Lucretius's own words and art endure, attract the reader, engage him both emotionally and intellectually, induce his understanding and own creative response, and remain forever with him. Such engagement—by analogy to procreation in the natural world—is *generative*, begetting thought and understanding through the intellect's own attractive and procreative reach. Lucretius makes the entreaty with characteristic alliterative emphasis: quo magis **aeternum d**a **d**ictis, **d**iva, **leporem**. The pointedness of the plea shows Lucretius himself in Venus's thrall, his own imagination straining to her influence, as strains Nature everywhere and throughout. All nature submits to Venus; sentient life thrills and quickens to her summons. Beasts in both senses *join* in her procreative retinue. Lucretius thus concludes, ita capta **lepore** / te sequitur cupide quo quamque inducere pergis 'thus captivated by [your] **charm**, they eagerly follow where you seek to lead [them] each'.

As Lucretius is drawn to Venus, he hopes his readers will be drawn to *him*, that Venus's **charm** throughout his verse—this time her *venustas* (the word bearing Venus's own name)—will enthrall his readers to Lucretius's *own* lead. As charmed nature instinctively yields to love's generative impulse, the intellect is attracted to and seeks union with that to which Venus's **charm** is given—in this case a philosophical poem on the nature of things. "Mating" further occurs at the level of form and content. Suffused with the **charm** of artistically generative power, the *De Rerum Natura* is able to "wed" poetic form to philosophic content. This is a most unlikely and challenging union and, for the 7,500 lines of poetry that follow, a most successfully accomplished and *enduring* bond. '**Eternal charm**' (*aeternum . . . leporem*)—i.e., the attractive power of love— thus also bespeaks the desired prolongation of all generative process: human, natural, and artistic (see *TLL* 91–95; cf. Vanita, 20–25).

Venus, in the opening line, is *voluptas*: voluptuousness, satisfaction, enjoyment, pleasure, delight (Gr. *elpō*, Lat. *volo* 'hope, wish'). She is beauty incarnate, and the word suits her perfectly as goddess of love. I earlier translated *voulptas* 'pure ravishment'; but now 'enravishment', with a nod to W. Somerset Maugham:

> Beauty is a grave word. It is a word of high import. . . . It is very rare. It is a force. It is an enravishment . . . the heart and nerves are thrilled and shattered by the rapture of pure beauty.

Quoted by Curtis and Whitehead, eds., 406–407 (cf. "thrilled and quickened by your allure"; line 19, below).

§117

Aeneadum genetrix, hominum divomque voluptas,
alma Venus, caeli subter labentia signa
quae mare navigerum, quae terras frugiferentis
concelebras, per te quoniam genus omne animantum
concipitur visitque exortum lumina solis:
te, dea, te fugiunt venti, te nubila caeli
adventumque tuum, tibi suavis daedala tellus
summittit flores, tibi rident aequora ponti
placatumque nitet diffuso lumine caelum.

Nam simul ac species patefactast verna diei
et reserata viget genitabilis aura favoni,
aeriae primum volucris te, diva, tuumque
significant initum perculsae corda tua vi.
inde ferae pecudes persultant pabula laeta
et rapidos tranant amnis: ita capta lepore
te sequitur cupide quo quamque inducere pergis.
denique per maria ac montis fluviosque rapacis
frondiferasque domos avium camposque virentis
omnibus incutiens blandum per pectora amorem
efficis ut cupide generatim saecla propagent.

Quae quoniam rerum naturam sola gubernas
nec sine te quicquam dias in luminis oras
exoritur neque fit laetum neque amabile quicquam,

te sociam studeo scribendis versibus esse,
quos ego de rerum natura pangere conor
Memmiadae nostro, quem tu, dea, tempore in omni
omnibus ornatum voluisti excellere rebus.
quo magis aeternum da dictis, diva, leporem.

Effice ut interea fera moenera militiai
per maria ac terras omnis sopita quiescant;
nam tu sola potes tranquilla pace iuvare
mortalis, quoniam belli fera moenera Mavors
armipotens regit, in gremium qui saepe tuum se
reiicit aeterno devictus vulnere amoris,
atque ita suspiciens tereti cervice reposta
pascit amore avidos inhians in te, dea, visus
eque tuo pendet resupini spiritus ore.

Hunc tu, diva, tuo recubantem corpore sancto
circumfusa super, suavis ex ore loquellas
funde petens placidam Romanis, incluta, pacem;
nam neque nos agere hoc patriai tempore iniquo
possumus aequo animo nec Memmi clara propago
talibus in rebus communi desse saluti.

◆

Mother of Rome, enravishment
Of men and gods, nurt'ring Venus,
Who under heaven's zodiac
Makes ship-decked sea and fruitful earth
To teem with life, since through you are
Conceived all forms of living things
Which, risen, contemplate the sun—
Before you, goddess, flee the winds,
Your presence hails the clouds' retreat,
And daedal earth makes spring to you
Its flowered scent. Upon you smile
The ocean plains, and placid skies
Shine offerings of outpoured light.

For when the day dons spring attire,

196

And western breezes rush to take
All living things to their embrace,
The birds from heights ethereal
First herald, goddess, your approach,
Thrilled and quickened by your allure;
Then beasts maddened with desire
Fast overleap their fertile fields
And swim across the swirling tides—
Thus all bound by your sorcery
They crave to follow where you lead.

At length through oceans and mountains,
Throughout rapacious river streams
And leaf-encircled homes of birds
And greening fields, do you make each
New generation grow afresh,
Instilling in the hearts of all
The eagerness of luring love.

Since you alone hold sway of life,
And nothing, wanting you, ascends
To reach the splendid shores of light
Nor has its share of joy or charm,
I ask for your companionship
In writing verse to explicate
The cosmos for our Memmius,
For whom, goddess, you have wished
All ornament of excellence
In all respects at every time—
The more so, goddess, may you grant
Grace everlasting to these words.

And as I write make works of war
To slumber soundly throughout earth.
For you alone with limpid peace
Dispel the pain by man endured,
Since Mars, renowned in weaponry,
Takes refuge on your sacred breast,
Subdued by love's enduring wound;
And tilting back his tapered neck,

With gaping parted lips regales
His eyes ablaze with love on you—
His breathing ling'ring round your mouth.

Pour down a sweet complaint on him
Reclining on your sacred breast
To bring, clear goddess, peace for Rome!
For strife, our state's iniquity,
Drives thought of writing verse away,
And noble Memmius must be free
To serve its causes as he may.

BAUDELAIRE, "LESBOS"

❧

The abyss: kisses in excess

Ever keen to heightened eroticism, Charles Baudelaire (1821–1867) focuses on Lesbos as a land of compulsive yet irresistible lesbian passion, a land of at once self-voyeuristic masturbatory fantasy and untiring amatory refinements. We may begin with the following five lines (literally translated):

§118

Lesbos, terre des nuits chaudes et langoureuses,
Qui font qu'à leurs miroirs, stérile volupté!
Les filles aux yeux creux, de leur corps amoureuses,
Caressent les fruits mûrs de leur nubilité,
Lesbos, terre des nuits chaudes et langoureuses.

◆

Lesbos, land of warm and languorous nights, which make the hollow-eyed girls, before their mirrors—sterile pleasure!—caress the ripe fruits of their amorous bodies' nubility; Lesbos, land of warm and languorous nights.

198

Baudelaire reached this fevered pitch by way of several drafts, first writing that the mirrored girls merely *contemplate* the fruits of their *nubilité* (in one version), and of their *virginité* (in another). At this point, as it appears, Baudelaire *ne voit pas encore dans le saphisme l'appel du gouffre, la recherche de l'infini, mais l'attirance d'un monde de beauté et de tendresse pures* 'does not yet see in Sapphism the call of the abyss, the search of the infinite, but the attraction of a world of pure beauty and tenderness' (Adam, 436). However, Baudelaire's final version (shown here) offers a marked surrender to the abyss and its infinitude—the same realms in his "Le Balcon" ("The Balcony") (below) holding recollective and redemptive promise. The first five (of fifteen) stanzas of "Lesbos" are here offered:

> Mère des jeux latins et des voluptés grecques,
> Lesbos, où les baisers, languissants ou joyeux,
> Chauds comme les soleils, frais comme les pastèques,
> Font l'ornement des nuits et des jours glorieux,
> Mère des jeux latins et des voluptés grecques,
>
> Lesbos, où les baisers sont comme les cascades
> Qui se jettent sans peur dans les gouffres sans fonds,
> Et courent, sanglotant et gloussant par saccades,
> Orageux et secrets, fourmillants et profonds;
> Lesbos, où les baisers sont comme les cascades!
>
> Lesbos, où les Phrynés l'une l'autre s'attirent,
> Où jamais un soupir ne resta sans écho,
> À l'égal de Paphos les étoiles t'admirent,
> Et Vénus à bon droit peut jalouser Sapho!
> Lesbos où les Phrynés l'une l'autre s'attirent,
>
> Lesbos, terre des nuits chaudes et langoureuses,
> Qui font qu'à leurs miroirs, stérile volupté!
> Les filles aux yeux creux, de leur corps amoureuses,
> Caressent les fruits mûrs de leur nubilité;
> Lesbos, terre des nuits chaudes et langoureuses,
>
> Laisse du vieux Platon se froncer l'oeil austère;
> Tu tires ton pardon de l'excès des baisers,
> Reine du doux empire, aimable et noble terre,

Et des raffinements toujours inépuisés.
Laisse du vieux Platon se froncer l'oeil austère.

◆

Greek amorous mother of profligate thrill,
Lesbos, languid the kisses or elated,
That with sun-immersèd warmth or melon's chill
Overwhelm the day, and leave night ne'er sated,
Greek amorous mother of profligate thrill.

Lesbos, where leap the kisses cascading down,
Heedlessly flung to a fathomless ravine,
That hasten unfearful in tumult profound,
With murmurs or sobs in their melee unseen;
Lesbos, where leap the kisses cascading down!

Lesbos, afire the courtesans face to face,
Where a fading sigh ne'er unechoed is left,
By the heavens admirèd in Paphos'* place,
Where Venus of rights is by Sappho bereft!
Lesbos, afire the courtesans face to face.

Lesbos, where balmy nighttimes langu'rously reign,
That—in mirror's view, infelicitous gain!—
Goad vacant-eyed girls to self-pleasured disdain,
Their ripened fruits gladdened where no man has lain.
Lesbos, where balmy nighttimes langu'rously reign.

Let old peering Plato from grievance refrain;
Your pardon is excess of kisses outpoured,
Queen of pleasured empire, belovèd terrain,
For ev'ry refinement forever adored,
Let old peering Plato from grievance refrain.

*Paphos, on the southwest coast of Cyprus, where
Aphrodite/Venus first rose from the sea.

Baudelaire depicts what he views as the torment and sterile pleasure of lesbian-
ism in two other poems, "Femmes damnées" and "Delphine et Hippolyte." His

attraction to the theme initially prompted him to the title *Les Lesbiennes* for what was ultimately published as *Les Fleurs du Mal*. Fantastically depicted lesbianism was the hallmark of the French fin-de-siècle literary imagination, as here seen in Baudelaire and, among others, Louÿs, Swinburne, Balzac, and Théophile Gautier. Baudelaire in fact dedicated *Les Fleurs* to Gautier, whose *Mademoiselle de Maupin* (1835) was that author's own apologia for lesbian love. Lesbian depictions "were born in the male imagination and intended, for all the conflicted authors' moralistic disapproval, to arouse the reader sexually." However, contemporary women of known lesbian inclination or practice would have thought the depictions "as strange and terrifying as they were to their creators and heterosexual readers, since the characters of those poems and novels had absolutely nothing to do with their lives and loves" (Federman, 268, 275–276).

Readers in a sexually restrictive society were enthralled by the kinship of sex and sin, and were *shocked!* at lesbians—"always young and lovely and arousing as they shuffle[d] off to hell" (Federman, 273). We are reminded that the image of lesbian love frequently reflected less an ideological or aesthetic program than the artist or writer's personal morality or attitude toward sexuality (Kosinski, 187). The then male obsession with lesbianism may be linked to the prevalent view that women in bed—see Courbet's *The Sleepers* (1866), painted in the aftermath of *Les Fleurs*—would not know what to do with each other, and that the male voyeur would show them. Be that as it may, *il faut épater le bourgeois* 'you have to shock the provincials'. This was surely an element of the strategy, one typically generating the always hoped for *succès de scandale*. For discussion of lesbians as "men in women's bodies," see Donoghue, xxxiv–xxxv. For probing discussion of *The Sleepers*, see Kosinski. We turn now to the redemptive side of *l'abîme* 'the abyss'.

BAUDELAIRE, "LE BALCON"

ᕫ

The abyss: kisses untold

Bygone kisses! How their memory is ever reborn, ever fresh, like suns cleansed and daily risen from ocean depths wherein they sank, with which they merged and were assumedly lost. But the kisses, sun-like, *reemerge*, saved from the liquid abyss. In "Lesbos," Baudelaire speaks of the gurgling and sobbing melee of kisses, cascading without return into *gouffres sans fonds* 'bottomless abysses'. But no matter, *l'excès des baisers* 'the excess of kisses' pardons all, leaving kisses in salvationally plentiful supply. Bespeaking the island's enduring refinements, the kisses will never languish nor run out. A supply of infinite kisses is also a Catullan death-challenging demand, both above, in my own "Catullan Caprices" (§§142–143, pp. 255–258), and elsewhere.

In "Le Balcon," by contrast, kisses, among other remembrances of pleasure, *return*, are reborn *d'un gouffre interdit à nos sondes* 'from a gulf forbidden our senses', [A]*près s'être lavés au fond des mers profondes* 'after having bathed in the depths of bottomless seas'. The consuming marine abyss here nightly cleanses and daily restores the kisses it but provisionally claimed—a redemptive occurrence (and recurrence) of its own kind. In "Lesbos," kisses in excess forever abide, *despite* the kisses forever lost; in "Le Balcon," the kisses sink and subside, but return with reassuring regularity upon the benevolent summons of memory. It is restorative and vivifying memory that strengthens the metaphoric bond between nature's and the soul's own seasons, and how they deal with loss—as in the opening chorus of Swinburne's "Atalanta in Calydon" (1865): "And time remembered is grief forgotten, / And frosts are slain and flowers begotten." It is further noted that the reassuringly summoned recollections of "Le Balcon" (among other poems of Baudelaire) anticipate the embrace of Proust's *A la Recherche du Temps Perdu* (Adam, 319–320). Indeed, and as Sappho herself reminds us (§6), recollection, rekindling the pleasures of love, assuages love's loss: "Be on your way, yet remember me now / and again. You know how / we have cared for you. / If not, I'd remind you / . . . of joyous times that we once knew" (the recollection here anticipated at the moment of separation).

It is noted that "Lesbos" and "Le Balcon" are two of only several Baudelaire poems in five-line stanzas, and the only two with the rhyme scheme a-b-a-b-a.

§119

Mère des souvenirs, maîtresse des maîtresses,
Ô toi, tous mes plaisirs! ô toi, tous mes devoirs!
Tu te rappelleras la beauté des caresses,

La douceur du foyer et le charme des soirs,
Mère des souvenirs, maîtresse des maîtresses!

Les soirs illuminés par l'ardeur du charbon,
Et les soirs au balcon, voilés de vapeurs roses.
Que ton sein m'était doux! que ton coeur m'était bon!
Nous avons dit souvent d'impérissables choses
Les soirs illuminés par l'ardeur du charbon.

Que les soleils sont beaux dans les chaudes soirées!
Que l'espace est profond! que le coeur est puissant!
En me penchant vers toi, reine des adorées,
Je croyais respirer le parfum de ton sang.
Que les soleils sont beaux dans les chaudes soirées!

La nuit s'épaississait ainsi qu'une cloison,
Et mes yeux dans le noir devinaient tes prunelles,
Et je buvais ton souffle, ô douceur! ô poison!
Et tes pieds s'endormaient dans mes mains fraternelles.
La nuit s'épaississait ainsi qu'une cloison.

Je sais l'art d'évoquer les minutes heureuses,
Et revis mon passé blotti dans tes genoux.
Car à quoi bon chercher tes beautés langoureuses
Ailleurs qu'en ton cher corps et qu'en ton coeur si doux?
Je sais l'art d'évoquer les minutes heureuses!

Ces serments, ces parfums, ces baisers infinis,
Renaîtront-ils d'un gouffre interdit à nos sondes,
Comme montent au ciel les soleils rajeunis
Après s'être lavés au fond des mers profondes?
— Ô serments! ô parfums! ô baisers infinis!

◆

Mother and mistress of memories all,
O resolute pleasure, allegiance pure!
Our blissful caresses will you recall,
The reposeful hearth, the evening's allure,
Mother and mistress of memories all!

The evenings illumined by charcoal's glow,
Evenings rubescent on the balcony,
What comfort your breast, your heart kindly so!
We vowed evermores imperishably,
The evenings illumined by charcoal's glow.

How welcome the warmth, the sun in descent!
The space how profound, the heart how availed!
Toward you, queen adored, inclining, intent,
Your perfumed blood, so I thought, I'd inhaled.
How welcome the warmth, the sun in descent!

Deepened the night, an enclosure of calm,
My eyes in the dark infusing your glance,
And I drank your breath, O venom, O balm,
Slumbrous your feet in my dutiful hands.
Deepened the night, an enclosure of calm.

Mine is the art of recollections gay,
I relive my past nestled at your knees;
For what langu'rous beauties might I survey,
Save those wherein your heart and body please?
Mine is the art of recollections gay!

These oaths, these perfumes, these kisses untold,
Will they from a void to our senses closed
Arise, cleansed suns from depths of ocean old
A'mount the skies, suns ever recomposed?
O oaths, O perfumes, O kisses untold!

Baudelaire's abyss is the realm of both love's irretrievable loss ("Lesbos")
and saving reclamation ("Le Balcon"). Antecedent to both, however, is
the realm of love's first awakening and, with it, a first awakened artistic
compulsion, one striving for, but always wanting, perfected expression.
This is seen in Baudelaire's longer-lived British contemporary Wilkie
Collins, who, with suggestive Lucretian overtones, probes the unknown
"void" in our spiritual natures, and love's entry and generative stirrings
therein (pp. 95–97).

It is interesting to note that Baudelaire's younger contemporary poet Paul Verlaine (1844–1896), in his "Sur le Balcon" ("On the Balcony") and other poems, takes a much more benign view of lesbianism than did Baudelaire and others of Baudelaire's fevered imagination.

Part V

Safe and Sound Ashore:

Horace, *Odes* 1.5, "To Pyrrha"

§120

ὥσπερ θάλασσα πολλάκις μὲν ἀτρεμὴς
ἕστηκ᾽ ἀπήμων χάρμα ναύτῃσιν μέγα
θέρεος ἐν ὥρῃ, πολλάκις δὲ μαίνεται
βαρυκτύποισι κύμασιν φορευμένη·
ταύτῃ μάλιστ᾽ ἔοικε τοιαύτη γυνὴ
ὀργήν, φυὴν δὲ πόντος οὐκ ἄλλην ἔχει.

As oft the sea by storm lies unbeset,
To sailors summertime delight, and yet
As oft o'erswollen roils in thund'rous threat;
Essentially so such woman's estate
Perfidious ocean to duplicate.

– SIMONIDES (6th and 5th centuries BC),
On the Types of Women

1. A Classic Classically Translated

Horace, writing in lyric and epic meters, was a Roman poet contemporary with Virgil, author of the *Eclogues* (pastoral poems), *Georgics* (farming poems), and epic *Aeneid* (the foundation poem of Rome). Both lived during the first century BC under the rule of Augustus at the outset of the Roman Empire. The two were friends, Virgil having secured Horace's introduction to and favor with Emperor Augustus. Horace wrote, among much else, four books of odes (poems in lyric measures) noteworthy for their consummate adaptation of Greek meters to Latin. Horace thus significantly enhanced the scope and luster of Latin poetry.

The fifth poem of Horace's first book of odes (hereafter *Odes* 1.5)

is the most famous of Horace's poems. Sir Ronald Storrs collected 451 versions of it in 21 languages, of which 144 were published under the title of Ad Pyrrham in 1959. The tally keeps rising. The poem plays upon the ancient practice whereby on retirement the huntsman would dedicate* his nets to Diana[,] and the prostitute her mirror to Venus. The miracles of the poem include its music, the many details of interplay between storms at sea and the storms of love, and the typical Horatian twist that Horace's first love poem in this collection is a farewell to one type of love.

*the dedicated offering being *ex voto*, in fulfillment of a *vow* made in thanks.

The poem, more broadly, describes the sexual relationship between unequal partners: an "inexperienced boy attempting the conquest of a girl experienced in such encounters, well able to cope with the situation as long as it amuses her." The theme, an initiatory commonplace, is rooted in the male imagination—in the recollection of overthrow, pain, and likely humiliation vis-à-vis the more insouciant or dismissive female. In *Odes* 1.5 Horace vividly, and most concisely, depicts a situation as universal as it is varied by particular instance.

Equally vivid and varied has been the poem's translation. My own translation is Victorian in idiom, and thus "classical" both by temperament and in recognition of the original's poetic pedigree. However, my critique, or take, is twentieth- and twenty-first-century urbane, offering a finer and more suggestive reading than has the secondary literature to date. Critic Lawrence Venuti has recently noted that "the occasional use of markedly archaic or markedly modern-sounding words can be a useful device to invite deeper reflection on the relationship of ancient to modern cultures." Using sometimes archaic diction, I proceed in a "classical mode," inviting just such reflection in the service of contemporary sensibility. Little has changed since Horace's own time: human nature, insight, and sexual experience remaining constant. At root, archaizing diction merely reflects the benign and prosodically necessary artificiality of Horace's (and all classical) verse from Homer onward. Translation and critique are yet, and alike, considerate of the Latinless reader and intended for ready comprehension.

Many of the poems in the Storrs collection, using a stanzaic rhyme form (usually the quatrain), "vary widely, not to say wildly, in their rendering of

Horace's diction, figures of speech, and even dramatic situation." Which is to say, they are imitations rather than translations. I have made no effort to determine how many hundreds of translations more have appeared in the near sixty years since, nor have I anywhere encountered a tally. My own rendering of *Odes* 1.5 is translation, *literary* translation; which is to say, one preserving the meaning and tenor of the original in as poetic an English as possible (here rhymed and metered), while providing English-language equivalents (alliteration, assonance, figures of speech) for what is untransferrable from the Latin (Lat. *transfero/translatus* 'bring over/brought over'; Eng. transfer, translate).

Though easily said in retrospect, it was with trepidation that I undertook to translate the single most frequently and freely translated Latin lyric from antiquity, even as Horace himself "has had more translators than any other poet, ancient or modern." The attraction, in the words of one pundit, owes to "the perversity of human endeavor," Horace's poetry being "about as untranslatable as you can get." By the number of its renderings, we further surmise that *Odes* 1.5, as Pyrrha herself, is especially alluring; the most exciting and exacting of Horace's poems; its pretenders, no less than Pyrrha's own, left in disarray. The prediction that "no poem of Horace will continue to attract the attention of critics more magnetically than his ode to Pyrrha" remains true today—though truer more of the poem's translators than of its critics. In over 1,500 JSTOR results surfacing from a "Pyrrha" search, translations continue apace, the last significant article apparently dating to 1985. Variations on the search—"Horace C. 1.5," "Carm. 1.5," "*Odes* 1.5"—do not appreciably alter the count. If the count is correct, this essay is the first major study in over thirty years, one further offering a new translation and focusing on translation method.

My initial reservations aside, the poem would have been conspicuous by its absence, relating, as it does, to my book's title and theme. The translation was first intended as unrhymed decasyllabics—with *ex voto* enough for that, if done well. It was ultimately rhymed, as follows:

§121

Quis multa gracilis te puer in rosa
perfusus liquidis urget odoribus
   grato, Pyrrha, sub antro?
   cui flavam religas comam,   4

simplex munditiis? Heu quotiens fidem
mutatosque deos flebit et aspera
    nigris aequora ventis
      emirabitur insolens,   8

qui nunc te fruitur credulus aurea,
qui semper vacuam, semper amabilem
    sperat, nescius aurae
      fallacis. Miseri, quibus   12

intemptata nites. Me tabula sacer
votiva paries indicat uvida
    suspendisse potenti
      vestimenta maris deo.   16

◆

What slim and sweetly scented lad, in such
Roses, Pyrrha, roses, crowds thee now, lush
Throughout your grotto grown? For whom stylest
Thou that flaxen hair o'erflown, thus artless   4

In your elegance? Guileless lad, Alas!
How ofttimes gasping in waters amassed,
Gales glowering, will he, aghast, repent
Your grace bygone and heaven's grim intent,   8

Who assesses thee gold, caresses thee,
Who fancies—poor naïf—that ever free
Will'st ever loving be, unoccupied;
Wide-eyed the while, by trait'rous winds untried.   12

Hapless they for whom thou gleam'st untested!
But votive plaque to vestibule applied
Avers that I, unshipwrecked, here abide,
Threads drenched, but by Neptune unmolested.   16

    Horace's poem is all of sixty-five words; my translation, one hundred and five. As any translation of Latin or Greek poetry (or prose), and for reasons to be explained, the translation of a classical language *inevitably* runs longer than the original (here by about 40 percent). Further, of Horace's sixty-five words, fully—almost inordinately—twenty-one are adjectives (30 percent). And not one of them appears immediately adjacent to the noun it modifies, there being one or more intervening words (with the minor exception of *mutatosque deos* 'and [-*que*] changed gods'). The issue, of course, is one of Latin's flexible word order.

2. Learning Latin As You Go

For the beginning student of Latin (others may skip this and the following section), I offer a number of Latin-language basics before turning to matters of style and interpretation. The first issue, though largely mechanical, is significant.

Latin nouns belong to different systems called declensions (five of them). Latin adjectives also belong to declensions (three of them). Nouns and adjectives "decline" (Lat. *de* + *clino* 'lean') by "leaning away" from the *nominative* case (Lat. *nomen* 'name'), the case containing the sentence's *subject*. Each case has its own ending, and different cases sometimes share the same ending. I use words appearing in *Odes* 1.5.

Example 1
(1st decl. noun)

We use the following word:

    aura (fem.), 'breeze, wind, gale'

Singular

Nominative:	aura, breeze [subject]
Genitive:	aurae, of the breeze [possession]
Dative:	aurae, to/for the breeze [interest]
Accusative:	auram, breeze [direct object]
Ablative:	aurā, by/from the breeze [agency]
Vocative:	[O] Pyrrha [direct address]

Plural

Nominative:	aurae, breezes
Genitive:	aurarum, of the breezes
Dative:	auris, to/for the breezes
Accusative:	auras, breezes
Ablative:	auris, by/from the breezes

Example 2
(1st & 5th decl. nouns and 1st decl. adj.)

We use the following words:

> *aureus* (masc.), *aurea* (fem.), *aureum* (neut.), 'golden'
> *rosa* (fem.), 'rose'
> *fides* (fem.), 'hope'

Note that noun/adj. "agreement" from one declension to another does not necessarily involve identical noun/adj. endings.

Singular (only)

	1st decl. fem.		5th decl. fem.	
Nominative:	aurea	rosa	fides	golden rose/trust
Genitive:	aureae	rosae	fidei	of a golden rose/trust
Dative:	aureae	rosae	fidei	to/for a golden rose/trust
Accusative:	auream	rosam	fidem	golden rose/trust
Ablative:	aureā	rosā	fide	by/for a golden rose/trust

Example 3
(1st decl. fem. & 2nd decl. neut. nouns and 3rd decl. adj.)

We use the following words:

> *aura* (fem.), 'breeze, wind, gale'
> *aurum* (neut.), 'gold'
> *fallax* (nom., fem., & neut.), 'false, deceptive'

	1st dec. fem.	2nd decl. neut.	3rd decl. adj.	
Nominative:	aura	aurum	fallax	false gale/gold
Genitive:	aurae	auri	fallacis	of false gale/gold
Dative:	aurae	auro	fallaci	to/for false gale/gold
Accusative:	auram	aurum	fallax	false gale/gold
Ablative:	aurā	auro	fallaci	by/from false gale/gold

Even this limited example shows the potential for confusion—and need for training in the language that dominated Europe for one thousand years after the fall of the Roman Empire. Is *aurae* genitive or dative singular, or nominative plural? Only the context tells. Is *aura/aurā* nominative or ablative singular, given that Latin texts typically omit the long mark of the ablative *ā*-ending? Context again determines. The matter is helped in poetry by metric scansion (i.e., the poetic determination of long and short vowels/ syllables for purposes of rhythm). But scansion for modern readers takes time, interrupting the pace and sense of disclosure by which the poem's meaning is meant to unfold. Moreover, nouns and adjectives in different declensions—*though not always displaying the same case endings*—"agree" in (1) case (nom., gen., etc.); (2) number (sing. or pl.); and (3) gender (masc., fem., or neut.).

Thus the three "easy" examples from the poem's opening lines are these: *multa . . . in rosa* 'in much [many a] rose' is readily identified as an ablative phrase, comprised of an identically declined first-declension noun and adjective; the phrase governed by the preposition *in* + ablative. Scansion confirms that both final *a*-endings are long: *multā . . . in rosā*. Similarly, *grato . . . sub antro* 'beneath a pleasing grotto' (abl. sing., 2nd decl.); and *flavam . . . comam* 'flaxen/auburn hair' (acc. sing., 1st decl.). One thus need know not only the noun or adjective declension (five noun and three adjective declensions) or verb conjugation (four of them), but the often overlapping endings proper to each. The dictates of Latin vocabulary are stringent (and those of Greek more so), and much memorization is required. But all becomes quite second nature with study and focused reading. Back when Latin was part of elementary or junior-high-school education (as it was in many boys schools), it became second nature by young adulthood.

Because Latin syntax—prose and especially poetry—is not predicated on the sequential presentation of phrases, or units of thought, but on a free and open word order dependent on coordinated word endings, Latin differs significantly from English. This is a matter of considerable difficulty albeit some reward to the contemporary reader. In sum, "inflected" languages— Lat. *in* + *flecto* 'bend in(ward), change, curve, vary by change of form'—allow for the intricate (yet always metrical) interlocking of words, resulting in a texture richer than anything known to English verse or verse translation. The effect, in Nietzsche's famed formulation of Horace, "is in certain languages not to be hoped for":

> This mosaic of words, in which every word, by sound, by placing, and by meaning, spreads its influence to the right, to the left, and over the whole; this minimum in extent and number of symbols, this maximum thereby achieved in the effectiveness of the symbols—all this is Roman, and believe me, elegant par excellence.

And as amplified:

> The energizing tension between the static "mosaic" quality of the diction, which invites you to pause and admire every word, every stanza individually, and the forward-moving pull of his long arcs of thought is what gives Horatian verse its great distinction.

What we lose in translating such poetry is the original's "music, its cultural resonance, and the special pace at which it surrenders its information."

A further element in the compression of *Odes* 1.5 (and of Latin and Greek overall) is Latin's general absence of subject pronouns—*I, he, we, they*, etc. (which are generally "contained" or understood in verb endings)—and of prepositions (only two in 1.5: *in*, line 1; *sub*, line 3). Verb endings typically convey the subject pronoun: *nito* 'I shine', *nites* 'you shine'; and case endings typically convey the unexpressed preposition. Thus *antro* or *in antro* both equally mean, in context, 'in a/the cave', though *antro* or *ab antro* can both equally mean, in context, 'from a/the cave'. Whether a preposition is expressed or implied typically depends on stylistic preference or metrical need (a beat too many with the preposition; the right number without). English has none of these resources or concerns. Thus, the inevitable clutter, or "flotsam," of little words in English—syntactically significant, but substantively meaningless: *in, to, for, by, with, I, you, they*, etc. One can little avoid but only minimize the effect of such occurrences by attempting to distance inconsequential words, one from the other, avoiding monosyllabic runs.

3. The Latin Learned Applied

Here, stanza by stanza, with syntactically paired words italicized, bolded, or underscored, etc. (in that order), is a literal, necessarily clumsy translation. The various ellipses (. . .) indicate that words consecutively rendered in English are interrupted by, or interlocked with, Latin words or phrases otherwise comprising the sense. Words consecutively rendered in English may, in the Latin, appear in two or three different lines within the stanza (such occurrences indicated by stanza-break backslashes). To understand the poem as readily in Latin as in translation—i.e., to understand it as readily as would a literate reader of Horace's time—today's reader would need know, *while reading*, which words go together, the poem's sense ever "suspended" from one word or phrase to the next. But it is a daunting task, even for the well-schooled contemporary reader of Latin. Indeed, figuring which words go together *takes time*, constituting a "sub-task" prerequisite to meaning.

> Quis *multa* **gracilis** te **puer** in *rosa*
> perfusus <u>liquidis</u> urget <u>odoribus</u>
>   *grato*, Pyrrha, sub <u>*antro*</u>?
>   cui **flavam** religas **comam**,

> Quis . . . gracilis . . . puer
> Which   slender   boy

> multa . . . in rosa
> many   in rose

> perfusus   liquidis . . . odoribus
> suffused [with] liquid   odors

> te . . . / urget / Pyrrha
> you / presses / Pyrrha

> grato . . .   sub   antro
> [a] pleasing beneath cave?

> cui . . .   religas
> [for] whom [do you] bind back

> flavam . . .   comam
> [your] flaxen hair

◆

simplex munditiis? Heu quotiens fidem
mutatosque deos flebit et <u>aspera</u>
  <u>nigris</u> aequora <u>ventis</u>
  emirabitur insolens,

simplex   munditiis?
simple [in your] elegance?

Heu quotiens fidem
Alas, how often faith [in you]

mutatosque deos flebit   et aspera
changed and gods he will weep and harsh

nigris   aequora ventis
[with] black waters   winds

emirabitur   insolens,
he will wonder at   unaccustomed,

◆

qui nunc *te* fruitur credulus *aurea*,
qui semper **vacuam**, semper **amabilem**
  sperat, nescius <u>aurae</u>
  <u>fallacis</u>. Miseri, quibus

qui nunc te   fruitur credulus   aurea,
who now you enjoys believing [you] gold

qui semper vacuam, semper amabilem
who always available, always able to be loved

sperat,   nescius   aurae
hopes [you], unknowing [of] breeze

fallacis. Miseri,   quibus
false.   Wretched   to whom

◆

intemptata nites. Me *tabula* **sacer**
votiva **paries** indicat <u>uvida</u>

215

suspendisse _potenti_
vestimenta maris _deo_.

intemptata   nites. Me   tabula   sacer
untested [you] shine. Me [on] tablet [the] sacred

votiva paries indicat   uvida
votive wall   indicates wet

suspendisse   potenti
[to have] hung [to the] potent

vestimenta   maris deo.
garments [of the] sea   god.

Horace, here as elsewhere, shows the impossibility of Latin syntactic breadth to create formal effects in English. The most intricate of these effects appears in the final stanza, where the word arrangement itself creates a visual _mosaic_ impression of the poem's own imagery. The visual image created is that of the temple wall itself, set about with _ex voto_'s. "In the arrangement of words, two interlocking pairs on either side of the main verb, we can see the very design of a _tabula votiva_. English, with its articles and greater reliance on explanatory prepositions, baffles so direct an effect":

> intemptata nites. Me _tabula_ **sacer**
> _votiva_ **paries** INDICAT uvida
>   suspendisse _potenti_
>   vestimenta maris _deo_.

The above stanza shows the main verb INDICAT, enclosed to either side by two interlocking pairs: _tabulā sacer_ & _votivā paries,_ and _uvida ... vestimenta_ & _potenti ... deo._ Truly a verbal mosaic (as is the first stanza). We further note INDICAT (Lat. _dico_ 'say, speak'), both meaning and _indicating_ that the personified wall "speaks out," announcing the _tabula_'s content in the poem's own words. It is _tabula votiva_ 'votive tablet' because offered "after the speaker has narrowly escaped drowning ... in fulfillment of a vow uttered in a moment of jeopardy." Horace has escaped the treacherous Pyrrha and swum ashore. The slender lad will go down with the ship.

Pretty dull stuff in literal translation, serving again to recall the long-standing precepts earlier cited in this volume (p. 173):

> I did not think it required to translate word for word, but have retained the spirit and force of the passage. For I saw it my duty not to count but weigh out the words for the reader.

> It is not [the translator's] business to translate Language into Language, but Poesie into Poesie.

4. The Meter Makes the Poem

What heightens the difficulty—and finesse—of Horace's odes is his effortless adaptation of Greek meters to Latin poetry (here, the "Third Asclepiadian," non-indigenous to Latin). Horace, in fact, showcases his ability by writing each of the first nine poems of *Odes*, Book I, in a different Greek meter, the so-called Parade Odes (the Muses nine in number). The Third Asclepiadian for the Book's first poem on an amatory theme—Horace doesn't really write "love poems"—marks the meter as especially appropriate to the theme; the meter further used in fourteen poems throughout Horace's four books of odes. The Third Asclepiadian was, nonetheless, not the metric preference of other Latin poets of the time or after. It runs as follows:

$$— —\,|—\smile\smile—\,|—\smile\smile\,|—\smile\,\text{x} \quad \text{[12 syllables]}$$
$$— —\,|—\smile\smile—\,|—\smile\smile\,|—\smile\,\text{x}$$
$$— —\,|—\smile\smile—\,|\,\text{x} \quad \text{[7 syllables]}$$
$$— —\,|—\smile\smile—\,|\smile\,\text{x} \quad \text{[8 syllables]}$$

—	long vowel/syllable
$\smile$	short vowel/syllable
x	long or short

$$— \quad —|— \,\smile\smile—|—\smile\smile\,|\,—\smile—$$
Quis multa gracilis te puer in rosa

$$— —|— \quad \smile\smile—\,|\,—\smile\smile|—\smile\smile$$
perfusus liquidis urget odoribus

$$— —| — \smile \quad \smile —|—$$

grato, Pyrrha, sub antro?

$$— —|— \quad \smile\smile — | \smile \smile$$

cui flavam religas comam.

We recall that classical meter is *quantitative*, determined by the long or short quantities of the line's vowels/syllables—vowels long "by nature" or "position"; by position when naturally short but followed by consonants. The poetic meter/rhythm is superimposed, as it were, on the words' spoken stress to the extent reasonably required to prevent the line from sounding prose-like, or sounding simply prosaic. This is to say that the avoidance of excessive coincidence between poetic beat and spoken stress is paramount. The "play" between beat and stress is thus what gives classical poetry its particular effect. English poetic meter, by significant contrast, is determined by spoken stress alone; poetic beat occurring as it would in spoken discourse, regardless vowel quantity, long or short. Though English recognizes naturally long and short vowels, it does not recognize vowels long "by position." Unelaborated spoken stress in English poetry (barring good dictional choices and other incidences of verse) can and often does lead to dreary results. Nor is there any rhyme (end-rhyme, at least) in classical poetry, Greek or Latin. The rhythm is *all*, and all that is needed to make the poetry *poetry*.

The Third Asclepiadian done, if rarely, in comparable English meter, produces the following, as per Colin Anderson's noble undertaking. Stress marks (/) appear instead of long marks (—) to indicate the solely stress-based nature of English poetry:

$$/ \quad / \ || / \ \smile\smile \ / \ || \ / \quad \smile \ \smile|| / \smile \quad /$$

What young slip of a boy, head   all anointed with

$$/ \ / \ || / \ \smile \ \smile \ / \ || / \ \smile\smile | / \smile /$$

perfumed oil, cuddles you, Pyrrha, upon a soft

$$/ \ \ / \ || \ / \ \smile\smile / || \smile$$

rose-bed heaped in a cavern?

$$/ \quad / \ || \ / \ \smile \ \smile \ / \ || \smile\smile$$

Whose love puts up your golden hair . . .

5. Making a Literary Translation

In *literal* translation the words often hasten as they will, making no particular difference or impression. Paramount in *literary* translation is the attention to *every* word, and the awareness that such translation does not occur in a vacuum. Rather, it looks to earlier efforts to see what is "out there"—to see how such efforts might be bettered (as in my "Epiphany," §144, p. 258) and to borrow or adapt judiciously. The key is *judiciously*, both in acknowledgment of one's predecessors and to keep from reinventing the wheel. One does not plunder a prior translation's *bons mots*, but integrates them to the ends of purposeful innovation. In the dedication and acknowledgments of his *Iliad* translation (2007), Rodney Merrill writes,

> I must also acknowledge the indispensable contributions of commentators, translators, and lexicographers listed in the bibliography. I have constantly had at my side the versions of Richmond Lattimore [1906–1984] and A. T. Murray [1886–1940]—the latter revised [in 1999] by William F. Wyatt—and have plundered them freely for felicitous phrasing.

This, if other than humorous, is self-indicting. Translators typically reference and borrow from their predecessors, but without "plundering" them. Pope's indebtedness to Dryden is of this kind, even as the King James translators looked to the earlier Wycliffe and Tyndale bibles. But if a new translation does not provide abundant felicitous phrasing of its own, why bother? Why even suggest it does not? The contributions of others being "indispensable," Merrill urges that *his* best is *their* best.

My own rendering is thus indebted to:

> **John Milton's** *gold . . . gales* (lines 7 and 9). This nicely reflects Horace's punning *aureā* 'golden' . . . *aurae* 'wind, gale'. This is the kind of *luck* between languages that rarely, if ever, presents. At the same time, Milton's rendition has met with a contentious reception since first penned. Thus Milton:
>
>> Who now enjoys thee credulous, all **gold**,
>> Who, always vacant, always amiable
>>> Hopes thee, of flattering **gales**
>>> Unmindful. Hapless they . . .

W. G. Shepherd's *crowds you* (line 2). "Crowds" for Lat. *urget* 'urge, press, coax, prod, prompt'—"hedges" (Mayer, 86)—conveys just the right sense of spatial and bodily proximity ("the lovers are not merely talking"). The word denotes amatory advance, the "moving in" for that first kiss or, by "euphemistic suppression," coital positioning. At the same time, it is a verb indicating something amiss, since "rarely used in such an amatory sense." Pyrrha, readily crowded or "put upon," affects acquiescence—as if trapped, confined, unable to move. But no matter. The grotto is *her* private getaway, the place to which she brings her "boy toys." They are *grato . . . sub antro* 'beneath a pleasing grotto'—pleasing *to Pyrrha,* for the pastimes she indulges there (thus, "convenient" in Shepherd's translation). Pyrrha may now be "crowded, pressed," but it is the "slender innocent," the "scented stripling," the "slim youngster" who will ultimately be crushed. Thus Shepherd:

> What slender boy besprinkled with fragrant oils
> now **crowds you,** Pyrrha, amid the roses
> in some convenient grotto?
> For whom do you dress that yellow hair . . .

Joseph P. Clancy's *What slim and sweetly scented boy* (line 1). The rendering is perfect but for Clancy's *boy,* which I change to *lad* for the alliteration. No sense in improving on perfection, but for a slight adjustment. Thus Clancy:

> **What slim and sweetly scented** boy
> presses you to the roses, Pyrrha,
> in your favorite grotto?
> For whom is your blond hair styled . . .

Cedric Whitman's *among roses, roses,* changed to *in such roses* [Pyrrha,] *roses. . . .* Whitman's brilliant locution captures the multitudinous sense of *multa . . . in rosa* 'in much rose, in many a rose, in many roses', etc. I adopt the phrasing, while spacing the iteration. I would not otherwise have thought to repeat "roses." Thus Whitman:

> What slim youth, Pyrrha, drenched in perfumed oils,
> Lying in an easy grotto **among roses, roses**
> Now woos, and watches you
> Gathering back your golden hair . . .

(Also appealing is Michie's "ensconced in a / Snug cave curtained with roses.")

Colin Anderson's *dripping duds* changed to *threads drenched* (*uvida . . . / vestimenta* 'damp[ened] clothing', line 16), my consonant-heavy phrase conveying water's weight and slosh. This either-way unlikely colloquialism conveys the familiar "down home" manner of one's "kicking off his shoes" (to change the metaphor) and taking hearth-bound comfort after perilous voyage. Thus Anderson:

> . . . I won't be caught by that!
> Votive plaques to the sea god on the wall of his
> sacred shrine show that I have
> hung up my **dripping duds** for good.

It is further worth noting that Anderson (2010) translates all the odes of Book I into English metric equivalents of the Latin—a daunting task with variable, though always admirable, results. Less successful is J. B. Leishman's translation (1956) of thirty odes in original meters from *Odes*, Books 1–4, e.g.:

> For me,
> yonder sanctified wall's picturing tablet shows
> I survived to uphang there
> oozy garments to Ocean's god.

Anderson and Leishman are, however, alike excellent in their detailed meter-explanatory and other introductory matter (Anderson offering a detailed review of Leishman). Also translating into English metric equivalents are Charles E. Passage (1983); Guy Lee (1998); and, selectively, James Michie (1963).

6. Select Literary Elements

I have translated into rhymed decasyllabics, as noted, changing the rhyme scheme in the last stanza from a-a-b-b to a-b-b-a, wakening the reader to Horace's summation and giving it edge. The changed rhyme scheme conveys a "take note" quality.

Also, in the first stanza: "roses . . . *lush* / Throughout *your* grotto grown." *Lush* and *your* capture the otherwise untranslated sense of *grato . . . sub antro* 'in [your] pleasing grotto'. Nothing is to be made of Lat. *grato* 'pleasing' (abl. neut. sing.) and Eng. *grotto*, the similarity pure coincidence. Though "grow/ grown" does not appear in the Latin, the idea is implicit. "Grotto grown," moreover, conveys the alliterative and anagrammatic quality of *grato . . . sub antro. O'erflown*, internally rhyming with *grown*, does not appear in the Latin, but is implicit as well: "for whom," asks Horace, "do you bind <u>back</u>"—*religas*—your flaxen hair"? Pyrrha sports no pageboy, but longish hair, needing to be backward set or pinned—exposing an erogenous neck (as imagined) and marking "an assertion of detached control of the situation." *Flaxen* was chosen over *yellow* or *golden*—both too common and otherwise implicit throughout the poem—for the *f*- alliterative *for . . . / flaxen . . . o'erflown*. More on Pyrrha's grotto and flaxen hair below.

The translation's formal qualities aside, internal rhymes appear in *Alas—gasping—amassed—aghast* (2nd stanza); *assesses—caresses, free—be, unoccupied—wide-eyed—untried* (3rd stanza); and otherwise in the iterative end-rhymes of stanzas three and four: *unoccupied—untried/applied—abide.*

A word is required on the poem's most heralded phrase: *simplex munditiis* 'simple/artless in your elegance'. No elaborate "do" for Pyrrha; her flowing hair looks great with the slightest containing gesture, as casually gathered in a knot behind or aside her head. The phrase moreover "implies the chic conferred by sure, simple taste—and also that the simplicity is an illusion." *Simplex* (voc. fem. sing.) refers to Pyrrha. Milton's "Plain in thy neatness" gets it just right (not "plain in *its* neatness"). Clancy's "For whom is your blond hair styled, / deceptively simple" gets it wrong. It is, in fact, surprising just how many Latinists do—taking vocative *simplex* (referring to Pyrrha) as though accusative *simplicem* (referring to *comam* 'hair'; trisyllabic *simplicem* unsuited to the meter). The problem is easily neutralized by a certain ambiguity: "For whom those auburn tresses bindest thou / with simple care?" or "For whom do you dress that yellow hair / so simply neat?" Such approaches leave the referent (Pyrrha or hair) acceptably vague.

As further concerns Pyrrha's *comam*, it is *flavam* 'yellow, golden, flaxen, tawny, reddish'. The adjective *flavam* (acc. fem. sing.) is phonetically similar to *flammam* 'flame' (acc. fem. sing. of *flamma*), which it here suggests. For this reason, the poem likely omits the word *flamma*, its import also apparent in both the name *Pyrrha* and Gr. *purrós* 'flame-colored, yellowish-red'. Thus, and again, the suitedness of Gladstone's "auburn tresses" (so also "auburn haired"). (Of interest in this connection is the hair color of Poynter's *The Cave of the Storm Nymphs*, which serves as the cover art of this volume.) There is thus, depending on light and viewing point, a variable aspect to the color of Pyrrha's hair; even as combustion is of variable hues—the variable Pyrrha herself causing dramatic changes of fortune. Alternatively (or concurrently), "The female protagonist, as her name adumbrates, is alluring for the blond beauty of her hair (*flavam*), and, in the eyes of the entranced lover, for her golden character (*aurea*). But she soon is changed . . . into a beacon fire whose flames lure unsuspecting devotees to their doom, shipwrecked in love's treacherous waters."

Reddishness of hair was rare in antiquity, then considered a barbarous characteristic suggesting feral origins in Scythia or Thrace. The Athenian comic playwright Aristophanes (5th century BC) chides his countrymen for rejecting the best of their own citizens for *brazen/bronzed* foreigners and *redheads*, calling them odious offspring of odious parents. The word there used for "brazen" is Gr. *chalkois* 'bronze' (dat. masc. pl.)—which in Eng. brassy continues the millennia-old opprobrium. Eng. bronze likely derives from Ger. *brunst* 'fire/conflagration' (and related cognates), which brings us back to Horace's *Pyrrha,* for it is precisely the Gr. *purríais* (dat. pl. from the rare *purrías* 'red-colored serpent') that Aristophanes uses to designate redhead:

> τοῖς δὲ **χαλκοῖς** καὶ ξένοις καὶ **πυρρίαις**
> καὶ πονηροῖς κἀκ πονηρῶν εἰς ἅπαντα χρώμεθα
> ὑστάτοις ἀφιγμένοισιν, οἷσιν ἡ πόλις πρὸ τοῦ
> οὐδὲ φαρμακοῖσιν εἰκῇ ῥᾳδίως ἐχρήσατ᾽ ἄν.

> But the **brazen** foreigners and **redheads,**
> worthless offspring of worthless parents, to these we
> everywhere resort, these recently arrived, whom
> the city earlier would not have thought to use as
> random scapegoats.

Further built into Pyrrha's name, then, are the dangers of fire and its doings; of fire's unpredictable spread; of its searing and consuming power; of its unwanted dying, or extinguishment by water—fire as necessary as it is untrustworthy.

Horace's verbal dexterity continues with play—and crossover imagery—between *aureā* 'golden' (abl. fem. sing.) and *aurae* 'of [the] wind' (gen. fem. sing.). Lat. *aura* 'breeze, wind' (nom. fem. sing.; gen. *aurae*) has a secondary meaning, as in English, of "aura," meaning *glow, sheen, shine*—an *emanation*; "'charm', that which fascinates about a woman," or even *sex appeal*. Aura as *emanation* encompasses *mood, disposition,* or *character,* all as changeable as *aura* 'wind' itself. *Aureā* 'golden', on the other hand, agrees with *tē* (pers. pro. abl. fem. sing.), the direct object of *fruitur* 'he enjoys', i.e., "he enjoys you." Thus, *qui nunc te fruitur credulus aureā* 'who now, credulous, enjoys you [as] gold' (line 9); or, 'who now enjoys you believing you gold'; or, 'who now enjoys you, believing in the gold you are'—the same lad being *nescius aurae / fallacis* 'unknowing of false wind' (gen. fem. sing), or, 'of [your] false aura/quality/ [golden] disposition'. The pairing of *fruitur . . . aureā* (abl. fem.) and *aurae/fallacis* (gen. fem.) thus plays on (and into) the multivalent untrustworthiness—of gold, wind, mood; fire and water—that is Pyrrha.

There follows *Miseri quibus / intemptata nites* 'wretched they for whom [*quibus*] you shine [*nites,* 2nd pers. sing. from *niteo* 'shine') untested' (*intemptata,* perf. pass. part. from *tempto* 'try, prove, attempt, essay, assay, experiment upon'). "All that glitters isn't gold"; and 'gold' (*aurum,* nom. neut. sing.) and the 'golden' (*aureus-aurea-aureum,* nom. masc.-fem.-neut.) *deceive*—as much as any gale, wind, or mood (nom. *aura*) (the gale/gold collocation Milton's, as seen). It is noted that cognates of *nites* 'you shine' are often used by Horace to indicate seductive beauty and its consequences.

The Romans, aware as we of fool's gold, devised ways still used today of assaying the element. In the passage examined in part above, Aristophanes elaborately compares the assay of gold and that of character, concluding the Athenians ever choose the baser metal/mettle. Our golden girl—be she flaxen, auburn-tressed, or golden-red—thus shines unassayed, at least by her next and nearing victim. She appears truly minted, coin of the trusted realm, with gold's own gleam or sunny aura for noonday sail. But the naïve and sentimental lover has yet to suffer her mutations. As quickly as weather's change, the lad will have departed the cool and placid surfaces, the glistening shales and shallows of Pyrrha's rose-strewn grotto, for roiling storm-swept depths. No exit, and no *ex voto* for him.

7. Thematically Reinforcing Alliterations

"*Grotto grown*" unleashes the translation's dominant hard "g" (and "l") alliterations: *grotto grown—elegance—guileless—gales glowering—aghast—gasping—grace bygone—grim—gold—gleam'st.* The stick-in-the-throat "*g*" alliteration (recalling contextually resonant words such as *groan, grief, agony*; cf. Gr. góos 'lament') is particularly suited to the context. Other alliterative patterns are readily found throughout the translation. Their abundance, by way of equivalence in translation, reflects comparable qualities in the original, by stanza and throughout. The original has a pervasive and, if you will, stormy or crashing "k" sound in interrogatory and relative pronouns beginning with "q" (entire word bolded); in words containing "q" (letter alone bolded); and words containing "c" (letter alone bolded; "c" always *hard* in classical Latin). Thus, in the order appearing:

> **Quis** ('which'?)—*graçilis* ('slender')—*liquidis* ('liquid')—*cui* ('for whom'?)—**quotiens** ('how often'?)—*aequora* ('water')—*qui* (who)—*çredulus* ('believing')—*qui* ('who')—*nesçius* ('unknowing')—*fallaçis* ('false')—**quibus** ('to whom')—*saçer* ('sacred')—*indiçat* ('indicates').

The crackling insistently interrogatory or disbelief-conveying "q" and "c" bespeak warning and catastrophe—the crash and shipwreck to come. We note that Lat. *naufragium* 'shipwreck' does not itself appear in the poem, though translators often include it, naming the avoided disaster. The omission of shipwreck may be due to the votive tablet's own likely depiction of that very event. "In an illiterate age, the plaque often told its story by means of a picture." The interrogatories also recall—for us, perhaps, though not necessarily for Horace—the repeated questions in Sappho's "Hymn to Aphrodite" ("Who now?" "Whom this time?", etc.—repeated or run-on questions conveying urgency). Likewise—as recollected from high-school Latin, and so affecting in its verbal assault—the famed inquisitional opening of Cicero's First Catilinarian Oration (1st century BC). The great statesman and orator saves the Roman Republic from conspiratorial overthrow, thus beginning his denunciation of the renegade senator Catiline:

Quo usque **t**andem abutere, **C**atilina, patientia nostra? **Quam d**iu etiam iste tuus furor nos elu**d**et? **Quem ad f**inem sese effrenata ia**c**tabit auda**c**ia? [*sese* duplicated emphatic for *se* 'itself']

How long, pray tell, O Catiline, will you exploit our patience? By what means yet will that madness of yours mislead us? To what length, alack, will [your] unbridled effrontery flaunt itself?

The other marked alliterative pattern in *Odes* 1.5 is an extraordinary run of the mild and flowing consonants "m" and "n." These, together with "l" and "r" (also present), are referred to as "liquid consonants" because of their smooth and rolling sounds. And fittingly so, as often noted, because *Odes* 1.5 is "saturated" with liquid (scents), waters, and sea. Such sounds, it may be argued, reflect the proverbial calm before the storm. In the order presented throughout the poem ("m" and "n" alone highlighted):

> *multa* ('many')—*flavam* ('flaxen')—*antro* ('cave')—*comam* ('hair')—*simplex munditiis* ('simple [in your] elegance')—*quotiens fidem* ('how often faith')—*mutatosque* ('changed')—*nigris* ('black')—*ventis* ('winds')—*emirabitur* ('he will marvel')—*insolens* ('unaccustomed')—*nunc* ('now')—*semper vacuam* ('always available'), *semper amabilem* ('always lovable')—*nescius* ('unknowing')—*Miseri* ('miserable')—*intemptata nites* ('untested you shine')—*Me* ('me')—*indicat* ('indicates')—*suspendisse potenti vestimenta maris* ('have hung my clothes to the potent [god] of the sea').

Alliteration is as richly abundant at the stanzaic level, as the closing stanza indicates with its insistent *t-p-r-v-d-n-m* iterations, as follows (number of occurrences in brackets):

("**t**" [11] – "**p**" [4])

intem**p**ta**t**a nites. Me **t**abula sacer
votiva **p**aries indicat uvida
  suspendisse **p**otenti
  vestimenta maris deo.

("**r**" [3] – "**v**" [4] – "**d**" [4])

intemptata nites. Me tabula sace**r**
votiva paries in**d**icat u**v**ida

suspendisse potenti
vestimenta maris deo.

("n" [6] – "m" [4])

intemptata nites. Me tabula sacer
votiva paries indicat uvida
suspendisse potenti
vestimenta maris deo.

Similar qualities, aside those already noted, are apparent in the translation (yielding, among other alliterations, 26 "r" sounds, 14 "s" [including letter "x"], and 11 "d").

("r" [12] – "s" [14])

What slim and sweetly scented lad, in such
Roses, Pyrrha, roses, crowds thee now, lush
Throughout your grotto grown? For whom stylest
Thou that flaxen hair o'erflown, thus artless

("l" [8] – "m" [3] – "n" [7], "r" [6])

(the liquid consonants)

In your elegance? Guileless lad, Alas!
How ofttimes gasping in waters amassed,
Gales glowering, will he, aghast, repent
Your grace bygone and heaven's grim intent,

("w" [4] – "f" [3] – "d" [6] – "tr" [reiterative])

Who prizes thee as gold, caresses thee,
Who fancies—poor naïf—that ever free
Will'st ever loving be, unoccupied;
Wide-eyed the while, by trait'rous winds untried.

("p" [5] – "v" [4] – "d" [6] – "t" [11] – "r" [6])

Hapless they for whom thou gleam'st untested!
But votive plaque to vestibule applied
Avers that I, unshipwrecked*, here abide,
Threads drenched*, but by Neptune unmolested.

*final "d" with "t" sound

8. The Danger Without

The imminence of danger is also apparent in such descriptives as *gracilis* 'slender'; *insolens* 'unaccustomed, unprepared'; *nescius* 'unknowing'. The boy knows not where, what, or with whom he is; knows nothing of what to expect. He lives on 'hope' alone (*sperat*, line 11). There will be nothing *gratum* 'pleasing' for this *gracilis . . . puer* 'wisp of a lad' in Pyrrha's hideaway embrace—the hideaway concealing, the embrace enfolding the boy therein, his tomb twice sealed from the outset. (How different the *puer furens* of *Odes* 1.13.11–12, leaving his telltale teeth marks on Lydia's lips; Lydia 'hoping' [*speres*, line14] that he will be forever hers.) Further in this vein, the exclamatory *Heu* 'Alas' and unique [*e*]*mirabitur* 'he will [fully] wonder' (fut. act./dep. indic. from *miror* 'wonder'; Eng. admire, miracle)—unique because the only attested instance (as often noted) of emphatic *e*-prefixed *miror* (Lat. *e/ex* 'from, from out of, outside of'). *Emirabitur* thus signals "he will be outside of himself with wonder" or, more idiomatically, "beside himself in wonder," "stupefied."

Emirabitur further strengthens context as the poem's sole pentasyllabic—wonder being manifold. Renowned British classical scholar of his time Richard Bentley (1662–1742), writing in Latin, much objected to the words, *Heu quotiens . . . / emirabitur insolens*, arguing that one cannot repeatedly (*quotiens*) be utterly amazed (*emirabitur*) and, in the process, remain unaccustomed (*insolens*) to it all. But that is doubtless the point. Horace intends ever recurring stupefaction, the betrayal *ever initially* registered, the pain renewedly felt. This is tantamount to perpetual prelude, the kind of pain Dante would later devise for the sinners of his *Inferno*. "The sound of the pentasyllabic *emirabitur* excellently evokes [a] state of long and stunned amazement." One may compare Catullus's *conturbabimus illa* 'we will confound them' [the kisses], lest they be subject to count (§111, p. 186); similarly, my own "multitudinous kisses" (§145 [2nd stanza], p. 259); cf. J. A. Symonds's "multitudinous pinions" (Addendum [3rd stanza], p. 167). So too is love's fire, a'race beneath the skin, "accelerated" by Sappho's hexasyllabic *pur up-a-de-drom-ēk-en* 'flame [slips] racing neath' (§2, p. 109, in a prefixed reduplicated verbal form).

Yes, the boy's fate is from the outset sealed. Pyrrha—in one manner of speaking (the other below)—has already consumed him. His designation as *puer* 'boy' dictionally *subsumes* him—i.e., places him beneath or within—**Pyrrha**'s fiery name (Gr. *pur* 'fire'): he is kindling; moth to the flame. The wordplay ingeniously continues in the intervening prefix **per-**: *puer* ... / *per-fusus* ... / *Pyrrha*. The *puer* is *perfusus* ... *liquidis odoribus* 'doused through with liquid scents' (possible hint of *doloribus* 'griefs' in *odoribus* 'scents'), thinking he'll score with that extra splash of cologne. It is an idle thought in the already rose-saturated grotto. The boy, in sum, "belongs to *jeunesse dorée* ['gilded youth'], is heavily scented, and got up accordingly." It is overkill, to say nothing of diffidence, opposite the artlessly elegant Pyrrha, her "appearance. . . . due to careful, though unobtrusive, grooming."

The verb *perfusus* 'doused, flown through with'—(perf. pass. part. of *perfundo*; Lat. *fundus* 'bottom'; Eng. fund, profound, foundation; perfuse, perfusion)—is prelude to the "soaking" to come and the *uvida* / . . . *vestimenta* 'drenched garb' the boy will not survive to hang *ex voto*. *Liquidis* (abl. masc. pl. of *liquidus*) is a word explicitly associated—more often in Latin than in English—with bodies of water, bad weather, and tempest. Lucretius refers to the sea as *liquida moles* 'liquid mass'; to a torrential downpour as *liquidissima caeli tempestas* 'a "liquidinous" fury of the sky'; while Propertius refers to an ocean voyage as *liquidum iter* 'liquid way'. *Boy overboard, applying cologne*. Also involved are contexts (too numerous to mention) associating *liquidus*, in Latin as in English, with what is pure, pristine, positive, transparent—their opposites all here awaiting, including fire itself.

9. The Danger Within

That fragrantly enrosed—that lushly *gratum* 'pleasing, favor rendering' and quintessentially female-enflowered entryway! What there awaits *multa* ... *in rosa* 'amid many roses'—as urged by their color (and the suggested flaxen or auburn color of Pyrrha's hair)—but the fiery element in Pyrrha's very name? The grotto, as we now suggest, is not merely an opening in the ground, but Pyrrha's own "portal"—little inviting for all the grotto's gardened care and adornment.

Antrum 'grotto, cave, cavern' as bodily portal, entry, or arrival point, would have been as intuitively apparent to the ancients as to us. *Antrum* was given to such use even in antiquity and is so used today, primarily in medical contexts. Three examples follow. I first selectively quote from a lengthy

Virgilian passage, replete with associations for our Horatian context, ending with the phrase *exesae arboris antrum* 'grotto of an age-worn tree' (where bees make their home):

> Saepe etiam **effossis**, si vera est fama, **latebris**
> sub terra fovere larem, penitusque repertae
> pumicibusque cavis **exesaeque arboris antro***.

> Oft **in burrowed coverts**, if tale be true,
> They make their comfy habitats neath ground,
> And deeply lodged in hollow rocks are found,
> Or in **arbored grotto by age worn through**.

> **exesae* 'eaten out', perf. pass. part. of *ex-edo/ex-esus*
> 'eat/eaten'; gen. fem. sing. agreeing with gen. fem.
> sing. *arboris* (nom. *arbor* 'tree').

We see, then, in Horace's own contemporary Virgil the nearly biological, warmth- and comfort-bearing association of *antrum*. The bees, moreover, are *penitusque repertae* 'deeply lodged' (*repertae* lit. 'discovered, found').

Similarly, in the Roman satirist Juvenal (1st century AD), we find *claustro . . . antro* 'enclosed grotto' in the sense of *litter, sedan*, i.e., where the elite take their seated and secluded comfort. Juvenal thus complains of his friend's extravagantly expensive fish, which were forgivable if, instead of bought for himself, were

> . . . magnae si misit amicae,
> quae vehitur **clauso** latis specularibus **antro** . . .

> . . . sent to some great lady who rides in a **closed off** broad-windowed **litter**.

Rather later, in the writings of Sidonius Apollinaris (5th century AD, Gallo-Roman poet, diplomat, and bishop), we find *antrum* in the actual bodily cavity sense, i.e., *narium antra* 'nasal passages' (lit. 'grottoes of the nostrils'). This matches the sense in which *antrum* has been applied in contemporary medical usage, e.g., antrum, antral; gastric (antral) ulcer. Responding at length to his brother-in-law's request for a description of Theoderic the Great, King of the Goths (454–526 AD), Sidonius thus writes in relevant part:

Si forma quaeratur. . . . nasus venustissime incurvus. Labra subtilia nec dilatatis oris angulis ampliata. Pilis **infra narium antra** fruti-cantibus cotidiana succisio.

If features are the issue. . . . The nose is finely aquiline; the lips are thin and not enlarged by angulated dilation of the mouth. Every day the hair sprouting **from his nostrils** is cut back [lit., because of the hairs sprouting **from under his nasal passages,** there is a daily cutting. . . .]

It is noteworthy that the position- or spatial-related associations of *an-trum* have persisted over time: *grato . . . **sub** antro* (Horace); ***infra** narium antra* (Sidonius). The *antrum* itself being *beneath* or *within* the ground/ cliff/facial structure, there is typically something under or inside the *antrum* itself (be it person, beast, or growth). Even the passage from Juvenal sug-gests those implicitly beneath the *antrum* 'litter'—bearing it. Though there are large *antra*—e.g., Calypso's cave, the Cyclops's cave, Sir Edward John Poynter's *Cave of the Storm Nymphs* (see cover)—the *antrum* is typically narrow and entered in a crouching position (e.g., Juv. *clauso . . . antro*, above); crawled through on belly, hands, and knees; a lurking space, narrowly if at all escaped, and typically with sexual connotations, all as in *Odes* 1.5. Today's medical terminology designating the female reproductive organs is replete with such notions: cervical *canal*, internal *os* (mouth), uterine *tube*, fallopian *tube*, uterine *cavity* (Lat. *cavus* 'hollow'; cf. cave, cavity, cavern [and preced-ing note]). The Latin root with its associated English etymologies has an analogue in Heb. ה ב קּ נ (NIKĀVAH) ('female', Gen. 1.27) and ב קּ נ (NE**KEV**) 'perforation'; the anagram NQV–QVN yielding such words as *queen*; Old. Eng. *cwene* 'woman, prostitute, wife'. "Grotto," more poetic than "cave" in our context, derives, as seen, via Italian, from Gr. *krupto/kruptos* 'hide/hidden' (Eng. crypt).

It is all one and the same for what is itself properly deemed the ety-mological encryption of Lat. *antrum.* The boy has entered the cave: the structural formation itself and/or bodily passageway within it—points of both entry and internment. Upon entering the passageway, however con-strued, he is *grato . . . sub antro* 'beneath/(within) a pleasing grotto'. One commentator suggests "*sub*: 'in'; lit., 'under (the cover of)'," incidentally giving credence to the notion of *antrum* as a physical passageway. In that sense alone is the *antrum* "pleasing" to the boy; otherwise, and as noted, it is solely Pyrrha's whim, pleasure, and convenience that govern. Horace, however, has all inferences and implications covered.

Within the seafaring context of *Odes* 1.5, the figurative sense of *antrum* as bodily passage (see §126, p. 248) makes of Pyrrha a "port" or "harborage" (cf. §150, p. 263) where men take their comfort or, in ribald terms, "drop anchor." This much analogizes the lover to a vessel; secure the while, but shipwreck-bound. Alternatively, *woman* is the vessel of love's venturing, the sexual handling of woman a form of seafaring (as it is a form of horsemanship, §§ 51, 94); the sea god Neptune, an inventor with Minerva of the chariot, is also associated with horses. The imagistically multivalent Pyrrha thus represents the totality of aquatic disaster, being at once sea, harbor, and vessel. She is both the shipwreck and the sea in which it occurs—(Dylan Thomas's "Let me shipwreck in your thighs")—the Shipwreck Sea itself. As old, then, as the inequality of partners in sex—the situation in *Odes* 1.5—is the marine/nautical imagery used by analogy to the act itself. The beauty of *Odes* 1.5 resides in just how deftly Horace conveys it all, merely suggesting that which itself intends to suggest.

What we have in the opening stanza, in one sense, is shipwreck in reverse, or where least expected; shipwreck at, and merely for being in, port—the port providing no harbor, but engulfed, tsunami-like. The stripling, for his part, is from the outset unmarked for survival, his scented suffusion not only predictive of a watery fate but also embalming him as dead upon arrival. There he lies, sprawled prone—and thus again in reverse—on the pyre that is Pyrrha. The roses, so viewed, are not merely amorous accoutrement. They are part of a cremation ceremony; while the flame and *ardor* are of death rather than love. The oppositions are as forceful as those between fire and water, the elements driving the poem. In Latin literature, to be "in the roses and violets" means to experience carefree pleasure or luxurious living. At the same time, while roses had funerary significance in Greece, "they were particularly associated with death and entombment among the Romans. As a symbol of both blooming youth and mourning, the rose often marks a death experienced as untimely or premature." So the lad in *Odes* 1.5—whether in the geological or physical *antrum*—is buried or burnt alive/deluged and sinking fast. The associations are no less assured than allusive; as changeable as Pyrrha herself, the "Eternal Feminine" in reverse—drawing us not *hinauf* 'upward', but *unten* 'down' (see p. 26–27).

10. The Poem's Predecessors

We round out these considerations with a view toward the opening of the sixty-fourth of Catullus's edition-numbered poems: the 408-line epyllion or "little epic" dealing with the marriage of Peleus and Thetis (parents of Achilles) and, by way of narrative "inset" (though longer), the marriage of Theseus and Ariadne. Catullus 64 displays a marine-sexual context as overt as Horace's *Odes* 1.5 is subdued—sexual entry the key to both, and Horace well knowing his Catullus.

It is, preliminarily, the simple house door that initially signals sexual access or rebuff, the lover either gaining, or more often denied, entry by the beloved or her parental "gatekeeper." Augustan poetry features the *paraklausithyron*—call it the "portal complaint"—i.e., the excluded lover (*exclusus amator*) outside the beloved's "door," lamenting denied "entry"; door and entry both with double entendre (*para* 'beside' + *klaus*- 'wept' [past simple stem of *klaiō* 'weep', seen repeatedly below] + *thuron* 'door'; *paraklaiō* 'weep beside'). The *paraklausithyron* endured into troubadour poetry and remains to this day, notably in twentieth-century songs, e.g., Steve Earle's "Hard Core Troubadour" ("Girl, don't bother in lockin' door / He's out there hollering. . . . You always let him in before.") and Bob Dylan's "Temporary Like Achilles" ("Well, I lean into your hallway / Lean against your velvet door / I watch upon your scorpion / Who crawls across your circus floor / Just what do you think you have to guard?"). Doorway entry presaging bodily access is seen in the example, discussed below (p. 238), from Terence. *Doorless* entry, e.g., into a cave, "abbreviates" the imagery to suggest direct and unimpeded sexual access, as in *Odes* 1.5 and related contexts. "The house and its humble counterpart, the cave, figure among the poet's [here Horace's] favorite female sexual emblems."

Especially pronounced in poetry, classical and other, are marine-sexual conceits. These include woman as sea; male as ship, and penis as ship's prow, beak, ramming rod, or oar; sailing as coition; woman sailing (dominant partner); woman the vessel (subordinate partner); woman or vagina as harbor, port; and the like. These often appear in comic contexts as determined by author disposition. One need look no further than Aristophanes to appreciate the scope. Sailing as coition takes a vividly imaginative turn in the Alexandrian, and thus recherché, Catullus 64. Knowing Catullus's poetry, as mentioned, Horace was himself influenced by the Alexandrianism that shaped it (though himself more conservative in its practices).

Catullus 64 is aptly described as "precious and mannerist in style and bizarre in form," "a feast for the senses," "[of] seductive sensuality," and "luxuriously beautiful and strange." It is within such framework that we specifically look to the poem's opening thirty lines. The poem begins amid marked sexual innuendo, starting with the description of the first-constructed ship, the Argo, on its maiden voyage (pun inevitable). Its lusty crew (the Argonauts) embark to faraway and exotic Cholcis in daring quest of the Golden Fleece, the *auratam . . . pellem*. The female pubic analogue of Lat. *pellis* 'fleece' [acc. fem. *pellem*] is clear, highlighted by *aurata = aurea* 'golden' [acc. fem. *auratam*], as earlier discussed. The quest, given its goal, is markedly antiheroic, a Homeric send-up. The maiden voyage of a mythic past, it "deflowers" the ocean on and in which it proceeds.

The crew is described as *Argivae robora pubis* 'the might of Argive youth'. Lat. *robor* (Eng. robust) literally means "hard wood, oak," here conveying a sense of erotic hard(i)ness. Lat. *pubes* (gen. *pubis*), meaning "body hair" of puberty (Eng. pubic), by metonymy designates "youth." The Argo is built of pine, Lat. *pīnus* suggesting *pēnis* 'penis'. The pines themselves are (alliteratively) *prognatae* 'born, engendered' atop a mountain peak, conveying a sense of both towering firmness and progenitive power. The ship cuts the surge with its prow, its fir-fitted oars 'dragging [and churning] the bluish water' (*caerula verrentes . . . aequora*)—and 'the oar-writhened water whitened with foam' (*tortaque remigio spumis incanuit unda*). We think in this context of Gr. *aphros* 'foam', suggesting semen, as in Hesiod's sea-born birth of *Aphro*dite from the severed genitals of Ouranos.

From the Argo's wake, i.e., from the cloven waterway, emerge the Nereids, as though vaginally "delivered." Their birth is highly eroticized because occurring, like Aphrodite's, in foam. The Nereids have risen *nutricum tenus* 'as far as their breasts', and are thus prominent at water level. Lat. *nutrix* (gen. *nutricis*, gen. pl. *nutricum*), here uniquely used of "breasts," means one who nurtures or suckles, a wet nurse. The locution thus literally means 'as far as their nurturers', bizarrely giving the Nereids, as firstborn of seafaring, an imagined breastfeeding capacity—they are "potential mothers." The Nereids suckle the Argonauts' imaginations and sexual appetites. Nereids and men thus stand stupefied in mutual surprise and admiration, the Nereids *monstrum . . . admirantes* 'admiring the apparition' that is the Argo (cf. *Odes* 1.5.8, *emirabitur insolens* 'unaccustomed will he wonder at'; a *monstrum* being something to which one is *insolens*).

Foremost of the Nereids is Thetis. Peleus espies her from the ship, and the two are instantly in love. This is one of the rare mortal/immortal unions in classical mythology, here reflecting the merged opposites—sea/land, liquid/solid—occasioning the very encounter. Peleus for his part is apostrophized as *Thessaliae columen* 'peak, height, summit [stay, support], of Thessaly'—*columen* from the same root (*cel-*, cf. *excellere* 'surpass, rise high, excel') as *columna* 'column, pillar, post'. Peleus's designation as *columen* 'rod' strengthens the notion of his towering firmness and ardor. He is, moreover, *incensus amore* 'aflame with love'. Such characterizations share in what we might call the erotics of the Argo's construction and its most purposefully erotic mission, i.e., the tragic passion of Jason and Medea (narratively enfolded into the passions of Peleus and Thetis, Theseus and Ariadne).

The first-time incursion (or immersion) of phallic wood/strength into yielding or submissive ocean is ocean-invasive, violative. It is "rape" in a tale suffused with sex and perfidy. The Argo was

> The first boat that gave the innocent sea
> Experience. When her beaked prow cut the surge
> And the waves, oar-wounded, whitened, the sea-nymphs
> Peered out of the gullies of the foam,
> Amazed at the apparition [Lat. *monstrum*]. Never before
> Or since have men's eyes seen the Nereids
> Stand nipple-naked in the green-grey swell.

The nautical-sexual conceit has a long-recognized agricultural counterpart in "plowing"—dormant earth blade-upturned, inseminated, parturitive. Catullus uses the verb *proscidit* 'tore, cleaved, broke up' (cf. 'cut the surge'; Michie, above)—the verb *proscindo* regularly used of first plowing and as sexual slang.

Horace further looks to his Greek predecessors' treatment of caves, grottoes, ravines, and the like. Caves in antiquity, and in general, often portend woe (Gr. *antron* or *speos*, Lat. *antrum* or *spelunca* 'cave, cavern'). A singular Homeric exception is the Cave of the Nymphs described in Ithaca upon Odysseus's return. It is there, with Athena's help, that Odysseus stashes the treasures given him by the Phaeacians. It is described as *antron epēraton ēeroeides* [pron. *ay-eh-raw-áy-des*] 'a lovely shaded cave' (Lattimore), from which description Horace may have taken the initially inviting notion of *gratum* 'pleasing' with reference to Pyrrha's cave (*epēraton* 'most lovely' from *ep(i)* 'upon' + *eros/eratos* 'love/beloved'; *ēeroeides* 'shady', or even 'dim/ cloudy/murky' [with a hint of menace] from *aēr* 'air' + *eidos* 'shape/form/ appearance'). We further note the connection between caves and eroticism in the collocation **eros**/**ēeroeides**—an ancillary tie, but one as surely built into the long-developed and thus associative diction that is Homer's.

Turning from such description to more typically sinister fare, Horace appears to have had Calypso's cave in mind (*Od.*, Book 5) when composing *Odes* 1.5—the name *Calypso*, as noted, from Gr. *kalupto/kalupso* 'conceal/ will conceal'. That is what the grotto-dwelling nymph does to Odysseus, making love to him for a year, after his shipwreck on her island. Like Horace's Pyrrha, Calypso is fair-haired and associated with things golden; while Odysseus, reduced to a child, *klaie* 'wept' looking out over the sea, lamenting his thwarted homecoming. The scene is predictive: Horace's lad, in tears (*flebit* 'will weep'), will himself be shipwrecked, never quite making it home (see the following Appendix for further points of comparison). The enchantress Circe, by contrast, lives in a well-appointed mansion of polished stone, nonetheless situated—from Gr. *baino/bēsomai* 'go/will go'—*en bēssēisi* 'in a ravine', ravines (tunneled enclosures resembling grottoes or caves) associated with torrents, lurking danger, and pillage. Those of Odysseus's companions whom Circe has already converted to swine sit about *klaiontas* 'weeping'. There are also tears aplenty when a number of Odysseus's crew, trapped in the Cyclops's cave, are smashed to the ground, dismembered, and devoured. Their remaining companions, witnessing the scene, are described as *klaiontes* 'weeping', holding their hands forth to Zeus. And when they finally escape, Odysseus forbids his men *klaiein* 'to weep' their missing comrades, the better to hasten escape. The association is enduring, a poignant example Keats's "La Belle Dame sans Merci": "She took me to her Elfin grot, / And there she wept and sighed full sore."

Given such contexts, Horace immediately arouses suspicion. *Grato . . . sub antro* 'beneath a pleasing grotto'? No, thanks! Associated with grottoes, caves, and the beauties or beasts that inhabit them are tears aplenty. Not for nothing will Horace's stripling weep, alas, time and again: (*Heu . . . quotiens*

/ ... *flebit*). Indeed, a late-eighteenth-century political imitation of *Odes* 1.5 (by George Howard) makes Pyrrha's *antrum* a threatening "bloodstain'd den"; the "'lair' ... wherein dangerous beasts lurk." Pyrrha, proverbial man-eater and, for all her beauty, figurative cyclops, is herself the beast. She will eat the boy alive, *consume* him, as already reflected by the dictional ingestion: the *puer* subsumed beneath or within *Pyrrha's* fiery name (p. 229).

In this way, too, Pyrrha's grottoed setting or *self* conforms to the archetype of cave (with one entry) as place of imprisonment and dwelling of harmful being; so too the motif of the hero-type's retreat into a cave followed by death. No retreat for Horace's boy, but a place from which retreat is foreclosed; the boy no type of hero, but sacrificial victim. In Sophocles's plays of the same names, the steadfast Antigone commits suicide by self-entombment in a cave, and the wounded and ever suppurative Philoctetes inhabits one.

It is, of course, in a cave (*speluncam* = *antrum*) that Dido and Aeneas consummate one of the most ill-fated love affairs in literary history. In Virgil's account, the cave is refuge from severe weather; in Horace's, the harbinger of the same to come. In Virgil, the hunting party fearfully flees helter-skelter in search of shelter (*tecta metu petiere* 'fearfully sought they cover'), leaving Dido and Aeneas to fend for themselves in the wilds:

> ... ruunt de montibus amnes.
> **Speluncam** Dido dux et Troianus eandem
> **deveniunt**: prima et Tellus et pronuba Iuno
> dant signum; fulsere ignes et conscius aether
> conubiis, summoque ulularunt vertice nymphae.
> Ille dies primus leti primusque malorum
> causa fuit ....

> ... Torrents outrace the ravines.
> Dido and the Trojan prince **descend** the same **cave;**
> First signals Mother Earth and then marriage-marking
> Juno. Fires th' air throughout consent illumining
> The union; and wood nymphs, from high their cresting trees,
> wailed wedding songs: the dire premiere of death that day
> And heartache's cause to come.

Of the word *deveniunt* (*Aen.* 4.166) 'descend, come down into, reach' (*de* + *venio*), the famed Vergilian commentator Servius (5th century AD) notes:

Bene subprimit rem pudendam: sic Terentius, "quid tum, fatue?" "Fateor."
'He [Virgil] does well to omit the shameful act: thus Terence [in the ex-
change]: [Chaerea] "What *then*, [are you an] idiot?" [Antipho] "Admitted,
I am'" (*Eun.* 604). The cryptic reference is to *Eunuchus* (*The Eunuch*) by the
comic playwright Terence (2nd century BC). Antipho has begun by asking
Chaerea an obvious question, *Quid tum*? 'What *then*?'—i.e., What did you
then do after bolting the door of your beloved's bedroom, disguised as her
eunuch? After upbraiding him (in the words quoted by Servius), Chaerea
responds clearly enough, but without specifics: "Was I to squander the won-
drous opportunity offered me, so brief, so desired, so unexpected? In truth, I
really should have been the person I was counterfeiting." What Chaerea did
in the bedroom—an enclosure, for Servius's purpose, analogous to Virgil's
speluncam 'cave', with its foregone sexual promptings—is thus clear without
elaboration (the comic dialogue moving to a different topic). Virgil, accord-
ing to Servius, allows the nature and traditional associations of a cave to
speak for themselves.

The Dido and Aeneas encounter is nonetheless elaborately anticipated
in the forested inlet and cave arrival of Aeneas's fleet toward the start of the
poem. The description utilizes, among other double entendres, the key term
antrum and speaks of a naturally formed *portum* 'port'. Similarly, and in terms
reflecting sexual release, the approaching surf is dashed on the inlet's outly-
ing breakers, receding into eddies—*quibus omnis ab alto / frangitur inque
sinus scidit sese unda redactos*. The *antrum* prefigures not only the *speluncam*
in which Aeneas and Dido will consummate their passion, "but, surely, the
intimate Dido herself." Virgil, as is known, looked to the marriage of Jason
and Medea as a model for his own story. They too consummated their most
ill-fated union Gr. *antroi en ēgatheōi* 'in a sacred grotto'; a cave, as in *Odes*
1.5, strewn with flowers and (torch) flame; the cave thereafter celebrated as
antron / Mēdeiēs 'Medea's antrum'.

11. Horace's and the Other Pyrrha

The name *Pyrrha* decidedly recalls the myth of Pyrrha and Deucalion, the
only two survivors of the Bronze Age flood sent by Zeus to destroy a de-
praved mankind; water, like fire, an untrustworthy necessity. Deucalion is the
son of Prometheus who brought *pur* 'fire' to mankind; Pyrrha, the daughter

of Pandora who opened her namesake box, loosing travails throughout the world. The pedigree and "backstory" of this antecedent couple heighten the sense of disaster inhering in Horace's Pyrrha. She incorporates the opposing elements of fire and water, which is to say she is *elemental*. Whether Pyrrha is ultimately associated with water more than fire is irrelevant. Being protean, she is now one, now the other, and both. We recall, in this connection, the anatomical aspect of Pandora, inhering in or suggesting the *antrum* of Horace's Pyrrha. Pandora's "box"—the word, as slang, long connoting female sexual anatomy—is in the original telling a *pithos* 'jar', its tapered neck suggesting vaginal entry; the space itself a trap, cavernous and danger-filled. The biblical tale offers an upright tree, a phallic snake, a ruddy breast-like apple. Eve offers her fruit, Pandora opens her box, and so on.

As the flood's sole female survivor, the mythical Pyrrha is the "first woman" archetype. As a liquid symbol alone, Horace's Pyrrha is "not merely comparable to the behavior of the sea in its inconstancy, but . . . metaphorically . . . is the sea, a natural force blind to morality." She is "the natural phenomenon 'woman' in its essence, the principle of *das ewig-Weibliche* [though downward not upward drawing]. There is, then, "as little control of Pyrrha . . . as there is of the sea"; "her tempers and whims are like a law of nature, inevitable and immutable." Escape from such a sea, if at all possible, occasions votive offerings.

The prismatic *Odes* 1.5 yields further reflections reprising Pyrrha's own. The boy's "liquid confidence" (*perfusus liquidis . . . odoribus*) will yield to tears and near-drowning in stormy seas, while Pyrrha, like her primordial flood-surviving predecessor, will remain "high and dry"—a siren in a cave. This interpretation makes Horace's Pyrrha a survivor, unperishing, imperishable; indeed, vampirish—the relentlessly preying incarnation of her havoc-related namesake. One may compare Barine in *Odes* 2.8, "a woman whose sexuality is seemingly—and for Horace, almost uniquely—unaffected by time"; her "public status as a kind of timeless object of desire . . . made to seem monstrous."

The first Pyrrha, though the good woman archetype, and thus *saved* from the flood, is havoc-related by association with the flood itself, as elsewhere recollected by Horace. The poet there fears

> . . . grave ne rediret
> saeculum Pyrrhae nova monstra questae

omne cum Proteus pecus egit altos
visere montes.

the return of the dread age of Pyrrha bewailing
new prodigies, when Proteus drove his entire herd
[of seals] to view towering mountains.

This is the sea-and-mountains-merged, world-upside-down chaos of the flood, vividly described by Ovid in *Metamorphoses,* Book One. It is survived by primordial Pyrrha; her mother, Pandora (as noted), having loosed her own chaos on the world; Pandora subsequently grandmother to her own namesake—Pyrrha's daughter, Pandora (II). Horace's Pyrrha thus bears a marked chaotic namesake and association, herself signaling chaos emergent. The two Pyrrhas are thus and again one and the same in each subsequent age, embodying what one commentator refers to, vis-à-vis the flood itself, as the "gemination theme," the ever biding fear and likelihood of the flood's— of chaos's—return, be it personal or political (so the boundaries-shattering social wreckage of Barine).

Pyrrha is further a *phenomenon,* both alluring and disastrous, whose powers of seduction evoke the "culture of spectacle" in ancient Rome. Herself spectacular, Pyrrha is a psycho-cultural attraction; a sexual stunner of Circus-Maximus or triumphal-parade dimensions, the delirious desire of every man—his fantastical delectation and dread (so "Barine's public status as a kind of timeless object of desire . . . made to seem monstrous"). Though Pyrrha's amours occur beneath cover of grotto, every man is her voyeur, her type and archetype known and, ultimately, transparent. The universality of the situation, referenced at the outset, is, in one commentator's gloss, "of cosmic significance." Thus, the import of *Heu quotiens fidem / mutatosque deos flebit* (lines 2–3): 'Alas, how often he'll lament your faith and the gods transformed'. Pyrrha's shipwrecking fits of rage will seem cataclysmic, the upending of heaven's disposition, once favoring gods now opposed.

Conclusion

Odes 1.5, as noted, has attracted many, including the likes of John Milton (1608–1674) and former British Prime Minister William Ewart Gladstone

(1809–1898); both steeped in the classics from youth. Milton, aside his epic undertakings, wrote poetry in Latin; Gladstone translated, among other things from Latin and Greek, the complete *Odes* of Horace. Curiously, Milton's version has never been much in favor, while Gladstone's efforts were excoriated in an 1824 review. Thus have "the greats" been lured to the enterprise with middling or poor results, even as lesser hands have enjoyed varied successes.

The allure of Horace's *Odes* resides in their wit, worldly wisdom, and absolute economy of expression ("compression," as Gladstone notes). For ancient audiences, it resided as well in Horace's deft adaptation of Greek meters to Latin poetry, by which he heightened the cachet and significantly advanced the development of Latin poetry (the first nine odes of Book 1, as noted, programmatically announcing the meters to follow). Within so exacting a scope, *Odes* 1.5 appeals with its exquisite choice, ordering, and interlocking of words; the sweeping and thematically reinforcing alliterative patterns; the dextrous exploitation of conventional imagery; the amatory mise en scène; the sexual entendres and double entendres; and, not least, the wry, understated, and self-effacing wit that a life-seasoned Horace— seasoned because *cautious*—brings to a pervasively recurring theme. The theme is that of the trusting lover *in* over his unknowing head with a libertine partner, one known for (and knowing) her own appeal, one both predatory and readily acquiescent. Playing with Pyrrha, the lad, to mix the metaphor, is shipwrecked on the shoals of his own callow fervor.

But not Horace. *He* has escaped the like disaster, dedicating his ocean-drenched vestments as votive offering to Neptune. The wall-attached dedication of vestments or other precious objects after a trying experience comes with a pedigree as old as Homer (c. 750 BC). We thus find that the nefarious Aegisthus—having seduced Clytemnestra (wife of the long-absent Agamemnon, still returning from Troy) and killed off the bard Agamemnon assigned to watch her—made just such an offering. As Homer relates, Aegisthus

> on the sacred altars of the gods . . . burned many thigh
> > bones and hung up*
> many dedications, *gold and things woven,*
> for having accomplished this monstrous thing he never hoped for.

*"hung up": Gr. *anēpsen* = *an* + (*h*)*aptō* / *ēpsa* 'hang up/hung up'

From earliest times, then, the hung or fastened dedication of vestments and valuables was the rule for those escaping danger. Here, however, it underscores the irony of Aegisthus's miscalculation, Aegisthus thinking he has *escaped his crimes*—by analogy to one *escaping the sea*—for which he will be slain by Orestes. We wonder whether his hanging of gold is not somehow reflected in the *flavam . . . comam* 'flaxen/golden hair', which is Pyrrha's prized asset. The shearing and hanging of Pyrrha's hair would indeed make a fine—and golden—*ex voto*. But that won't happen here. It is, in any case, sooner the woman who shears the man (Samson and Delilah) or, better, decapitates him (Judith and Holofernes). Escaping Pyrrha with one's shirt on is escape enough.

It is noteworthy that in this, the first "love poem" of Horace's *Odes*, the poet does not pine for unreciprocated love but disavows love's very risk. Here is no Dylan Thomas's "Lie down, lie easy. Let me shipwreck in your thighs," but a self-satisfied poet pleased to have escaped the ordeal. How very much like Horace—by contrast to Catullus's thrilling-to and riding out the storm—to hunker down in the captain's quarters, chart the safer course, and boast the storm's and life's avoidances. Horace's love poems are sweetly impressive confections—*"jeux d'esprit* of the sort that for the moment lighten and clear the spirit"—emotionally constrained, even as his poetry is verbally compressed; the consensus that "as a love poet, [Horace] has been for a century and a half [now two centuries] more often derided and patronized than praised." Horace offers no impassioned outpouring: no tongue "breaking" or "unhinged" and no cold sweat or racing subcutaneous flame (Sappho); no "shameful fits of parching rage" (Ibycus); none the annoyance nor bittersweetness of love's iterations: "Why this time?" "Whom this time?" (Sappho); no resignation in the face of love's assaults: "Again does Love . . . " (Anacreon). He sooner says, *never again* and *whew*! And yet there is the utter charm, resourcefulness, and sophistication of it all, attracting centuries of translators (and critics) to *this* Siren's song in particular, even as preternatural Pyrrha beguiles and beckons—poem and portal alike quasi-*intemptati nitentes.*

APPENDIX

❧

Possible Influences on Horace, *Odes* 1.5

Odyssey 5.55–84 (R. Lattimore, tr.)

Hermes Arrives at Calypso's Island
Grotto to Secure Odysseus's Release

ἀλλ᾽ ὅτε δὴ τὴν νῆσον ἀφίκετο τηλόθ᾽ ἐοῦσαν,   55
ἔνθ᾽ ἐκ πόντου βὰς ἰοειδέος ἤπειρόνδε
ἤιεν, ὄφρα **μέγα σπέος** ἵκετο, τῷ ἔνι **νύμφη**
ναῖεν ἐυπλόκαμος· τὴν δ᾽ ἔνδοθι τέτμεν ἐοῦσαν.

But after he had made his way to the far-lying island,
he stepped then out of the dark blue sea, and walked on over
the dry land, till he came to the **great cave**, where the **lovely-haired
nymph was at home,** and he found that she was inside . . . .

πῦρ μὲν ἐπ᾽ ἐσχαρόφιν μέγα **καίετο**, τηλόσε δ᾽ **ὀδμὴ**   59
κέδρου τ᾽ εὐκεάτοιο θύου τ᾽ ἀνὰ νῆσον **ὀδώδει**
δαιομένων· ἡ δ᾽ ἔνδον ἀοιδιάουσ᾽ ὀπὶ καλῇ
ἱστὸν ἐποιχομένη **χρυσείη κερκίδ᾽ ὕφαινεν**.

            There was
a great **fire blazing** on the hearth, and the **smell** of cedar
split in billets, and sweetwood **burning**, spread all over
the island. She was singing inside the cave with a sweet voice
as she went up and down the loom and **wove with a golden shuttle**.

ὕλη δὲ **σπέος** ἀμφὶ πεφύκει τηλεθόωσα,   63
κλήθρη τ᾽ αἴγειρός τε καὶ **εὐώδης** κυπάρισσος.
ἔνθα δέ τ᾽ ὄρνιθες τανυσίπτεροι εὐνάζοντο,

σκῶπές τ᾽ ἴρηκές τε τανύγλωσσοί τε κορῶναι
εἰνάλιαι, τῇσίν τε θαλάσσια ἔργα μέμηλεν.

There was a growth of grove around the **cavern**, flourishing,
alder was there, and the black poplar, and **fragrant** cypress,
and there were birds with spreading wings who made their nests in it,
little owls, and hawks, and birds of the sea with long beaks
who are like ravens, but all their work is on the sea water;

ἡ δ᾽ αὐτοῦ τετάνυστο περὶ **σπείους** γλαφυροῖο   68
ἡμερὶς ἡβώωσα, τεθήλει δὲ σταφυλῇσι.
κρῆναι δ᾽ ἑξείης πίσυρες ῥέον ὕδατι λευκῷ,
πλησίαι ἀλλήλων **τετραμμέναι ἄλλυδις ἄλλη.**

and right about the hollow **cavern** extended a flourishing
growth of vine that ripened with grape clusters. Next to it
there were four fountains, and each of them ran shining water,
each next to each, **but turned to run in sundry directions;**

ἀμφὶ δὲ λειμῶνες μαλακοὶ ἴου ἠδὲ σελίνου   72
θήλεον. ἔνθα κ᾽ ἔπειτα καὶ ἀθάνατός περ ἐπελθὼν
θηήσαιτο ἰδὼν καὶ τερφθείη φρεσὶν ᾗσιν.
ἔνθα στὰς θηεῖτο διάκτορος ἀργεϊφόντης.

**and round about there were meadows growing soft with parsley
and violets,** and even a god who came into that place
would have admired what he saw, the heart delighted within him.
There the courier Argeïphontes stood and admired it.

αὐτὰρ ἐπεὶ δὴ πάντα ἑῷ **θηήσατο** θυμῷ   76
αὐτίκ᾽ ἄρ᾽ εἰς εὐρὺ **σπέος** ἤλυθεν. **οὐδέ μιν ἄντην
ἠγνοίησεν** ἰδοῦσα Καλυψώ, δῖα θεάων·
οὐ γάρ τ᾽ ἀγνῶτες θεοὶ ἀλλήλοισι πέλονται
ἀθάνατοι, οὐδ᾽ εἴ τις ἀπόπροθι δώματα ναίει.
οὐδ᾽ ἄρ᾽ Ὀδυσσῆα μεγαλήτορα ἔνδον ἔτετμεν,
**ἀλλ᾽ ὅ γ᾽ ἐπ᾽ ἀκτῆς κλαῖε καθήμενος, ἔνθα πάρος περ,
δάκρυσι καὶ στοναχῇσι καὶ ἄλγεσι θυμὸν ἐρέχθων.
πόντον ἐπ᾽ ἀτρύγετον δερκέσκετο δάκρυα λείβων.**   84

but after he had **admired** all in his heart, he went in
to the wide **cave, nor did the shining goddess Kalupso**
fail to recognize him when she saw him come into her presence;
for the immortal gods are not such as to go unrecognized
by one another, not even if one lives in a far home.
But Hermes did not find the greathearted Odysseus indoors,
but he was sitting out on the beach, as before now
he had done, breaking his heart in tears, lamentation, and sorrow,
as weeping tears he looked out over the barren water.

Part VI

In a Classical Mode:

Poems / Catullan Caprices / Sapphics / Reproof / Envoie / Aforetime / From the Hebrew

POEMS

℘

§122

Love's glory day is past
and I to pasture placed
who in love's course held fast
nor equaled nor outpaced.

I mounted high the vale
descended the divide,
and snorting did assail
love's rampart opened wide.

Yes, I who stayed love's course,
to whom no steed drew near,
am petted now perforce,
a hayseed in my ear.

§123

Love's glory day be sung
resplendent to the lyre,
strings taut and neatly strung
aglow with bygone fire.

So range the bard's report
of epic ecstasies
wherein I did disport
once, nestled at your knees.

§124

Tamara, demon of my brain
exquisite torment wreaking Cain
with seething song, incarnate fright,
my mind's disruption, mind's delight;
sing stinging strains that lash my brain
refrains of unrelenting pain
until my mind completely flayed
with scourge of Siren serenade
will bleed to have you far away
while pleading, stay, Tamara, stay.

§125

The murmured chant
"I want you now . . ."
pounds frantically
beneath my brow.
Your wanton nails
assail my back,
the tightening hold
impales me to the rack
where, torn and tense,
resounding cadence
makes me crack!—
a heathen din
a harrowing hymn

crushing my marrow
limb by limb,
confounding the power
of my will, reduced to dust,
these two, within the mill
and ground with sweat and tears,
a mound to spill
insensate from the gears
of you.

§126

Speed me, Tamara, to the shore,
doomed feral reef of nevermore,
listing low on the bellied swell
toward devastation's certain knell.

Catch my course in the nethergrip
batter my passage hip to hip
inter me at the salted slip
be this my last apprenticeship,

that torn asunder stem to stern
aground the berth of no return,
abide I unanesthetized,
blessing the shipwreck at your thighs.

What need have I of seven seas
athwart the main between your knees?
Fount and vortex, my world entire,
there be I borne and there expire.

§127

Oh, were the world entire mine,
by oceans bounded and defined,
the whole of it would I forsake
that mighty England's queen awake
in my arms intertwined.

Casting off her queen's attire
to seamanship may she aspire,
and I become her ship of state
her mast and tiller and first mate,
in sum, her world entire.

Hair hastening from her diadem,
bare foot bereft of jeweled hem,
my voyager insatiate,
our course her realm and rich estate,
and say the saints, Amen.

§128

Here manifest is God's design,
your body undulant under mine;
writhing within the reel and roll
be stalwart, my prophetic soul!

Played havoc with upon the tide
I mount now high the wave, now low,
a'waste in waters open wide,
now left to thrash, now drawn below,

where fathoming what mortal man
might only muse upon or wish,
cavort I with Leviathan
(past prodigious that fabled fish,

or mammal, if of warmer blood)
from breakers high atop the tide
to depths within the swaddling flood,
in whom Jehovah did confide

aforetime when he sought to probe
the heart of disputatious Job,
or set the jaded Jonah free
to furnish Nineveh's prophecy.

§§129–133, *Five Duban Songs* (see Preface)

§129

Beneath a gazing gossamer,
this body sunned and brown,
with puberty begins to stir
amid a nascent down.

Oh, may it to full flower come
before the sun is set,
Oh, how the bud grows tiresome
were better to forget.

§130

Not in gold admired
nor silk to sight displayed,
my greeting stands attired
in nature's kiss conveyed.

My hair hangs fallen free,
my lips wear dawn's first gaze,
find upward from my knee
pasturage where to graze.

Explore me north and south,
feast fully on my breast,
fasten me to your mouth
north, south, east, and west.

§131

When I kiss doting Daphnis, fair,
my soul strides to my lips;
constrained the daring spirit there
yet past the gateway slips.

§132

How clearly does the cup delight,
fast coupled to the lips
of Lalagē, delicious sprite,
whose mouth the droplet drips.

Blessed cup! Were lips of hers fast-bound
to lips my very own,
I would her soul entire draw down,
throughout my being sown.

§133

Unclothed athwart a limb,
bark moistened by the rain,
I grip the bough within
thighs darkened by the stain.

The bough is firmly hewn,
where strain my slender hips,
within do we commune
where open lie my lips.

§134

Taking hold of her
as of a pitcher—
handles her trim ears—
I venture a sip
from off her lips
and slake the thirst of years.

Petaled pitcher mine
cup incarnadine,
resplendent, I implore,
from bount'ous hips
slumb'ring in my grip
be surfeit evermore.

§135

I know not whom to choose
of rivals lacking peer,
the one my radiant muse,
wondrous the other near.

Each holds one hand, one breast;
to whom give I my mouth?
To whom my heart confess?
I would enfold them both.

Lucina I prefer,
but won't bear Galla gone;
what would become of her
when breaks the darkened dawn?

Thus do we persevere,
the three beneath one roof,
on Lesbos ever dear
as objects of reproof.

This drama shall I end
aside some other friend?

§136

Sleep at the door remains
when girls together room.
Night's hurried hour wanes.
"My dearest, tell me whom,"
she said, "you most adore."
Bold in this blandishment
did she confess the more:
"I know, my heart's content,
whom most thou holdest dear,
close now your eyes and say
'This is my Lykas near.'"
I touched her where she lay,
and touching said for shame,

"I know thee only by
such charms as maidens claim.
Here's jest by which to die."
But she: "Just close your eyes,
here find his lips and limbs,
it's here your Lykas lies,
submit and I am him."

§137

By naught asunder torn
were we, strewn o'er the bed,
by love's unrest outworn
till dawn had risen red.

§138

I'll leave the bed in which we slept
disheveled ever and unkept,
gathering to my anguished breast
her figure there impressed.

Fragrance and fashion I'll forswear
nor fuss foolishly with my hair;
treasure on features unrepaired
caresses she left there.

Nor will I eat the morning through,
nor makeup use nor rouge renew,
that on my lips her kisses strewn
retain the rosebud's hue.

The doorway will I bolt secure
and mark the shutters shut for sure,
that midnight's wasting winds without
not fasten memory round about.

§139

"Oh, would that I might lover be!"
Thus ardently had Love implored.
But finding his appeal ignored,
his shafts in golden quiver stored,
flew Love attired combatively,
to punish my inconstancy.
Responding I my corselet seize,
protective oxhide and stout spear,
to bring Love suppl'ant to his knees,
his dread Achilles drawing near.
Our ranks fast close, he fires, I flee;
next finding arrows vainly spent,
does he, a jav'lin, fly at me,
loath from the onslaught to relent.
Love tears my corselet open wide,
strikes to my heart, cries, "Woe betide!"
What good this war waged openly,
myself at war where none can see?

§140

This hidden spot is spot accursed
that spied our kiss—that very first—
conveyed by moonbeam to the lake,
that night of it might notice take.

It first became the boatman's lore,
a tale for telling once ashore.
He made it to a woman known
wherein were seeds of scandal sown.

She rumored it about the town
where seed was grown to rank renown,
converting our ecstatic sport,
to scuttlebutt and rank report.

Boatman, retire that wretched oar
and speak to woman nevermore.

§141

Callimachean Echo

I despise the cyclic epic
nor in the path delight
that leads the masses aimlessly,
proceeding where it might.

I loathe the sauntering lover,
shun the frequented spring,
detest coarse commonality's
hyped and deceitful ring.

Lykas, fairer than fair art thou!
To this my ardent vow
from afar responds the echo:
"Another has him now."

CATULLAN CAPRICES

❦

(See §§111–112, pp. 186–187)

§142

Lesbia, you ask:

What count of kisses does it take
full reckoning of which to make?

As many as the grains of sand
which dormant wait upon the wind
where Libya's dunes deserted stand.
Of these not one would I rescind.

As many as are swirling borne
suffusing every eye and pore

when sands ascend the desert's storm.
By that amount I set my store.

As many as from dune to dune
aloft beneath a noontime sun
from Negev to Namib are strewn.
Of that amount not less the one.

On these bestow as many more
as from Morocco to Sudan
the vast Sahara hungers for,
its appetite gargantuan.

As many as on coast and shore
comprise the littoral therefore,
as many as on ocean's floor
conspiring seethe to come ashore.

On kisses such may we be fed
the while that they unreckoned be
as streams of sand through fingers fled
to mock our cold accountancy.

Presume not of this sum to ask—
apply yourself but to the task.

§143

Lesbia, again you ask:

What sum throughout the Zodiac
the constellations keep in store
that we of kisses nothing lack
nor craving be the poorer for.

As many as are kisses stored
within the Dippers ere outpoured,
or such as Libra's laden state
unteetering does tolerate.

As many as dispersed reside
twixt Scorpio's pincers opened wide,
the sum between the Pisces twain
ere to their stations swum again.

Those sidelong sifting by the ton
from Cancer's exoskeleton,
the legions that emblazoned rain
shaken from Leo's regal mane.

Of these in heaven's barreled vault
let none know languor or default,
or in its dome bejeweled throughout
delinquent be or done without.

The measure Virgo as she pants
does feign abjure but fully grants
(then claiming, after light years past,
that she was sexually harassed,
withal recoils from and recants.)

The sum that Sagittarius
dispatches taking aim at us,
man above, lewd beast below,
unbettered but by Cupid's bow.

As many as the Ram and Bull
ill-joined to cart with kisses full
do butt and snort the load to pull.
Of these the lot without a lull.

The count by which the lusty Goat
gives lovers leave the while to gloat,
trim harbinger in his caprice
of ardor reeling toward release.

And all the excess plenitude
bestrewn the reach of heaven's rood
as constellations interact
a'thrill throughout the Zodiac,

Aquarius will wash away,
withholding for another day,
lest heaven woebegone repent
that these its kisses wasting went.

SAPPHICS

ॐ

(On Sapphic meter, see *TLL* 246–251.)

§144

Epiphany

Last night dreaming spoke I with Aphrodite,
drank the dulcet blend of her lips decanted,
deft amalgam suave interfused with laughter
      winsome, malignant;

Dreaming saw the mythic physique resplendent;
peered through pendent drape of her sheer attire,
saw the flesh aglow, saw the form afire which
      stunned and unnerved me;

Saw through mesh diaphanous awe inspiring
curvature, exquisitely ranged to inward,
whence the transport so commandeered my stricken
      soul as to slay me;

Saw the glinting foot and the dazzling ankle
bound by patterned Lydian straps, distinctive
handiwork of locals in lieu of footworn
      gift of Hephaestus;

Saw the grace from garlanded forehead issue,
skin the while the whiter than milk or snowdrift,
shrine revered of soul resolute within me,
      bowed to her bidding;

Marked th' untethered tide of her wayward tresses
—Botticelli's own in their flown profusion—
stream to windward, streaking the morning sky with
      cincture of dawn-fire;

Glimpsed the steadfast eye, and with blinded daring
raised my sight to hers, glanced begetting's rapture,
saw creation's spark and the steel that strikes it,
      swooned and was nothing.

§145

Gone, Unkissed

All I ever wanted was once to kiss you,
feel the petaled pulse of your lips upon me,
taste the russet rose of your breath exhalent
      limpid within me;

pass my tongue between tiers of chiseled iv'ry,
guardians, implacable, interdictive,
barring multitudinous kisses ever,
      one kiss excepted;

wanted but to imbibe upon that instant,
Muses' gift of memory unrelenting—
mind dismantled, dumbstruck in adoration,
      loosed and afire in

your arresting stature, the lissome presence,
tow'ring neck, the nightingale's throated passion,
Sappho's singing "Once did I love thee, child, once,
      Atthis, aforetime."

Come, O lyre divine, and dispel within me
midnight's pang, the pulsating discomposure;
hold me not as trifle nor in despite for
      daring to love thee.

§146

To One Impossibly Beautiful

Nude disposed, recumbent, let me behold you,
gasp as did old masters renowned aforetime,
stupefied, undone by the sight inspired of
          form in perfection;

hair cascaded, rounded the breasts to sideward,
legs elongate, fingers arrayed to center,
languidly conspiring in your self-pleasure,
          thighs gathered inward;

pendant-pearled your earlobe adorèd bounty,
peer you God-knows-where past my famished person,
Titian-bred not sea-born of Botticelli,
          bedroom-dominioned;

pillowed elbow bent to the silken bed sheet,
vacant glance proclaiming your vast indifference,
virginal despite the enticements offered
          fools everlasting.

Sooner be you statue than flesh configured,
pedestaled, delectable Galatea;
suffer not this heart to endure the mortal
          pulse of its offspring.

§147

Innocence Repaid

Child ahead the years practiced in your pleasures,
bounteous attendant to my tumescence,
languid seated balanced astride my kneecaps,
          thighs loosely parted;

agile-fingered grip yours the wrist resourceful,
gaze transfixed and gaping in coy amazement

signals transport o'erspread your face, proclaiming
   joy self-assurèd.

Rhythm-raptured weight on my finger balanced,
hand the other—foiling the longed for ingress—
slight atop my own; indecisive guard'an
   failing its duty;

Oh, so mastered, *Oh*, the strain thus abated!
Lax the hands now—listless the one acquitted,
and indiff'rent even the other fallen
   weak to the wayside.

Tense yourself, dear child, for the dire encounter,
penetration's spite to your cunt delivered;
I the thrashing swan, you the Leda yielding,
   thighs thrust asunder.

REPROOF

§148

Embrace my promise made sincere
That I'd as lover hold you dear,
And know that I entreat you true
Your trust to pledge the nighttime through,
Our every kiss, sigh, and caress
A testament to steadfastness.
A stone your stillness in reply,
Disdain the drift of your goodbye.

My proffered kiss does irritate
You, fidgeting you remonstrate,
In dudgeon high at my offense
You herald me thrice-banished hence,
Then indignation seal my fate,

#MeToo-indicted, reprobate,
Who but obeying courtship's law
Ordained your beauty fit for awe.

Enough! My fate would chosen be
Apart disdain and calumny
Between your blouse upbuttoned full
And fabric yielding to my pull;
Between your legs linked at the knee
Or at my neck insatiately.
From indications such as these
I'll certify you fully pleased.
Be not indignant, curb reproof,
Atop its dwelling spare the roof.

ENVOIE

§149

Thighs upthrust to my either side,
poised pistons chafing to the chore,
consign me to the great divide,
there be my passage evermore.

Oh, vast and teeming continent,
luxuriance East to Occident,
be where my wanderlust is spent
triumphant and impenitent;

and I from ridge to trestle blessed
astride the adamantine rail,
your thund'rous Orient Express
a'wasting to the whistle's wail.

AFORETIME

❧

§150

Woman's Harborage

(On a theme from Nikos Kazantzakis, *Odusseia*, 6.773–786)

The stars begin to tinkle, strung like bells,
The prow-sown sea lies supine neath her swells,
The slumb'ring soul in search of dreams unmoors,
Its hold to weight with wares from distant shores.

Across the crust of crumbling thirsting earth
Death's ensign reigns affixed atop its berth,
But soul its banner wraps about the world,
From woman's harb'rage voyaging unfurled.

It glides from lavish longitudes o'er-crossed,
Cargoed with kisses, kisses flame-embossed,
Each kiss untiring, each kiss evermore
Protesting the loss of the kiss before.

§151

Not Sighing Gone, MH

(On a theme from Ernest Dowson, 1867–1900)

We have walked in love's land a little way
We have learnt his lesson a little while,
I thought, "We will part at the end of day
With a sigh, a smile."

I thought love would end as it had begun
With a sigh, a smile, a last merriment,
But the sigh was mine only when day was done
And affection spent.

We took no vow, no vow was e'er broken,
"Love while it pleases" our erstwhile intent;
No word unsaying that we had spoken
This I question, yet:

Why did you so want at the end of day—
Who had so loved and lingered for the while
Who never once wanted for what to say—
For a sigh, a smile?

Were you sighing gone, last breath to the lyre,
Day's parting were ended, why further dwell?
Wanting that sigh, wanting you, I expire,
Past words to tell.

§152

To an Unborn Daughter*

(On themes from Jeanne and Jean)

Sow the seed of corn
let the grain be sown
let the root be born
be the stem high grown;
bear seed corn alike
bear grain high its spike
till the summer dies
and youth be lost in sighs.

Little daughter freed
from inside of me
moisture-sucking need
eyes too new to see;
yours I pray god's speed
warmth on which to feed,
tender tendril mine
outlasting this my vine.

O'er fields of years to be
to time's end scatter me.

§153

Do Not Stand at My Grave and Weep

(On a theme from Mary Elizabeth Frye, 1905–2004)

Do not stand at my grave and weep
I am not there, I do not sleep
I am the agile wind aflow
The diamond's glint upon the snow
I am the springtime's nurt'ring rain
Its sunlight on the ripened grain;

When you waken in morning's hush
Amid the swift uplifting rush
Of circling birds in blissful flight
I spark the fire of their delight
My colors fleck the flower bed
Forbidding tear of yours be shed.

Seek not my grave whereat to mourn,
I live within you, each day reborn.

*A poem to her unborn daughter (Jean) was written by my late wife, Jeanne A. Petrek, MD (1948–2005), sometime in 1981. I had never known Jeanne to write a poem. While still a girl, Jean found and memorized it, the written copy then disappearing. Learning of this only during the writing of this book—Jean reciting parts of it—I asked her to write out as much of it as she remembered. This, in non-consecutive segments, was somewhat less than half the present version. The rest is my "restoration," following what was apparent of the fragments' rhyme, meter, and spirit. The poem "Do Not Stand at My Grave and Weep" is my own version, read at Jeanne's ash scattering, of an original poem by Mary Frye, which Jean first brought to my attention.

JEFFREY M. DUBAN

FROM THE HEBREW

❧

(On themes from Rachel Bluwstein, 1890–1931)

§154

The Garden

In my garden have I planted you,
thus humbly in my heart;
your roots and branches winding through
have touched my every part.

And from sunrise until evening
it knows not peace nor calm;
yourself ever in it singing,
a thousand birds your psalm.

§155

Summer Mornings

Summer mornings find the world in violet-fresh array,
with compassion aflow;
perhaps I'll get up, shake of the dust of yesterday,
trust in tomorrow,
and bless the burden in a humbled heart someway,
accept the sorrow.

A girl between the flower beds and furrows walks,
sprinkling the dew;
she scatters beads of life, and in their thirst the stalks
are all attended to.
Might I pardon God his heart that mocks,
might I start anew?

§156

Aforetime

Just so am I, calm—
still-watered as a pond,
of idle days and children fond,
and poems of Francis Jammes.

There once was a time when my soul
was appareled in purple,
and aloft the mountain peaks
I was at one with supple
winds and eagles' shrieks.

But that was once upon a time;
the seasons come and go
and now—I am just so.

—fin—

Notes

NOTES TO THE PROSE portions of this book are arranged by paragraph, with italicized beginnings preceded by the page number on which the paragraph appears. The text to which a note attaches is in bold.

xxiv *This book explores both*
"the idealized . . . of art." The inherent connection between art and civilization is a leitmotif of *The Lesbian Lyre*.

xvii *The inquiry was spurred*
***because* they are women.** The inquiry becomes more complex when gays are considered. The claim then arises that gays are more "qualified" to treat gay matters and, more exactly yet, that gay men are more qualified to treat gay men's matters; and lesbians, lesbian matters. So what is done or reasonably considered in the prominent case of Marcel Proust, himself gay, treating of both gay and lesbian relationships in *Remembrance of Things Past*? Does he accurately convey lesbianism and its concerns, or intend the same, or have it seem an "inversion" of homosexuality—his own? For discussion, see Ladenson, esp. Introduction, "Pussy Galore and the Daughters of Bilitis."

Classicist and Sappho scholar
"has almost . . . academia." An example of a theorizing work is Ellen Greene, ed., *Women Poets in Ancient Greece and Rome* (2005), seeking to locate the typically feminine in each poet's work with frequent reference to Freudian or Lacanian psychoanalysis. A book of earnest intent, its review by Simone Viarre is deservedly mixed, with criticism of its "gender and genre" approach by a predominance of female authors, and of the case made by one contributor for "sexuality" (i.e., Eros/love) as "the only tool for interesting . . . students in ancient literature." "Gender and genre"/"texuality and sexuality" (Greene, xiii) suffice as catch(y) phrases, but not as approaches to the arts. Says Viarre, echoing the sentiment herein, the "originality [of female voices] does not need to be proved by long demonstrations if we have a good approach to literature and problems of aesthetics." It is thus perspective, not demonstration or literary-sexual gerrymandering, that is key. As noted over fifteen years ago by veteran classicist Peter Green (2002), "Sappho, like Shakespeare, has a remarkable quality of attracting idolaters, pseudo-moralists, spinmeisters (mostly with a feminist agenda), and a wide range of crackpot theorists, ranging from the benignly dotty to the angrily obsessive. Her case has also been taken up ferociously by serious feminists of just about every persuasion." And more recently, author and cultural critic Michael Walsh, noting the attack of critical theory on sexually attained transcendence: "Tellingly, the word 'sex' came to mean the same thing as 'gender', an impersonal grammatical term that means masculine, feminine, and neuter. Primal notions of masculinity and femininity were redefined and 'nuanced', which in practice meant shattered and rendered meaningless" (Walsh [2015], 82–83).
***enfants* . . . Hélène Cixous.** Of passing interest to this study is the French feminist-critic

Hélène Cixous's (b. 1937) *écriture féminine* ('women's writing'). This much revered triumphalist-misandrist theory posits a "mode" of female writing so contorted and impractically theoretical as to defy practice. Such manner of writing, if ever implemented, would be laughably incomprehensible. For a helpful overview, see Wortmann (2012) (pamphlet essay). It is, of course, not *how* women write, thus setting themselves apart from "oppressive patriarchy," but what and how well they write. As ever in literary and critical studies of the past fifty years, the more arcane and theory-bound the feminist scholar, the more militant, misandrist, and tenure-assured. (See Paglia [2017], 60, for views of feminist wannabes who "don't come up to Simone de Beauvoir's anklebones, that damp sob sister, Hélène Cixous, with her diarrhea prose," etc.)

A more reasonable case for a female writing style—"whether to write as a woman or a man"—was made by female authors of the eighteenth century. This involved "a calm, plain, unimpassioned voice. Also a disembodied voice, for the style calls attention to everything but the writer: Not 'I fear' but 'it is to be feared,'" etc.; and "a rhetorical triumph . . . a neutering operation by which, without pretending to be a man, [the female author] nevertheless ceases to be a woman." So, too, "the balanced, judicious style of 'manly' writing" (in a Johnsonian mode). The style had its drawbacks, to say the least, including extreme depersonalization and the cumbersome noncommittal use of passive verb constructions. See McCarthy, Ch. 7: "An Intruder on the Rights of Men: Piozzi as Arbiter of Style and Stylist."

"Largely . . . Lesbian writers." Vanita, 39–41. Woolf elsewhere laments the discrepancy between the depiction of women in literature and the reality of their lives, e.g., "Some of the most inspired words and profound thoughts in literature fall from her lips; in real life she could hardly read; scarcely spell; and was the property of her husband." Woolf, *A Room of One's Own* (1929, 1992), 56. *A Room* argues that women are kept from realizing their potential as fiction writers because of severe societal biases; that what they require foremost is space of their own and a decent income to succeed. Coming to young adulthood in the final third of the lengthy Victorian Era (1837–1901), Woolf (1882–1941) experienced the severity and lingering aftermath of its restrictions on women. Though *A Room*'s observations are now dated, it has attained hallowed feminist standing, quotable by chapter and verse for almost any proposition (see, e.g., Hussey/Gubar, 2005). This largely results from the indeterminacy of a work as much concerned with Woolf's random perceptions as with her perceptions about them—the personal voice overlay muddying the import. For an excellent appreciation of Woolf's Hellenism, see Fernald, 17–42.

xviii *To illustrate these principles*

archaic Greek lyric. Gr. *archaios* 'archaic, old'; Eng. archaeology. The terminus for the archaic period may be placed at the landmark of Xerxes's invasion of Greece, 480–479 BC (Snodgrass, 212). Archaic literature is generally distinguished from the classical literature of the "Golden Age" of Athens (5th century BC), followed in turn by Hellenistic literature in the aftermath of Alexander (4th century BC). Writers nonetheless often use *classical* or *ancient* to include *archaic*, though archaic provides a significant chronological and cultural referent.

"For it is . . . the words." Sir John Denham, Preface, *The Destruction of Troy.*

xxi *Akin to the distress of*

Les Chansons de Bilitis. By Pierre Louÿs (1870–1925)—among the most famous literary hoaxes of all times. In 1894, the French author and poet Pierre Louÿs published 143 prose poems which he claimed were translations of texts by one Bilitis, whom he offered up as a courtesan contemporary with Sappho. The texts, claimed Louÿs fantastically, were discovered inscribed on the walls of a tomb on Cyprus—*and credibly enough,* as Cyprus is the island onto which Aphrodite, goddess of love, was conveyed following her birth from the sea (*Th.* 173–200). Sapphic love was Louÿs's theme—his prose poems mellifluous, languid, and erotically charged. The work, at once a tremendous hoax and irresistible indulgence, was an overnight sensation. Few doubted the fabrication, or perhaps wanted to, and the work achieved cult status. Even after the hoax was known, the work retained its cachet, as it does to this day. In 1897, three years after the work's publication, Louÿs's good friend Claude Debussy scored three of the poems as songs for piano and female voice—*Trois Chansons de Bilitis*—the work since a mainstay of the mezzo-soprano repertoire. See further p. 86, and Rumph.

xxii *These works have in*
the Greek Anthology. Also known as the *Palatine Anthology* (see Glossary).
If I am ... of poetry. Bernstein, 201.

INTRODUCTION: FIVE ARCHAIC GREEK LYRIC POETS

SAPPHO

1   *Sappho is the first love*
"simply nothing ... all." Swinburne, 228 (posthumous publication).
preferable to any translation. See, e.g., Swinburne's magnificent fifteen-stanza sixty-line "Sapphics."

Sappho's Lesbos—well-wooded
Sappho's poetry apolitical. See Friedrich, 108; *Contra*, Parker, "Sappho's Public World" in Greene, ed. (2005), 3–24.
famed for their beauty. See *Il.* 9.129–130, 664, and on the beauty contests on Lesbos, see the stanza by Alcaeus (p. 129).

2   *Ancient criticism of Sappho*
Adonis in ... the blessed. The reference is to Adonis, son of Cinyras (King of Cyprus) by an incestuous union with his (Cinyras's) daughter (*Met.* 10.298–559, 708–739). Adonis, a paragon of Greek male beauty, was beloved by Aphrodite. See further Friedrich, 69–71; Grigson, 55–62; and Boardman & La Rocca, 132–133, 142.

Sappho was praised as well
Greek comic playwrights. It has been noted of Sappho's unsparing treatment at the hands of the Greek comedians that, with six known comedies written under the title *Sappho,* and her history furnishing material for at least four more, "it is not strange that much of their substance should in succeeding centuries have been regarded as genuine" (Wharton, 22–24, 37–39). Wharton's *Sappho* (1885, 1887, 1895)—memoir, Greek text, literal translation, selected renderings, and bibliography—was the first edition of Sappho written not "solely by scholars for scholars" but for "those who have neither leisure nor power to read her in the tongue in which she wrote" (xix). The volume, of biding interest, is readily available in reprint. Wharton himself could have been no more eminent a Victorian: a Master of Arts (Oxford), Member of the Royal College of Surgeons, a Fellow of various medical associations, Honorary Surgeon of Kilburn Dispensary and of Queen Charlotte's Convalescent Home, the writer of various scientific papers (on, e.g., ornithology and mushrooms), *and* the author of *Sappho*—collecting and translating all her extant writings. **"What did ... was safe."** Lesbia quid docuit Sappho nisi amare puellas? / tuta tamen

270

Sappho ... (*Tristia* 2.365–366). The *Tristia* (*Sorrows*) are five books of poems addressed to Emperor Augustus, to Ovid's wife, and to other unnamed persons at Rome. Ovid wrote these highly autobiographical materials while in exile at Tomis on the Black Sea. Somewhat monotonous in tone, they reflect the poet's preoccupation with the miseries of banishment. As concerns the condoning of homosexuality, the notion of theory versus practice is difficult to maintain, as those professing love are wont to practice it. Comment on the nature of Sappho's relationships with women does not begin until Hellenistic times (4th century **BC**) and may derive from fifth-century Athenian social, moral, and cultural attitudes. See Dover (1987), 18, 174.

"Sappho-Phaon Epistle." The fifteenth and most famous of fifteen *Heroides* of Ovid. The *Heroides* (*Heroines*) is a collection of poems in letter, or "epistolary," form composed in elegiac couplets. They are presented as though addressed by various aggrieved mythological heroines—Penelope, Dido, Helen—to their heroic lovers who have abandoned or mistreated them. The poems are highly rhetorical and somewhat overwrought, though compelling in their sympathetic portrayals of "hearts submissive to the power of love." See Showerman (1963).

"Not Pyrrha's . . . alone." Pyrrha is located in central Lesbos; Methymna, on the northeast coast. Sappho herself came from Mytilene, on the southeast coast. For Atthis and Anactoria, see §§4, 10. At line 200 of Ovid's poem, Sappho invokes the "Daughters of Lesbos whom I have loved to my disgrace."

"But is not ... of Lesbos." *Maximus of Tyre*, 167 (*Oration* 18.9); see Campbell (1982), 21.

Forests . . . comparison. The loves of Socrates and Sappho are yet the subject of an excellent master's thesis by Elizabeth Baxter (2007, 2011). The remainder of the paragraph is adapted from Friedrich, 115–117.

preparation for ... society. As supported by de Beauvoir:

> Sapphic loves in no way contradict the traditional model of the division of the sexes: in most cases, they are an assumption of femininity and not a rejection of it. We have seen that they often appear in the adolescent girl as an ersatz form of heterosexual relations she has not yet had the opportunity or audacity to experience: it is a stage, an apprenticeship, and the one who most ardently engages in such loves may tomorrow be the most ardent of wives, lovers, mothers. What must be explained in the female homosexual is thus not the passive aspect of her choice but the negative side: she is not characterized by her preference for women but by the elusiveness of this preference [420].

ARCHILOCHUS

4   *Archilochus of Paros*

often deviates ... outlook. See Barker and Christensen, 9–41.

I omit two ... poems. The two omitted poems are translated and discussed by Rankin, 61–64.

As concerns poetic meter

As concerns ... meter. On Archilochus and poetic meter, as quoted herein, see Will, 94.

5   *Direct evidence of Lycambes*

Direct evidence ... daughters. The paragraph on Lycambes and his daughters is summarized from Nagy (1976).

"assumed personality ... genre." Even as "Archilochus" may be a literarily "assumed personality," Lycambes is "a character constructed to question the value and status of the iambist [i.e., the vituperative poet in iambic meter] within the social space of contemporary Paros." See also Hawkins, 93–114 (Lycambes being "a voice that rivals" Archilochus's own; "reject[ing] Archilochean poetics in an invective voice of his own"). The phrase "assumed personality and the imaginary situation" is often ascribed to Dover (1964). Its two components, however, are found in a turn-of-the-century essay on Shakespeare's sonnets (Price [1902]).

5   *Archilochean in its invective*
have the "boor". . . Horace. See Horace, *Satires* I.9.

6   *Satire and vituperation*
"is the . . . of his advice." Snodgrass, 173.
of private versus public. On the cultic aspect of Sappho's poetry, including the private-versus-public nature of her poetry, see Segal (1996), 63–64; Hallett (1979/1996), 139–142; Winkler (1981/1999), 89–109 (public-male versus private-female spheres); and Petropoulos, 43–56 (focusing on the Hymn's "affinities with magical discourse").

7   *Some urge that Sappho*
"feminine . . . of Archilochus." Bowra, 240; Gerber, 161. Comparisons between Archilochus and Sappho derive from Bagg, 44–46.

ALCMAN

Alcman of Sparta is
Musician and poet Terpander. Terpander was reportedly the first winner of lyre-accompanied song at the Karneia, a revered Spartan festival, dating to the early seventh century BC, in honor of Apollo. On Terpander's victory there, see Nagy (2004), 35.
"centers of musical excellence." See G. Ferrari, 8–9.
"strong . . . parochial" flavor. Campbell (1967), 194.

8   *The longest of Alcman's*
"No poem in . . . preference." Gerber, 85.

Despite such diffidence
"Although it is . . . universe." G. Ferrari, 17.
"music . . . spheres" theory. G. Ferrari, 4–6.
"Here several . . . other." Hallett, 462. For a summary of views concerning what the chorus members are doing or celebrating, see G. Ferrari, 11, n. 36.

ANACREON

9   *According to Pausanias*
"the first . . . love poems." Levi, 70 (1.25.1).

IBYCUS

Ibycus came from Rhegium
Ibycus came from Rhegium. My overview takes its departure from Symonds, Vol. I, 326–327.
"Foremost . . . mindfulness." *Th.* 116–122. On Gr. *lusimelēs* 'limb-loosing' as used by the lyric poets, see West, 196.
"primal notions . . . femininity." Walsh (2015), 82–83.

PART I: FEMALE HOMER AND THE FALLACY OF GENDERED SENSIBILITY

12   *Female Homer and the Fallacy*
"And will virtue, as virtue." On the unity of virtue in Plato—ungendered virtue (its quality and quantity) and ungendered souls—as expressed through the character of Socrates, see Scaltsas.

13   *Though Sappho is known*
"Lesbos may . . . evidence." Friedrich, 110.
"a sort . . . vision of love." Friedrich, 122.

14   *By the same token, Aphrodite*
both types . . . work and life. Some of the observations in this paragraph concerning Sappho's sexual person (or persona) are tracked and elaborated by Porter (19–22) in an excellent overview of scholarship and Sappho interpretation.
in its . . . indeterminate *pais*. On the vagaries of the word *pais* 'child', see *TLL* 578.
likely . . . (putative) daughter. *TLL* 578. Sappho's marriage to one Cercolas and her daughter Cleïs are of late provenance and comically derived (Parker, 309–310; Prentice, 348–349). Those disinclined to see Sappho as married and with a child look to the word *pais*, which Sappho uses to designate her daughter. The word means 'child', and, as in many languages, either in a biological or affectionate sense. In the latter case, *pais* may also designate a sexual playmate. Sappho, in what remains of her poetry, uses *pais* in both senses. The word is used in an expressly homoerotic sense by Anacreon (§52, there translated 'lad'). Plato regularly uses *pais* with reference to the object of homoerotic desire, i.e., an *erōmenos* 'beloved' (young male). In any poetic context, considerations of meter would dictate the use of *pais* over *thugatēr* 'daughter'—though the Muse is prominently invoked as *thugatēr Dios* 'daughter of Zeus' at the start of the *Odyssey*, and the formula is otherwise frequently used of Aphrodite and Athena and, once, tellingly, of Helen (see Clader, 43, 53). The above-mentioned Maximus of Tyre refers to Cleïs as Sappho's *thugatēr*. In the *Iliad*, Hector wishes he were a *Dios païs* 'son of Zeus' (*Il.* 3.825), or is otherwise accused of too proudly wishing such parentage (*Il.* 13.54).
　　In the opening stanza of Sappho's "Hymn to Aphrodite," the goddess is invoked as *pai dios* 'child [i.e., daughter] of Zeus'. This last reference is to the union of Zeus and the obscure goddess Dionē, by a parentage less vaunted than that of Hesiod's birth of Aphrodite from Ouranos's severed genitals (*Th.* 173–200). Derived from *Di-*, the same verbal root as *Zeus* (Genitive *Dios* 'of Zeus'), *Dionē* is merely a feminine of Zeus. She makes an isolated appearance as Aphrodite's mother at *Il.* 5.370. In the penultimately discovered Sapphic poem (§39), Sappho invokes her *paides*—'dear children, companions, friends'—in the generic sense. A similar flexibility is apparent in the English word *mate*. For other views and attestations supporting a mother-daughter relationship, see Hallett (1982).
　　A sexually quixotic interpretation takes *Kleïs* as a by-form of Gr. **klei-tōr* 'closer, door-keeper', the equivalent of *clitoris*. Reviewing the linguistic data, one outspoken critic concludes: "Sappho's daughter was her daughter, not her clitoris, not her girlfriend." See Parker (1993), 206, and *contra* Bennett (seeking to "dismiss the putative daughter"). See also F. Ferrari, 34–37.
though mentioned . . . *Iliad*. *Il.* 22.466–472 (Andromache's marriage to Hector strategically mentioned directly before she laments his death).
"leap . . . ferryman Phaon." "The story of Sappho's . . . leap . . . so long implicitly believed, does not seem to rest on any firm historical basis. . . . [M]ore than one epigrammatist in the Greek Anthology expressly states that [Sappho] is buried in an Aeolic

grave" (Wharton, 15; cf. Prentice, 349). By *Aeolic*, Wharton means that which pertains to *Aeolia*, the northern part of Asia Minor and its nearby islands, Lesbos included. *Aeolic* also designates the dialect of Greek spoken by Sappho and others on Lesbos and throughout the area—the other two principal dialects being Ionic (i.e., Homeric Greek), and Doric (little preserved). The Attic dialect, or Attic Greek, would develop and predominate by the fifth century BC (in the district of Attica on the Greek mainland, with its capital, Athens).

Of Sappho's leap, one commentator states with fine skepticism:

> She followed Phaon, failed to gain his love, and so travelled from Sicily to the west of Greece and threw herself off the two-thousand-foot-high rock of Leucadia on the coast of Epirus, a favorite point of adieu for lovers keen to cure themselves of desire.... Quite apart from the implausible geography—that she pursued him from Sicily to the east [sic] coast of Greece—judging from the poems that survive, this is unlikely. If Sappho died around 550 BC, as most scholars believe, her suicide would have taken place when she was in her seventies, by which time she might have been expected to have learned restraint [Schmidt, 181–182].

That Sappho leapt from a promontory on Lesbos, if she leapt at all, is thus entirely possible. On the tomb for sightseers, see Campbell (1982), 26, n. 1.
"to be at . . . matter is love." Greer (1995), 8.

15   *However we think to allocate*
"All poetry . . . transmitted." Bowman, 17. Bowman's discussion of "the mechanism of dissemination of female authored poetry into the main-stream" (referencing works on Sappho by classicists Marilyn Skinner and Eve Stehle) strangely omits mention of the eminent superiority of Sappho's poetry. One would not know from such scholarship or analyses that Plato deemed Sappho the Tenth Muse.
Gregory Nagy elaborates. Nagy (2010), 34.

There are women's concerns
however . . . in the process. See R. West (1931, 2006), arguing that while "there is no inherent reason in the constitution of woman why she should not equal the performance of man as thinker and artist," she has not done so, owing to the mandate of biological factors and men's responses to them.
Songs of . . . and Deborah. Exodus 15:1–18, esp. 20–21; Judges 5:2–31.

16   *The Greek genre of parthéneia*
"the personality . . . voice." Klink, 276.
lament, love . . . and lullaby. Genres identified by Gutzwiller, 202–203. See further Karanika, Ch. 6 ("From Lullabies to Children's Songs: Some Diachronic Perspectives").

The "lament," as a subgenre
Prominent Homeric examples. The lament texts referenced in this paragraph, or mentions of lament and its singer (third-person accounts without lament text), appear in the *Iliad* as follows:

> 6.407–439: Andromache/Hector (anticipatory lament).
> 6.487–502: Hector lamented "though still living" (third-person related).
> 18.50–64: Thetis laments Achilles while still alive.
> 19.282–300: Briseis/Patroclus.

19.314–337: Achilles/Patroclus.

22.429–436: Hecuba/Hector.

22.477–514: Andromache/Hector (seeing him dead).

23.6–23: Achilles urges and next leads lament; Thetis strengthens it.

24.507–514: Priam/Hector; Achilles/Patroclus and his own father (third-person related).

24.718–722: Bards' formal lament upon arrival of Hector's corpse into Troy.

24.723–745: Andromache/Hector.

24.746–760: Hecuba/Hector.

24.761–775: Helen/Hector.

17   *Further, though the Iliad*

Iliad's only mention of a *thrēnos.* *Il.* 24.718–723. For discussion of the various types of lament and the difference between *thrēnos* and *góos*, see Alexiou, 11–13, 103 ("In the classical period, the *thrēnos* was still remembered as a distinct type of lyric poetry, but it was interchangeable with *góos*, especially in tragedy, and could be used to refer to any kind of lament, not necessarily for the dead."). See also the sources collected by Pantelia 21, n.1 and works by Dué. For the Greek "mourning that never ends," see Fernald, 28–30.

found only once . . . *Odyssey.* *Od.* 24.60–61.

or Muse-inspired bards. See *Th.* 1–115.

***Iliad's* sole warrior-musician.** See *Il.* 9.182–191.

sorrow has no place . . . Muses. " . . . It ill befits that there by a song of mourning (Gr. *thrēnon*) <in the house> of those who attend the Muse; such would not suit us" (LP 150; Maximus of Tyre XVIII, 9). For the possibly programmatic intent of this sentiment in Sappho's poetry, see F. Ferrari, 144.

Where epic merely relates

"the definitive . . . of tragedy." Nagy (2010), 31.

"so realistic . . . barely noticeable." Nagy (2010), 31.

mythic/primordial . . . male poet. See Bergren 70–71, further arguing "the degree to which [the poet] attempts to demote, divide, or expel the 'female' at the same time he takes on her powers, and then . . . proceed[s] as if they had always been his own."

18   *Accordingly, parthéneia maiden*

"men who . . . really are." Nagy (2010), 32 (referencing Plato, *Republic* 111.395d–e). See further Dué (2006), 23 n. 58 (dangers to the state, as perceived by Plato, of onstage female impersonation).

Male lament, coming full

development from epic lament. Nagy (2010), 26–30. Nagy shows "elegy in perfect convergence with lament"—the "evolutionary relation" between them—in Euripides's *Andromache.* The (male) actor there playing Andromache moves effortlessly from iambic trimeter (lines 91–102), the meter of tragic dialogue, into couplets of alternating dactylic hexameter and pentameter (103–116), the meter of elegy. See Nagy (2010), 28. On the development of genres, one from the other—in the Greek and Western literary traditions, all beginning with Greek epic—see *TLL* 63–64 (discussion here elaborated by that involving the extraction of elegy from the epic subgenre of lament).

"[t]he sensuality . . . of elegy." Nagy (2010), 42, with reference to Euripides, *Andromache* 87–90:

> But I, filled as I ever am with laments, wailings and outbursts of tears,
> will make them reach far off, as far as the aether. For it is natural

for women, when misfortunes attend them, to take pleasure
in giving voice to it all, voicing it again and again, maintaining the
voice from one mouth to the next, from one tongue to the next.

For men's tears, again with reference to Euripides, see Segal (1992), 148–157.
embraced a . . . of topics. The fuller and quite varied subject matter of lament is de-
scribed as follows:

> The earliest Greek elegies deal with a variety of themes: war, politics, the pleasure
> and pains of life in general, love, friendship, death. They communicate a variety of
> moods: joy and sadness, hope and despair, deeply personal beliefs and common
> thought. Such [Greek] fragments as we have do not tell a story for the sake of the
> story; they do not compete with epic. An early Greek elegy is at the same time
> more personal and less straightforward than epic; it reveals more of the poet's
> personality, his tastes, his experiences, his philosophy of life [Luck, 20–21].

Elegy further evolved to include mythological narratives of a personal and even highly
emotional character and, ultimately, during the Augustan period (1st century **BC**–1st
century **AD**), to become the preferred medium of love-poetry. Ennius (3rd–2nd cen-
turies **BC**) was the first Roman author to compose elegy. Epic matter could be and
at times was conveyed in elegiac couplets, elegy described as "a variation upon the
heroic hexameter, in the direction of lyric." See Campbell (1993), xxiv–xxv (citing W.
R. Hardie, *Res Metrica* 49). The foremost example of such elegy is what survives of the
Spartan poet Tyrtaeus (late 7th century **BC**).

19 *For the larger purposes*
designate *mascula Sappho.* Horace, *Ep.*1.19.28.

There are no Miriams or
initiative-taking women. See Cooke.

20 *Meter is of the essence*
makes classical . . . poetry. See *TLL* 10, 241.
"rhythmic stylization." Nagy (2010), 14.
regularization . . . derived. Summarized and paraphrased from Nagy (1974), 143–145.
"language of Achilles." See Parry, Martin.
"language of Hector." See Duban (1980), Martin.
Iliad's **"Embassy scene."** *Il.* 9.177–668.
"verge on . . . figures." Beye (1966), 131–137.
"Meeting . . . Andromache." *Il.* 6.369–502.

Says one critic, A female
"A female . . . that usage." Gutzwiller (2014).
(as noted by Euripides). Thus, the female chorus in his *Medea*:

> Phoebus [Apollo] leader of songs, has from our understanding withheld the lyre's
> song divine [*thespin aoidan*], or else would I a song have sung responsive to the
> race of men. Length of time has as much to say of our and men's fortunes alike
> (lines 424–430).

Gr. *thespin aoidan* 'song divine' (above) is reminiscent of the *audēn thespin* 'voice divine'—
with specific reference to epic poetry—with which the Muses inspire Hesiod (*Th.* 27–28).

performance masculinization. Nagy (2010), 34 ("A salient example of such professionalization by way of masculinization is the poetry and song making of Sappho.... The tradition of singing Sappho's songs, which required virtuoso lead singing that leads into choral singing and dancing, became professionalized as a tradition of monodic singing [i.e., solo as opposed to choral song] as performed by men at symposia [i.e., drinking parties]..."). The development is vividly memorialized in an anecdote over a thousand years after Sappho's time. The Macedonian Greek anthologizer Joannes Stobaeus (5th century AD) relates an event supposed to have occurred at a symposium. Hearing his nephew sing one of Sappho's poems, the Athenian lawgiver Solon (7th–6th centuries BC) wished to learn it. Asked why he should thus waste his time, Solon replied, "That I might learn it and die." The anecdote is thought to reflect the introduction of Sappho's poetry into Athens. More than this, it conveys the effect Sappho's poetry had on near contemporaries, such as Solon. See further *TLL* 406 and 685 (vis-à-vis the feminist spin on Sappho's Athenian reception).

21 *Thus, and with parthéneia*
contradistinction ... concerns. See Rissman.

Three to four hundred
"had the result ... speak." Gutzwiller, 207.

Perhaps so, but the male
reputation rests ... Distaff. On the *Distaff* and the peculiarity of its name, see Cameron and Cameron.

23 *Greer elaborates on artistic*
vis-à-vis poetic inspiration. My summary of Greer in this and the following paragraph derives from Greer (1995), xii–xv, 5, and 23.
115– ... Hesiod's Theogony. The Muses, as described by Hesiod, inspire the poet—Hesiod himself—with divine voice, that he might sing of creation and the gods. Inspiration, as the word indicates, is the *in-breathing* of poetic voice (Lat. *in + spiro*; Gr. *en + pneō*). Thus, *enepneusan de moi audēn / thespin, (h)ina kleioimi* 'they breathed within me voice divine, that I might celebrate' ... (*Th.* 31–32).
fertilizing ... living poem. In the process as similarly described by Ann Bergren, the Theogony's poet is "cast simultaneously as 'male' in social and judicial authority by the *skēptron* ['staff', given him by the Muses] and as 'female' in terms of reproductive capacity by the infusion of *audē* ['voice']." Bergren, 89–90, n. 18.

24 *Thus, and as the following*
theoretical ... narratology. Lanser, 341–342.
feminism ... keep company. Lanser, 343.

25 *Though best known for his*
The Authoress of the Odyssey. Samuel Butler, *The Authoress of the Odyssey* (London: Jonathan Cape, 1922). Reprint, Univ. of Chicago Press (1967).
"because [it] so ... not think." Beard, 335. Parts of this paragraph are otherwise indebted to Beard. Butler's theory motivated Robert Graves, *Homer's Daughter* (Garden City: Double Day, 1955)—a novel in which Graves credits Butler as "irrefutable." The novel is told from the viewpoint of Nausicaa—on Sicily, where Butler places her—beset by suitors in her father's absence. In a different vein, see Downes (with discussion of Butler), and Dalby (positing the gendered authorship of both Homeric poems). Downes explains his "subterranean" endeavor as follows:

Another important, shadowy character in these chapters is Anyte of Tagea (fl. c. 280 BCE), the "female Homer" mentioned by Antipater of Thessalonika (first century BCE). As the female Homer, Anyte serves as Muse throughout this book, and as a kind of Virgilian guide through the underworld or Great Below of literary history. She calls us from across her two millennia of fragmentation as one of many earlier muses, women and "women-Homers" denied us by the erasures of time and history. Like so many women poets of the past, including her more illustrious ancestress Sappho (c. 630–570 BCE), she works in a darkness caused in part by our own obscured horizons, our traditional hallucinations of gender, of women, of epic poetry, and of the past. These hallucinations, I claim, keep us from a better understanding not only of Anyte of Tagea, but of all women epic poets, all the "female Homers" of literary history [Downes, 15–16, footnotes omitted].

The feminist argument can sometimes be strangely silent on *Authoress,* and all but neglectful of Homer (e.g., Beshero-Bondar).

"acknowledged . . . contrary." *TLL* 435. The study of writings by or about women developed in the 1970s under the rubrics of women's studies and feminist theory. It is not so much a discrete literary endeavor (i.e., an academic discipline) as a feminist bailiwick in the identity politics of the late twentieth-century and presently ongoing culture wars. The same period witnessed the rise of African American studies, queer theory, post-colonial studies, and other discipline-fragmenting group-identity inquiries—one's *oppressed* and increasingly self-insulating *self* the focus of inquiry. It is, thus, not only women writers/artists but minority writers/artists who lay claim to special consideration. The focus conveyed by the long-regnant "women and minorities" sorely pits all "others" against the Caucasian male. The various journals, organizations, conferences, and prizes encouraging writings by and about women in no way validate the idea that women's writing—what appears on the page—is discernibly different from men's or worthy of gendered consideration by virtue of female authorship alone. This is not to say that women writers and artists do not warrant attention as women; see, e.g., Nochlin (1988), Chapter 7, "Why Have There Been No Great Women Artists?" (an article supporting my arguments on key points).

Nochlin's essay originally appeared in *ARTnews* (January 1971), lavishly illustrated with masterworks, and with no ax to grind. She subsequently published "'Why Have There Been No Great Women Artists?' Thirty Years After" (2006), in which she "declares" as a feminist—"fear[ing] this moment's overt reversion to the most blatant forms of patriarchy, a great moment for the so-called real men to assert their sinister dominance over 'others,'" etc., etc. She lauds women's studies and the theory that enables it; her "update" illustrated with some of its more mundane and ever execrable byproducts: e.g., one of Cindy Sherman's (b. 1954) *Sex Pictures*—here an anatomically correct mannequin vulgarly positioned and disturbingly portrayed, as though having undergone a bilateral transpelvic amputation. Sherman here follows in the footsteps of male shock artists Andrea Serrano, Chris Ofili, and Damien Hirst, quite surpassing them, as feminist art comes full circle to the worst of what seeks to pass for art. A bit of "sinister dominance" is surely in order.

As further concerns the excess of theory, recent decades have witnessed a concerted effort to determine "The 'Women's Tradition' in Greek Poetry," as seen, e.g., in an exhaustive article of the same title by classicist Laurel Bowman. "Poetry from this tradition is argued to be distinguished by style, subject matter, and alternate modes of subjectivity from the poetry of the public, and predominantly male-authored poetic tradition" (Bowman, 3–4). Given the paucity of women's poetry surviving from antiquity, and the pervasive uncertainties even as to those texts and contexts, the results remain inconclusive. For one thing, the focus is skewed, being on "ancient women's poetry" (Bowman, 23) rather than on ancient poetry that may have been female-authored, i.e., being on author gender rather than poetic merit. For another, and doubtless owing to the dearth of evidence, the inquiry is excessively theory-reliant. The argument thus resorts to "French feminist thought" and the likes of "Lacanian psychoanalytic theory" (Bowman, 5–7)—the former positing that "language, and the entire Western symbolic order is a male-ordered construct." Enter deconstruction: "out with old, in with the new." The recourse to modern(ist) theory, moreover, posits that ancient poetry, for all its penetrative simplicity, has necessarily waited these twenty-five hundred years and more for theorist special pleading, mostly by feminist scholars, to light the way.

What the inquiry ultimately yields is questionable. After page upon heavily foot-noted page, we read in Bowman's conclusion:

> It remains to ask whether the extant evidence indicates the existence of a public text-based women's poetic tradition. The answer to this question must be made for each poet individually. However, one factor that must be taken into account . . . is that no female poet was *only* influenced by her female predecessors. All female poets whose work has survived were strongly influenced by their male predecessors. All female poets whose work has survived have more in common with their male contemporaries than with any female predecessor [Bowman, 23].

So where does that leave us? Moreover, the argument, by English-speaking scholars for language as a male construct generally ignores the implications of gender-encoded European languages, with their masculine, feminine, and even neuter nouns; and masculine and feminine rhymes (for insightful discussion, see Engleking, 82–87). Sappho, owing to her supreme merit, needed no warrant of "women's tradition," but was accepted as canonic.

26 *Butler's thesis developed*
perception . . . the *Odyssey*. More recently, celebrated author John Fowles (1926–2005), acknowledging Butler and Graves, has expressed his own "heretic" view of the *Odyssey*'s female authorship:

> Transparently also the writer is obsessed by all the things—especially young female things—that keep husbands away from their proper place at home. There is that repeated vivid eye for the interior decor and life of the palaces of Nestor, Menelaus and Alcinous—how guests are received, how they are bathed, how dressed, how fed, even how the laundry is done; that ubiquitous sympathy for the feminine ego, from the glittering *grande-dame* entry given Helen of Troy to Calypso's sadness; the love of describing clothes and jewellery; the sympathy shown older women, the flagrant greater interest, in the Land of the Dead, taken in the female ghosts.

> . . . the little touches of humor, the psychological accuracy underlying the delight in the fabulous (the ability to make fabulous beings behave humanly), the obsession with domestic behavior and domestic objects, the preponderant role played by the relationship between men and women . . . a shared sense of sensibilities and preoccupations that we know, in the latter case, did not belong to a man.

> Even if one must take the orthodox scholarly view, and make Homer the male bard that tradition has always maintained, it seems to me certain that he was composing quite as much for a feminine audience as a masculine one, and from an

essentially feminist point of view: that is, a civilizing one" [Fowles (1978), 52, 58; and generally on Homer, 51–74].

As noted by one critic, Fowles's feminism, which is to say his regard for women and their abilities, is "characterized not by political activism but chiefly by admiration for and allegiance to women (at least for those women who demonstrate what Fowles calls the 'feminine principle'), especially in marked opposition to society's general admiration of men." Fowles deemed feminism, thus viewed, as a "requisite part of civilized society" (Aubrey, ed. [1999], 4–6). Fowles's notion of feminism—connoting the feminine—as a civilizational predicate is refreshing; one rarely if ever echoed by patriarchy-indicting feminists. Aubrey elsewhere elaborates:

> They have fought against the Trojans, driven by masculine greed, bloodlust and aggression. What the Odyssey shows is that they ought to have stayed at home with their wives; men on their own are brutish creatures who become civilized only under the influence of women. This is Homer's overall message, says Fowles, and in his view, it is one of the main reasons for believing that the author of the Odyssey was female rather than male [Aubrey, ed. (1999), 37].

Had the Greeks stayed home, there would, of course, have been no Trojan War, no Greek and Roman literature, and no Western culture (as we know it), and likely no John Fowles's opining on Homer's gender as predicate to the treatment of women in his novels. For a female-authored *Odyssey* as the "template" for all Fowles's novels, and "a gesture toward a lost androgyny, an attempt to recover the faculties and sensibilities he names female," see Tarbox, in Aubrey, ed. (1999), 54.

technical . . . clumsily handled. For elaboration, see Manguel, Chapter 18, "Madame Homer."

at the core . . . perpetuation. "Even though the protagonists of both the *Iliad* and the *Odyssey* are men, at the core of each poem are extraordinary women. . . . The action is driven by the fighting men, the justification they give for it lies with the women: the relationship between the two weaves the story into the future. Helen is magically aware of her emblematic role. She says to Paris: 'Zeus planned a killing doom within us both / so even for generations still unborn / we will live in song'" (Manguel, 164).

26 *Butler had bucked the tide*
(Rosalind/Ganymede; Viola). See Donoghue, 29–32, 35–36, 64–66.
"Mme . . . including Balzac." Faguet, 107.
Goethe ended . . . *uns hinan.* For discussion, see Manguel, Chapter 15, "The Eternal Feminine."
his proverbial better half. For *das ewig-Weibliche* as spousal "better half," see Walsh (2015), 91, in Walsh's Chapter 6: "The Eternal Feminine."

27 *This, however, little contents*
disdain . . . regard or need. The notion of *das ewig-Weibliche* is disdained as condescending precisely because it makes woman the means of man's uplift (no pun intended) instead of an autonomous force in her own right. The attack on *ewig-Weibliche*—that which inspires and motivates men to self-improvement and protection of the biologically weaker sex—is an attack on normative heterosexuality, as explained by Michael Walsh:

> And yet this most elemental force in human life, *das ewig-Weibliche*, is routinely scorned and denigrated by the offspring of the Unholy Left, the increasingly deracinated "feminist" harpies whose anti-male rhetoric bespeaks not so much

impotent rage as sexual jealousy.

The attack on normative heterosexuality—led by male homosexuals and lesbians, and invariably disguised as a movement for "rights," piggybacking as a movement for rights on the civil rights movement of the 1960s—is fundamental to the success of Critical Theory. . . . The reason was simple: If a wedge could be driven between men and women, if the nuclear family could be cracked, if women could be convinced to fear and hate men, to see them as unnecessary for their happiness or survival—if men could be made biologically redundant—then the political party that had adopted Critical Theory could make single women one of their strongest voting blocks" [Walsh (2015), 87–88].

For Critical Theory as a means to this end, see pp. 29–30. The attack on normative sexuality is tantamount to an attack on sex itself—"the most powerful engine in human existence," etc. It is *particularly* an assault on the "citadels of Western culture." See Walsh [2015], 75; cf. *TLL* 680 (note to "case for a third gender").

"Fools . . . than the whole." *WD* 40.

dealing with . . . "appropriators." The Roman poet Ovid (43 BC–17 AD) is the Western literary forebear of what is sometimes called "other-voiced verse," poetry of known male authorship assuming a female persona. He wrote, among other things, *Heroides* (*Heroines*), a collection of poems in letter or "epistolary" form, composed in elegiac couplets. The first fourteen poems are spoken by mythological female figures to their unfaithful lovers. The fifteenth alone is spoken by a historical figure, Sappho, addressing her lament to Phaon. Was Ovid a Sapphic voice or a mere "appropriator"? Classical formalist poet and translator Daryl Hine (1936–2012) notes (echoing Virginia Woolf) as follows:

Heroines in name, the passive but vocal victims of Ovid's epistolary elegiacs might better, if less neatly, be termed women of the Heroic Age, grandes dames, or famous females. In lieu of an anachronistic feminism, they display . . . a wounded femininity, ambiguous because imagined by a man—an avowedly heterosexual man at that. Never is the feminine mystique more cruelly traduced, indeed parodied, than in the singular instance of Sappho, the sole subject in this gallery to have left a self-portrait, less fragmentary in Ovid's first century than in our twentieth [Hine, ix].

For the feminist/theoretic attempt to mitigate the fact of Ovid's male authorship, see Janan, 427, n. 3, and 432 (seeking to establish a uniquely female concept of desire with recourse to radical feminist authors and the founders of deconstructionism and poststructuralist thought, e.g., Andrea Dworkin, Julia Kristeva, Catharine MacKinnon, Jacques Derrida, and psychoanalyst/psychiatrist Jacques Lacan, Lacan a decisive influence in Janan's work). See further pp. 28–29.

In academic feminism, the male does not so much appropriate, or even adopt, a female voice, as well he might, as engage in a "discourse [or fiction] of female desire," or "appropriate a *woman's right* to articulate female desire" (emphasis added) (DeJean, 3, 7)—as if the "right" were exclusively a woman's, or a woman were actually ever *deprived* of it, or deprived of the right to counter or *better* a male appropriation, rather than simply complain about it. DeJean otherwise establishes a persuasive Sappho–Ovid–Racine–Baudelaire continuum ("Racine set Phèdre on a course modeled after that elected by Ovid for his Sappho"; "Racine had contaminated Ovid just as Ovid had contaminated Sappho"; "only Baudelaire reveals something of the uncanny identification that resonates in Ovid and in Racine" [DeJean, 7, 12, 17]).

DeJean astutely notes that Ovid's version of Sappho gradually became more prominent than any authentic remains of Sappho herself (DeJean, 12). Thus, so *authentic* was Ovid's articulation of Sappho's voice that he came to *speak for her*, and be credited, without corroboration, and for over five hundred years after her death, as the sole source of her leap from the Leucadian Cliff. DeJean, in the end, essentially *credits* the male-appropriative enterprise:

> Historically, the most influential fictions of Sappho have been those conceived by male authors, like Racine, who are *somehow* able to identify with the original female writer—'Sappho c'est moi, selon moi', to rephrase that often cited aphorism that, it appears, is appropriately beyond origin" (emphasis added) [DeJean, 19].

DeJean's "somehow" would equally apply to a female author, and with no discernibly different result, assuming equal gifts.

occasionally . . . white female. The latest viral furor at the time of this writing was an 18-year-old Utah student who attended her prom wearing a traditional Chinese dress (Amy Qin, "Furor Over a Prom Dress in America Baffles Chinese," *NYT*, 5/3/2018). Thereafter, Asians and the media alike reveled in the all Asian(-American) cast assembled for the movie adaptation of *Crazy Rich Asians* (Roberto Ito, "25-Year Wait To See a Cast Like This," *NYT* [Arts&Leisure], 8/12/2018). Vociferous protests long greeted *Miss Saigon* (1989), among other reasons, for the choice of Jonathan Price (Caucasian) to play the lead role of the Eurasian pimp, the "Engineer" (Michael Paulson, "The Battle of 'Miss Saigon', Yellowface, Art, and Opportunity," *NYT* [Theater], 3/17/2017). Similar controversy has of late marred Puccini's *Madama Butterfly* (1904)—of which *Miss Saigon* is a latter-day incarnation—both as concerns casting and perceived stereotypes (Jason Victor Serinus, "Cultural Controversy swirls around Seattle Opera's 'Madame Butterfly,'" *The Seattle Times*, 8/2/2017). Meanwhile, the Smithsonian has appointed a Caucasian (following a Caucasian retiree) as curator of its Asian galleries (Peter Libbey, "Smithsonian Appoints Head of Asian Galleries," *NYT* [Arts, Briefly], 8/22/2018).

Complaints of stereotyping and appropriation have accompanied *Porgy and Bess* from its 1935 premiere to date (Safiya Merchant, "'Porgy and Bess' symposium to tackle cultural appropriation," *Michigan University Record*, 1/8/2018). The prospect of a mid-1930s black-authored *Porgy and Bess* is unlikely; but being so, would likely have made all well with the world, whatever the work's quality. The Gershwins themselves stipulated that the leads be played by blacks in all U.S. performances (folly to play the show otherwise). The point, here in particular, is that genius necessarily trumps identity politics. In fact, nowadays, just about any use or referecne to anything non-indigenous to onesself raises a hue and cry. See Maureen Callahan, "The Insane War on 'Appropriation,'" *NYP* [Post Opinion], 10/25/2018. The Gershwins and Heywards (the Heywards authors of book and libretto alike) were musical, librettist, and theatrical geniuses, creating a work at once irresistibly impassioned, painful, tender, and sentimental. In a lesser key, appropriational outcry recently accompanied the use of black vernacular by a white poet (Jennifer Schluessler, "A Measure of Contrition for a Poem: An attempt at black vernacular in the The Nation draws criticism," *NYT* [Arts], 8/2/2018).

By contrast to all the above, the perennially popular *Fiddler on the Roof* (1964), suffused with old-world Jewish types/stereotypes, has been singularly lacking in Jewish complaint, even as it has virtually defined Jewish identity in the decades following its release. The plot, based on a series of stories (in Yiddish) by Sholem Aleichem (1859–1916), the chronicler of Jewish village life in Tsarist Russia, highlights Jewish "Tradition"—the eventual musical's signature song—and the preservation of Jewish identity in the face of a daughter's marrying "for love" outside of the faith (her father ultimately relenting). The situation has long resonated with Jewish parents, but less so of late as intermarriage continues to win the day. One nonetheless wonders how *Fiddler* would have fared if other than Jewish-authored and composed.

27 *The classicist author of*
"a contemporary . . . *thiasos*." McEvilley, 383.
"has almost . . . discourse." McEvilley, 383 (and n. 6 for quotation).
invited sympathetic few. A conspicuous exception is Laurence M. Porter's *Women's Vision in Western Literature: The Empathic Community* (2005), a chapter book of broad learning and range from a master critic, in the Praeger "Contributions to Women's Studies" series. With Bernard Schweizer, also cited herein, Porter is only one of two men recently publishing in this series.

The sisterhood seeks to
"The perfection of . . . emotion." Tucker, 85.

28 *In sum, the common sense*
"purely . . . complex scenarios." Karanika, 220.
"Feminist theory . . . propaganda." Paglia (2017), 98.

29 *The times are deliciously*
"Feminism has . . . or fate." Paglia (2017), 5.

By theory is meant Critical
"And when in . . . the void." Scruton (2015), 16.

30 *The sisterhood has thus*
as I would myself learn. I was an appropriator over whose work British classicist Edith Hall, on behalf of the sisterhood, raised her territorial hindquarter, reviewing my *The Lesbian Lyre*. See Hall, *Times Literary Supplement* 1/6/2017. The review was accompanied by a snarky post on Hall's "Edithorial" (blog) beginning, "I've never been asked by a reputable journal to review such a bad book as Jeffrey Duban's *The Lesbian Lyre*." Subsequent review by Sandra Kotta overtly disavows Hall's assessment (*Quillette*, 5/17/2017, Part II) (a tradition-reviving "ambitious, pugnacious, eccentric book. . . . Duban has a great deal to say; much of it immensely valuable"). See further the detailed assessment (in French) by Michel Briand, *Revue des Études Anciennes*, 119.2 (2017), 701–706 ("*The Lesbian Lyre* by Jeffrey M. Duban offers a most stimulating reading. It richly documents, at the outset of the 21st century, the long list of uses and misuses that Sappho has known since Antiquity. To be sure, Duban has many examples to offer.").

Hall's lavishly partisan review and blog show that she had done nothing more than skim the book. One instance suffices. Hall faults the book for its stance that translators of classical Greek *know Greek*, and know it *well*. She objects that such a requirement disallows the likes of Alexander Pope. The book, however, early notes and elaborates on the exception that is Pope, later deeming him "the greatest imitation or version of Homer" (*TLL* 499). Barely three pages into the Preface, one reads, "There have of course been rare and outstanding exceptions: witness Alexander Pope (1688–1744), who, with minimal Greek and an unfailing poetic sensibility, completed one of the most successful and enduring translations of Homer" (*TLL* xxvii). The book's index shows discussion of Pope in twenty subdivisions covering nearly fifty pages.

If the issue is not
"Homer . . . unmitigated fools." Bell, 318–319.

31 *An Odyssey might have*
"**Epic has been ... perspective.**" Alexander Alter, *NYT*, 4/7/2018 (Arts, C1) (review of Miller's *Circe*, quoting Miller).

32 *The growth of Man, says*
"**the growth ... preponderance.**" Fuller, 169.
"**The lineaments ... and light.**" Swinburne (1913), 61.
though ... vastly differently. The essential thesis of Martin van Creveld, *The Privileged Sex.*
Coleridge's then ... mind. See Paley, 169–172 (from which my use of "avuncular"). Coleridge in the same poems bids Betham, "Fly, ostrich-like, firm land beneath thy feet, / Yet hurried onward by the wings of fancy / Swift as the whirlwind, singing in their quills." The image, intentionally or not, is inescapably comedic (the cleverness of *quills*, in context, aside). It is *height* and its sensation that are traditionally associated with poetry, the eagle most frequently evoked. The clumping ostrich will not do. One feminist writer does as best she can with this. "She [Betham] is not to fly in the air but to run like an ostrich, always on the ground. While the advice imposes limits, Coleridge's patriotic British reference to Sappho does assert Betham's potential importance as a national poet" (Beshero-Bondar, 94).
"**a closer ... a woman.**" The piece, by Mary Colum, was hastily published in the *Saturday Review* two days after the Baudelaire publication by coauthors Edna St. Vincent Millay and George Dillon (see Milford, 398). Millay's Baudelaire was otherwise enthusiastically received (see Freer).

A continuous prose narrative
with origins in epic. At the beginning of the eighteenth century, the prose translations of Homer by Ann Le Fèvre Dacier (1654–1720) brought Homer, as a forerunner of the modern novel, to an appreciative French-reading public. Ancient prose narratives, often described and taught today as "ancient novels," include Petronius, *Satyricon*; Lucian, *True History* (a prose narrative parodying the fantasies of Homer's *Odyssey*); Apuleius, *The Golden Ass*; Heliodorus, *Ethiopian Story*; and Longus, *Daphne and Chloe*.
      Notwithstanding the now classic prose narratives of Richardson, Swift, and Defoe, Henry Fielding (1707–1754) is considered the first to write English prose fiction in the form of the novel (verse and drama previously the only sanctioned genres). In the Preface to *Joseph Andrews* (1742), Fielding describes his fictional form as a "comic *epic* poem in prose" (or "comic romance"). However, Fielding's *Tom Jones* (1749) is generally considered the first novel in the modern sense. Fielding there describes the work as a "*heroical*, historical prosaic poem" (IV, 1); a form of "prosaic-comi-*epic* writing" (V, 1) (emphases added). Fielding's prose fiction-as-epic, however expansively treating of an era, emphasizes not its heroism but foibles. The title page bears the tag, *Mores hominum multorum vidit* 'He [Tom Jones] saw the ways of many men.' This references the third line of the *Odyssey*: "He saw the cities of many men and knew their minds" (see p. 47). Further seeking to establish his epic credentials, Fielding makes particular use of comically extended Homeric similes, out-Homering Homer as, e.g., in the portrayal of *pater familias* Squire Thomas Allworthy, the first appearance of Mrs. Deborah (I, 6), and the "battle" of Tom and Blifil & Thwackum (V, 12). For the epic influence on Fielding, with reference to Homer, Virgil, and Milton, see Stovel. On Fielding and the classical tradition see Mace; also Powers.
author V. S. Naipul. See "How ig-Nobel! Winner raps gal writers," *NYP*, 6/2/2011 (conveying British newspaper report). In a distinguishable case, Charles Dickens, after reading the first two of the three tales of George Eliot's *Scenes of Clerical Life* (1857), wrote her as follows: "I should have been strongly disposed, if I had been left to my own

devices, to address the said writer as a woman. I have observed what seem to me to be such womanly touches, in those moving fictions, that the assurance on the title-page is insufficient to satisfy me even now." Letter to George Eliot, 18 Jan. 1858; see Hartley, ed., 331–332. Eliot had sent Dickens a copy of the book through an intermediary. It was her first work of fiction.

So identifiably female. For reasons Eliot made clear; see Eliot (1856).

34 *The progenitor of the*
its feminist supporters. *Frankenstein* is a story that lends itself to strong feminist interpretations (see Hollinger).

It was not only Charlotte
unbridled . . . so sheltered. Though overcoming the insulation of her woman's life, Elizabeth Barrett Browning (1806–1861)—the Brontës' older contemporary—early claimed that seclusion from real life had been an impediment to literary achievement; that she had been "blind," as Homer and Milton, and would thus seek to emulate them (Hurst, 111). One can only wish all women thus impeded. Eroticism emergent from and despite reclusiveness is apparent in Dickinson's (c. 1861).

> Wild nights! Wild nights!
> Were I with thee,
> Wild nights should be
> Our luxury!
>
> Futile the winds
> To a heart in port,
> Done with the compass,
> Done with the chart.
>
> Rowing in Eden!
> Ah! the sea!
> Might I but moor
> To-night in thee.

35 *In the United States*
under her own name. We know, of course, that male and female authors alike have regularly used pen names for various reasons—as actors use stage names—and do so to this day. Pseudonymous author names include Agatha Christie, Henrik Ibsen, C. S. Lewis, George Orwell, and Ayn Rand; and perhaps most famously, Mark Twain, Stephen King, and Joyce Carol Oates. While pen-name motive may vary, it is especially clear from the British examples here examined that the motive was most often gender-driven. In more contemporary cases, motive is name-driven, e.g., "Joyce Carol Oates" sexier than "Rosamond Smith"; "Ayn Rand" more catchy than "Alisa Zinov'yevna Rosenbaum"—the supposition strengthened by the fact that neither pseudonym is male.

The Brontës were women
dashing, dissolute . . . Byron. See Gérin.
in appearance and effect. See Paglia, Chapter 13: "Speed and Space: Byron"; Chapter 17: "Romantic Shadows: Emily Brontë."
model for Rochester. See Wilson, 162–166; Brown, 374–381.
Emily's *Wuthering Heights*. Completed in 1846, *Wuthering Heights* was published in

December 1847, after *Jane Eyre.*
"mad, bad and . . . know." Of interest is Stowe (1870), preceded by Stowe (1869). These writings temporarily turned Stowe's famous life upside-down. In response to disparaging remarks against Lady Byron by Byron's last mistress, Countess Teresa Guiccioli, Stowe claimed in the *Atlantic* article that Byron was sleeping with his half-sister. The ensuing outrage and derision prompted Stowe to the larger and still vainly self-exculpatory work. Stowe claimed that she and Lady Byron were disbelieved because they were women. This was a strange case of wanting it both ways—Stowe's *Uncle Tom's Cabin*, published under her own name, then outsold (as believed) only by the Bible.

36 *The Brontës, however*
skeletons . . . in the attic. The reference is to Rochester's wife, Bertha, whose mental illness is unknown to him when the couple weds. Bertha is secretly housed, with a live-in attendant, in an upper room at Thornfield Hall. See Gilbert and Gubar.
"In Wuthering . . . interesting." Anonymous, *Douglas Jerrold's Weekly Newspaper*, 15 *Jan. 1848*. Contemporary reviews were decidedly mixed, wavering between admiration, disgust, and disbelief. The work, in sum, was a great success.

37 *No one at the time*
Thackeray divined . . . pen. Letter of William M. Thackeray to W. S. Williams (Charlotte's publisher), 23 Oct. 1847. Thackeray first queries whether the author be a woman, then so concludes (Harden and Hill, eds., 141).
dramatically opposed natures. "Linton's [soul] is as different [from Heathcliff's] as a moonbeam from lightning, or frost from fire" (E. Brontë, 95).
"To you . . . your judgement." Letter of Charlotte Brontë to W. S. Williams, 16 Aug. 1848 (Smith, ed., 235).

Which is to say that
"What . . . impracticable." E. Brontë, 96–97 (emphasis added). The idea is announced earlier in the chapter: "I love the ground under his feet, and the air over his head, and everything he touches, and every word he says. I love all his looks, and all his actions, and him entirely and all together" (92), and "I love him: and that, not because he's handsome.... but because he's more myself than I am. Whatever our souls are made of, his and mine are the same" (95).
"This is the . . . universe." De Beauvoir, 693.

38 *The totalizing unification*
"*Herz an Herz* . . . breath." Wagner, *Tristan und Isolde*, Act II, Scene 2.
"With your fair . . . breath." Michelangelo, Sonnet XXX.

39 *Positing complete union and*
convulsed in rippling habit. For the orgasmic quality of Bernini's depiction, see Schama, 114–120 (the seraph "turns her body inside-out so that the habit—the protecting garment of her chastity, the symbol of her discipline—becomes a representation of what is taking place deep within her," etc.). It is Schama who, in the first instance, refers to Teresa as voluptuous.

Rubens painted an ecstatic Teresa (1612–1614), depicting (less sensually) Teresa's autobiographically described vision. The Magdalen is more than once depicted in ecstasy (Rubens, Caravaggio), as are certain male figures, Saint Francis in particular (Caravaggio, Bellini, El Greco). Danaë's receiving the shower of Zeus's gold (semen) is a repeated subject of ecstatic depiction (Artemisia Gentileschi, Orazio Gentileschi, Corregio,

Rembrandt, Klimt); also Judith (Artemisia, Klimt), and most especially, perhaps, Jupiter and Io (Corregio).

with sacred or profane love. The ambiguity between religious and sexual fervor, in a way reminiscent of Bernini's *Teresa*, is supremely captured in the climactic lesbian sex scene of the film *Disobedience* (2017), a scene that need not be overtly graphic (it isn't) to be perfectly effective and most sympathetically erotic. The story, set within a London Jewish orthodox community and household, was female written; the movie, male produced and male cowritten. The movie was not, and need not have been, female produced for its riveting and entirely persuasive depiction of love between two women. It is noted, more recently, that "no one blended the sacred and sexual quite as Ms. Franklin did" (Cinque Henderson, "Aretha on Heaven and Earth," *NYT* [Op-Ed], 8/17/2018) (the song "Natural Woman" showing that a "natural woman can know God and erotic longing, ravenous spiritual and sexual need all at once").

39 *This is one manner of*
"**mercurial and malicious.**" The phrase, used of Girodet's Eros (Stafford, 194), is equally apropos of Bernini's seraph. Both are accomplices to acts of amorous possession.
"**The wonder of . . . nature.**" Stafford, 197.

40 *Neoplatonism, starting with*
Plotinus (3rd century AD). This paragraph in part indebted to Celenza, 632–634.

41 *Incorporating his creatures*
"**O House of . . . Israel.**" Jer. 18:6.

Further to the biblical
basár achád 'one flesh'. Gen. 2:24.

42 *Returning, then, to Brontë*
"**At first when . . . gender.**" Greer (1995), 5. We further note in this connection that "a vision," as Virginia Woolf observes, that "becomes too masculine or . . . too feminine . . . loses its perfect integrity and, with that, its most essential quality as a work of art." Woolf (1929/1958), 80. In her "Women and Fiction," Woolf further laments the limitations of early nineteenth-century female-author experience as an impediment to creativity. The essay, however (1) fails to account for the extraordinary characters and events portrayed by women authors of that era; (2) makes no mention of the gender anonymity under which the women's works first appeared; (3) is unmindful of the respective works' successes upon publication and thereafter; and (4) intones the since perennial complaint that "until lately, women in literature were the creation of men". On Woolf's signature *A Room of One's Own* (1929), see p. 269.
"**Whatever pure . . . soul.**" *PL* 8.622–629 (Rafael to Adam).

43 *Catherine's stance has*
Brahms . . . Schumann. Sixten Sparre and Elvira Madigan (real-life figures portrayed in three movies) might be added to the list, as well as any number of other young women in thrall to older military men, perhaps especially Sarah Woodruff in John Fowles's *The French Lieutenant's Woman* (1969) (see p. 98).

44 *Hawthorne also describes*
"**As a first . . . evaporated.**" Hawthorne, 218–219.

male author's psyche. However sympathetic and predisposed to Hester Prynne, Hawthorne in *The Marble Faun* (1860) is less generous toward female writers and artists.

44 *We take but passing note*
"**poetry of sensibility.**" See Knowles, Chapter 5.
"**The problem ... by women.**" Greer (1995), 259.

45 *Poetic beacon of her day*
"**authoritatively ... view.**" Hurst, 110.
lacking in ... and concern. The argument for *Aurora Leigh*'s epic standing is made by Bailey, in Schweizer, ed. 117–137. More to the epic point is Eleanor Porden Franklin's earlier published *Coeur de Lion, or, The Third Crusade: A Poem* (1822). This sixteen-book epic features cross-dressing women warriors succumbing to Richard I and his forces—foil to the "ultimately triumphant English social order of the Lionhearted" (Beshero-Bondar, 1–3).

We further mention two
feminist apologists aplenty. See especially the opening essay in Gladstein and Sciabarra, eds.; and in the same volume, the essays by Branden ("Ayn Rand: The Reluctant Feminist"), Gladstein ("Ayn Rand and Feminism: An Unlikely Alliance"), Brownmiller ("Ayn Rand: A Traitor to her Own Sex"), and others. The book is part of Penn State University's "Re-Reading the Canon Series." A feminist cottage industry, the series presently offers close to forty volumes on everyone from Plato and Aristotle to Jane Addams and Hanna Arendt. With the exception of the Addams and Rand volumes, the series is entirely female-edited.
"**I myself ... prostitute.**" See West (1913; reprint 1982), 218–222.

46 *West and Rand were writing*
West and Rand were writing. My discussion is indebted to the succinct and engaging Bernard Schweizer (2002).
"**epics are ... framework.**" Schweizer, 3.
"**misotheistic ... composition.**" Schweizer, 144.

Thus seeking to designate
"**extraordinary ... civilization.**" Schweizer, 7–8.

Schweizer yet injects a
"**how the ... epic calling.**" Schweizer, 12. This and the preceding quote are from Schweizer's introduction. He makes the full case in his Chapter 4, "Black Lamb and Grey Falcon: A Modern Female Epic."

47 *Moreover, spiritual and*
"**citizens who ... in women.**" North, 47.
"**commended ... aggressiveness.**" North, 48.

48 *Wisdom is ultimately*
Rarely ... by brain alone. The outstanding exception is the Greek philosopher Epicurus—as described in Lucretius's *De Rerum Natura* (*On the Nature of Things*)— seen as an intellectual hero conquering the *moenia mundi* 'walls/ramparts of the universe':

§157

Thus prevailed the enlivening powers of his
Mind, and far proceeded he the flaming ramparts
Of the universe beyond, traversing the All
Immense in spirit and in mind, whence as victor
Reports he that which can arise, and what cannot,
The finite forcefulness of each created thing,
Its rationale and deeply anchored boundary.

[ergo vivida vis animi pervicit et extra
processit longe flammantia moenia mundi
atque omne immensum peragravit mente animoque,
unde refert nobis victor quid possit oriri,
quid nequeat, finita potestas denique cuique
qua nam sit ratione atque alte terminus haerens.]

[*DRN* 3.25–30; Duban (1982) and pp. 193–198]

"Human 'nature' . . . before." Auden, 32.

49 *In preindustrial society*
In preindustrial . . . limited. See van Creveld, 73–76. There is a significant di-chotomy, argues van Creveld, in the treatment of women in the criminal justice system and in the military. As concerns the latter, "[A]s long as armed forces were meant for combat and occasionally engaged in it, the few women who served were not expected to fight and hardly ever did. But as the armed forces' role as a fighting machine all but came to an end, the number of female soldiers who served in them rapidly rose" (van Creveld, 187). Similarly, the "reluctance on the part of both men and women to see a field . . . littered [with female bodies] is a cardinal reason why women have very seldom fought in war" (van Creveld, 196). To this may be added the male protective instinct toward women, the reluctance of men in combat to see female comrades harmed, and the distraction that comes from the concern and its avoidance. War being hell, "women . . . have hardly ever been conscripted to serve. [S]ince one of the most important, if not the most important, objectives of war is to preserve the life of the community, [the conscription of women] would be both absurd and counterproductive." Insulating women from combat, as from all harm, is psychologically rooted in the prohibition—"drummed into boys from the moment they are old enough to understand the meaning of no"—against hitting girls (van Creveld, 203).

51 *The female expects heroism*
"deserved sexual prerogative." Roberts, 108–109.
The paradigm . . . its failings. Roberts, 73–84.

This "princess and the dragon"
"illicit and . . . transcendent." Newman, vii.

52 *The restorative post-rescue*
"So speaking . . . stilled him." *Il.* 14.346–353 (R. Lattimore, tr.).
"She most . . . of revenge." *PL* 454–466.

53 *Satan's proximity to Eve*
"Interspecies ... Darrow." Walsh (2018), 137.
Beauty tames the beast. See Walsh (2018), Chapter 7: "La Belle et la Bête: For each Beauty a Beast."

54 *There, as in the quest paradigm*
Smooth and ... beholder. Smith, 84.
sex ... they "got the girl." We briefly consider pop culture hero James Bond, whose questing wrap-up is typically a tumble in the sack (or hay)—not with the woman who inspired or was object of his life-and-death adventuring—but with his female antagonist, often of dangerously foreign or seductively exotic origin, who has tried to thwart his every turn. This is sweet and playful comeuppance, a buoyant assertion of life, and great high jinx. How fittingly yet daringly named is Bond's in-the-hay-taken *Goldfinger* (1964) antagonist Pussy Galore: the most off-color, and thus famous, Bond girl name (almost vetoed by U.S. censors). The name was in every way predictive of the Bond ethos, though recent talk of Bond as misogynist and rapist is quite over the top. Bond, the ultimate winner, does not so much "get the girl" as get laid. The rule holds. As *Goldfinger's* Sean Connery more bluntly put it over thirty years later in another movie, "Losers always whine about [having tried] their best. Winners go home and fuck the prom queen" (*The Rock*, 1996).

The combat hero quests
woman's sex ... sovereignty. Roberts, 88.
Having wagered ... produce. One of the sexes, as the quest paradigm shows, is *necessarily* brawny. Cf. the tendentious and self-flagellatory lament of famed art historian Linda Nochlin, rejecting "the return of manly men.... The operative word is men. Brawny heroic, manly men" (2015, 320; quoting and responding to *The New York Times*).

55 *Other circumventions*
"As Homer ... of Homer." Quoted by Hurst, 113.

The aspiration toward
interest to *humanity*. As noted by Scottish classicist, poet, novelist, and literary critic Andrew Lang (1844–1912), Homer "is a poet all of gold, universal as humanity, simple as childhood, musical now as the flow of his own rivers, now as the heavy plunging wave of his own ocean" (Lang, 87–88).

Says Isobel Hurst
"The most ... violence." Hurst, 113. *Contra*, Nochlin:

> Another attempt to answer the question ["Why have there been no great women artists?"] involves shifting the ground slightly and asserting, as some contemporary feminists do, that there is a different kind of "greatness" for women's art than for men's, thereby postulating the existence of a distinctive and recognizable feminine style, different in both its formal and expressive qualities and based on the special character of women's situation and experience [148].

> If there actually were large numbers of "hidden" women artists, or if there really should be different standards for women's art as opposed to men's—and one can't have it both ways—then what are feminists fighting for? If women have in fact achieved the same status as men in the arts, then the status quo is fine as it is [1988, 150].

A similar *apologia* is made for the lack of great Antebellum literature by women; see Baym, ix–xlii (Introduction to the Second Edition).

56 *Epic reflects an age*
causal tale of Helen's. Its argued shortcomings as a depiction of the Trojan War aside, the movie *Troy* (2004) has the Greek commander, Agamemnon, make this very point—that Helen is irrelevant; that control of Troy and its wealth is the goal, i.e., that the Trojan War (albeit on a grand scale) is essentially a taking war.

vastly exceeding . . . inception. The same may be said, e.g., of the *Chanson de Roland* (*Song of Roland*, 11th century **AD**), climaxing in the Saracen ambush of Charlemagne's rear guard at the pass of Roncesvalles/Fr. Roncevaux, Spain (778 **AD**). The pass was valiantly defended by Roland, the Twelve Peers, and a vastly outnumbered contingent of Franks, all of whom were killed. The battle, such as it was, grew in legend to heroize Roland and become the first French epic. The events as recounted are at variance with the historical record, including Einhard's *Vita Karoli Magni* (*Life of Charles the Great* [i.e., Charlemagne], c. 833) and the *Annales Regni Francorum* (*Annals of the Kingdom of the Franks*, c. 800). The glorification of Roland and the Twelve Peers has an analogue in that of Arthur and the Knights of the Round Table.

The taker in such brutal
for the kleos . . . fame. *Kleos* 'glory, fame, repute', of paramount concern in Homer, comes in many forms. Though the collocation *kleos* + *aphthiton* 'fame . . . undying' appears only once (spoken, appropriately, by Achilles; *Il.* 9.413), all *kleos* is meant to endure. The topic is immense and much written about (see *TLL* 185–205, 608–620). **paramount prize—life itself.** As breathtakingly put in Achilles's pursuit of Hector:

> They ran beside these, one escaping, the other after him.
> It was a great man who fled, but far better he who pursued him
> rapidly, since here was no festal beast, no oxhide
> they strove for, for these are prizes that are given men for their running.
> No, they ran for the life of Hector, breaker of horses.
>
> [*Il.* 22.157–161, R. Lattimore, tr.]

"gendered writing . . . hegemony." Alwes, 56.

57 *As man is a history-making*
The quest, often . . . city. "The only characteristic common to both images [those of one's "open future" and "unforgettable past"] is a sense of purpose; a road, even if its destination is invisible, runs in a certain direction; a city is built to endure and be a home" (Auden, 32). Precious objects obtained in the quest (including a "princess bride") typically inure to the benefit of the city (Auden, 37).

questing Trojan . . . roots. Continuum and interconnection are ever prominent in the epic enterprise—from one epic and epic tradition to another. The *Iliad* and later Greek sources make a survivor of Trojan Aeneas, though not mentioning his later-developed migration (see Lang, 51–64). Glorifying Emperor Augustus and his Julian ancestry (i.e., his relationship, as posthumously adopted son and heir, to his maternal great-uncle Julius Caesar), Virgil places Trojan ancestry in Italy itself, thus making Aeneas's arrival there a return home of sorts (*Aen.* 3.163–168; 7.195–196, 205–211; 8.126–136), if not a mandate (*Aen.* 7.239–242). Moreover, King Evander of Italy, from whom Aeneas seeks help, had once hosted Trojan King Priam and Aeneas's own father, Anchises, as they passed through the then young Evander's realm (*Aen.* 7.153–171).

This created the sacrosanct guest-host relationship, obliging the since aged Evander to befriend Aeneas. Across the oceans and ages, Spenser made Brute/Brutus, grandson of Aeneas, the founder of England and progenitor of the British monarchic line, culminating in Elizabeth.

57   *Dido, who commits suicide*
"**a long view . . . for Man.**" Beshero-Bondar, 2.

A "feminine of Homer"
facile and counterintuitive. It is not, as tellingly told, the lack of genius that has impeded women in the arts, but a misguided educational system and the strictures of social institutions (including art academies and systems of patronage). See Nochlin (1988), 150–152, 157–158, 163; cf. George Sand, *Letters to Marcie* (letter VI): "Women are allowed a deplorable education. That is man's worst crime. Masculine abuses against women are everywhere, supported by the most sacred institutions" (as quoted by Federman, 263).

58   *Moreover, the Iliad is the*
epic-combat . . . containing. It is believed that epic narrative originated in descriptions of martial encounter, one-on-one, single or successive—i.e., in Gr. *aristeiai* (pl. noun; sing. *aristeia*: "the feat of the hero that won the mead of valour" [Liddell & Scott Greek-English Dictionary]). The word and notion derive from Gr. *aristos* 'best'; hence, a mortal contest in which the fighter supremely excels. See Highet (tr.), 74–75; Johansen, 28, 42, 46; and Krischer, 9–10.
introduction . . . contain him. "The Wrath of Achilles had probably been an epic subject for generations before Homer found it, and the germ of its meaning, the conflict between personal integrity and social obligation, must always have been inherent. But Homer's development of the theme squeezes the last drop of psychological and metaphysical meaning out of the old material" (Whitman, 82). On the singular nature of Achilles, see Whitman's chapter "Achilles" (181–220).
singular *mater dolorosa*. Thetis cradling Achilles's head (*Il.* 18.71, 23.136) is "the primal Pietà" (Beye, 45–46). See also Bodkin, 161–162.

In the same vein, the
Nunc leti . . . viae. Tibullus, *El.* 1.3.50.

59   *There is, in short, no*
"**relative . . . greatness.**" Hurst, 113.
of death, love, hate. See p. 91 and *TLL* 624–626.
but never quite achieved. Though showing great compassion for Priam (Hector's father) in the moving final book of the *Iliad* (the ransoming of Hector's body), Achilles at one point loses his temper, threatening the king; and when the ransoming is done, prays to his beloved Patroclus (whom Hector had slain, triggering Achilles's revenge) to forgive his actions. One senses that Achilles's revenge (slaying Hector and chariot-dragging him around the walls of Troy) has failed to sate his bloodlust, and that he is yet the reluctant ransomer of Hector's mutilated corpse (however much preserved in appearance by the gods)—that Achilles's full redemption, within reach, remains elusive.

Women, as the source of
may have been female bards. See Downes, as quoted in the opening note, above.
This is not male chauvinism. The thought is corroborated in a female author's discussion of erotic art. "In the nineteenth century, and still today, the very idea—much less

an available public imagery—of the male body as a source of gentle, inviting, satisfaction for women's erotic needs, demands, and daydreams is almost unheard of, and again *not because of some 'male-chauvinist' plot in the arts*, but because of the total situation existing between men and women in society as a whole" (Nochlin [1988], 141–142; emphasis added).

are of Darwinian import. The case is briefly and insightfully made by P. Jones (2012). Noting that Homer always speaks deferentially of women—Agamemnon of Chryseis, Achilles of Briseis, Patroclus of Briseis [as reported by her], Odysseus of Penelope—he finds "no misogynistic conception of a humiliated woman bossed by her contemptuous man." Crediting Homer as a "feminist pioneer," Jones merits quotation as follows:

> The point is this. Population stability in the ancient world was a life-or-death matter. Unless every woman produced about eight children to ensure that two or three survived, the state would collapse; so essential was the unseen biological imperative of giving birth. Female roles, in other words, were limited in the main because the very existence of the state depended on a woman's fertility.

> So it was just not possible for a woman to hold down a tightly scripted chat show or run a top law firm. Her work as mother was far too important to society for that. Homer understands this, and the result is that husband-wife relationships are painted in terms of the Hector-Andromache scene—two worlds, each entailing different responsibilities, skills, and demands, with both parties united in respect for and commitment to each other, the family and its needs. Humiliation and subjugation do not come into it.

> It is in later authors that the battle of the sexes flourished . . . [a] male-generated public image [that] is not exactly unknown today. But Homer, the first and greatest author of the classical world, bucked the trend as a feminist pioneer in delineating the unique capacities and abilities, with their associated duties and responsibilities, of women, in reciprocal and complementary terms to those of men.

60   *The male sex, both human*
     competes for the female. See van Creveld, 38–41, 47.

     There is to be sure
     "conspicuous . . . world." Alwes, 56.

61   *In late-Renaissance painting*
     repellent . . . hundred years. Straussman-Pflanzer, 29.
     feminist movement . . . history. Straussman-Pflanzer, 31. The feminist revision of art history—the many works of Norma Broude and Mary D. Garrard aside—is apparent in the highly theoretical collection of her own essays by art historian doyenne Linda Nochlin, *Representing Women* (1999). For the "tidal wave" in the poetic tradition of the 1970s Women's Movement and Gay Liberation, see Donoghue, xlii–xliii.
     "An unresolved . . . life." This and the immediately following quotation from Straussman-Pflanzer, 11, 28.
     threatened female characters. Bal, 194–195.
     "She knew quite . . . to do." Bal, 18.

62   *Artists being extraordinary*
     "something . . . womanhood." Greer (1979), 191.

63　*In the perennially painted*

older men . . . event. The chronology is offered as follows, that the 1610 *Susanna* "reflects a rare visual expression of female victimization, metaphoric testimony to the artist's own resistance to the sexual harassment she endured from a community of Roman males in the year preceding her rape by Agostino Tassi" (Garrard, 77). The rape, in other words, did not occur in a vacuum. Artemisia was a conspicuous and estimably beautiful artist.

"Only she . . . understood." Greer (1979), 191.

"women are . . . activities." Greer (1979), 195.

There is considerable

"expressive . . . acquiescence." See Garrard in Broude & Garrard eds. (1982), 150.

"She does not . . . convention." Garrard, 79.

65　*Susanna depictions are thus*

nude . . . inviting attention. The classic distinction between *nude* and *naked* is made by premier twentieth-century art historian Kenneth Clark: "To be naked is to be deprived of our clothes, and the word implies some of the embarrassment most of us feel in that condition. The word 'nude,' on the other hand, carries, in educated usage, no uncomfortable overtone. The vague image it projects into the mind is not of a huddled and defenseless body, but of a balanced, prosperous, and confident body: the body reformed" (Clark, "The Naked and the Nude," 3). Straddling these definitions is Paul Emile Chabas's highly controversial *Matinée de Septembre* (*September Morn*) (1911) (Metropolitan Museum) (plate 20). The side-view depiction is of a standing, slightly forward-leaning young woman bathing in a mutedly sun-lit lake. Her arms are arranged so as to reveal, while giving the impression of seeking to conceal, her breasts (the painting a clever mockery of innocence). Cf. the *Capitoline Venus* (statue).

"the Bible's . . . concubine." Stocker, 29, 32.

amorous garden settings. See Garrard, "Susanna in the Garden of Love," in Garrard, 81–86.

67　*More recently, the work of*

her artifice . . . sensibility. Nochlin (1988), 115. See also Nochlin, "Florine Stettheimer: Rococo Subversive" (2015), 133–152, 1st pub. *Art in America*, 7 (1980).

"exist[s] apart . . . time." Nochlin (1988), 132.

mural . . . Diego Rivera. Nochlin (1988), 123.

work of Marc Chagall. See Schwartz.

"She was . . . of the term." Nochlin (1988), 117.

68　*Genre art of the twentieth*

The Dinner Party (1979). My own discussion is quite critical. For a sympathetic appraisal of this work, with commendations and criticisms alike, see A. Jones, in Broude and Garrard, eds. (2005), 409–433. As earlier noted, politics, and sexual politics in particular, little make for inspiring art. For a Chicago biography—as overwrought as *The Dinner Party* itself—see Levin (2007) (on which I rely solely for Chicago quotations).

Such art is no more

"pure artist . . . suggestions." Swinburne, 103 (note).

69　*Indeed, Courbet's painting*

metonymically essential. Author's paraphrase and elaboration of discussion in Nochlin

(2007), 145, 149 (citing sources).
"'trace back' . . . original." Nochlin (2007), 149.
Hesiod's cosmic . . . Eros.

§158

Foremost of all then was Chaos born, followed by
Broad-breasted Earth, the ever steadfast seat of all
The gods atop snowy Olympus resident;
Then murky Tartarus, creviced in spacious earth,
And Eros, fairest among the immortal gods,
Looser of limbs, crushing in gods and humankind
Within their breasts all sturdy thought and mindfulness.

[*Th.* 115–122]

70   *While Courbet depicts it*
"the forbidden . . . itself." Nochlin (2007), 147.
"make . . . simultaneously." Quoted by Levin, 252.
"twenty-five . . . Supper." Quoted by Levin, 250–251.

The stack of dishes, before
"would like the . . . freedom." Quoted by Levin, 251.
"The growing . . . representation." Nochlin (1988), 143.
"Feminist art . . . woman did it." Quoted by Levin, 251.

71   *Female nudes are often*
clyster by her maid. "The servant girl is giving her mistress an enema. This process allows her impatient guest to satisfy his curiosity and examine parts of her body that might normally be less accessible." See Althaus, ed., 114 (commenting on the like depiction by artist Pierre Maleuvre, *Le Curieux* 'Peeping Tom' [1779]; the practice both common and voyeuristically purposeful in eighteenth-century France). The "remedy," notes Donald Posner, was at the time "as common to medical practice as aspirin today"; and further, "In Watteau's work it illuminates the erotic aura of the female presence. Watteau's naked, long-limbed beauty awaiting her cure is the image of voluptuous receptivity" (Posner, 387–388).

As for William Etty
"he was . . . marble limbs." Mass, 166.
"finding God's . . . in her." Smith, 86, quoting Alexander Gilchrist, *The Life of William Etty* (1855, 1978), 36.
depict . . . female pubic hair. The Victorian Era was extremely well shaven. See p. 69.

72   *One allows for qualification*
allows for qualification. Paragraph in part indebted to Hyde, 4–5, 150–156.
entertainment . . . pleasure. See Althaus, 11.

73   *Angelica Kauffman*
"inimitable femininity." See Häusle, et al.
"truth to nature . . . Paris." Bindman, 66, quoting M. Missirini, *Della Vita di Antonio Canova* (Prato, 1824), 231–232.
"light grace . . . the subject." Bindman, 70, quoting M. Quatremère de Quincy, *Canova*

et ses Ouvrages ou Mémoires historiques sur la vie et les travaux de ce célèbre artiste (Paris, 1834), 37.

74   *The Woodmere Art Museum*
Extend our . . . to sculpture. The discussion extends to music as well, of which we may summarily note the following. If Clara Schumann's (1818–1896) works are inferior to Robert's (1810–1856), it is because she lacked his gifts, not his anatomy. Clara's was the work of any good to excellent male composer, which is not to discount her towering musical acumen and the performance idolatry she enjoyed from youth to old age. Again, the issue is not what a female artist might do, but whether what she does reflects a gendered sensibility. No female composer, by virtue of her sex alone, has been incapable of composing enduring works of acknowledged genius. None, however, has. Had it been otherwise, the *mores* of earlier times would have little conceded the result.

Clara's care for the couple's eight children, both during their marriage and after Robert's death at age 46, was a dire constraint on her artistic creativity. Similarly constrained—as any female painter of the time—was Fanny Mendelssohn (1805–1847), older sister of the acclaimed Felix, her works sometimes published under his name (cf. p. 77). Prolific composer and piano prodigy, she was thought to have "played like a man." One also thinks of older sister Maria Anna ("Nannerl") Mozart (1751–1829), whose prodigious gifts were systematically back-burnered to her brother's greater glory. Noteworthy as well—for posthumous lack of fame, though remaining "known," even as she was revered in her lifetime—is the infant prodigy Amy Beach (1867–1944): the first significant American composer of classical music, who was also acclaimed for piano performance.

Beach's musical milestone was her *Gaelic Symphony*, the first symphony composed and published by an American woman. Premiering October 30, 1896, with the Boston Symphony, it was an exceptional success, though "whatever the merits or defects of the symphony were thought to be, critics went to extraordinary lengths in their attempts to relate them to the composer's sex" (Gates, 4) (also referencing the "double standard of sexual aesthetics" and "conformity to the prevailing stereotypes of ideal femininity").

The contemporaneous evaluation of outstanding female performer-composers was, then, typically made with the critic's awareness of their sex. Barring such awareness, the critique—both in approach and conclusions—would doubtless have been other than it was. The situation particularly recalls the reception of Charlotte Brontë (p. 37), depending on whether her sex were known. Gates's excellent (and excellently researched) article on Beach may be read in connection with the different forms of female artistic endeavor discussed herein.

Contemporary American composer, concert pianist, and conductor Joan Tower (b. 1938) has been hailed by *The New Yorker* as "one of the most successful women composers of all times." Yet there is nothing identifiably female in her works, including those of a specified female inspiration, e.g., her four-part (later five) *Fanfare for the Uncommon Woman*—a response to Aaron Copeland's *Fanfare for the Common Man*—each part dedicated to an "adventurous, risk-taking woman." The work is actually more emphatically masculine for its heavy brass and percussive scoring, including tuba. Nor would one know, but for its title, that Tower's *Amazons* concerns fierce warrior queens. Tower is otherwise a frequently serial composer, further removing her from conventional considerations, whether of gender or composition. Though the comparison is necessarily skewed, owing to their overwhelmingly greater numbers, male composers consistently compose with a lightness, sweetness, and tenderness one would instinctively think female. By the same token, no female opera composer ever composed, or might compose, more beautifully for the female voice than did Verdi, Bellini, Donizetti, and Puccini.

75 *Nor is Power's The Greek*
    "pure because . . . of shame." Smith, 84.

78 *Also exhibited was Adrienne*
    social . . . institutions. Nochlin (1988), 150–152, 158.

    However, the then traditional
    training: the nude model. A pioneering exception is the British painter Evelyn
    Pickering De Morgan (1855–1919), a vividly colorist Pre-Raphaelite, who studied at
    the (then as now) prestigious Slade School of Fine Art (London). The Slade was first
    to (controversially) admit female students into "life drawing" classes, where they might
    draw from partially clad nudes, including male nudes. Curiously, De Morgan turned
    down a Slade scholarship, not because it required her to execute such drawings, but
    because the required medium was charcoal, for which she did not care. Her paintings
    range from elaborately garmented to nude female figures. De Morgan studied at Slade
    with Sir Edward John Poynter, whose images appear as cover art for both this volume
    and *The Lesbian Lyre.*

79 *Finally, though other*
    incontrovertibly . . . style. Nochlin (1988), 174.

80 *Returning to poetry and*
    poem by Michelangelo. See Cox, 288 (n. 110); also 63.
    'a man in a woman'. The notion morphs in science fiction into the "female man," as ex-
    pounded by feminist author Joanna Russ in her 1975 novel of the same title (cf. Queen
    Anne as a "female man" in Jonathan Swift, *Gulliver's Travels*, Ch. 4). The novel's "Joanna"
    calls herself the female man, believing she must abandon her female identity to be taken
    seriously (Russ, 5). This is an extreme recalibration of the nineteenth-century female
    author's recourse to pseudonym. "Joanna" states that "there is one and only one way to
    possess that in which we are defective. . . . Become it" (Russ, 139).

81 *Colonna and her poetic*
    "the ineluctable . . . Sapphos." Cox, 64.
    "finer and . . . a woman." Cox, 70–71.

    The masculine imprint
    Katherine Philips (1632–1664). My comments on Philips adapted from Andreadis,
    55.

82 *Of further note is Colonna's*
    abdomen taut and rippling. Paglia designates the androgyn *Giuliano de' Medici* as one
    of "Michelangelo's provocative works of sexualized theater" (Paglia, 162–165, with
    photo and mention of Colonna).

83 *Conlon's essay, however*
    "The rich . . . observations." Conlon, 42.

84 *Not to belabor the obvious*
    Sonnets from the Portuguese. Robert Browning deemed Elizabeth's collection of forty-
    four love sonnets the best sonnet collection since Shakespeare's own. And the twentieth
    century's greatest formalist poet and literary translator, Richard Wilbur (1921–2017),

deemed Edna St. Vincent Millay (1892–1950), with her 138 sonnets, the century's premier sonneteer.

Philosopher George Santayana (1863–1952) considered the sonnet "the most classic of modern poetical forms" for the way it "synthesiz[es] the phrase and make[s] the unexpected seem inevitable" (Santayana, 131). This the sonnet does by the consistency of its metric and interlocking patterns of rhyme, analogous to the texture-enriching interlock of inflected classical diction. As it is the most classic, the sonnet form has been the most assayed since its thirteenth-century beginnings, with what one prominent critic deems a success rate of one in a thousand (Trench, xi–xii).

Those incapable of rhyme dismiss its "tyranny" for free verse (*TLL* 236–238): "The Feminine Romantics shared a distaste for the sonnet with its Romantic precursors who found the sonnet's restrictions too stifling for their abundant lyricism." Thus, and in the words of one female poet, the sonnet was a "brilliant shackle" belonging "only to men" (Engelking, 80). This is a feminist rejection of "patriarchy," by lowered bar, similar to the argument for epic on themes of female concern (as discussed above).

84   *Poet Sara Teasdale's*
"I have included . . . own." Teasdale, ix.
Sappho-influenced "Fatima." Considered among the most erotically charged of Tennyson's poems, "Fatima" was prefixed upon publication with a transliteration of the opening verse of Sappho's electrifying *phainetai moi* 'He appears to me' (see *TLL* 309–328). The title "Fatima" was later added.
"once he . . . drinketh dew." The classics-steeped Tennyson likely found inspiration for these lines in the *Palatine Anthology*:

> The wine-cup sweetly rejoices, and says that it touches
>   the garrulous mouth of sensual Zenophilia.
> Blessed cup! If only she would place her lips on my lips now
>   and drink in my soul without stopping for breath.

> [Meleager, *PA* 5.171; A. Gosetti–Murray John (tr.)]

> Kissing Agathon, I checked my soul at my lips;
>   for she came, wreckless (or wretched), as though intending
>   to cross over.

> [Plato[?], *PA* 5.78; A. Gosetti–Murray John (tr.)]

85   *Poet, translator, and essayist*
"in the . . . nature." Hamalian, 352.
If the ruse . . . women. Hamalian, 352.

86   *Highlighting the available*
Highlighting the available. For less familiar other-voiced verse, see Overton.
"the uniquely . . . sensitivity." Louÿs, 11–14. The poems were immediately denounced by the great German philologist Ulrich von Wilamowitz-Moellendorff (1848–1931), whose detailed rebuff of Louÿs began with an ardent exclamation: *Und nun Sappho! Eine vornehme Frau, Gattin und Mutter. . . .* 'And now Sappho! An honorable lady, wife, and mother. . . .' (Wilamowitz, 73). See also Highet, 458 (Wilamowitz falling on Louÿs "like a hawk on a rabbit"). The Sapphic legend influenced Marcel Proust (1871–1922), contemporary with Wilamowitz (see Ladenson, Introduction: "Pussy Galore and the Daughters of Bilitis," in *Proust's Lesbianism*). The reviews, however, were sometimes

mixed: "In recent years, Pierre Louÿs in *Les Chansons de Bilitis* (1895) made Mytilene [the capital of Lesbos] a Sodom, and Sappho a mistress of courtesans, and so has interpreted the Lesbian poetess too pornographically, we believe, yet with lyric charm" (Miller and Robinson, 63). For detailed discussion of the hoax and its reception, see Venuti, 34–46.

We return, in ring-
"encod[ing] the ... spaces." Lawrence, 2.

Nor for its hardened
"There is ... pine tree." Lang, 84.
Helen, despising herself. The referenced scenes—Helen's self-loathing, the meeting of Hector and Andromache, the ransoming of Hector's corpse—appear in *Iliad*, Books 3, 6, and 24.

87 *There are tears enough*
"brushed ... sleeping child." *Il.* 3.128–132 (R. Lattimore, tr.).
"lies ... ankles beneath them." *Il.* 3.142–147 (R. Lattimore, tr.).

88 *The description of Menelaus's*
extended simile ... Book 16. The simile, long regarded a scene of mother-daughter domesticity in peacetime, has been argued to reveal the destruction of normal life for a mother and daughter on the verge of capture by ancient Greek warriors (Gaca).
"There ... whisper together." *Il.* 22.125–128 (R. Lattimore, tr.); see further Van Nortwick.

There is, further, a
"Telemonian ... tree-top." *Il.* 4.473–481 (R. Lattimore, tr.). There are two Greek heroes named Ajax (Gr. *Aias*). Ajax, son of Telemon, is second mightiest of the Greeks after Achilles (and mightiest during Achilles's absence). Ajax, son of Teucer, is the "lesser" Ajax. Troy lay on a plain between two rivers, the Simoeis and Scamander (aka Xanthus). Both are semi-personified as the battle rages in anticipation of Achilles's slaying Hector.

The simile is parodied by Henry Fielding in *Tom Jones* (describing a free-for-all cemetery brawl, a skull used as weapon):

> Recount, O Muse, the names of those who fell on this fatal day. First, Jeremy Tweedle felt on his hinder head the direful bone. Him the pleasant banks of the sweetly-winding Stour had nourished, where he first learnt the vocal art, with which, wandering up and down at wakes and fairs, he cheered the rural nymphs and swains when upon the green they interweaved the sprightly dance; while he himself stood fiddling and jumping to his own music. How little now avails his fiddle! He thumps the verdant floor with his carcass.
>
> [*Tom Jones* IV, 8, 97]

The section heading reads: "A Battle Sung by the Muse in the Homeric Style, and Which None but the Classical Reader Can Taste."
"If either ... of war." Taplin, 32.

89 *Such vignettes, on a*
smaller scale throughout. See, e.g., *Il.* 5.69, 6.20–22, 14.443–444, and 20.382–383.

The lengthier Simoeisios description, occurring in *Iliad,* Book 4, sets the stage for the similar but briefer depictions that follow.
"If anything . . . the living!" Hugo, 298–299.

90   *Except as earlier noted*
Odyssey's . . . sensibility. See, e.g., Cohen and, of earlier vintage, Perry. See also Symonds (1882), Ch. 4, "The Women of Homer," inspiring Oscar Wilde's *The Women of Homer* (1st pub. 2008).
"As regards . . . guided me." Butler, 268.

Butler thus haplessly ends
"Slaying of the Suitors." See *Odyssey*, Book 23. The episode with its improbabilities was perplexing to the rhetorician and literary critic Longinus (1st century **AD**), who cites it as an example of the foolishness into which genius descends with the onset of age. In a lengthy aside, he focuses on the *Odyssey's* less realistic, more mythological or fantastical materials:

> It was, I imagine, for the same reason that, writing the *Iliad* in the heyday of his genius [Homer] made the whole piece lively with dramatic action, whereas in the *Odyssey* narrative predominates, the characteristic of old age. . . . [I]n great writers and poets, declining emotional power passes into character portrayals. For instance, his character sketches of the daily life in Odysseus's household constitute a sort of comedy of character [i.e., of "manners"].
>
>   [Longinus, *On the Sublime,* 195]

As Longinus ascribes the *Odyssey* to a later phase of Homer's life, instead of to a different author, Butler (apparently) makes no mention of Longinus. As concerns the slaying of the suitors, neither Butler nor Longinus concedes suspension of disbelief as Odysseus's long-delayed—indeed, otherworldly—revenge at last unfolds (see Duban [1980], 22).
"a woman . . . man can." Butler, 268.
"she is . . . the raunch." Wills, *NYRB*, 3/12/2009.

91   *Sexual union—life's*
Self . . . incandescence. Scruton (2009).
"the most . . . gained." Walsh (2015), 75.

92   *The sexes can and do*
biological . . . the minds. Cf. Lawrence Durrell's (1912–1990) fuller formulation:

> . . . And then (listen) I think that very few people realize that sex is a psychic and not a physical act. The clumsy coupling of human beings is simply a biological paraphrase of this truth—a primitive method of introducing minds to each other, engaging them. But most people are stuck in the physical aspect, unaware of the poetic rapport which it so clumsily tries to teach. That is why all your dull repetitions of the same mistake are simply like a boring great multiplication table, and will remain so until you get your head out of the paper bag and start to think responsibly [Durrell, *Balthazar*, 292].

It bears emphasizing that Durrell's percipient depictions of women—Justine (*Justine* and *Balthazar*), Leila (*Mountolive*), and Clea (*Clea*)—are the mainstay of his

perspective-laden ("Rashomon"-style) *Alexandria Quartet.*
French-... querelle des femmes. Balance of paragraph paraphrasing Jordan, 200–201 (discussing François Billon's *Le fort inexpugnable de l'honneur du sexe féminin* (*The Unassailable Fortress of the Female Sex's Honor*) (1555).

For whatever biological
"an embodiment...form." Smith, 119.
male form ... male artist. Certain iconic exceptions are noted, e.g., Michelangelo's *David* and *The Creation of Adam*, and the depictions of Greek heroes, including Achilles, Perseus, Prometheus, etc.

93 *The veneration to which*
rococo color...cosmetics. Hyde, 4–5 (as is evident in the title of her book "*Making Up the Rococo*").

In Greek mythology, the
"When I see...her skirt." Quoted by Goldberg, *NYT*, 8/11/1996.

We earlier noted that
"with a preference...revolt." R. West, 21.

94 *It is the excess or*
forwardness...impulse. As Paglia observes, "My explanation for the male domination of art, science, and politics, an indisputable fact of history, is based on an analogy between sexual physiology and aesthetics. I will argue that all cultural achievement is a projection ... and that men are anatomically destined to be projectors." Also, "Man, the sexual conceptualizer and projector, has ruled art because art is his Apollonian response toward and away from woman.... Phallic aggression and projection are intrinsic to western conceptualization" (Paglia [2017], 17, 31). No friend of liberals and feminists, Paglia takes the "indisputable fact of history" as her logical (i.e., Apollonian) starting point. See generally Paglia's introductory chapter, "Sex and Violence, or Nature and Art," elaborating on male "projection" and female interiority.
homo faber 'man the maker'. "When I cross the George Washington Bridge or any of America's great bridges, I think: *men* have done this. Construction is a sublime male poetry.... If civilization had been left in female hands, we would still be living in grass huts" (Paglia [2017], 38).
"breasts and...development." De Beauvoir, 177.
generative and moribund nature. See further de Beauvoir, 376–377 (the adolescent girl's affinity to and participation in nature as a particular "project" of her sex).

As earlier seen, Plato's
"All beauty...beat of all." Du Maurier, 99.

The male artist's obsession
"The woman...the pen." Collins, 52; see further Santayana.
"And so was...penetrate." Proust, 109.
"I loved...any association." Proust, 109.

96 *Proust's revelatory*
"as you thought...in mine." Collins, 52.

97 *One cannot generalize*
as I ... demonstrated. See Rickey (excellent and appropriately indeterminate review of the Sofia Coppola remake of *The Beguiled*).

A recently politicized area
in my earlier publication. See *TLL* 435–438 (assessing a Dryden-compared passage by Ruden with the same passage by Dryden himself).
"When judging ... tells all." *TLL* 452.

98 *There is finally the case*
"The ideological ... women." Michael, 225–236. The issue is thorny. For elaboration with reference to Michael, and in sympathy with the views herein, see Lenz, 20–25.

99 *The truest art in all*
"extract[ing] ... from chaos." *TLL* 416.
"By Man ... divine thought." Fuller, 14.

PART V: SAFE AND SOUND ASHORE: HORACE *ODES* 1.5, "TO PYRRHA"

207 *The fifth poem of*
(Hereafter "*Odes* 1.5"). Bibliographical references sometimes refer to *Odes* 1.5 as "*C* 1.5" ("*C*" for Lat. *carmen* 'song') or *Carm.* 1.5; and sometimes to "*Lib.* 1" ("*L*" for Latin *liber* 'book').
"is the most ... type of love." West, 141.
"inexperienced boy ... her." Quinn (1980), 130.

Equally vivid and varied
"the occasional ... cultures." Wilson, 15.

Many of the poems in
"vary widely ... situation." Bowditch, 357.
imitations ... translations. I discuss and illustrate the difference throughout *TLL*. With a title punning on *Pyrrha/pyrotechnics*, Bowditch "analyzes several English versions of the Pyrrha ode ... from the perspective of Ezra Pound's threefold distinction between logopoeia, melopoeia and phanopeia [sic] as categories of poetic language captured in a good translation." I discuss the idleness of Pound's terminology in *TLL*.

208 *Though easily said in*
"has had more ... modern." Showerman, 146.
"about as ... you can get." Kates, 1.
no poem of ... to Pyrrha. Putnam (1971), 251.

209 *Horace's poem is all of*
twenty-one are adjectives. These include: one "substantive," i.e., an adjective used as a noun, Lat. *miseri* (line 12) 'wretched (they), the wretched ones', and two predicative adjectives, *vacuam ... amabilem / sperat* (lines 10–11) 'hopes you [will be] unoccupied and lovable', i.e., available (or free of other lovers) and able to be loved. In the translation by Nielsen and Solomon (1993): "Who hopes you always free and there for love."

302

212 *Because Latin syntax*
"This mosaic . . . excellence." Wilkinson, 41 (translating Nietzsche).
"The energizing . . . distinction." Mendelsohn, 166. In a related formulation:

> Horace has an almost infallible instinct for poetic form, an unerring sense of his own potentialities and limitations, and a profounder intuitive understanding of the genius of Latin than any other writer. The formal perfection of the odes derives from the concentration of the language—its pregnant brevity which enables it to say more in fewer words than any other European tongue; from the extreme flexibility of word-order which allows Horace to move his words about like pieces of a jig-saw puzzle within the strict metrical control of his stanza-structure; and from the beauty of sound, especially the pure vowels, which makes it the worthy progenitor of modern Italian, the most musical language we are ever likely to hear [Wormell, 12].

"music . . . its information." Anderson, *New York Magazine*, 10/3/2010.

213 *A further element in the*
little words in English. Thus, of the 105 words of my translation, fully 20 (nearly 30 percent) are necessarily prepositions or subject pronouns (unexpressed, since implied, in the Latin). Had it been possible to omit them, the translation, at 85 words, would have been only twenty words more than the original, or longer by only c. 25 percent.

216 *Horace, here as elsewhere*
"In . . . direct an effect." Commager, 35, cf. Anderson, 35–36.
as in the first stanza. See Commager, 51–52.
"after the . . . of jeopardy." Putnam (2006), 30.

217 *Pretty dull stuff in literal*
"I did not . . . the reader." "In quibus non verbum pro verbo habui reddere, sed genus omne verborum vimque servavi. Non enim ea me adnumerare lectori putavi opportere, sed tamquam appendere." Cicero, *De Optimo Genere Oratorum* (*On the Best Kind of Orators*), 4.14.
"It is not . . . into Poesie." Sir John Denham, Preface, *The Destruction of Troy*.

What heightens the difficulty
fourteen poems . . . odes. On the disposition of Third Asclepiadian throughout the *Odes*, with particular references to *Odes* 1.5, see Knorr, 154–157.

We recall that classical
The . . . particular effect. The play between poetic beat and spoken stress detailed at *TLL* 85, 230–236, and elsewhere.

219 *In literal translation*
"I must also . . . phrasing." Merrill, v.

My own rendering is
"the lovers are . . . talking." Nisbet-Hubbard (NH), 73.
"euphemistic suppression." Vessey, 459.
"rarely used in . . . sense." Putnam (1970), 253. Cf. Minadeo (1982), 147 (*urget* "signals a physical, thrusting motion").
Pyrrha . . . "crowded, pressed." For the three formulations that follow, see the translations of Moore (1902), Chorlton (1910), and Michie (1963).

now crowds you. It is difficult, in speaking of *urget* 'urges, presses, crowds' ('clasps', below), to sidestep John Boyle's (1710–1762) lengthy paraphrase/imitation (Storrs, 45–46). Lines 9–12 (of fifty-four) summarily and ingeniously convey much of Horace's import, to say nothing of the thematic double entendre of "Sinks."

> What gaudy Stripling, eager to be blest
> Sinks a glad victim on thy perjur'd Breast?
> And, while essential Sweets their Odours spread,
> Clasps thee with Ardour on the rosy Bed?

221 *Also in the first stanza*
"an assertion . . . situation." Quinn (1980), 151.

222 *A word is required on the*
"implies the . . . an illusion." Quinn (1980), 151. The "illusion" of this simplicity resides in the plural *munditiis* (sing. *munditia* 'clean elegance'), which "suggests the effect is not as simple [*simplex*] as it looks" (Garrison, 211).
"For whom . . . simple care." Gladstone, tr.
"For whom . . . simply neat." Shepherd, tr.

As further concerns Pyrrha's
so also "auburn haired." Bennett, 155; NH, 74.
"The female . . . waters." Putnam (2006), 142.

223 *Reddishness of hair was*
τοῖς δὲ . . . ἐχρήσατ᾽ ἄν. *Frogs* 729–733.

224 *Horace's verbal dexterity*
glow, sheen . . . emanation. Mackail, 67.
"'charm' . . . about a woman." Quinn (1980), 152.
even *sex* appeal. "But *aurae* [nom. *aura*] also applies to Pyrrha the girl, as that subtle, undefinable but distinctive atmosphere that emanates from and surrounds her person; in short, we might say, somewhat loosely, her sex appeal" (Fredricksmeyer, 182, citing Horace, *Odes* 2.8 [line 24] and 4.13 [line 19]). Writing over fifty years ago, Fredricksmeyer thus states the case, abashedly, yet ahead of his time. More recently, "Aura . . . can have a specific sexual sense: an emanation arising from sexual arousal" (Ancona, 81–82, also referencing Barine in *Odes* 2.8.23–24; Barine "a near doublet of Pyrrha," Minadeo [1982], 51). Similarly contemporaneous is the formulation of Pyrrha, a "courtesan . . . [who] is working on (or being worked on by) an innocent young victim" (Garrison, 210). The presence and effect of such *aura* equate with pheromonal emanation or primal scent, which is air- or *aura*-borne (*pheromone*—Gr. *pherō* 'carry' + (h)*ormaō* 'move, drive on'); *aura* being that which *wafts* or moves gently through the air (*wafts*—Ger. *waken*, *wechen* 'wake [someone] up/rouse/arouse [an interest, anger]' [Eng. waken]; PIE root *weg- 'to be strong, lively'; cf. *wachsen* 'grow'). *Waft* as noun is the conveyance of odor, scent, or perfume carried through the air; its effects fateful: "Meanwhile, the wafts from his old home pleaded, whispered, conjured, and finally claimed him imperiously" (Kenneth Grahame, *The Wind in the Willows* [1908]); and, synesthetically, "And so was wafted to my ears the name of Gilberte, bestowed on me as a talisman . . ." (Marcel Proust, *Swann's Way* [1922], Scott Moncrieff, tr.) (see further below on this famed "awakening"). So, we imagine, Pyrrha's intoxicant aura.
'he enjoys' . . . "enjoys you." *Fruitur* 3rd pers. sing. pres. act./dep. indic. from *fruor* 'I enjoy'; one of a handful of Latin verbs taking an ablative object.

There follows Miseri quibus
'you shine'... consequences. Putnam (1970), 252.

The Romans, aware as
elaborately... of gold. States Aristophanes:

> Often it seems to us the city has done the same thing with the best and the finest of its citizens as with established coinage and the *new gold*. For these, in no way counterfeit, but the finest, it seems, of all coins, and alone with the proper stamp, of sound metal amongst Greeks and foreigners everywhere, we never use, but the *base bronze coinage* instead, struck but yesterday or so ago, with the basest stamp. So too the citizens—whom we know to be wellborn and principled, of right-mindedness, truth and quality, trained in the palaestra in dancing and music; these we disdain, but the brazen foreigners and redheads, worthless offspring of worthless fathers, to these we everywhere resort, these recently arrived, whom the city earlier would not have thought to use as random scapegoats. But now, dimwits, change your ways, using the good ones once again. And praise to the successful. But if you somehow fail, at least [you will hang] from a respectable tree. So will the wise deem you to have fared, should thus you fare (emphases added).*

> *It is clear that Aristophanes intends "new gold" as fool's gold, for he later refers to it as "base bronze coinage."

225 *"Grotto grown" unleashes*
tablet's own... depiction. Hopkins, 57, n. 11; 62.
"In an illiterate... picture." NH, 77.

228 *Emirabitur further strengthens*
"The sound of... amazement." Vessey, 466.
pur up-a-de-drom-ē-ken. 'Flame [slips] racing neath' (§2). The perfect tense of consonant-initial ancient Greek verbs is formed by initial consonant reduplication (**de-drom**) and "**k**"-added stem ending. The hexasyllabic verb is here divided to distinguish syllables. Otherwise parsed—**pur upa-de-dromēk-en**—the verb shows prefix **upa-** 'beneath' (alliterative with **pur** 'fire'); reduplicated **de-**; perfect tense stem **dromēk-**, and 3rd pers. ending **-e(n)**. The present tense is *trecho* 'I run'. The perfect of *trecho*, *dedramēka* 'I have run', is formed (as are the other tenses of *trecho*) as if from **dromeō** 'I run' (not found in the present tense). Sappho's use of **dedromēken** for **dedramēken** appears to track the irregular poetic perfect of **dromeō**, i.e., **dedroma** 'I have run' [reduplicated, but without "**k**"]; *dromos* 'race, course'; Eng. dromedary, hippodrome). The Greek perfect, though indicating completed action, often has present force, i.e., the flame has run and *is still running*.

Yes, the boy's fate is
"belongs to... accordingly." Mackail, 66.
"appearance... grooming." NH, 76.

229 *The verb perfusus 'doused'*
liquida moles 'liquid mass'. DRN 4.1259, 6.405.
liquidissima caeli tempestas. DRN 4.168.
liquidum iter 'liquid way'. El. 3.20.
Boy overboard... cologne. The boy's perfumed overkill (*profusus liquidis... odoribus*, line 2) bespeaks excessive ardor and inexperience vis-à-vis the cool and simple chic

of Pyrrha—restraint the secret of chic (see Quinn [1963], 69–70, excellent discussion). Moreover, Latin *profusus* (Eng. profuse) and *odoribus* 'scents' (versus *odoratus* 'scented') are pejorative (Quinn [1980], 150). One thinks, in this connection, of scent, dress, hairstyle, and/or the application of makeup as prelude to disaster from, e.g., the excitable and cross-dressed Pentheus in Euripides's *Bacchae* (405 BC) to the soulful homosexually besotted Gustav von Aschenbach in Thomas Mann's *Death in Venice* (*Der Tod in Venedig*) (1912) (see Rutledge, 19). Canio/Pagliaccio, as tragic made-up clown, also comes to mind.

229 *Antrum 'grotto, cave, cavern'*
Antrum . . . bodily portal. Support for this argument, based on sources other than those here discussed, appears in Adams, 85, *caverna = antrum = cunnus* or *culus* 'cunt/ anus'. Among the secondary sources consulted herein, only one suggests (without elaboration), "Of all possible vaginal symbols, a cave or grotto is among the most certain"(Minadeo [1975], 394; [1982], 17). So too Adams, 93, citing Ap. *Met.* 2.17: *glabellum feminal rosea palmula . . . obumbrans* 'covering her [bit of a] hairless mount with her rosy palm' (*glabellum* 'hairless, smooth shaven' a diminutive acc. neut. of *glabrum*; hence, "a bit of"). The words appear in a salacious seduction scene with reference, as in *Odes* 1.5, to roses (not just the "rosy palm"), tresses (released and flowing), and the sea (the seductress compared to a marine Venus).

Glabellum is a post-classical word. *Feminal*, also post-classical, is an Apuleian invention (Apuleius, 2nd century AD, author of the *Metamorphoses* aka "The Golden Ass"). The words' collocation supports the present argument—*glaber* 'smooth' (nom. masc. sing.) from Gr. *glaphō* 'hollow out', *glaphuros* 'hollow'. The adjective is most frequently used of ships in Homer but, notably, also of caves (e.g., Calypso's, *Od.* 1.5 and elsewhere), which, if not lovemaking locales, are amorously suggestive.
lengthy Virgilian passage. The passage is *G.* 4.8–50; the lines quoted are *G.* 4.40–43.
penitus repertae **'deeply lodged'.** For the sexual connotations of *penitus* 'deep/deeply', see *TLL* 275–276.

230 *Similarly, in the Roman*
magnae si . . . specularibus antro. Juv. 1.4.21.

Rather later, in the writings
Si forma . . . cotidiana succisio. Sid. *Ep.* 1.2.

231 *It is noteworthy how*
The Latin . . . prostitute, wife. Mozeson, 115; Clark, 161.

It is all one and the same
One commentator suggests. See Bennett, 155.

232 *Within the seafaring context*
woman a form of seafaring. Jocelyn, 333–335.

What we have in the
flame and ardor . . . death. Putnam (1970), 253.
pleasure or luxurious living. Henriksén, 59; Quinn (1980), 150.
"They were . . . or premature." Brenk, 87–88, 102.

233 *It is, preliminarily, the simple*
example . . . from Terence. Cf. Adams, 89.

"The house ... sexual emblems." Minadeo (1982), 4.

Especially pronounced in poetry
harbor, port; and the like. Cf. Minadeo (1982), 4, vis-à-vis Horace.
appear in comic contexts. Murgatroyd, 10–12; cf. Adams, 89.

234 *Catullus 64 is aptly described*
precious and mannerist, etc. Fitzgerald, 142–143.
pellis **'fleece' ... is clear.** Cf. *pellis* 'foreskin', Adams, 73–74.

The crew is described as
Lat. *pīnus ... pēnis* **'penis'.** Cf. *Odes* 2.3.9–15 and Minadeo (1982), 71–72, 228.

From the Argo's wake, i.e.
are "potential mothers." Fitzgerald, 151.
'admiring the apparition'. On the thematic importance of the gaze in C. 64, see Williams, 142.

235 *Foremost of the Nereids is*
'column, pillar, post'. See Adams, 16–17.

The first-time incursion
"The first boat ... swell." 64.11–18 (J. Michie, tr.).
first plowing ... slang. Fordyce, 279 (citing sources) and Adams, 82–85, 150.

Horace further looks to
Cave of the ... in Ithaca. Cf. *Aen.* 1.157–174 (discussed below).
given him ... Phaeacians. *Od.* 13.100–112, 345–351.

236 *Turning from such description*
a child, *klaie* **'wept'.** *Od.* 5.82.
en bēssēisi **'in a ravine'.** *Od.* 10. 208–211.
forbids his men *klaiein*. *Od.* 9.294, 469.

Given such contexts, Horace
threatening "bloodstain'd den." Storrs, 53.
"'lair' wherein ... beasts lurk." Bowditch, 358.

237 *In this way, too, Pyrrha's*
dwelling of harmful being. Abrahamian, 98.
a cave followed by death. Aston, 350.

It is, of course, in a cave
ruunt de ... causa fuit. *Aen.* 4.164–169.
associations of a cave. Though the *antra* (sing. *antrum*) of Virgil's *Eclogues*, e.g., *E.* 6.13 and 9.41, are more benign.

238 *The Dido and Aeneas encounter*
quibus omnis ... redactos. *Aen.* 1.157–174 (*sinus* 'folds, hollows' [masc. acc. pl., 4th decl.] [Eng. sinus]; on *scidit* [here] and *proscidit* [Catullus 64], see p. 235).
"but, surely ... Dido herself." Minadeo (1982), 9.

antroi . . . 'in a sacred grotto'. For *Argonautica* references, see *Arg.* 4.1131, 4.1128–1160, and 4.1153–1154.

238 *The name Pyrrha decidedly*
with water . . . is irrelevant. See Lee, 113.
Pandora's "box" . . . anatomy. Paraphrasing discussion in Glenn and Lachs.
original telling a *pithos* 'jar'. WD 90–95.

239 *As the flood's sole female*
"as little . . . is of the sea." Fredericksmeyer, 184. Nielsen and Solomon (NS) (1993) decry the traditional reading of *Odes* 1.5 as "a man's proto-autobiography and censure of the emotional or physical infidelity of one woman, part of a *fiction* called 'das ewig weib-liche'" (64, citing Fredericksmeyer, 184; NS italics). Insofar as portraying Everyman's "Pyrrhic" obsession, the poem is well described as "man's proto-autobiography." By the same token, however, Pyrrha is not simply "one woman" but, archetypally, every woman. Nor is *das ewig-Weibliche* a "fiction." That NS so view it owes to their discomfort with the objectification of woman for which the abstraction appears to allow.

NS thus explore three imitations of *Odes* 1.5 by British poet, playwright, and transla-tor Aphra Behn (1640–1689), conscripting the ode to feminist service. They proceed on the perennially polarizing assumption of "an entropic motion . . . between a male writer and any female body, because his words are distanced from *her experience* which, in male amatory poetry, can exist merely as a translation into his metaphors, imagery and projec-tions" (65) (emphasis added). Referring to "her experience," NS make *Pyrrha* the *victim*: she exists "only as the youth's target, a body" (65); she is "treat[ed] . . . as less than equally human" (67), "a silenced object" (69); she is, by the poem's opening question—"What slim and sweetly scented lad . . . ?"—"unfairly pressed towards dialogue about the youth's identity as she is pushed into love-making by the military metaphor [in] *urget* (69)." The opening question is, of course, rhetorical—Pyrrha shrugging it off, if she has at all heard it; the youth someone, anyone, the next of Pyrrha's infatuations. The intended focus of *Odes* 1.5 is the poor lad, not poor Pyrrha. Behn's *is* a smart take on Horace. But NS go too far in an argument better suited to PART I of this volume than to Horace.
"her tempers . . . immutable." Whiteborne, 42.

The prismatic Odes 1.5 yields
"high and dry" . . . a cave. Lee, 57.
"a woman . . . seem monstrous." Ancona, 77, 87, 161–162.

The first Pyrrha, though
grave . . . altos visere montes. *Odes* 1.2.5–8; the reference is to Proteus, the ever-changeable "Old Man of the Sea"; see *Od.* 4.363–484.
Ovid in *Metamorphoses*. *Met.* 1.240–429.
as the "gemination theme." Frantantuomo, 94, n. 44.
so the boundaries- . . . Barine. *Odes* 2.8; Ancona, 81.

240 *Pyrrha is further a*
"culture of spectacle." Bowditch, 358.
"Barine's . . . monstrous." *Odes* 2.8; Ancona, 87. See Horace's assessment of Barine, *iuvenumque prodis / publica cura* 'and you walk the streets a public menace of young men' (West, tr.); lit., 'and you go forth, the public concern [i.e., open preoccupation] of young men'. One thinks in this connection of Alcman's Astymeloisa 'Concern of the town', whose "sweetness serves no idle whim" (§41, pp. 136–137).
her type and archetype. "Pyrrha is a type, after all: the beautiful, irresistible woman who

goes through life accepting and rejecting admirers, turning before long on those who claim to conquer her with an impersonal violence that it is almost arrogant of us to find cruel" (Mason, 50). To this statement—ascribed by Mason to an otherwise work-unreferenced Kenneth Quinn—Mason registers "my disgust." Quinn's insight, however, was ahead of its time. The sensibility is nowadays embodied in songwriter Billy Joel's (b. 1949) "She's Always a Woman," e.g., "She can ruin your faith with her casual lies . . . She can lead you to love, she can take you or leave you . . . She just changes her mind . . . Oh, she takes care of herself, she can wait if she wants . . . She is frequently kind and she's suddenly cruel / She can do as she pleases, she's nobody's fool." Or, as imagined by the writer "Willy" (in the movie *Colette*, 2017), who has his wife of the same name ghostwrite the semi-autobiographical story of a witty and brazen country girl named Claudine: "He first sees her, Monna, held aloft on the shoulders of her admirers. She's eighteen, beautiful, wild and she's from the streets, eats men up, never wears a corset. . . . She seduces [Renault] in her shabby rooms—five entire days of carnal bliss. . . . She instinctively understands his base desires."

241   *The allure of Horace's*
wry . . . self-effacing wit. Wherein precisely does Horace's wit reside, and what does it say of his attitude toward the scene described in *Odes* 1.5? In addition to remarks in my own conclusion, we may note how Horace justifiably

> distinguishes himself not only from the wretched men who, like the slender youth, have yet to learn [Pyrrha's] true nature, but also from the foolish lover he once was. Nevertheless, the mixture of sympathy and gentle condescension which Horace exhibits toward the *gracilis puer* he extends, implicitly, to his former self. The attitude is characteristic of the witty self-irony in which Horace regularly indulges, in the *Odes* and elsewhere: he often detaches himself from the very situation in which he is most involved and includes himself among those whose foibles he fondly records and gently knocks [Hoppin, 57].

In the same vein, "The poetic *ego* demonstrates an interest in simultaneously concealing and revealing his own past emotional distress" (Sutherland, 441).

But not Horace. He
"on the sacred . . . hoped for." *Od.* 3.273–275 (R. Lattimore, tr., emphasis added).
rule . . . escaping danger. Closer to home, we find the following in Virgil, Horace's contemporary (with bolded words indicating similar phrasing):

§159

Virgil, *Aen.* 12.766–769   Horace, *Odes* 1.5.13–16

Forte **sacer** Fauno foliis oleaster amaris   intemptata nites. Me tabula **sacer**
hic steterat, nautis olim venerabile lignum,   ***votiva*** paries indicat uvida
servati ex undis ubi figere dona solebant   suspendisse potenti
Laurenti divo et ***votas*** suspendere **vestis**;   **vestimenta** maris deo.

Perchance positioned there, by Faunus sacred viewed,
An oleaster, bitter-leaved in brambled barb,
Esteemed by seamen, whereon ocean rescuèd,
Were they glad-given to surrender votive garb
And gifts to Latium's favored god in gratitude.

Dryden's translation of Virgil runs as follows, referencing Horace's *tabula* 'tablet(s)' (not mentioned by Virgil), and expressing Dryden's mention of "shipwrack" (implied in Horace):

> Within the space, an olive tree had stood,
> A sacred shade, a venerable wood,
> For vows to Faunus paid, the Latins' guardian god.
> Here hung the vests, and tablets were ingrav'd,
> Of sinking mariners from shipwrack sav'd.

The first three books of Horace's *Odes* were published in 23 BC (a fourth in 13 BC). Virgil, at an average rate of four to five lines a day, composed his *Aeneid* from 29–19 BC (dying in the year of its completion). As the Virgilian passage appears toward the end of the last book of the *Aeneid*, Virgil's description of the sacred oleaster likely looks to Horace.

242 *It is noteworthy that in*
   "**jeux d'esprit . . . the spirit.**" Showerman, 152–153.
   "**as a love poet . . . than praised.**" Wormell, 59.
   utter charm, resourcefulness. To recall Dryden,

> There appears in every part of his [Horace's] diction . . . a kind of noble and bold purity. His words are chosen with as much exactness as Virgil's; but there seems to be a greater spirit in them. . . . But the most distinguishing part of his character seems to me to be his briskness, his jollity, and his good humor; and those I have chiefly endeavored to copy; his other excellences, I confess, are above my imitation.
>
> [Preface to *Sylvae* (1685)]

Glossary to Ancient Sources

THE FOLLOWING LIST briefly identifies the authors whose works preserve so much of extant Greek lyric (all except what is preserved on papyri and parchment, and in one case on pottery). Citations are adapted from N. G. L. Hammond and J. J. Scullard, eds., *The Oxford Classical Dictionary* (Oxford: Oxford Univ. Press, 1970).

Aelian (2nd and 3rd c. AD) Pontifex at Praeneste, taught rhetoric at Rome, wrote works of a moralizing nature.

Alexandrian Age (4th – 1st c. BC) The period when Alexandria in Egypt, thanks to its library and museum, was the literary capital of the Greek world.

Ammonius (2nd c. BC) Pupil and successor of the great Alexandrian scholar Aristarchus, grammarian and commentator on the works of Homer.

Antigonus of Carystus (3rd c. BC) Athenian writer connected with Plato's Academy, author of anecdotal writings.

Apollonius Dyscolus (2nd c. AD) Alexandrian grammarian in Rome under Emperor Marcus Aurelius, known for his exactitude, obscurity of style, and asperity (Gr. *dyskolos* 'harsh, severe').

Apollonius of Rhodes (3rd c. BC) A leading figure of the Alexandrian Age; author of the first fully extant account of Jason and the Argonauts.

Apollonius the Sophist (2nd c. AD) Alexandrian Homeric scholar.

Aratus (4th and 3rd c. BC) Best known for his major extant work, an astronomical poem entitled *Phaenomena* 'appearances'.

Augustan Age (27 BC–14 AD) The golden age of Roman rule and culture under Emperor Augustus.

Chrysippus (3rd c. BC) With life devoted to elaboration of the Stoic system, his philosophy became identified with Stoic orthodoxy.

Clement of Alexandria (2nd and 3rd c. AD) Alexandrian churchman, author of extant works arguing the merits of Christianity over pagan religions and philosophies.

Demetrius (4th and 3rd c. BC) Author of a treatise *On Style*. The work, elaborating upon the meager, florid, grand, and fearsome classes of rhetoric, quotes poets, historians, orators, and numerous minor fourth-century figures.

Dio Chrysostom (1st and 2nd c. AD) Called *Chrysostomos* (*Golden-mouthed*) for his rhetorical prowess. Author of some eighty speeches on a variety of themes. Many of these are display-pieces extolling Stoic ideals.

Diodorus (1st c. BC) Greek author, under Julius Caesar and Augustus, of a *World History* in forty books from the earliest times to Caesar's Gallic War (54 BC).

Dionysius of Halicarnassus (1st c. BC) Greek rhetorician and historian who taught at Rome for many years. His treatise *On Literary Composition*, the only surviving ancient work on word arrangement and euphony, preserves one of the few surely complete poems of Sappho, "The Hymn to Aphrodite."

Etymologicum Magnum A lexicon of uncertain date used by the great twelfth-century AD classical scholar and churchman Eustathius, Archbishop of Thessalonica.

Eustathius (12 c. AD) Deacon at St. Sophia in Constantinople and commentator on classical works, the *Iliad* and *Odyssey* in particular.

Galen (2nd c. AD) Court physician in Rome to Emperor Marcus Aurelius. Author of philosophical treatises and medical books.

Hellenistic Age (4th–1st c. BC) Period following the death of Alexander the Great (323 BC), which marked the spread of Greek culture throughout the known world (see Alexandrian Age).

Hephaistion (2nd c. AD) Greek metrist whose mammoth forty-eight-volume treatise, *On Meter*, was reduced by successive abridgments to a single volume, *Handbook* (Gr. *Encheiridion* 'in the hand'), in which form it is extant.

Heraclitus (6th c. BC) Pre-Socratic philosopher who conceived the universe as a ceaseless conflict of opposites, regulated by the unchanging law which he designated as *Logos*. His work survives in fragments only.

Hermogenes (2nd c. AD) Author of *On Forms*, dealing with seven qualities of style, all seen as ingredients in the perfected style of the orator Demosthenes.

Herodian (2nd c. AD) Son of Apollonius Dyscolus (above), he wrote on the accentuation of the *Iliad* and *Odyssey*. Ranks with his father as one of the greatest, as he is the last, of the original Greek grammarians.

Hesychius (5th c. AD) Alexandrian lexicographer, author of a comprehensive word list preserved as a "glossary" in a sole fifteenth-century manuscript. Despite its badly preserved state, the glossary remains a valuable source for words whose meanings are otherwise lost or obscured.

Himerius (4th c. AD) Greek rhetorician practicing most of his life in Athens. Author of eighty speeches (forty-two survive) on contemporary subjects. Largely displays a talent for saying nothing, gracefully and at length.

Julian (the Apostate) (4th c. AD) Highly colorful figure. Successful general, statesman, and classical scholar/enthusiast. Responsible for the reinstitution of pagan cults and the advocacy of a pervasive classicism over Christianity. Proclaimed "Caesar" by Emperor Constantius II and placed in charge of Gaul and Britain. Later proclaimed "Augustus" by his adoring troops, when the emperor sought to restrict his growing power and popularity.

Longinus (1st c. AD) Author of the highly creative and influential *On the Sublime*, exploring the qualities of thought and style that mark writing as "sublime." A serious and original mind.

Lucian (2nd c. AD) Rhetorician turned author. Best known for his satiric dialogues and for his extant *True History* (whose only truth, he tells us at the start, is that all which follows is false).

Maximus of Tyre (2nd c. AD) Sophist and itinerant lecturer. Author of forty-one extant *Lectures* which, though showing no philosophic originality, are eloquent exhortations to virtue, decked with quotations chiefly from Plato and Homer.

Menander (4th and 3rd c. BC) Writer of New Comedy. Only one of his approximately 100 plays, *Dyskolos* (the *Misanthrope*), survives intact.

Palatine Anthology The greatest anthology of classical literature, consisting of Greek poetic epigrams. So called because the only manuscript was discovered at the Count Palatine's library at Heidelberg (1606). The work is thought to have been compiled by Byzantine scholars c. 980 AD. It contains some 3,700 epigrams arranged in fifteen books.

Pindar (5th c. BC) Lyric poet whose Epinician (or Victory) Odes survive almost complete. Pindar composed them on commission from victors of the Olympian, Nemean, Pythian, and Isthmian Games. The victors' accomplishments, qualities, and pedigree were extolled within the framework of divine myth.

Plutarch (1st and 2nd c. AD) Philosopher and biographer. A most prolific writer, many of whose works survive (though even more are lost). Most influential in Byzantine times and during the Renaissance. His minor works were collected in medieval times under the heading of *Moralia* (*Moral Pieces*), a title now used to cover everything apart from his *Lives*.

scholiast An author of notes—or *scholia*—preserved in the margins of texts, which expound on or criticize the language or subject matter at hand.

Servius (4th and 5th c. AD) Author of an extensive commentary on the poems of Virgil. The work, designated for school purposes, shows great erudition in its treatment of grammatical, rhetorical, and stylistic matter.

Stobaeus (4th and 5th c. AD) Author of an anthology, intended for the instruction of his son, Septimius, of poets and prose writers. Topics range from metaphysics to household economics. The second two of four books deal largely with ethical questions.

Strabo (1st c. BC – 1st c. AD) Greek Stoic geographer whose *Geography* is extant in seventeen books. His work is a storehouse of information, at once a historical geography and a philosophy of geography.

Synesius (4th and 5th c. AD) Christian Neoplatonist, orator, and poet. Author of hymns, letters, and rhetorical discourses.

Syrianus (5th c. AD) Philosopher and rhetorician; author of a commentary on Aristotle's *Metaphysics*.

General Bibliography

Adam, Antoine, ed. *Les Fleurs du Mal: Les Épaves, Bribes, Poèmes divers, Amoenitates Belgicae* (Paris: Editions Garnier Frères, 1961).

Alexiou, Margaret. *The Ritual Lament in Greek Tradition* (Cambridge: Cambridge Univ. Press, 1974).

Althaus, Frank and Mark Sutcliffe, eds. *The Triumph of Eros: Art and Seduction in 18th-century France* (London: Fontanka, 2006).

Alwes, Karla. "Virginia Woolf and the Modern Epic" in Schweizer, ed., 55–68.

Andreadis, Harriette. "The Sapphic-Platonics of Katherine Philips, 1632–1644," *Signs: Journal of Women in Culture and Society*, 15.1 (1989), 34–60.

Athenaeus, *Deipnosophistae*, C. B. Gulick, ed. and tr. (Cambridge: Harvard Univ. Press, Loeb Classical Library [VII Vols.], 1927–1941).

Aubrey, James R. Preface, "Fowles and Feminism," in Aubrey, ed., *John Fowles and Nature: Fourteen Perspectives on Landscape* (1999).

Auden, W. H. "The Quest Hero," in Rose A. Zimbardo and Neil D. Isaacs, eds., *Understanding The Lord of the Rings* (2004), 31–51.

Bagg, Robert. "Love, Ceremony and Daydream in Sappho's Lyrics," *Arion*, 3.3 (1964), 44–46.

Bailey, Peggy Dunn. "'Hear the Voice of the [Female] Bard': Aurora Leigh as a Female Romantic Epic," in Schweizer, ed., 117–137.

Bal, Mieke. *The Artemisia Files: Artemisia Gentileschi for Feminists and Other Thinking People* (Chicago: Univ. of Chicago Press, 2005).

Barker, Elton T. and Joel P. Christensen. "Flight Club: The New Archilochus Fragment and Its Resonance with Homeric Epic," *Materiali e discussioni per l'analisi dei testi classici*, 57 (2006), 9–41.

Baxter, Elizabeth. *Sappho and Socrates and the Nature of Eros* (Dalhousie Univ. Master's Thesis, 2007) (Library and Archives Canada, 2011).

Baym, Nina. *Woman's Fiction: A Guide to Novels by and about Women in America 1820–1870* (Urbana: Univ. of Illinois Press, 1993 [2nd ed]; 1st pub. Cornell Univ. Press, 1978).

Beard, Mary. "Why Homer Was (Not) a Woman: the Reception of the Authoress of the Odyssey," in James G. Paradis, ed., *Samuel Butler: Victorian Against the Grain: A Critical Overview* (2007), 317–342.

Bedggood, Daniel. "John Fowles and the Writing Process," in James Acheson, ed., *John Fowles* (2013), 49–62.

Bell, Peggy Ullman. *Sappho's Song: A fictionalized biography of Psappha: The Poetess of Lesbos* (Auckland: Upstart Press, 2000).

Bennett, Curtis. "Concerning 'Sappho Schoolmistress,'" *Transactions of the American Philological Association*, 124 (1994), 345–347 (in response to Holt Parker, 1993).

Bernstein, Charles. *Attack of the Difficult Poems* (Chicago: Univ. of Chicago Press, 2011).

Beshero-Bondar, Elisa. *Women, Epic, and Transition in British Romanticism* (Lanham: Univ. of Delaware Press, 2011).

Beye, Charles R. *The Iliad, the Odyssey, and the Epic Tradition* (Garden City: Doubleday, 1966).

———. *Ancient Greek Literature and Society* (New York: Anchor, 1975, 1987).

Bindman, David. *Warm Flesh, Cold Marble: Canova, Thorvaldsen, and Their Critics* (New Haven: Yale Univ. Press, 2014).

Bloch, Ariel and Chanah Bloch. *The Song of Songs: A New Translation with an Introduction and Commentary* (Berkeley: Univ. of California Press, 1995).

Bloom, Harold, Henry W. Berg and Albert A. Berg, eds. *The Brontës* (New York: Chelsea House, 1987).

Boardman, John, Antonia Mulas, and Eugenio La Rocca. *Eros In Greece* (London: John Murray, 1978).

Bodkin, Maud. *Archetypal Patterns in Poetry: Psychological Studies of Imagination.* (London: Oxford Univ. Press, 1934).

Boedeker, Deborah B. "Sappho and Acheron," in Glen W. Bowersock, Walter Burkert, and Michael Putnam, eds., *Arktouros: Hellenic Studies Presented to Bernard Knox* (1981), 40–52.

Bowman, Laurel. "'Women's Tradition' in Greek Poetry," *Phoenix*, 56.1/2 (2004), 1–27.

Bowra, C. M. *Greek Lyric Poetry: From Alcman to Simonides* (Oxford: Oxford Univ. Press, 1967).

Brontë, Emily. *Wuthering Heights* (New York: Random House, Modern Library Edition, 1950).

Broude, Norma and Mary D. Garrard, eds. *Feminism and Art History: Questioning the Litany* (New York: Harper & Row, 1982).

———. *Reclaiming Female Agency: Feminist Art History After Postmodernism* (Berkeley: Univ. of California Press, 2005).

Brown, Christopher G. "To the Ends of the Earth: Sappho on Tithonus," *Zeitschrift für Papyrologie und Epigraphik*, 178 (2011), 21–25.

Brown, Helen. "The Influence of Byron on Emily Brontë," *Modern Language Review*, 34.3 (1939), 374–381.

Burnett, Anne P. "The Race with the Pleiades," *Classical Philology*, 59 (1964), 30–31.

Butler, Samuel. *The Authoress of the Odyssey* (London: Jonathan Cape, 1922). Reprint, Univ. of Chicago Press (1967).

Cameron, Averil and Alan Cameron. "Erinna's Distaff," *Classical Quarterly*, 19.2 (1969), 285–288.

Campbell, David A., ed. *Greek Lyric Poetry: A Selection of Early Greek Lyric, Elegiac and Iambic Poetry* (New York: St. Martin's, 1967; London: Bristol Classical Press, 1982).

———, tr. *Greek Lyric, Vol. 1, Sappho and Alcaeus* (Cambridge: Harvard Univ. Press, Loeb Classical Library, 1982).

———, ed., tr. *Greek Lyric, Vol. 5, The New School of Poetry and Anonymous Songs and Hymns* (Cambridge: Harvard Univ. Press, Loeb Classical Library, 1993).

Carson, Anne. *Eros, the bittersweet* (Princeton: Princeton Univ. Press, 1986).

Celenza, Christopher. "Neoplatonism," in Anthony Grafton, Glenn W. Most and Salvatore Settis, eds., *The Classical Tradition* (2010), 632–636.

Chadwick, Whitney. *Women, Art, and Society* (London: Thames & Hudson, 1990; 2012, 5th ed.).

Clader, Linda and Helen Lee. *The Evolution from Divine to Heroic in Greek Epic Tradition* (Leiden: E. J. Brill, 1976).

Clark, Kenneth. "The Naked and the Nude," in *The Nude: A Study in Ideal Form* (New York: Pantheon Books, 1956), 3–29.

Clay, Diskin. "Fragmentum Adespotum 976," *Transactions of the American Philological Association*, 101 (1970), 119–129.

Clay, Jenny S. "Sappho's Hesperus and Hesiod's Dawn," *Philologus*, 4 (1980), 302–305.

Cohen, Beth. *The Distaff Side: Representing the Female in Homer's Odyssey* (New York: Oxford Univ. Press, 1995).

Collins, Wilkie. *The Woman in White*, Edited with an Introduction and Notes by Matthew Sweet (London: Penguin Books, 1999; 1st pub. 1860).

Cooke, George Albert. *The History and Song of Deborah: Judges IV and V* (Rochester: Scholar's Choice, 2017; 1st pub. 1923).

Copland, Perry Walter. *The Women of Homer* (London: William Heinemann, 1898).

Cox, Virginia. *Women's Writing in Italy: 1400–1650* (Baltimore: Johns Hopkins Univ. Press, 2008).

Curtis, Anthony and John Whitehead. *W. Somerset Maugham: The Critical Heritage* (London: Routledge & Kegan Paul, 1987).

Dalby, Andrew. *Rediscovering Homer: Inside the Origins of the Epic* (New York: W. W. Norton, 2006).

Davies, Malcolm. "Symbolism and Imagery in the Poetry of Ibycus," *Hermes*, 114.4 (1986), 399–405.

Dawson, Christopher M. "Spoudaiogeloion: Random Thoughts on Occasional Poems," *Yale Classical Studies*, 19 (1966), 60.

De Beauvoir, Simone. *The Second Sex*, Constance Borde and Sheila Malovany Chevallier, trs. (New York: Random House, 2011). First published as *Le deuxième sexe* (Paris: Les Éditions Gallimard, 1949).

DeJean, Joan. "Sappho c'est moi, selon Racine: Coming of Age in Neo-Classical Theater," *Yale French Studies*, 76 (1989), 3–20 (anticipating the author's *Fictions of Sappho: 1554–1937* [1989]).

Delon, Michel, ed. *The Libertine: The Art of Love in Eighteenth-Century France*, John Goodman, tr. (New York: Abbeville Press Publishers, 2013).

Denham, Sir John. *The Destruction of Troy, an essay upon the second book of Virgils Æneis. Written in the year 1636* (London: Printed for Humphrey Moseley, 1656; Ann Arbor, Text Creation Partnership, 2007–2010).

Dodds, E. R. See Euripides.

Donoghue, Emma, ed. *Poems Between Women: Four Centuries of Love, Romantic Friendship, and Desire* (New York: Columbia Univ. Press, 1997).

———. *Inseparable: Desire Between Women in Literature* (New York: Random House, 2010).

Dover, Kenneth. "The Poetry of Archilochus," in Jean Pouilloux, et. al., *Entretiens Sur L'Antiquité Classique. Tome X. Archiloque. Sept Exposés et Discussions* (1964), 182–212.

———. *Greek Homosexuality* (London: Duckworth, 1987).

Downes, Jeremy D. *The Female Homer: An Exploration of Women's Epic Poetry* (Newark: Univ. of Delaware Press, 2010).

Duban, Jeffrey M. "Distortion as a Poetic Device in the 'Pursuit of Hector' and Related Events," *Aevum*, 54 (1980), 3–22.

———. "Les duels majeurs de l'Iliade et le langage d'Hector," *Les Etudes Classiques*, 49 (1981) 97–124.

———. "Venus, Epicurus, and the naturae species ratioque," *American Journal of Philology*, 103 (1982), 163–177.

———. *The Lesbian Lyre: Reclaiming Sappho for the 21st Century* (West Sussex: Clairview Books, 2016).

DuBois, Page. *Sappho* (London: I. B. Tauris, 2015).

Dué, Casey. *The Captive Woman's Lament in Greek Tragedy* (Austin: Univ. of Texas Press, 2006).

———. *Homeric Variations on a Lament by Briseis* (London: Rowman & Littlefield, 2002).

Du Maurier, George. *Trilby, A Novel, with illustrations by the author* (New York: Harper & Brothers, 1895).

Durrell, Lawrence. *The Alexandria Quartet* (London: Faber and Faber, 1962; first one-volume edition).

Euripides. *Bacchae,* Edited with Introduction and Commentary by E. R. Dodds (New York: Oxford Univ. Press, 1960).

Evelyn-White, Hugh G. *Hesiod, the Homeric Hymns and Homerica* (London: William Heinemann, 1914; Cambridge: Harvard Univ. Press, Loeb Classical Library, 1914, 1970, 2017).

Faguet, Emile. *Flaubert,* R. L. Devonshire, tr. (Boston: Houghton Mifflin, 1914).

Farnell, Lewis Richard. *The Cults of the Greek States,* V Vols. (Oxford: Clarendon Press, 1896–1909).

Federman, Lillian. *Surpassing the Love of Men: Romantic Friendship and Love Between Women from the Renaissance to the Present* (New York: William Morrow, 1981).

Fernald, Anne E. "O Sister Swallow: Sapphic Fragments as English Literature in Virginia Woolf," in *Virginia Woolf: Feminism and the Reader* (2006), 17–50.

Ferrari, Franco. *Sappho's Gift: The Poet and Her Community,* Benjamin Acosta-Hughes and Lucia Prauscello, trs. (Ann Arbor: Univ. of Michigan Press, 2010).

Ferrari, Gloria. *Alcman and the Cosmos of Sparta* (Chicago: Univ. of Chicago Press, 2008).

Foley, John Miles. "Reading Homer through Oral Tradition," in Kostos Myrsiades, ed., *Approaches to Homer's Iliad and Odyssey* (2010), 15–42.

Fowles, John. *The French Lieutenant's Woman* (London: Jonathan Cape, 1969).

———. *Islands* (Boston: Little, Brown, 1978).

Freer, Agnes Lee. "Baudelaire in English: review of *Flowers of Evil, from the French of Charles Baudelaire,* by George Dillon & Edna St. Vincent Millay," *Poetry*, 48.3 (1936), 158–162.

Friedrich, Paul. *The Meaning of Aphrodite* (Chicago: Univ. of Chicago Press, 1978).

Fuller, Margaret. *Woman in the Nineteenth Century* (New York: Greeley & McElrath, 1845; New York: W. W. Norton, 1971).

Fyfe, W. H., tr. See Longinus.

Gaca, Kathy L. "Reinterpreting the Homeric Simile of 'Iliad' 16.7–11: The Girl and Her Mother in Ancient Greek Warfare," *American Journal of Philology*, 129. 2 (2008), 145–171.

Gaisser, Julia Haig, ed. *Oxford Readings in Classical Studies: Catullus* (Oxford: Oxford Univ. Press, 2007).

Garrard, Mary D. *Artemisia Gentileschi Around 1622: The Shaping and Reshaping of an Artistic Identity* (Berkeley: Univ. of California Press, 2001).

Gates, Eugene. "Mrs. H. H. A. Beach: American Symphonist," *The Kapralova Society Journal: A Journal of Women in Music*, 8.2 (2010), 1–10.

Gerber, D. D. *Euterpe: An Anthology of Early Greek Lyric, Elegiac, and Iambic Poetry* (Amsterdam: Hakkert, 1970).

Gérin, Winifred. "Byron's Influence on the Brontës," *Keats-Shelley Memorial Bulletin*, 17 (1966), 1–19.

Gilbert, Sandra and Susan Gubar. *The Madwoman in the Attic: The Woman Writer and the Nineteenth Century Literary Imagination* (New Haven: Yale Univ. Press, 1984; 2d ed., 2000).

Gladstein, Mimi Reisal and Chris Matthew Sciabarra. *Feminist Interpretations of Ayn Rand* (University Park: Penn State Univ. Press, 1999).

Glenn, Justin. "Ariadne's Daydream (Catullus 64.158–163)," *Classical Journal*, 76 (1981), 113–116.

Goldberg, Vicki. "A Sculptor's Obsession, A Model's Devotion," *The New York Times* (Arts), 8/11/1996.

Gorman, Robert J. and Vanessa B. Gorman. *Corrupting Luxury in Ancient Greek Literature* (Ann Arbor: Univ. of Michigan Press, 2014).

Gosetti, Murrayjohn A. "Sappho's Kisses: Bibliographical Tradition and Intertexuality in 'AP' 5.246 and 5.236," *Classical Journal*, 102.1 (2006), 41–59.

Green, Peter. "On Fire with Longings," review of Anne Carson, tr., *If Not, Winter: Fragments of Sappho,* and Stanley Lombardo, tr., *Sappho: Poems and Fragments, New Republic,* 10/7/2002.

Greene, Ellen, ed. *Reading Sappho: Contemporary Approaches* (Berkeley: Univ. of California Press, 1996a).

———. *Re-reading Sappho: Reception and Transmission* (Berkeley: Univ. of California Press, 1996b).

———. *Women Poets in Ancient Greece and Rome* (Norman: Univ. of Oklahoma Press, 2005) (reviewed by Viarre).

——— and Marilyn B. Skinner, eds. *The New Sappho on Old Age: Textual and Philosophical Issues* (Washington, D.C.: Center for Hellenic Studies and Harvard University Press, 2009).

Greer, Germaine. *The Obstacle Race: The Fortunes of Women Painters and Their Work* (New York: Farrar, Straus & Giroux, 1979).

———. *Slip-Shod Sibyls: Recognition, Reflection and the Woman Poet* (New York: Viking, 1995).

Grigson, Geoffrey. *The Goddess of Love: The Birth, Death and Return of Aphrodite* (London: Constable, 1976).

Gutzwiller, Katherine. "Genre Development and Gendered Voices in Erinna and Nossis," in Yopie Prins and Maeera Shreiber, eds., *Dwelling in Possibility: Women Poets and Critics on Poetry* (1997), 202–222.

Hallett, Judith, P. "Beloved Cleis," *Quaderni Urbinati di Cultura Classica*, n.s. 10 (1982), 21–31.

———. "Sappho and Her Social Context: Sense and Sensuality," *Signs: Journal of Women in Culture and Society*, 4 (1979), 447–464. Reprint, Greene, ed. (1996a), 125–142.

———. "Catullan Voices in Heroides 15: How Sappho Became a Man," *Dictynna* [En ligne], 2/2005.

Hamalian, Linda. *A Life of Kenneth Rexroth* (New York: W. W. Norton, 1991).

Harden, Edgar F. and Mike Hill, eds. *Selected Letters of William Makepeace Thackeray* (New York: New York Univ. Press, 1996).

Harris, William. Sappho: *The Greek Poems* (www.community.middlebury.edu).

Hartley, Jenny. *Selected Letters of Charles Dickens* (Oxford: Oxford Univ. Press, 2012).

Hawkins, Tom. "Out-Foxing the Wolf-Walker: Lycambes as Performative Rival to Archilochus," *Classical Antiquity*, 27.1 (2008), 93–114.

Hawthorne, Nathaniel. *The Scarlet Letter* (Philadelphia: Henry P. Altemus, 1892).

Henderson, Jeffrey S. *The Maculate Muse: Obscene Language in Attic Comedy* (New Haven: Yale Univ. Press, 1975).

Highet, Gilbert, tr. *Paideia: The Ideals of Greek Culture, III Vols.* (Oxford: Oxford Univ. Press, 1939–1944), Vol. I (1944, 1986). Originally, Werner Jaeger, *Paideia: die Formung des griechischen Menschen* (Berlin: Walter de Gruyter, 1933–1947).

———. *The Classical Tradition: Greek and Roman Influences on Western Literature* (New York: Oxford Univ. Press, 1949).

Hine, Daryl. *Ovid's Heroines: A Verse Translation of the Heroides* (New Haven: Yale Univ. Press, 1991).

Hollinger, Veronica. "Putting on the Feminine: Gender and Negativity in *Frankenstein* and *The Handmaid's Tale*," in Daniel Fischlin, ed., *Negation, Critical Theory, and Postmodern Textuality* (1994), 203–226.

Hugo, Victor. *Les Misérables*, Julie Rose, tr. (New York: Random House, 2008).

Hurst, Isobel. *Victorian Women Writers and the Classics: The Feminine of Homer* (Oxford: Oxford Univ. Press, 2006).

Hussey, Mark, ed. *Virginia Woolf: A Room of One's Own, Annotated and with an Introduction by Susan Gubar* (New York: Harcourt, 2005).

Hyde, Melissa. *Making Up the Rococo: François Boucher and his Critics* (Los Angeles: Getty Publications, 2006).

Jacob, Christian. *The Web of Athenaeus* (Washington, D.C.: Center for Hellenic Studies, 2013).

Janan, Micaela. "There beneath the Roman Ruin Where the Purple Flowers Grow: Ovid's Minyeides and the Feminine Imagination," *American Journal of Philology*, 115.3 (1994), 427–448.

Johansen, Knud Friis. *Ajas und Hektor: Ein vorhomerisches Heldenlied?, Historisk-filosogiske Meddelelser*, 39.4 (Copenhagen, 1961).

Jones, Amelia. "The 'sexual politics' of the Dinner Party: A Critical Context," in Broude and Garrard, eds., 409–433.

Jones, Peter V. "A Woman's Place in Homer," *Spectator*, 12/15/2012.

Jordan, Constance. *Renaissance Feminism: Literary Texts and Political Models* (Ithaca: Cornell Univ. Press, 1990).

Karanika, Andromache. *Voices at Work: Women, Performance and Labor in Ancient Greece* (Baltimore: Johns Hopkins Univ. Press, 2014).

Klein, Theodore M. "Apollonius Rhodius, 'Vates Ludens': Eros' Golden Ball (Arg. 3.113–150)," *Classical World*, 74 (1981), 225–227.

Klinck, Anne L. "Male Poets and Maiden Voices: Gender and Genre in Pindar and Alcman," *Hermes*, 129.2 (2001), 276–279.

Knowles, Claire. *Sensibility and Female Poetic Tradition, 1780–1860: The Legacy of Charlotte Smith* (Burlington: Ashgate, 2009).

Krischer, Tilman. *Formale Konventionen der Homerischen Epik: Versuch einer Rekonstruktion, Zetemata*, 56 (Munich: C. H. Beck, 1971).

Kurke, Leslie. "The politics of (h)abrosúnē in Archaic Greece," *Classical Antiquity*, 11.1 (1992), 91–120.

Laing, Gordon L. "The Legend of the Trojan Settlement in Latium," *Classical Journal*, 6.2 (1910), 51–64.

Landeson, Elizabeth. *Proust's Lesbianism* (Ithaca: Cornell Univ. Press, 1999).

Lang, Andrew. "Homer and the Study of Greek," in *Essays in Little* (1891), 77–92.

Lanser, Susan S. "Toward a Feminist Narratology," *Narrative Poetics*, 20.3 (1986), 341–363.

Lawrence, Karen. *Penelope Voyages: Women and Travel in the British Literary Tradition* (Ithaca: Cornell Univ. Press, 1994).

Lefkowiz, Mary R. *The Lives of the Greek Poets* (Baltimore: Johns Hopkins Univ. Press, 1982).

Lenz, Brooke. *John Fowles: Visionary and Voyeur* (Amsterdam: Rodopi, 2008).

Levi, Peter, tr. See Pausanias.

Levin, Gail. *Becoming Judy Chicago: A Biography of the Artist* (New York: Harmony Books, 2007).

Longinus. *On the Sublime*, W. H. Fyfe, tr., revised by Donald Russell (Cambridge: Harvard Univ. Press, Loeb Classical Library, 1995).

Louÿs, Pierre. *The Songs of Bilitis*, Mitchell S. Buck, tr.; Intro., George Ross Ridge (New York: Capricorn Books, 1966), first English tr., M. S. Buck, 1928.

Luck, Georg. *The Latin Love Elegy* (London: Methuen, 1969).

Maas, Jeremy. *Victorian Painters* (New York: Harrison House, 1978).

Mace, Nancy A. *Henry Fielding's Novels and the Classical Tradition* (Newark: Univ. of Delaware Press, 1996).

Manguel, Alberto. *Homer's The Iliad and The Odyssey: A Biography* (New York: Atlantic Monthly Press, 2007).

Martin, Richard P. *The Language of Heroes: Speech and Performance in the Iliad (Myth and Poetics)* (Ithaca: Cornell Univ. Press, 1989).

Maximus (of Tyre). *The Philosophical Orations*, M. B. Trapp tr. (Oxford: Oxford Univ. Press, 1997).

McCarthy, William. *Hester Thrale Piozzi: Portrait of a Literary Woman* (Chapel Hill: Univ. of North Carolina Press, 1985).

McClure, Laura K. *Gender and Greek Literary Culture in Athenaeus* (New York: Rutledge, 2003).

McEvilley, Thomas. *Sappho* (Putnam: Spring, 2008).

Meeker, Natania. *Voluptuous Philosophy: Literary Materialism in the French Enlightenment* (New York: Fordham Univ. Press, 2006).

Michael, Magali Cornier. "'Who is Sarah?': A Critique of The French Lieutenant's Woman's Feminism," *Critique: Studies in Modern Fiction*, 28.4 (1987), 225–236.

Milford, Nancy. *Savage Beauty: The Life of Edna St. Vincent Millay* (New York: Random House, 2001).

Miller, Marion Mills and David Moore Robinson. *The Songs of Sappho* (New York: Frank-Maurice, 1925).

Morgan, Thaïs E., ed. *Men Writing the Feminine: Literature, Theory, and the Question of Gender* (Albany: State Univ. of New York Press, 1994).

Müller, Timo. "Gerty MacDowell, Poetess: Butler's *The Authoress of the Odyssey* and the Nausicaa Episode of *Ulysses*," *Twentieth Century Literature*, 55.3 (2009), 378–392.

Nagy, Gregory. *Comparative Studies in Greek and Indic Meter* (Cambridge: Harvard Univ. Press, 1974).

———. "Sappho's Phaon, and the White Rock of Leukas," *Harvard Studies in Classical Philology*, 77 (1973), 137–177. Revised and retitled, "Phaethon, Sappho's Phaon, and the White Rock of Leukas: 'Reading' the Symbols of Greek Lyric," Greene, ed. (1996a), 35–57.

———. "Iambos: Typologies of Invective and Praise," in Van Sickle, ed. (1976), 191–205.

———. "Transmission of Archaic Greek Sympotic Songs: From Lesbos to Alexandria," *Critical Inquiry*, 31.1 (2004), 26–48.

———. "Ancient Greek Elegy," in Karen Weisman, ed., *Oxford Handbook of the Elegy* (2010) 13–45.

Natter, Tobias. *Angelica Kauffman: A Woman of Immense Talent* (Ostfildern: Hatje Cantz Verlag, 2007).

Newman, Francis X, ed. *The Meaning of Courtly Love* (New York: State Univ. of New York Press, 1968).

Nochlin, Linda. "Why Have There Been No Women Artists?" (seminal article), in Nochlin (1988). Reprint, Reilly, ed., 42–68 (2015); 1st pub. ARTnews, January 1971.

———. *Women, Art, Power and Other Essays* (New York: Harper & Row, 1988).

———. *Representing Women* (London: Thames & Hudson, 1999).

———. "'Why Have There Been No Great Women Artists?' Thirty Years After," in Reilly, ed., 311–321; 1st pub. Carol Armstrong and Catherine de Zegher, eds., *Women Artists at the Millennium* (2006).

———. *Courbet* (London: Thames & Hudson, 2007).

North, Helen F. "The Mare, the Vixen, and the Bee: 'Sophrosyne' as the Virtue of Women in Antiquity," *Illinois Classical Studies*, 2 (1977), 35–38.

O'Hara, John Myers. *The Poems of Sappho: An Interpretative Rendition into English* (Portland: Smith & Sale, 1910).

Overton, Bill. "Lord Hervey, Poetic Voice and Gender," *Review of English Literature*, n.s. 62.256 (2011), 594–617.

Paglia, Camille. *Sexual Personae* (New York: Vintage, 1991).

———. *Free Women, Free Men: Sex · Gender · Feminism* (New York: Vintage, 2017).

Paley, Morton D. "To Matilda Betham from a Stranger," *The Wordsworth Circle*, 27.3 (1996).

Pantelia, Maria C. "Helen and the Last Song for Hector," *Transactions of the American Philological Association*, 132 (2002), 21–27.

Parker, Holt N. "Sappho Schoolmistress," *Transactions of the American Philological Association*, 123 (1993), 309–351. Reprint, Greene, ed. (1996b), 146–183.

———. Sappho's Daughter/Clitoris/Lover," *Rheinisches Museum für Philologie*, n.f. 149.1 (2006), 109–112.

Parry, Adam M. *The Language of Achilles and Other Papers* (Oxford: Oxford Univ. Press, 1989).

Patrick, James David. "Goldfinger: Subtext and the Rape of Pussy Galore" (third essay in a 24-part series about the James Bond cinemas, entitled "Of [In]human Bondage"). www.thejamesbondsocialmedia-project.com.

Pausanias. *Guide to Greece, Vol. 1: Central Greece*, Peter Levi, tr. (Harmondsworth: Penguin Books, 1971).

Peterson, Linda H. *Becoming a Woman of Letters: Myths of Authorship and Facts of the Victorian Marketplace* (Princeton: Princeton Univ. Press, 2009).

Petropoulos, J. C. B. "Sappho the Sorceress—Another Look at Fr. 1 (LP)," *Zeitschrift für Papyrologie und Epigraphik*, 97 (1993), 43–56.

Porter, Laurence M. "Make Love, Not War: Sappho," in *Women's Vision in Western Literature: The Empathic Community* (Westport: Praeger, Contributions in Women's Studies [Number 203], 2005), 17–34.

Power, Henry. *Epic into Novel: Henry Fielding, Scriblerian Satire, and the Consumption of Classical Literature* (Oxford: Oxford Univ. Press, 2015).

Prentice, William K. "Sappho," *Classical Philology*, 13.4 (1918), 347–360.

Price, Thos. R. "The Technic of Shakespeare's Sonnets," in B. L. Gildersleeve, ed., *Studies in Honor of Basil Lanneau Gildersleeve* (1902, 2016), 363–378.

Proust, Marcel. *Swann's Way*, in *Remembrance of Things Past (II Volumes)*, translated by C. K. Scott Moncrieff (1934; *Swann's Way* 1st pub. 1913).

Putnam, Michael C. J. "Throna and Sappho 1.1," *Classical Journal*, 56 (1960), 79–83.

———. "Catullus 11: The Ironies of Integrity," *Ramus*, 3 (1974), 70–86. Reprint, *Essays on Latin Lyric, Elegy, and Epic* (1982), 13–29.

Raby, Peter. *Samuel Butler: A Biography* (Iowa City: Univ. of Iowa Press, 1991).

Rankin, H. D. *Archilochus of Paros* (Park Ridge: Noyes, 1977).

Redfield, James. *Nature and Culture in the Iliad: The Tragedy of Hector* (Chicago: Univ. of Chicago Press, 1975).

Reilly, Maura, ed. *Women Artists: The Linda Nochlin Reader* (New York: Thames and Hudson, 2015).

Rickey, Carrie. "The Male gaze? What of the Female's?: 'The Beguiled' is remade, with a woman behind the camera," *New York Times* (Film), 6/25/2017.

Rissman, Leah. *Love as War: Homeric Allusion in the Poetry of Sappho* (Königstein: Anton Hain, 1983).

Roberts, Mary Louise. *What Soldiers Do: Sex and the American GI in World War II France* (Chicago: Univ. of Chicago Press, 2013).

Robinson, David M. and Edward J. Fluck. *A Study of the Greek Love-Names, Including a Discussion of Paederasty and a Prosopographia* (Baltimore: Johns Hopkins Univ. Press, 1937).

Rubin, Nancy. "Radical Semantic Shifts in Archilochus," *Classical Journal*, 77 (1981), 6–7.

Rumph, Stephen. "Debussy's Trois Chansons de Bilitis: Song, Author, and the Death of the Subject," *Journal of Musicology*, 12.4 (1994), 464–490.

Russ, Joanna. *The Female Man* (New York: Bantam, 1975).

Ruyer, Raymond. *Homère au féminin* (Paris: Copernic, 1977) (*Réalism fantastique*, collection dirigée par Jean Mabire, Vol. 2).

Santayana, George. *The Sense of Beauty: Being the Outlines of Aesthetic Theory* (New York: Charles Scribner's Sons, 1896, 1936).

Scaltsas, Patricia Ward. "Virtue without Gender in Socrates," *Hypatia*, 7.3 (1992), 126–137.

Schama, Simon. *The Power of Art* (New York: HarperCollins, 2006).

Schmidt, Michael. *Lives of the Poets* (New York: Random House, 1998).

Schwartz, Sanford. "Taking Her Place in American Art: Florine Stettheimer, Painting Poetry," *New York Review of Books*, 7/13/2017.

Schweizer, Bernard. *Rebecca West: Heroism, Rebellion, and the Female Epic* (Westport: Greenwood, Contributions in Women's Studies [Number 199], 2002).

———, ed. *Approaches to the Anglo and American Female Epic, 1621–1982* (Aldershot: Ashgate, 2006).

Scruton, Roger. *Beauty* (Oxford: Oxford Univ. Press, 2009).

———. *Fools, Frauds and Firebrands: Thinkers of the New Left* (London: Bloomsbury, 2015).

Segal, Charles P. "Eros and Incantation: Sappho and Oral Poetry," *Arethusa*, 7 (1974), 139–160. Reprint, Greene, ed. (1996a), 58–75.

———. "Euripides' *Alcestis*: Female Death and Male Tears," *Classical Antiquity*, 11.1 (1992), 142–158.

Showerman, Grant. *Ovid Heroides • Amores* (Cambridge: Harvard Univ. Press, Loeb Classical Library, 1963). Revised, J. P. Goold.

Skinner, Marilyn B. "Women and Language in Archaic Greece, or, Why is Sappho a Woman?" in Nancy Sorkin Rabinowitz and Amy Richlin, eds., *Feminist Theory and the Classics* (1993), 125–144. Reprint, Greene, ed. (1996a), 175–192.

Smith, Alison. *The Victorian Nude; Sexuality, Morality and Art* (Manchester: Manchester Univ. Press, 1996).

Smith, Margaret, ed. *The Letters of Charlotte Brontë, Volume Two, 1848–1851* (Oxford: Oxford Univ. Press, 2000).

Snodgrass, Anthony. *Archaic Greece: The Age of Experiment* (Berkeley: Univ. of California Press, 1980).

Stafford, Barbara. "Endymion's Moonbath: Art and Science in Girodet's Early Masterpiece," *Leonardo*, 15.3 (1982), 193–198.

Stanley, K. "The Role of Aphrodite in Sappho Fr. 1," *Greek, Roman, and Byzantine Studies*, 17 (1976), 309–310.

Stigers, Eva S. "Retreat from the Male: Catullus 62 and Sappho's Erotic Flowers," *Ramus*, 6 (1977), 83–102.

———. "Romantic Sensuality, Poetic Sense: A Response to Hallett on Sappho," *Signs: Journal of Women in Culture and Society*, 4 (1979), 465–471.

———. "Sappho's Private World," *Women's Studies*, 8 (1981), 47–63.

Stocker, Margarita. *Judith Sexual Warrior: Women and Power in Western Culture* (New Haven: Yale Univ. Press, 1998).

Stovel, Bruce. "Tom Jones and the Odyssey," *Eighteenth-Century Fiction*, 1.4 (1989), 263–280.

Stowe, Harriet Beecher. *Lady Byron Vindicated: A History of the Byron Controversy from Its Beginnings in 1816 to the Present Time* (New York: Wallachia, 2015; 1st pub. 1870); cf. Stowe, "The True Story of Lady Byron's Life," *The Atlantic Monthly* (August, 1869).

Straussman-Pflanzer, Eve. *Violence & Virtue: Artemisia Gentileschi's "Judith Slaying Holofernes"* (Chicago: The Art Institute of Chicago, 2013).

Swinburne, Algernon Charles. *A Pilgrimage of Pleasure: Essays and Studies* (Boston: Richard G. Badger, 1913).

———. "Sappho," *Saturday Review*, 117 (1914), 228 (posthumous publication).

Symonds, John Addington. *Studies of the Greek Poets, II Vols.* (New York: Harper & Brothers, 1882).

———. *The Sonnets of Michael Angelo Buonarroti: Now for the first time translated into Rhymed English* (London: Smith Elder; New York: Charles Scribner's Sons, 1904, 2nd ed.).

Taplin, Oliver. *Homeric Soundings* (Oxford: Clarendon Press, 1992).

Tarbox, Katherine. "John Fowles's *Islands*: Landscape and Narrative's Negative Space," in Aubrey, ed., 44–59.

Teasdale, Sara. *The Answering Voice: One Hundred Love Lyrics by Women* (Boston: Houghton Mifflin, 1917).

Trapp, M. B., tr. See Maximus (of Tyre).

Trench, Richard Chenevix. *The Sonnets of William Wordsworth, Collected in One Volume* (London: Suttaby, 1884).

Tucker, T. G. *Sappho: A Lecture Delivered Before the Classical Association of Victoria, 1913* (Melbourne: Thomas C. Lothian, 1914). Reprint, Leopold Classical Library (2015).

van Creveld, Martin. *The Privileged Sex* (Mevasseret Zion: DLVC Enterprises, 2013).

Vanita, Ruth. *Sappho and the Virgin Mary: Same-Sex Love and the English Literary Imagination* (New York: Columbia Univ. Press, 1996).

Van Sickle, John, ed. *The New Archilochus, Arethusa*, 9.2 (1976).

Venuti, Lawrence. *The Scandals of Translation: Towards an ethics of difference* (London: Routledge, 1998).

———. *The Translator's Invisibility: A history of translation* (London: Routledge, 1995).

Viarre, Simone. Review of Ellen Greene ed., *Women Poets in Ancient Greece and Rome*, Bryn Mawr Classical Review at www.bmcr.brynmawr.edu/2005/2005-11-05.html.

von Wilamowitz-Moellendorff, Ulrich. *Sappho und Simonides, Untersuchungen über griechische Lyriker* (Berlin: Weidmannsche Buchhandlung, 1913).

Walsh, Michael. *The Devil's Pleasure Palace: The Cult of Critical Theory and the Subversion of the West* (New York: Encounter Books, 2015).

———. *The Fiery Angel: Art, Sex, Politics, and the Struggle for the Soul of the West* (New York: Encounter Books, 2018).

West, M. L., ed. *Hesiod Theogony, with Prolegomena and Commentary* (Oxford: Clarendon Press, 1966).

West, Rebecca. "Mr. Chesterton in Hysterics," *The Clarion* (14 November 1913). Reprint, Jane Connor Marcus, ed., *The Young Rebecca West: The Writings of Rebecca West, 1911–1917* (1998), Part II: *Essays (complete) from The Clarion*, 218–222.

———. "Woman as Artist and Thinker" (1937), in *Woman as Artist and Thinker* (Lincoln: iUniverse, 2006).

Wharton, Henry Thornton. *Sappho: Memoir, Text, Renderings, and a Literal Translation* (London: David Stott, 1885, 1887, 1895; Chicago: A. C. McClurg, 1887).

Whitman, Cedric H. *Homer and the Heroic Tradition* (New York: W. W. Norton, 1958).

Wiesner-Hanks, Merry E. "Women and the Creation of Culture" in *Women and Gender in Early Modern Europe* (Milwaukee: Univ. of Wisconsin Press, 2008, 3rd ed.), 174–206.

Wilde, Oscar. *The Women of Homer*, Edited by Thomas Wright and Donald Mead (London: The Oscar Wilde Society, 2008; second impression with corrections, 2011).

Wills, Garry. "Closer Than Ever to Virgil" (review of Sarah Ruden, tr., *The Aeneid*), *New York Review of Books*, 3/12/2009.

Wilson, Lyn Hatherly. *Sappho's Sweet Bitter Songs: Configurations of Female and Male in Ancient Greek Lyric* (London: Rutledge, 1996).

Wilson, Romer. *The Private Life and History of Emily Jane Brontë* (New York: Albert & Charles Boni, 1928).

Winkler, Jack. "Gardens of Nymphs: Public and Private in Sappho's Lyrics," in Helene P. Foley, ed., *Reflections of Women in Antiquity* (1981), 63–90. Reprint, Greene, ed. (1996a), 89–109.

Woodbury, Leonard. "Gold Hair and Grey, or The Game of Love: Anacreon Fr. 13G," *Transactions of the American Philological Association*, 109 (1979), 277–287.

Woolf, Virginia. *A Room of One's Own* (New York: Oxford Univ. Press, Oxford World's Classics, 1992; 1st pub. 1929), 76–84.

———. "Women and Fiction," in *Granite & Rainbow: Essays by Virginia Woolf* (1958; 1st pub. 1929).

Wortmann, Simone. *The Concept of Ecriture Feminine in Helene Cixous's 'The Laugh of Medusa'* (Norderstedt: Grinn, 2012).

Standard Editions of Greek Lyric Texts

D = Diehl, E. *Anthologia Lyrica Graeca* (Lipsiae: Teubner, 1925, 1942, 1949–1952).

G = Gentili, B. *Anacreon* (Roma: Edizioni dell'Ateneo, 1958). Introduction, critical text and apparatus, translation, studies on papyrus fragments (Italian).

LP = Lobel, E. and D. L. Page. *Poetarum Lesbiorum Fragmenta* (Oxford: Clarendon Press, 1955, 1968). Critical texts, apparatus, word indices, manuscript catalogues, and testimonia for the complete works of Sappho and Alcaeus.

P = Page, D. L. *Poetae Melici Graeci* (Oxford: Clarendon Press, 1962).

T = Tarditi, G. *Archilochus* (Roma: Edizioni dell'Ateneo, 1968). Introduction, testimonia, critical text, apparatus, and translation (Italian).

V = Voigt, E. M. *Sappho et Alcaeus* (Amsterdam: Polak Van Gennep, 1971). Exhaustive critical edition, supersedes Lobel and Page, whose numberings it largely follows.

W = West, M. L. *Delectus ex Iambis et Elegis Graecis* (Oxford: Oxford Univ. Press, 1980).

Supplemental Bibliography

(Works consulted but not cited.)

Adler, Sabine. *Lovers in Art* (London and New York: Prestel, n.d.).

Aldersey-Williams, Hugh. *Anatomies: A Cultural History of the Human Body* (New York: W. W. Norton, 2013).

Angier, Natalie. "A Society Led by Strong Females: Bonobos, closely related to humans, have evolved a matriarchal hierarchy that punishes male misbehavior," *The New York Times* (ScienceTimes), 9/13/2016.

Beer, Anna. *Sounds and Sweet Airs: The Forgotten Women of Classical Music* (London: Overworld, 2016).

Brisson, Luc. *Sexual Ambivalence: Androgyny and Hermaphroditism in Greco-Roman Antiquity,* Janet Lloyd tr. and intro. (Berkeley: Univ. of California Press, 2002).

Chicago, Judy and Edward Lucie-Smith. *Women and Art: Contested Territory* (Hertfordshire: Eagle Editions, 2004; 1st pub. 1998).

Collecott, Diana. *H.D. & Sapphic Modernism* (Cambridge: Cambridge Univ. Press, 1999).

Crispin, Jessa. *Why I Am Not a Feminist: A Feminist Manifesto* (Brooklyn: Melville House, 2017).

Deakin, Michael A. B. *Hypatia of Alexandria* (Amherst: Prometheus, 2007).

Döpp, Hans-Jürgen. *Music & Eros*, Niels Clegg, tr. (Ho Chi Minh City: Baseline, 2012).

———, et al., eds. *30 Millennia of Erotic Art* (New York: Parkstone International, 2012).

———, Joe A. Thomas, and Victoria Charles. *1000 Erotic Works of Genius* (New York: Parkstone Press, 2008).

Drinker, Sophie. *Music & Women: The story of women in their relation to music* (New York: The Feminist Press at the City Univ. of New York, 1948, 1995).

Elliott, Bridget and Jo-Ann Wallace. *Women Artists and Writers: Modernist (im)positionings* (London: Rutledge, 1997).

Friedman, Susan Stanford, and Rachel Blau DuPlessis. *Signets: Reading H.D.* (Madison: Univ. of Wisconsin Press, 1990).

Garrard, Mary D. *Brunelleschi's Egg: Nature, Art, and Gender in Renaissance Italy* (Berkeley and London: Univ. of California Press, 2010).

Ginsberg, Elaine K. and Laura Moss Gottlieb. *Virginia Woolf: Centennial Essays* (Troy: Whitston, 1983).

Goldstein, Lawrence, ed. *The Male Body: Features, Destinies, Exposures* (Ann Arbor: Univ. of Michigan Press, 1994).

Harkins, E. F. *Famous Authors (Women)* (Boston: L. C. Page, 1901).

Harris, Ann Sutherland. *Women Artists, 1550–1950* (exhibition catalogue) (New York: Alfred A. Knopf, 1976).

Hoganson, Kristin L. *Fighting for American Manhood: How Gender Politics Provoked the Spanish-American and Philippine-American Wars* (New Haven: Yale Univ. Press, 1998).

Johns-Putra, Adeline. *Heroes and Housewives: Women's Epic Poetry and Domestic Ideology in the Romantic Age (1770–1835)* (European University Studies Series 14: Anglo-Saxon Language and Literature, Volume 374).

Kestner, Joseph A. "Edward John Poynter and the Expansion of the Mythological Tradition," in *Mythology and Misogyny: The Social Discourse of Nineteenth-Century British Classical-Subject Painting* (1989).

Lardinois, André and Laura McClure, eds. *Making Silence Speak: Women's Voices in Greek Literature and Society* (Princeton: Princeton Univ. Press, 2001).

Lucie-Smith, Edward. *Sexuality in Western Art* (London: Thames and Hudson, 1972, 1995).

Lyons, Deborah. *Gender and Immortality: Heroines in Ancient Greek Myth and Cult* (Princeton: Princeton Univ. Press, 1997).

Manca, Joseph, Patrick Bade, and Sara Castello. *1000 Sculptures of Genius* (New York, Parkstone Press, 2007).

Mancoff, Debra N. *Danger! Women Artists at Work* (London: Merrell, 2012).

Marche, Stephen. "The Hollow Patriarchy," in *The Unmade Bed: The Messy Truth about Men and Women in the 21st Century* (2017) (read with van Creveld).

McLeod, Glenda. *Virtue and Venom: Catalogs of Women from Antiquity to the Renaissance* (Ann Arbor: Univ. of Michigan Press, 1991).

Miller, Shannon. *Engendering the Fall: John Milton and Seventeenth-Century Women Writers* (Philadelphia: Univ. of Pennsylvania Press, 2008).

Parisi, Joseph and Kathleen Welton, eds. *100 Essential Modern Poems by Women* (Chicago: Ivan R. Dee, 2008).

Peterson, Linda H. *Becoming a Woman of Letters: Myths of Authorship and Facts of the Victorian Market* (Princeton: Princeton Univ. Press, 2009).

Prins, Yopie. *Victorian Sappho* (Princeton: Princeton Univ. Press, 1999).

Quinn, Bridget. *Broad Strokes: 15 Women Who Made Art and Made History (in That Order)* (San Francisco: Chronicle Books, 2017).

Roberts, Mary Louise. *Civilization without Sexes: Reconstructing Gender in Postwar France, 1917–1927* (Chicago: Univ. of Chicago Press, 1994).

Russ, Joanna. *How to Suppress Women's Writing* (Austin: Univ. of Texas Press, 1983).

Smith, William J. and Louise Bogan. *A Woman's Words: A Lecture Delivered at the Library of Congress May 4, 1970* (Washington: Library of Congress, 1971).

Snyder, Jane Macintosh. *Lesbian Desire in the Lyrics of Sappho* (New York: Columbia Univ. Press, 1997) (Epilogue: "Sappho and Modern American Women Poets").

———. *The Woman and the Lyre: Women Writers in Classical Greece and Rome* (Carbondale: Southern Illinois Univ. Press, 1989).

Tate, J. P. *Feminism is Sexism* (CreateSpace, 2014).

Van Nortwick, Thomas. "Like a Woman: Hector and the Boundaries of Masculinity," *Arethusa*, 34.2 (2001), 221–235.

West, Rebecca. *Woman as Artist and Thinker* (Carbondale: Southern Illinois Univ. Press, 1971) (reissue of selected essays).

Zuffi, Stephano. *Love and the Erotic in Art*, Stephen Sartarelli, tr. (Los Angeles: Getty Museum, 2010).

Annotated Bibliography (Horace)

Abrahamina, Levon. "The Cave and the Labyrinth," *Iran and the Caucasus* 11.1(2007), 89–99 (includes discussion of Greek myths of subterranean or mountain-peak internment or punishment).

Ancona, Ronnie. *Time and the Erotic in Horace's Odes* (Durham: Duke Univ. Press, 1994).

Anderson, Colin. *Harvesting the Day: Horace for the 21st Century, Odes Book I, translations and commentaries* (Wellington: Steele Roberts, 2010) (translations into comparable English meters with excellent commentary and metrical analyses).

Anderson, Sam. "Knee-Deep in 'Bovary': Flaubert's obsessive masterpiece finally gets the obsessive translation it deserves," *New York Magazine*, 10/3/2010.

Aristophanes. *Frogs*. Edited with Introduction, Revised Text, Commentary and Index by W. B. Stanford (London: Bristol Classical Press, 1958).

Bennett, Charles, E., ed. *Horace Odes and Epodes* (Atlanta: Allyn and Bacon, 1901, 1965) (a solid commentary for the intermediate reader of Latin).

Beye, Charles Rowan. "Horace in English," *Parnassus: Poetry in Review*, 14.1(1987), 164–186 (review of then recent translations of Horace).

Bowditch, P. Lowell. "Horace and the Pyrotechnics of Translation," *Classical World*, 104.3 (2011), 355–362 (Horace by Poundian analysis).

Brenk, Frederick E. *Clothed in Purple Light: Studies in Vergil and in Latin Literature* (Stuttgart: Franz Steiner, 1999).

Brown, Jerrold C. "The Verbal Art of Horace's Ode to Pyrrha," *Transactions of the American Philological Association*, 111 (1981), 17–22 (laborious analysis based on Russian formalist and Prague structuralist thought; better made, for all it offers, without the theoretical scaffolding).

Bulwer-Lytton, Robert (1st Earl of Lytton). *The Odes and Epodes of Horace: Metrical Translation into English with Introduction and Commentaries* (London: Longmans, Green, 1872) (of a different era and sensibility).

Burnett, Archie. "The Fifth Ode of Horace, Lib. I. and Milton's Style," *Milton Quarterly*, 16.3 (1982), 68–72 (brief but excellent article beginning, "Widely differing judgments have been passed on nearly every aspect of Milton's translation of Horace, *Odes* 1.5.").

Carne-Ross, D. S. and Kenneth Haynes, eds. *Horace in English* (London: Penguin Books, 1996) (560-page anthology of translations over time from all of Horace's works; detailed introduction by Carne-Ross whom I discuss at length in *TLL*).

Cicero. *De Inventione, De Optimo Genere Oratorum, Topica. Cicero in 28 volumes* (Vol. 2), H. M. Hubbell, tr. (Cambridge: Harvard Univ. Press; London: William Heinemann, Loeb Classical Library, 1976; 1st pub. 1949).

Clancy, Joseph P., tr. *The Odes & Epodes of Horace*, rev. John C. Rolfe (Chicago: Univ. of Chicago Press, 1960).

Clark, Matityahu (Rabbi). *Etymological Dictionary of Biblical Hebrew: Based on the Commentaries of Rabbi Samson Raphael Hirsch* (Jerusalem: Feldsheim, 1999).

Coffta, David J. "Programme and Persona in Horace, *Odes* 1.5," *Eranos* 96 (1988), 26–31. (*Odes* 1.5 a programmatic disavowal of elegy and the elegiac voice; a bow to Alexandrianism: "The *puer* has the potential to represent good poetry (*gracilis*) but is also excessive. Pyrrha is like Callimachean poetry (*simplex munditiis*), but involvement with her is also like a disastrous foray into epic poetry (*aspera aequora*).")

Commager, Steele. *The Odes of Horace: A Critical Study* (New Haven: York Univ. Press, 1962) (landmark study ranking with Fraenkel).

Conington, John, tr. *The Odes and Carmen Saeculare of Horace* (London: Bell and Daldy, 1872, 5th ed.) (still serviceable preface on method and goals in translating the metrical variety of Horace's *Odes*).

De la Mare, F. A. and S. Eichelbaum, eds. *The Old Clay Patch: A Collection of Verses Written in and Around Victoria (University) College, Wellington, N.Z.* (Wellington, Melbourne, and London, 1910); Forgotten Books Classic Reprint Series (with charming imitation of *Odes* 1.5 by A. F. T. Chorlton [see p. 303 herein], not contained in Storrs).

Denham, John (Sir). *The Destruction of Troy: an essay upon the second book of Virgils Aeneis, written in the year 1636* (London: Printed for Humphrey Moseley, 1656); Ann Arbor, Text Creation Partnership, 2007–2010.

Duban, Jeffrey M. "Verbal Links and Imagistic Undercurrent in Catullus 64," *Latomus*, 39.4 (1980), 777–802.

———. Review of C. Whitman, *CO*, 59.2 (1981–1982), 57–58 (highlighting *Odes* 1.5).

———. *The Lesbian Lyre: Reclaiming Sappho for the 21st Century* (W. Sussex: Clairview Books, 2016).

Elbon, D. S. *Horace Fully Parsed Word by Word: Books I and II of Horace Odes Grammatically Analyzed and Literally Translated* (Wauconda: Bolchazy-Carducci, 2003); originally published by Elbon in 1917 under slightly different title. Reprint (2003) with Introduction by Thomas J. Sienkewicz.

Eyres, Harry. *Horace and Me: Life Lessons from an Ancient Poet* (New York: Farrar, Straus & Giroux, 2012) (an absorbingly sympathetic work by one steeped in his author's time, place, and poetry—by one who has lived and acutely conveys his own sense of the Horatian life [the book's sole fault and anomaly being the Poundian translation of Horace]).

Ferry, David, tr. *The Odes of Horace: A Bilingual Edition* (New York: Farrar, Straus & Giroux, 1997) (I bypass this edition because Ferry, the present darling of Latin verse translation—most recently of Virgil's *Aeneid*—is an essentially Latinless "poet-translator"; see further *TLL*).

Fitzgerald, William. Review of R. Ancona, *Classical Philology*, 91.4 (1966), 388–399.

———. *Catullan Provocations: Lyric Poetry and the Drama of Positions* (Berkeley: Univ. of California Press, 1995) (see esp. Ch. 6: "Gazing at the Golden Age: Belatedness and Mastery in Poem 64"; persuasively analogizing the "luxuriousness of Catullus' poem, its virtuosity, its imitation of visual art, its play with frames and with different modes of representation" to the representational power of the Boscotrecase panels at the Metropolitan Museum, NYC).

———. "Horace: The Sensation of Mediocrity," in *How to Read a Latin Poem (If You Can't Read Latin Yet)* (2013) (disarmingly astute insights).

Fordyce, C. J. *Catullus, a Commentary* (London: Oxford Univ. Press, 1961, 1973).

Fraenkel, Eduard. *Horace* (Oxford: Oxford Univ. Press, 1957) (among the most authoritative books in English on Horace overall; little on Horace's love poetry and nothing on *Odes* 1.5).

Fratantuomo, Lee and Cynthia Susalla. "Drowned Doublets: Virgil's Doomed Sailors and the Archytas Ode of Horace," *Maia*, 66 (2014), 84–96 (discussing "significant affinities" [p. 94] between *Odes* 1.5 and *Aeneid*, Book 5, including the "progression from the danger of fire ... to the hazard of stormy, tempestuous seas").

Fredericksmeyer, Ernst. "Horace's Ode to Pyrrha (Carm. 1.5)," *Classical Philology*, 60 (1965), 180–185 (excellent and frequently cited study).

————. "Horace's Chloe (*Odes* 1.23): Inamorata or Victim," *Classical Journal*, 89.3 (1994), 251–259.

Garrison, Daniel H. *Horace, Epodes and Odes: A New Annotated Latin Edition* (Norman: Univ. of Oklahoma Press, Oklahoma Series in Classical Culture, 1991) (revision and update of 1934 Bennett edition of Horace, considering "different assumptions about the poet and the business of reading him").

Gladstone, William Ewart, tr. *The Odes of Horace* (New York: Charles Scribner, 1894). Reprint Kessinger Publishing (n.d.).

Glenn, Justin. "Pandora and Eve: Sex as the Root of All Evil," *Classical World*, 71.3 (1977), 179–185 (myths of Pandora and Eve signify not so much man's suspicion of woman as society's suspicion of sex; "the image of Pandora opening her jar is the exact equivalent of Eve offering Adam her fruit"—a distorted representation of the sexual act; see also Lachs).

Glover, T. R. *Horace: A Return to Allegiance* (Cambridge: Cambridge Univ. Press, 1932) (Lewis Fry Memorial Lectures, Univ. of Bristol, 1932).

Gold, Barbara. "Mitte Sectari, Rosa Quo Locorum Sera Moretur: Time and Nature in Horace's Odes," *Classical Philology*, 88.1 (1993), 16–31 (emphasizing the rose in *Odes* 1.5).

Henriksén, Christer. *A Commentary on Martial: Epigrams Book 9* (Oxford: Oxford Univ. Press, 2012).

Hoppin, Meredith Clark. "New Perspectives on Horace *Odes* 1.5," *American Journal of Philology*, 105.1(1984), 54–68 (focuses on the antecedents for, nature of, and depictions on an ancient votive tablet within the context of Roman painting in Horace's time).

Jocelyn, H. D. "Boats, Women, and Horace *Odes* 1.14," *Classical Philology*, 77.4 (1982), 330–335.

Kaimowitz, Jeffrey, H., tr., Introduction by Ronnie Ancona. *The Odes of Horace* (Baltimore: Johns Hopkins Univ. Press, 2008) (containing a well-rendered 100-word translation of *Odes* 1.5; but see Nagle).

Kates, J. "Getting Horace Across," *Harvard Review Online*, www.harvardreview.org, 3/1/2016 (brief and cocky comparison of several *Odes* 1.5 translations; cf. Thayer, below).

Kiernan, V. G. *Horace: Poetics and Politics* (New York: St. Martin's Press, 1999).

Knorr, Ortwin. "Horace's Ship Ode ("Odes" 1.14) in Context: A Metaphorical Love-Triangle," *Transactions of the American Philological Association*, 136.1 (2006), 149–169.

Lachs, Samuel Tobias. "The Pandora-Eve Motif in Rabbinic Literature," *Harvard Theological Review*, 67.3 (1974), 341–345 (detailing parallels between the two myths; Pandora's "jar" originally containing scorpions or snakes; see also Glenn).

Lee, Guy, tr. *Horace Odes and Carmen Seculare* (Oxford: Francis Cairns, 1988)(translation into Horatian meters).

Lee, M. Owen. *Word, Sound, and Image in the Odes of Horace* (Ann Arbor: Univ. of Michigan Press, 1969).

Leishman, J. B. *Translating Horace: Thirty Odes translated into the original meters with the Latin text and an Introduction and Critical Essay* (Oxford: Bruno Cassirer, 1956).

Levi, Peter. *Horace: A Life* (London: Gerald Duckworth, 1997). ("I have adored Horace in the simplest manner since I was fifteen, and as undiscerning about poetry as anyone else, but he keeps pace with our years as he does with the ages of the world. Without being deep oneself, one can see depth in him, and he is one of the very few poets who always leaves one feeling wiser, better and more relaxed, with no diminution of energy or appetite.")

Levin, Donald Norman. "Thought-Progression in Horace, 'Carmina' 1.5," *Classical Journal*, 56.8 (1961), 356–358 (two progressions of thought; one forward- and the other backward-moving).

Lord Lytton (see Bulwer-Lytton).

Mackail, J. W. "A Lesson on an Ode of Horace," *Classical Review*, 35 (1921), 2–7. Reprint, John William Mackail, *Studies in Humanism* (Freeport: Books for Libraries, Essay Index Reprint Series, 1938, 1969), 60–69 (In a simple but learned student treatment, Mackail approaches *Odes* 1.5 "as though it were new to us and being read for the first time; dismissing the commentaries, ignoring the [later added] heading *Ad Pyrrham* . . . and dismissing modern punctuation." He commends the early versions of Fanshaw [1652, Storrs, 34] and Milton [1637, Storrs, 35] as "repay[ing] special attention," and is most critical of Conington [1863, Storrs, 68], notwithstanding Conington as a corrective to Milton).

Marris, W. S. *The Odes of Horace: Books I–IV & The Secular Hymn, Translated into English Verse* (London: Oxford Univ. Press, 1912).

Martindale, Charles and David Hopkins. *Horace Made New: Horatian Influences on British Writing from the Renaissance to the Twentieth Century* (Cambridge: Cambridge Univ. Press, 1993).

Mason, Harold A. "Horace's Ode to Pyrrha," *Cambridge Quarterly*, 7.1 (1976), 27–62 (good and varied points buried within the discursive autobiographical reflections of one of the great critics of his day [1911–1993]; classics-trained but relying in this essay on then contemporary classicists David West, Kenneth Quinn, and R. G. N. Nisbet as being the greater "masters" of Latin).

Mayer, Roland, ed. *Horace: Odes, Book I* (Cambridge: Cambridge Univ. Press, Cambridge Greek and Latin Classics, 2012) (commentary adding little in the aftermath of Nisbet).

McClatchy, J. D. *Horace, the Odes: New Translations by Contemporary Poets* (Princeton: Princeton Univ. Press, 2002) (benighted renderings, in an ill-conceived volume, by a majority of Latinless translators, one translation each; assembled upon the flawed premise that no one person can capture Horace's many moods; discussed at length in the preface to *TLL*).

McDonough, Christopher M., Richard E. Prior, and Mark Stansbury. *Servius' Commentary on Book Four of Virgil's Aeneid* (Wauconda: Bolchazy-Carducci, 2004).

Mendelsohn, Daniel. "The Strange Music of Horace," *New York Review of Books*, 5/13/2004. Reprint, Daniel Mendelsohn, *Waiting for the Barbarians: Essays from the Classics and Popular Culture* (New York: New York Review of Books, 2012), 159–178 (excellent chapter).

Merrill, Elmer Truesdell, ed. *Catullus* (Boston: Ginn and Co., College Series of Latin Authors, 1893).

Michie, James, tr., Introduction by Rex Warner. *Horace: The Odes and the Centennial Hymn* (New York: Bobbs-Merrill, 1963).

Minadeo, Richard. *The Golden Plectrum: Sexual Symbolism in Horace's Odes* (Amsterdam: Rodopi, Studies in Classical Antiquity – Band 4, 1982).

———. Sexual Symbolism in Horace's Love Odes," *Latomus*, 34.2 (1974), 393–424.

Mozeson, Isaac E. *The Word: The Dictionary That Reveals the Hebrew Sources of English* (New York: SPI Books, 1989, 2000).

Murgatroyd, P. "The Sea of Love," *Classical Quarterly*, 45.1 (1995), 9–25 (exhaustive and impressive study, including discussion of *Odes* 1.5 and of Greek and Latin marine and nautical metaphors, analogies, and allusions applied to love and sex).

Nagle, Betty Rose. Review of J. Kaimowitz and R. Ancona, *Vergilius*, 55 (1959) 138–146 (masterly review focusing and containing hypercritical remarks on K's translation of *Odes* 1.5—even while noting a "consistent strength" in K's "attention to the effects of word order and the repetition of key words" and "scattered throughout . . . many really nice turns." Nagle's objections largely (and unfairly) focus on K's use of archaisms and Latinate constructions. Discusses Horatian metrics and concludes with telling mentions of earlier translators, including Conington, Clough, McClatchy [ed.], Ferry, and Clancy).

Nielsen, Rosemary M. and Robert H. Solomon. "The Faith of Lover and Reader in Odes 1.5: Horace and Milton," *Revue Belge de Philologie et d'Histoire*, 67.1 (1989), 75–92 (solid discussion of *Odes* 1.5, followed by review of Milton's translation with reference to Pyrrha as model for Eve).

———. "Rescuing Horace, Pyrrha and Aphra Behn: a Directive," *Ramus*, 22 (1993), 60–77 (see discussion in Notes, p. 308).

Nisbet, R. G. M. "The Word Order of Horace's Odes," in Michèle Lowrie, ed., *Horace: Odes and Epodes* (2009), 378–400 (special emphasis on *Odes* 1.5, "the familiarity of this poem disguises its oddity").

NH = Nisbet, R. G. M. and Margaret Hubbard. *A Commentary of HORACE, Odes, Book I* (Oxford: Clarendon Press, 1970, 2001) (definitive commentary, offering numerous Greek and Latin literary sources for Horatian passages).

Otis, Brooks. "Horace and Housman," *Pacific Coast Philology*, 2 (1967), 5–24.

Passage, Charles E., tr. *Complete Works of Horace. Translated in the Meters of the Originals, with Notes* (New York: Frederick Ungar, 1983).

Polt, Christopher Brian. *Latin Literary Translation in the Late Roman Republic* (Master's Thesis, Univ. of North Carolina, 2007) (discussing the indebtedness to Catullus 64 of Apollonius's *Agonautica* [pp. 91–95]; specific reference to Catullus's lexical choices and coinages at poem's outset within context of novelty of seafaring).

Putnam, Michael C. J. "The Art of Catullus 64," *Harvard Studies in Classical Philology*, 65 (1961), 165–205.

———. "Horace Carm. 1.5: Love and Death," *Classical Philology*, 65.4 (1970), 251–254. Reprint, Michael C. J. Putnam, *Essays on Latin Lyric, Elegy and Epic* (1982), 95–98.

————. *Poetic Interplay: Horace and Catullus* (Princeton: Princeton Univ. Press, 2006).

————. "*Regina Aurea* (*Aen.* 1.697–98)," *Illinois Classical Studies*, 43.1 (2018), 176–178 (golden Dido's sumptuousness; *aurea* 'golden' used of Pyrrha in *Odes* 1.5; Dido and Pyrrha as "complements"). See also Weber.

Quinn, Kenneth. "A Reading of 'Odes' 1.5," *Arion* 2.3 (1963), 59–77 (excellent points on *Odes* 1.5, albeit in a tiringly wordy article).

————, ed., *Horace: The Odes* (London: St. Martin's, 1980) (introduction, revised text, and commentary with much valuable information).

Reckford, Kenneth. "Some Studies in Horace's Odes on Love," *Classical Journal*, 55.1 (1959), 25–31 (curiously without reference to *Odes* 1.5).

Rudd, Niall, ed., tr. *Horace: Odes and Epodes* (Cambridge: Harvard Univ. Press, Loeb Classical Library, 2004).

Rumford, James. *Carpe Diem: Horace De-poeticized; his odes in the original then rendered into Latin prose with many translated into English* (Honolulu: Manoa Press, 2015).

Rutledge, Harry, C. *The Guernica Bull: Studies in the Classical Tradition in the Twentieth Century* (Athens: Univ. of Georgia Press, 1989).

Shepherd, W. G., tr. *Horace: The Complete Odes and Epodes with the Centennial Hymn* (London: Penguin Books, 1983).

Showerman, Grant. *Horace and His Influence* (New York: Longmans, Green, 1922, 1931) (offering the author's own "airy" version of *Odes* 1.5 as alternative to Milton's "ponderous movement and excessive sobriety").

Stanford, W. B. See Aristophanes.

Storrs, Ronald. *The Memoirs of Sir Ronald Storrs* (New York: G. P. Putnam's Sons, 1937).

————. *Ad Pyrrham: A Polyglot Collection of Translations of Horace's Ode to Pyrrha* (*Book 1, Ode 5*) (London: Oxford Univ. Press, 1959; posthumously published) (introduction vividly explaining how this peculiar collection developed and how the translations were collected; contains an account of famed English classical scholar Richard Bentley's [1662–1742] tirade against Horace's "*emirabitur*" coinage; and recounts, among other things, the "changing phrases and values of the English language" with reference to renderings of "*gracilis puer*").

Sutherland, Elizabeth. "Audience Manipulation and Emotional Experiences in Horace's 'Pyrrha Ode,'" *American Journal of Philology*, 116.3 (1995), 441–452 (on the poem's emotional content vis-à-vis poet/audience interaction).

Thayer, Mary Rebecca. "On Translating Horace," *Classical Weekly*, 11.12 (1918), 90–94 (brief but incisive discussion of the difficulties in translating Horace; includes Milton's and Gladstone's *Odes* 1.5).

Trimpi, Wesley. "Horace's 'Ut Pictura Poesis': The Argument for Stylistic Decorum," *Traditio*, 34 (1978), 29–73.

Vessey, Thomas D. W. "Pyrrha's Grotto and the Farewell to Love: A Study of Horace Odes 1.5," *American Journal of Philology*, 105.4 (1984), 457–469.

Weber, Clifford. "Dido and Circe: Two Golden Women in 'Aeneid' 1.698 and 7.190," *Classical Journal*, 94.4 (1999), 317–327 (second half of article dealing with the gold and goldenness associated with Dido and Circe; *aurea* 'golden' prominent in Latin erotic terminology; a "lover's word" as noted of Pyrrha in *Odes* 1.5; a word often associated with Aphrodite). See also Putnam (2018).

West, David. *Horace: The Complete Odes and Epodes* (Oxford: Oxford Univ. Press, Oxford World Classics, 1997, 2008) (translation and commentary).

Whitehorne, J. E. G. "The Ode to Pyrrha," *Classical Outlook*, 52.4 (1974), 41–44 (soundly discussing the poem's word order and imagery).

Whitman, Cedric, tr. *Fifteen Odes of Horace* (Cambridge: Stinehour Press, 1980)(translations by a master).

Wilkinson, L. P. *Horace and His Lyric Poetry* (Cambridge: Univ. of Cambridge Press, 1945) (translating [p. 4] Nietzsche's famous Horatian dictum).

Wilson, Emily R. "A Doggish Translation," review of Barry B. Powell, *The Poems of Hesiod: Theogony, Works and Days, and the Shield of Herakles*, *New York Review of Books*, 1/15/2018.

Wormell, D. E. W. "Translations and Translators" *Hermathena*, 105 (1967), 5–20 (with particular emphasis on *Odes* 1.5).

Ziolkowski, Theodore. "Uses and Abuses of Horace: His reception since 1935 in Germany and Anglo-America," *International Journal of the Classical Tradition*, 12.2 (2005), 183–215.

Index

Z